The American Immigration Collection

The Second Generation Japanese Problem

EDWARD K. STRONG

Arno Press and The New York Times

NEW YORK 1970

Reprint Edition 1970 by Arno Press Inc.

Reprinted by permission of Stanford University Press

Reprinted from a copy in
The University of Illinois Library

LC# 73-129415

ISBN 0-405-00569-5

The American Immigration Collection—Series II

ISBN for complete set 0-405-00543-1

Manufactured in the United States of America

THE SECOND-GENERATION JAPANESE PROBLEM

THE

SECOND-GENERATION JAPANESE PROBLEM

By

EDWARD K. STRONG, Jr.

Professor of Psychology, Graduate School of Business
Stanford University

STANFORD UNIVERSITY PRESS
STANFORD UNIVERSITY, CALIFORNIA

LONDON: HUMPHREY MILFORD
OXFORD UNIVERSITY PRESS

STANFORD UNIVERSITY PRESS
STANFORD UNIVERSITY, CALIFORNIA

LONDON: HUMPHREY MILFORD
OXFORD UNIVERSITY PRESS

THE BAKER AND TAYLOR COMPANY
55 FIFTH AVENUE, NEW YORK

MARTINUS NIJHOFF
9 LANGE VOORHOUT, THE HAGUE

THE MARUZEN COMPANY
TOKYO, OSAKA, KYOTO, SENDAI

PRINTED AND BOUND IN THE UNITED STATES
OF AMERICA BY STANFORD UNIVERSITY PRESS

PREFACE

This report was made possible by a grant of $40,000 by the Board of Trustees of the Carnegie Corporation of New York, October 15, 1929, to Stanford University "in support of a study of educational and occupational opportunities offered to American citizens of Oriental races." It was the deep and genuine interest of President Ray Lyman Wilbur of Stanford University in the problems of Pacific relations which led to the specific determination of the grant. It was at his request and with his encouragement that the writer undertook the project.

Recognizing that some readers are interested in the detailed results and the procedures employed in obtaining these results, and that other readers are interested in the general conclusions, the entire project has been reported in such a way as to meet these two rather distinct requirements.

Three monographs have been published in the Stanford University Series, giving the detailed findings. They are entitled: *Vocational Aptitudes of Second-Generation Japanese in the United States; Japanese in California;* and *Public School Education of Second-Generation Japanese in California.*[1]

The first of these three reports includes data, primarily of interest to psychologists and educators, based on comparative results from Japanese-Americans and whites on various psychological tests and other measures of trustworthiness, delinquency, and crime. The second report is of interest more especially to sociologists and vocational counselors, reviewing, as it does, the data regarding birthplace, age, sex, size of family, births and deaths, and also the occupational and educational status of both the first- and the second-generation Japanese. The third report is concerned with the relative progress of Japanese and whites in the public schools and the effect upon that progress of segregating Japanese in certain special schools.

This book gives a brief summary of each of the three monographs (in chapters vi to ix), particularly as to how the findings bear upon the problem of adjustment of the second generation to life in California. In addition, chapters ii and iii give the historical setting of the present

---

[1] Stanford University Publications, University Series, Education-Psychology, Vol. I, Nos. 1, 2, and 3, respectively. Edward K. Strong, Jr., is the author of the first two and Reginald Bell of the third. Each will hereafter be cited by author and title merely.

situation, chapters iv and v discuss the nature of race prejudice and its bearing upon the problem, and many of the varied aspects of the problem set forth in chapter i are considered again in the light of the whole study in chapters x and xi.

Special mention must be made of aid and advice from Romanzo Adams and E. Lowell Kelley of the University of Hawaii; Wallace McK. Alexander, staunch friend of the Japanese; Saburo Kido, prominent leader of the second generation; T. Takimoto, secretary of the Japanese Association of America; Agnes Wilson, executive secretary of the International Institute of San Francisco; and the writer's colleagues, C. L. Alsberg, Reginald Bell, Eliot G. Mears, Robert E. Swain (at the time acting president of the University), Lewis M. Terman, and Y. Ichihashi. The following served as assistants in the study and contributed not only their assigned part but much of more general significance: Gladys Bond, Nora A. Blichfeldt, Malcolm Campbell, E. W. Field, John Hall, Alfred S. Lewerenz, R. B. McKeown, H. K. Misaki, Tsutomu Obana, L. J. Owen, H. Shimanouchi, Suma Sugi, M. Uyeda, C. Gilbert Wrenn, Sumie Yamamoto, and H. N. Young.

As a complete list of the Japanese throughout the state who have co-operated so generously has not been kept, it is unfair to give some names and omit many equally deserving of mention. Be it stated that without the aid of the Japanese leaders it would have been impossible to carry out certain portions of the study. The courtesy, generosity, and politeness of even the most ignorant Japanese, which was frequently commented on by our staff, converted an often trying task into one of genuine pleasure.

The specific suggestions of William Hawley Davis, editor of the Stanford University Press, were extremely helpful. Bruno Lasker and Eliot G. Mears were kind enough to read and criticize portions of the manuscript, with the result that several changes have been made for the better.

EDWARD K. STRONG, JR.

STANFORD UNIVERSITY, CALIFORNIA
March 1, 1934

TABLE OF CONTENTS

THE SECOND-GENERATION JAPANESE PROBLEM

I. THE PROBLEM

The origin of this study was the feeling that second-generation Japanese "had great difficulty in finding decent jobs" and the belief that some way should be found to remedy the situation. Consequently, the occupational opportunities of the Japanese are stressed in this book. It must be recognized, however, that the problem of the second-generation Japanese is adjustment to their environment; how they earn a living, although a very important aspect of the whole, is after all only one of many components of the entire problem.

Because racial groups differ from one another, it is most natural to suppose that their problems are rather distinct. The more one studies such groups the more one observes how clearly the similarities of their respective problems outnumber the differences. This is so true that one can substitute for "Japanese" in this book the name of any other immigrant group and find that in most cases the latter fits equally well. This is only another way of saying that every immigrant group is faced with many new situations: the newcomers are able to adjust themselves to only a limited degree; their children, the second generation, growing up in the new environment, adopt most of the prevailing customs and attitudes of those about them but are not able to free themselves entirely from the influence of their parents' foreign origin or from the effects of the inferior social and occupational status into which they are born.

For lack of space we have omitted many comparisons that could be made between the Japanese and other immigrant groups proving that the so-called Japanese second-generation problem is primarily a "second-generation" problem and only to a limited degree a "Japanese" problem. Yet in many respects this is the most important conclusion to be drawn from the study. With this in mind let us now consider some of the elements constituting the problem.

OCCUPATIONAL OPPORTUNITIES OF SECOND-GENERATION JAPANESE

There is a general impression that on the whole, with a few individual exceptions, white[1] business concerns will not employ either first- or

[1] Since the second-generation Japanese are American citizens, the term "American" is not sufficiently distinctive when reference is made to Caucasians. For lack

second-generation Japanese except for menial tasks. Kazuo Kawai, born in Japan but receiving his collegiate training in California, in discussing this subject, writes:

> I know of another American-born Japanese who was graduated after specializing in foreign trade in the college of commerce of the foremost university on the Pacific coast. But no American firm would employ him as long as white applicants were available, although they might not be quite so capable as he, and no Japanese firm in America was doing enough business to need a specialist in foreign trade, so for months this man was without work. Finally, the manager of the San Francisco branch office of the T.K.K. Steamship Lines took pity on him and gave him a position as a clerk in his office, at seventy dollars a month. Cases like these could be multiplied indefinitely.
>
> The minor positions which these college graduates finally secured would not be so bad if there were some chance for advancement, for young graduates must all start at the bottom of the ladder. But there is very little chance to rise, for the Americans make no distinction between the second generation Japanese and the older Japanese, and we are all treated equally badly. It is impossible, at least on the Pacific coast, to imagine a Japanese in any high position which would require Americans to work under him. If, in order to avoid troublesome contact with American workers, we man a whole industry from top to bottom with Japanese, as we have tried to do in some fields, such as farming, fishing, and in some cases the hotel and restaurant business, the cries of "yellow peril" and "peaceful penetration" are immediately raised, and august state legislators feel it their duty to safeguard the commonwealth by taking drastic steps to oust us from our business by legislative measures. Or if we limit ourselves to businesses which cater to only the Japanese community, we are accused of being unassimilable and clannish, an undesirable element in American society. But however that may be, the Japanese community here in America is too small to support many businesses or professions by itself.
>
> Our community is not self-sufficient. We can't stand off and live our own lives. We've got to find a place in American society in order to survive. And yet, no matter what our qualifications may be, evidently the only place where we are wanted is in positions that no American would care to fill—menial positions as house-servants, gardeners, vegetable peddlers, continually "yes, ma'am"-ing.[2]

---

of a better term the expression "white" is used to refer to the peoples living in the United States who are not Indians, Negroes, or Orientals.

The Japanese immigrants are designated as first-generation, and their children, born in either the Hawaiian Islands or continental United States, as second-generation Japanese, or as Japanese-Americans.

[2] Kazuo Kawai, "Three Roads and None Easy," *Survey,* LVI (1926), 164–65. Seven years after writing the foregoing statement Kawai was appointed assistant professor of geography at the University of California at Los Angeles.

As a general rule the author has quoted uncomplimentary remarks about the Japanese from writers who are sympathetic toward them and complimentary remarks about them from writers who are more or less antagonistic to them. In

Kawai is not complaining that whites will not hire Japanese at all but that they do not offer them opportunities to obtain the better-paid and more socially desirable positions. Thus far Japanese have been employed as common laborers and in some semi-skilled jobs, chiefly in farming and as fishermen. They have not entered the skilled trades nor have they been employed in manufacturing concerns. A few, particularly among the second generation, have obtained positions in offices and retail establishments.

Certain examples of the employment of technically trained Japanese by white concerns have been found. In such cases difficulties have been reported arising from the objections made by white fellow-employees. Thus, a highly trained electric welder (intending to capitalize his advanced Western technique upon returning to Japan) was engaged by the General Electric Company to demonstrate equipment in the West. Though he was the only available man qualified for certain marine work at Long Beach, his fellow-workmen made it so unpleasant for him that he quit the job and will hunt for his final construction experience in the East before returning to Japan. The interviewer[3] who reported this case adds that "the employer's sole consideration is that good work be done and usually he has no objection to Japanese. But he is not to be blamed if he bows to the feeling of his workmen—and his workmen cannot be blamed for feeling that a 'foreigner' (young citizen though he actually is!) is taking the place of a relative or friend who needs to work." Some qualified Japanese men have been accepted in technical departments of a county government, but there are no Japanese stenographers in county employ. The political aspect of such work undoubtedly explains this situation.

Eben T. Takamine reported the possibilities of employment of second-generation Japanese in New York City in 1928. His general conclusion was that such a one is "at a greater handicap in getting employment than any other American citizen of foreign descent. The reason for this being, that although he may be an American citizen, still in appearance he is a foreigner, and gives that impression when he calls upon anyone, whereas one of European descent may pass in appear-

chapter iv, dealing with specific complaints against the Japanese, the writers quoted are for the most part opposed to the Japanese.

[3] As a part of this investigation twelve assistants interviewed 9,690 Japanese living in California. The majority of these interviewers wrote reports giving their general impressions as based upon their interviews. This material has been drawn upon quite extensively. See the writer's *Japanese in California,* chapter ii.

ance as an American."[4] Mr. Takamine also emphasizes the point that employers are often unwilling to employ a member of the second generation because they believe he is a foreigner and will shortly leave them to return to Japan. He quotes this sentence from one letter received by him: "We cannot blame the Japanese for desiring to do this, as it is only natural, but employers would much prefer taking on men whom they can count upon as staying with the company as long as their work and progress are satisfactory."

Evidently one reason for not hiring Japanese is the opposition of fellow-employees, particularly when Japanese are promoted over them. There is also a fear on the part of employers that some customers may object to dealing with Japanese and that the business will lose thereby.

After considering the Japanese side of the case one of our interviewers added:

> A study of the economic opportunities of the second generation must take into consideration the interests of white labor and landowners as well as Japanese. These orientals are, after all, members of another race. In the coming years, extensive unemployment will undoubtedly continue while we readjust our productive forces to normalcy. It is only just that our white laboring population should receive first consideration. Therefore, Japanese should not be employed where white labor is equally effective and desirous of working.

There is nearly always something to be said on the other side of any contention. Young people—and the second-generation Japanese are young, averaging only ten years of age—overlook the fact that efficient performance of certain activities is not all there is to a job. In the case of very simple jobs, such as digging ditches, performance, it is true, is the principal part of the job. The more desirable jobs, however, involve adaptation to a complex working environment in which personal relations with subordinates, fellow-employees, and superiors play an important rôle, and very frequently contacts with customers and the general public are involved. The reader must certainly recall many examples from his own experience where an employee could do the work satisfactorily but could not be kept on the payroll because for one reason or another people didn't like him. The white employer is not to be blamed if he dismisses an efficient Japanese-American employee

[4] Americans living on the East Coast have never been able to appreciate the Oriental situation on the West Coast. To the former, Chinese are usually laundrymen and Japanese foreign diplomats; yet they cannot tell the two races apart on the basis of physical appearance. In one respect all whites, regardless of locality, are alike in that they do not recognize Orientals born in this country as American citizens.

merely because fellow-employees or customers do not like him or the general public disapproves of him.

Moreover, employers cannot rationally be censored when they discharge an inefficient employee unless they did not give him a fair chance to learn the work. It is a rare person, however, who does not blame his boss when he is discharged for inefficiency. It is then essential that the stories told by Japanese-Americans be taken with a grain of salt. Loss of position by Japanese employees does not always result from race feeling alone. In one case five Japanese young men were employed by a department store. In the course of several months three of them quit for different reasons, although they had been satisfactory to the store management. Some time later it was necessary to retrench, and in checking over the records of the employees the two remaining Japanese were found to be among the least efficient and they were discharged, together with several whites. About two weeks later several prominent Japanese waited upon the manager of the store and accused him of race discrimination and threatened loss of business if the young men were not reinstated. This he refused. From that time this store has had the policy of hiring no one who belongs to an organization that reviews employment and discharge of its members. Two other incidents of a similar nature have been reported to the writer, one involving interference by a consular representative.

It is well to recognize that Japanese are not the only immigrants who have suffered in these respects. Feldman[5] points out that "ever since the founding of this country the immigrant races have had to bear the accumulation of all the abuse that those who had arrived before could heap upon them," and then quotes from a letter of Benjamin Franklin, dated May 9, 1753, referring to the Germans in Pennsylvania as follows:

> Those who come hither are generally the most stupid of their own nation, and as ignorance is often attended with great credulity, when knavery would mislead it . . . . it is almost impossible to remove any prejudice they may entertain . . . . Not being used to liberty, they know not how to make modest use of it . . . . I remember when they modestly declined intermeddling with our elections; now they come in droves and carry all before them, except in one or two counties.[6]

Feldman adds that the "despised races of former decades regard themselves as the defenders of true America against the newcomers"

[5] H. Feldman, *Racial Factors in American Industry* (Harper & Brothers, 1931), pp. 134–36.

[6] Quoted by I. A. Hourwich, *Immigration and Labor* (B. W. Huebsch, Inc., 1922), p. 76.

and quotes Congressman Meyer Jacobstein in a speech before the House of Representatives:

> You contend that the present foreign element is less desirable than that of forty, fifty, sixty years ago. I call your attention to a report made to the House by a select congressional committee in 1838. It charged that "the country is being flooded with the outcasts of the jails, almshouses, and slums of pauper-ridden Europe." It asserted that at the time the jails of the capital were filled with these foreign-born people. It described them as "the most idle and vicious classes, in personal appearance most offensive and loathsome."
>
> But who were these "offensive and loathsome paupers and criminals"? Why, they were the scrappy Irishmen and Germans and British whose children today fear the influx of new foreign hordes.[7]

Feldman says that "the established custom has been that newcomers start at the bottom with unskilled work, no matter what their qualifications for better jobs might be. Nearly every race thus pays the price of immigration by the suffering of the first generation. The second and the third descendants usually overcome the handicaps of language and education, and graduate out of their lowly status."[8]

What are the prospects that second-generation Japanese may be employed by Japanese business concerns? One prominent Japanese informs us that Japanese-American commercial firms will employ these second-generation children, both here and abroad, provided they know Japanese, as well as English, sufficiently to carry on their work. However, there are not enough of these firms to take care of many second-generation children. It is very necessary, for the reason given above, that second-generation children learn Japanese quite well, but it is very difficult to get them to do so, for several reasons.

In the first place, Japanese is a very hard language to learn, especially to write. In the second place, Japanese-language school work is given after the American day-school work is done, in the late afternoon or on Saturday. Third, young Japanese do not see the need of learning Japanese until they are eighteen or nineteen years old, and by then it is rather late. Fourth, there are not enough of such schools; in some areas none are to be found, and, since they are pay schools, not all Japanese can afford to attend them.

---

[7] Quoted in an editorial on "Land of the Noble Free," *The Nation,* April 23, 1924, p. 468.

[8] H. Feldman, *op. cit.,* p. 137; quoted by permission of Harper & Brothers, publishers.

There are, then, difficulties in the placement of the second generation in either white or Japanese concerns in this country. Would they be better off if they went to Japan? Kawai discusses this possibility:

If it is so hard for us to get into suitable vocations here, why don't we go back to Japan? we are frequently asked. Only a few days ago I was walking across the Quad on our campus with an American classmate, and he turned around to me and said: "Gee! you fellows are lucky! Look at the great advantage you American-educated fellows have over the rest of your people when you go back to the old country." I suppose his attitude reflects that of most Americans. "Well," I should like to ask, "what do you mean by going *back* to our old country? We've never been there in the first place." Most of us were born here, and we know no other country. This is "our old country" right here. As to having advantage over the people in Japan, we have the wonderful advantage of being quite unable to speak their language or read their papers, of being totally ignorant of their customs, history, or traditions, of holding different ideals, of thinking in different ways. Yes, we have as much advantage over the people in Japan as a deaf mute has over a man in possession of all his faculties. An American would have an infinitely easier time in Japan than we would, for they would excuse a foreigner if he made mistakes, but we, with our Japanese names and faces, would have to conform to their rigid standards or else be "queer." As for advantage in education, with some of the universities over there like Imperial, Waseda, and others ranking with the leading universities of the world, *what chance have we products of the American rah-rah system against their mature scholars?* The trouble with us is that we have been too thoroughly Americanized. We have attended American schools, we speak English exclusively, we know practically nothing of Japan except what an average American knows; our ideals, customs, mode of thinking, our whole psychology is American. Although physically we are Japanese, culturally we are Americans. We simply are not capable of fitting into Japanese society, so we are destined to remain here.[9]

It has been suggested in certain quarters that the solution to the Japanese problem may lie in their widespread diffusion over the United States, especially in the East, where social prejudice is supposedly much less intense. The investigation of Takamine was undertaken with this possibility in mind. His conclusions do not support the idea that Japanese-Americans will find jobs awaiting them wherever they may go. And the actual condition, as brought out in chapters iii and x, is that the Japanese are not spreading throughout the country but rather are concentrating in southern California.

Another alternative, as has been pointed out, is for the second generation to work exclusively for those of Japanese ancestry. This is a possi-

---

[9] K. Kawai, *op. cit.*, p. 165.

bility for some, and we find Japanese physicians, dentists, insurance men, and the like who devote most of their time, if not all, to serving their fellows. But the Japanese are too few in number to be a self-contained community. The businesses they have so far built up are very small, averaging one-half employee to each, so that there is very little opportunity for the second generation to get ahead in this way, except by replacing their elders.

This situation is not peculiar to the Japanese alone; it applies equally to the second-generation Chinese, as is indicated by this excerpt from a letter of the San Francisco editor, Ng Poon Chew, to Samuel H. Cohn, dated July 4, 1929:

> The problem as to the livelihood of the coming generations of the Chinese born in this country is a serious one. There is considerable race prejudice existing today against the Chinese in the higher line of economic field. I know several Chinese young men graduates from our State University in engineering simply could not procure a position because the men of other, white skinned races would not work under or with them. One of them was employed by a large public utility corporation for a while and his work was found to be satisfactory, but eventually was discharged in order to keep peace and harmony in the camps among the men. Still there are a few graduates who have finally found permanent places with large firms in engineering line, and two are now holding engineering positions with city governments and are well liked by those who come in contact with them.
>
> These young people, like their American cousins, simply would not return to the farms or to agricultural work. They all want to stay in the cities and procure white collar jobs. And under no circumstances would they go to work as house servants or laundry work. There is now only one way open to them to procure a livelihood and that is in the commercial line and even in this line they have to confine themselves to their own people. Since the enactment of the Chinese exclusion laws in 1882 the number of the Chinese people in America is steadily decreasing until today we have less than sixty thousand in the whole United States, and it looks as though in ten or twenty years the Chinese population in this country will be so few that commercial activities will be so reduced that they will not be to any consequence.
>
> Perhaps the future of our American born Chinese will have to look to China for their life work. In this there is much hope. China will open thousands of lines for ambitious modernized young men to utilize their learning to help develop the country's resources.

Agriculture, a possible solution.—The first generation has demonstrated that they are successful agriculturalists. In fact, they have been altogether too successful to suit the whites, and so anti-alien land laws have been passed to curb their activities. The second generation are not subject to these laws and are as free to pursue agricultural work as anyone else. Why, then, do not the second generation turn to agriculture?

There is no doubt that this is the fond hope of many a first-generation Japanese who has toiled long and hard on a ranch and would like to see his sons seize the advantages denied him. It is also the solution most often offered by the older Japanese leaders. "There are unlimited opportunities for them in agriculture in this state," reports T. Takimoto, secretary of the Japanese Association of America. The trouble with this solution is that the second generation are like all other young people educated in American schools—they want white-collar jobs.

Takahashi takes the second generation to task for this view of theirs as follows:

> The time has come for the second generation to realize the strength of which they are capable, the utilization of which will determine their place in the business life of America.
>
> A certain amount of wishbone is a necessary requisite in any man's makeup, but along with this and even more important a factor is backbone. It is natural for youth to be idealistic . . . . much more than is practical. They are apt to scoff at the commonplace things around them and look to the far-away horizon for their inspiration. This, I believe, is the glaring weakness as it exists among the younger people of our community today.
>
> Frankly, the *second generation is afraid of honest to goodness toil.* The general trend is toward the gaining of "white-collar job" where a few manipulations will bring wealth and social recognition. This condition may be due to education, environment, or may be the result of reading too much idealistic fiction. No matter where the cause may be, the facts remain and the coming generation must come to life and face facts as they really are.
>
> Take a lesson from the first generation members of this community. They did not enter this country with Key to the City in their pockets. Far from it. They had to combat all the handicaps of a foreign tongue, different mode of living, and racial prejudice . . . . and how did they do it? By getting down on their knees and resorting to *common honest toil.*
>
> The result of their labors is the heritage which they are leaving behind them, and well may their children be proud of it. It is the bounden duty for the offsprings to carry on . . . . and it should be easier for them with the education and the various equipments which have been put into their hands.
>
> Here are facts worth remembering. A white collar job is not the bed of roses that it seems. The railroads, lumbering, fishing and agricultural industries are better paying jobs than they seem to be. For example, a young man enters the railroad payroll as a machinist's helper. Three years of hard conscientious labor and he is a machinist drawing wages that an office worker could never hope to get in ten years.
>
> Commonplace work is far from thrilling . . . . but the business of life is not all thrills. A person who cannot succeed in common undertakings will hardly make a good Captain of Industry.
>
> Hitch your wagon to the stars, dream your dream of success, but put your shoulder to the wheels of opportunity before you and push, brother, push! Thomas

Edison, whom we all know gives as his formula for Success, ten per cent inspiration . . . . and ninety per cent *perspiration.* Note the preponderance of the latter item, and make the most of it.[10]

Unquestionably, many second generation can earn a living on the ranch as their fathers have done before them, and when economic necessity compels them many will do so. Some will find the work satisfying though hard; others will merely endure it. In this, they will differ not at all from thousands of whites who enter occupations not so much from choice as from necessity.

Upon reading the preceding paragraphs in manuscript Mr. Bruno Lasker aptly suggested that the question is not how Japanese-American youths may be adjusted to the situation so as to find satisfaction in agricultural occupations but, rather, what technical changes are necessary in an agricultural system based on the use of cheap labor to emancipate it from that condition and make it available as a career for youths with engineering interests, mechanical skill, ambition, business ability, and high standards of living, accustomed to diversified recreations and intellectual pursuits. This is the problem confronting the sugar planter in Hawaii who would like to know how to attract Japanese youths educated in American schools. It is also the problem that must be solved for our own boys and girls who now so generally disdain farming. It is but a phase of the new adjustments coming in our social life as the oversupply of aspirants for professional life becomes more and more apparent. Graduates of our teacher-training institutions are being placed as household servants; graduates of law schools are taking positions as filling-station men. Everywhere it is plain that standards of occupational evaluation must be changed.

Legal restrictions.—All nations have restrictions regarding the occupational activities of foreigners within their borders. The first generation have been subject to such legal requirements. Certain other restrictions upon their activities were passed by California and several other Western states during the days of agitation against the Oriental, the most outstanding of which were laws against ownership or leasing of agricultural land and intermarriage with whites.[11] It must be emphasized that the second generation, born in this country, are American citizens and are

[10] C. T. Takahashi, *Japanese-American Courier* (Seattle, Washington), March 29, 1930.

[11] See E. G. Mears, *Resident Orientals on the American Pacific Coast: Their Legal and Economic Status* (1928). Hereafter cited as *Resident Orientals.*

therefore not subject to these restrictions any more than are white citizens, though each group is forbidden to intermarry with the other.

REACTIONS OF SECOND GENERATION TO OCCUPATIONAL SITUATION

The majority of our interviewers feel that the agitation against the Japanese has led them to withdraw among themselves and to seek for less contact of all sorts with the whites. "We are living today and carrying on in terms of the past more than other foreigners, if not in our actions, certainly in our thinking," said one second-generation Japanese. This may prove to be only a passing stage in their development. And it may be due primarily to the fact that the first generation are steadily growing older, for adults tend to live as they were brought up. It is a question whether the second generation will continue in the ways of their parents or will express themselves as Americans.

All this is typical of other immigrant groups in this country. Mr. Bruno Lasker reports that one of the most brilliant and respected of American rabbis, of an old and distinguished family, told him the other day that he met with non-Jews only about once a month and had no relation of friendship with any non-Jew. The pastor of one of the largest churches in New York, surrounded by a population of about 70,000 Italians, which maintains elaborate institutional provisions used almost exclusively by poor Italians, told him that in the many years of his pastorate he had never met an educated Italian. Yet in his neighborhood there are possibly more Italian doctors, lawyers, writers, and artists than in three or four of the largest Italian cities put together.

It is furthermore the belief of our interviewers that the period of agitation produced many changes in the Japanese. It awakened them to a situation of which they had been largely unconscious before. The criticisms heaped upon them made them aware of necessary changes in standards of living, mode of dress, customs, etc. There was also, during this period, whether due to the agitation or not, a continued change from common labor to business activities and toward more skilled professions. The whole Japanese community, assailed as it has been with all manner of views concerning every phase of life, has thus been unsettled. No wonder that it is difficult to find any two Japanese who hold the same opinion on as few as three general topics.

The second generation are bewildered, growing up as they are in an atmosphere of continual shifting, with parents who are not sure where they stand. "It is not to be wondered at," writes Galen M. Fisher, "that some of those who had looked forward with high hopes to happy and successful careers among a people that exult in freedom and in democratic opportunity should experience a revulsion of feeling and become pessimistic and critical of everything in the land which virtually disowns them."[12] Kawai gives us concrete pictures of this bewilderment, with resulting despair on the one hand and on the other hand determination to make good despite all obstacles. He writes:

So, many of my friends are giving up the fight. "Why get an education?" they say. "Why try to do anything at all? Probably we were meant to be just a servile class. We can't help it, so let's make the best of a bad bargain." These constitute the new shiftless, pleasure-seeking second-generation element in the heretofore industrious, thrifty Japanese community. The nicer individuals who accept this defeatist philosophy are a little more subtle. Instead of trying to drown out their unhappiness with mere pleasure-seeking, they turn to the church and religion to afford them comfort and relief from their economic and social misery, and they hold a cheaply optimistic, goody-goody idea that if they stay in their place, work hard and please the Americans and remain happy in the position where God has placed them, surely the Christian Americans, out of the generosity of their hearts, will throw out to them a few more crumbs to ease their condition. Personally, I see no use in the cheap optimism of that type of religion which would deaden the ambitions and aspirations of those who suffer from social injustice, so as to make them contented.

But others of our group intend to stay here and see the thing through. We don't intend to succumb to our environment. We believe that our duty is to stay here and make a distinctive contribution to American life just as other national groups have contributed to American life in the past. But in order to make this contribution we must be given the opportunity to develop ourselves normally. Our immediate outlook is of course very dark. But our policy is to get the best education we can, to hold to the highest ideals we know, and to keep ever before us the vision of what we might accomplish, even though for a while we cannot find vocations befitting our abilities. Then we shall be so dissatisfied with existing conditions that we shall be working continuously to change them. Only by such continuous hammering away will any change come about. Of course it is going to be hard on the individual who will have to plug away at an inferior position when he is really capable of something better. But this seems to be the only course which will bring any ultimate improvement. And to the credit of the American-born Japanese, many of them are following this policy, and a few of them are beginning to find their proper places in society.[13]

An editorial from the *Japanese-American Courier* emphasizes the need for character and sacrifice during the pioneering era which the second generation must pass through:

---

[12] Galen M. Fisher, *Relations between the Occidental and Oriental Peoples on the Pacific Coast of North America* (1928), p. 10; quoted by permission of the International Missionary Council, publishers.

[13] K. Kawai, *op. cit.*, pp. 165–66.

The duty of this generation is apparent. The responsibility is obvious. The second generation is fitted into a sacrificial position as pioneers to blaze the trail into American life to effect the proper recognition of themselves as genuine American citizens; to help the proper and easier amalgamation of the third generation into American life and not least of all to promote a better understanding between their country and the land of their parents.

The second generation era will yet be a stage of sacrifice and a stage of pioneering. Upon the shoulders of this first generation to be born in America will be the responsibility of building the proper foundation that the future generations of Americans of Japanese ancestry may be assured the fortunes of a better existence.

This sounds easy but the responsibility is heavy. It is a responsibility which will take the entire second generation era to discharge. The fact must not be misjudged.[14]

Another editorial, from the *Nikkei Shimin,* admits: "We are frankly pessimistic as to real good vocational opportunities which are open now for Japanese high school or college graduates," and closes with:

In technical or commercial vocations, we cannot afford to work with talents *inferior* to Americans. It is not enough even to be their *equals;* we must *surpass* them—by developing our powers to the point of genius if necessary.

We believe that the complaints against race prejudice in the matter of vocational opportunities *are not justified.* They only show that something is lacking in the initiative or ability of the one who complains.[15]

FACTORS DETERMINING CHOICE OF OCCUPATION

Choice of occupation is dependent first of all upon one's abilities and interests. Psychologists have not yet determined the basic abilities that pertain to vocational choice. There are some tests that throw light upon the problem. Thus, one who tests low in an intelligence test is unfitted for many occupations, particularly if they necessitate extensive educational preparation.

Although it is impossible to determine with any real degree of accuracy what career an individual should enter by the use of tests, it is possible to determine to a much greater degree whether one group is superior or inferior to another as far as certain mental traits are concerned. Chapter vii presents such comparative findings between Japanese and whites regarding intelligence, motor performances, interests, certain personality traits, and ability in art. These results indicate that there are relatively slight differences between the two groups, both of whom have been born in the United States and have been educated in the same

---

[14] *Japanese-American Courier* (Seattle).

[15] *Nikkei Shimin,* July 15, 1930.

schools in California. They suggest that as far as mental ability is concerned there should be approximately equal percentages of each racial group entering the various occupations and professions.

This conclusion does not take into account moral and personal traits which affect success to a large degree and unfortunately cannot be measured satisfactorily today. We can say that, other things being equal, two men of equal mental attainment should succeed equally well. But other things are seldom equal and frequently are the determining factors.

To throw light upon these moral factors investigation has been made of the honesty of Japanese as based upon mercantile credit ratings and the opinions of housewives who have employed them as servants, also regarding delinquency and crime (chapter vii).

Environmental factors play, however, an important rôle in vocational choice. One may have the ability and the disposition to enter a particular occupation, but, if it is already fearfully crowded or if the financial rewards are inadequate, it may be very unwise to consider it. Theoretically, vocational choice should involve the selection of the occupation for which one is best fitted and which will at the same time provide the best opportunity, which usually means the occupation in which there is the least probable competition. There is a woeful lack of information on the latter point. Today, in the midst of the business depression, every occupation seems greatly overcrowded. Who, then, is wise enough to counsel young people as to what will be the relative degrees of competition in all of the possible occupations ten years, twenty years, or thirty years hence!

There are many contributing elements in the total environment that throw some light on the future careers of the second generation. It is important to know how many Japanese there are in the United States and how many there will be as time goes on. The answer to this is dependent upon birth- and death-rates, whether many will return to Japan or move to Hawaii, whether those in Hawaii will come to the mainland, and so on. Will employers here and in Hawaii prefer to hire newcomers, i.e., Filipinos, Mexicans, or those of some other race, or will they decide to use natives? And will the native-born work at the menial tasks that somebody must do? The movement of Japanese population seems clearly to be toward Los Angeles, and away from the farm to the city. Is this movement a wise one, based on sound economic motives, or the reverse? If the Japanese should scatter widely throughout the country, they would set up one type of occupational problem—they would either have to work for whites or serve them in some business, professional, or personal way. If they are going to concentrate in a few localities, their occupational opportunities will be altered. Do they prefer to be in a warm climate and with their fellows, at the possible expense of economic advantage, or will they forego such preferences for wider occupational advantages?

Chapters viii and ix present many facts regarding the educational and occupational background of the second generation; also what their probable future will be in terms of their expressed preference for school subjects and occupations. As the second generation average but ten years of age and comprise very few adults, all this information gives slight basis for real prophecy. As a supplement there is added information gleaned from the graduates of Stanford University and the University of California. Here at least is recorded what a few of the vanguard of the second generation are doing.

MANY PROBLEMS FACED IN COMMON WITH WHITES

Mears concludes his discussion of the future of the second generation, occupationally speaking, with these words:

> The greatest handicap of the Oriental in America is the absence of any worthwhile direction or information regarding vocational opportunities. In this respect both American and Oriental private and official organizations have been notoriously lax. As a result, the second and third generations do not know what they are best fitted for, what they should train for, or what types of work would bring them into the least competition with others. They drift from calling to calling, from locality to locality, with little sense of how their particular talents or handicaps can be utilized to the best advantage. They spend time and money in higher education and in short technical and professional courses, but without any adequate knowledge of the likelihood of future positions . . . . The younger generation is vocationally embarrassed . . . . by sheer ignorance of their own unfitness, because they are without the benefit of any reliable information affecting the choice of their careers, derived from aptitude tests, interest tests, or organized occupational guidance.[16]

This is all true, but it applies equally to white young people. The writer personally handled thousands of qualification cards of enlisted men and officers in the American Army. One of the most noticeable things therein recorded was that most of these men had drifted from one job to another, seemingly without rime or reason. Judging from such records, "trial and error" is the chief method of finding one's occupational career. The question is, does one usually find just the best one? Even with college graduates there is much uncertainty and drift-

[16] E. G. Mears, *op. cit.*, p. 210.

ing along the lines of least resistance. Fully a third of the 1927 class at Stanford University did not know what they were going to do at the time of graduation. If a complete record could be obtained of college graduates ten years out of college, the aimlessness and lack of success of many would be amazing. But much of this is not disclosed in most follow-ups, for such men do not usually reply to questionnaires.

The many books and articles that have discussed the Japanese problem without reference to similar problems of other groups have unwittingly given the impression that the Japanese second generation are much more to be pitied than is the case. Most of the statements about them are equally true of all others of the same age. All human beings are far more alike than unlike. All persons growing up in the same community are faced with very much the same environmental conditions. Every study made has shown greater variation within a racial group than between it and any other social group. Most of the difficulties confronting the second-generation Japanese must be solved equally for all other groups. In solving their problems we are solving the problems of all, and vice versa.

Real work is being done throughout the country in the line of vocational guidance and personnel counseling. This is fine, for it is fearfully needed. There is danger, however, that enthusiasm will run ahead of common sense and scientific technique and that too many poorly prepared people will attempt to serves as guides. Where so little is known as in the case of counseling young people about their life careers, it is questionable whether poor counseling is really better than none.

The writer, furthermore, doubts the implication which Mears unwittingly makes that the second-generation Japanese have been denied the advantages of psychological tests. Knowing something of the extreme scrupulousness of the school men of California that no distinction shall be made because of color or race, one may consider it very doubtful if Japanese children have been denied the advantages of counseling open to their schoolmates. What Mears has written is true, nevertheless, because all children have been denied real vocational guidance, for the simple reason that this science is in its infancy.

OTHER FACTORS DETERMINING OCCUPATIONAL CHOICE

Problems faced in common with children of most immigrants.—Observers of many immigrant groups have pointed out the home difficulties which confront the second generation. There is the matter of the language, which few of the parents really master, so that they are separated from their children to a considerable degree, since each prefers a different language. There is the matter of low social environment out of which few of the first generation can rise. Miss Tuthill has emphasized this point:

> To the more sensitive Japanese children this situation develops a sense of shame of parents and home. Very often the houses which they can rent are not as up to date as those of their American schoolmates. The standard of living adopted by Japanese parents, because it often falls below that of Americans, is apt to cause American-born Japanese children to want to avoid having their American friends see or come to their homes. A shy little high school girl, every time she was taken anywhere with the family of her American friend, would insist that they leave her on the street corner or in some store near her home. She was ashamed of her home, no doubt, which was very respectable, although it sat back from the street and was surrounded with nursery stock set out in splendid order.[17]

There is the inability of the parents to interpret the American environment to their children, which must be an exceedingly important factor in the development of the child. There are many similar factors which need not be mentioned, all of which lead to misunderstandings and conflict between the two generations. That this is true of the Japanese there is no doubt. Their publications and their conversations are full of references to these ever burning questions which are increasingly discussed. One second-generation individual writes me that the interests of her group are widely diffused, "being concerned with education, socials, professions, and politics, whereas the first generation stress economy, work, money, going back to Japan, solemn quiet life, and the arrangement of marriages. They take life too seriously, always planning for the future, whereas the second generation want to enjoy life, forget the past, and let tomorrow come as it will." All of this sounds suspiciously like what young people in any generation say about their parents.

Much of what is involved in all this is common, as we have said, to all immigrants who settle in a foreign land, and some of it is the ever present conflict between youth and maturity. The confusion of ideals, motives, and aspirations is a serious matter and cannot be taken lightly. But it can hardly be charged solely to America. It seems unfortunate to the writer that the Japanese do not appreciate that other immigrant groups have had to contend with these things, and that they

---

[17] Gretchen Tuthill, "Japanese in the City of Los Angeles" (abridged from an unpublished Master's thesis, University of Southern California, 1924), p. 5.

attribute their troubles very largely to the fact that they are Japanese in origin. To be able to attribute one's failures to an external fact over which one has no control rather than to a possible deficiency in one's own character is more gratifying to one's self-esteem, but it destroys the impetus to self-improvement which might mean future success.

Race prejudice and preference.—Apparently every group exhibits prejudice toward the stranger. Certainly Americans are no exception; they have been accused of exhibiting this unpleasant trait much more than most peoples. And they show it not only to those distinctly different from themselves but even to those who are most nearly like them—many of my acquaintances testify to a prejudice against the English. The presence of the Negro first as a slave and later on up to the present time as for the most part an inferior has kept racial distinction to the fore. It is possible that this oversensitiveness on the part of Americans is due to the long period of fear of Indians and maltreatment of them, for those we ill-treat we also dislike. Regardless of cause, the American is prone to show race prejudice. (The nature and causes of this phenomenon are considered in chapter iv.)

The Japanese suffer from a stronger feeling of antagonism than is shown toward many other racial groups, largely because of the anti-Oriental sentiment stimulated for years in connection with California's insistence upon restriction of immigration. The feeling toward the Chinese has very largely died down since the passage of the Chinese restriction law in 1882 and the manifestations of animosity toward the Japanese have similarly largely disappeared since the Immigration Act of 1924. But there still remains a distinct prejudice to be found among the great majority of whites toward Japanese and Chinese.[18]

In discussing the Negro, Embree calls attention to two different ways in which prejudice is shown by two different classes of white people:

> There is on the one hand the bitterness of the competitive struggle by poor whites. Any group, desperate for existence and survival, fears and hates its competitors and will resort to every unfairness in order to climb upward upon the defeated backs of its rivals. Sportsmanship and honor are all right in games or by recognized superiors toward docile dependents. But questions of life and success disregard such artificial barriers as honor and fair play . . . .

---

[18] Newspaper advertising in support of Samuel M. Shortridge for re-election to the United States Senate stated: "He is against Filipino immigration; and has always been against Japanese immigration" (*San Francisco Chronicle,* August 28, 1932). Advertising of restaurants in some communities, particularly in the Northwest, points out that only "White help" is employed.

When the slave power was broken, the poor whites re-entered the fight for a place in the sun. To obtain bread and prestige they eagerly took every possible advantage of the Negro, who had been the means by which they had been driven physically into the hills and valleys and spiritually into the shadows. Fears were easily transformed into hate. Bitterness was further inflamed as the Negroes came into transient power during the Reconstruction Period. From that time forward the poor whites in the South, consciously or unconsciously, have used every means in their possession to handicap and thwart the Negroes. It is this class which has found representation in the Vardamons, Tillmans, Heflins, and Bleases, and their campaigns of racial abuse.

Quite another kind of discrimination has come from the old aristocracy. These people have been considerate of the Negro personally and helpful to him in his first struggles upward. The difference in status was so great that there was no question of competition. But with this sympathy has gone a patronizing and paternalistic attitude and the assumption that the Negro is clearly and inevitably inferior. "They are only children; we must be kind and patient with them." Unfortunately when people say this of another race, they always assume that these children will never grow up, that they are pleasantly feeble-minded . . . .

The patronizing attitude is really more damning than the competitive struggle. The stone wall of calm assumption of his inferiority is to the Negro a keener hurt and a greater obstacle than the battle which admits an adversary worth fighting against. It is hard to keep ambition alive and to maintain morale when those for whom you have fondness and respect keep thinking and saying that you are only children, that you can never grow up, that you are cast by God in an inferior mold.[19]

It is to be noted that those who espouse the patronizing attitude are themselves free from competition. There is no doubt that most in this group would change their attitude to that of open hostility if they were threatened by genuine competition. Thus, it has been the working classes in the West who have led the agitation against the Chinese and the Japanese, and it has been the business man, the large landowner, and the professional man who have been friendly. These suffered little or not at all, some even gained, by the presence of the Japanese.

Does this mean that as the Japanese aspire to higher and higher walks in life they are likely to meet larger and larger groups who will exhibit prejudice toward them? It may be so, but, on the other hand, it may be that other alleviating factors will be more potent. It is quite possible to feel race prejudice in general and yet to admire and associate with individual members of the race in question. It is entirely possible for Japanese as individuals to establish ever widening circles of acquaintanceship and friendship if they conduct themselves appropriately. And the white person with little prejudice may not become alarmed at the

---

[19] E. R. Embree, *Brown America* (1931), pp. 202–5; quoted by permission of the Viking Press, publishers.

gradual increase of competition from a few Japanese who establish themselves in a community as physicians, architects, florists, or what not. Personal liking for the individual and respect for his ability may be established before any evidence of competition is felt. It would seem that the interests of the second generation will be best served by slow, substantial advancement of its members without recourse to the spectacular.

Handicaps resulting from Japanese ancestry.—Because the second generation do not lose the distinguishing marks of their race as do so many immigrants, they are faced with a handicap peculiar to them and to races other than Caucasians. They may dress, behave, and speak like Americans, but they look different. This difference is not so great as with their fathers, owing to their Americanization, but it is still sufficient to be noted. Thus they are unable to escape the racial prejudice that attaches to their parents. What this means can best be told by a second-generation Japanese:

Ever since I was able to lick the pink water off of my rattle, it has been made known to me that I am a "Jap," was a "Jap," and always will be a "Jap"! . . . .

When I started school, there were no other "Japs" beside me so I had to learn to get along with my American companions or else play tiddely-winks with my toes. The latter idea didn't especially appeal to me—I played with the other kids.

My first tragedy was when our first grade dancing class was practicing in the music room. Every boy was paired off with a girl; mine was a yellow-haired, blue-eyed Swede (no disrespect meant) by the name of Dorothy. When she learned that I was to hold her hand and go through "Here we go Looby-loo—here we go looby-lai" she stamped her foot and shrieked, "I won't be his partner—he's a 'Jap'!"

Maybe I cried then—I don't remember. Since then, no more dancing for me.

My second air castle went to smashes when I went to a friend's house to play. We were building houses and having the time of our lives; just then the ogress (his mother) entered the scene and commanded, "Bobby, send that little 'Jap' home!"

I felt better when I noticed that Bobby was doing his best not to cry. I know I didn't try to hold back any moisture.

These little events took on colossal proportions as I dreamed about them. At that time I fully intended to become a soldier and buy me a big pistol and shoot all the people who had called me "Jap." I did get some satisfaction out of that.

After a time, I became calloused to insulting remarks, and vile epithets failed to arouse me to high pitch. (Maybe that was because I knew some pretty fiery cuss words myself and wasn't a bit bashful about using them.)

During my seventh grade days, an event took place that is funny now, but it wasn't any laughing matter then.

We were drawing pictures in art class and when the end of the period came, I passed my paper up. When my drawing reached Marion Doe, he held it up for the entire class to see (it was pretty poor art, I'll admit) and yelled, "Take a look at the work of a 'Jap'!"

Everyone in the class stared at me—I turned red—got out of my seat—took six steps (I counted 'em) and placed a solid upper-cut on Mr. Wiseguy's jaw. (My knuckles ached for days afterwards.)

I can still see those up-turned faces of my classmates; each one was dead white; the horrified silence hung thick.

"Why, why, Kay—" the teacher gasped at length.

That was my cue to cut loose with everything I had. I don't remember what I said, but what I said was plenty.

Marion and I are the best of friends now.

Funny? Now, yes; not then.

Two years ago, I almost socked my penmanship instructor on the beezer when she referred to me as "Jap." Afterwards I was glad I hadn't because she called me in after class and apologized for the slip.

After some seventeen years of living on this old planet of ours and being insulted some twenty-five hours a day by so-called "Americans," I still think the U.S. is a pretty darned good place to live after all. For the poor misguided "Americans" who try to be my enemy, I have only the deepest pity. And to the countless kids whose noses I have punched, I will add, "The pleasure was all mine."[20]

Jews encounter much the same situation. They are "foreigners" to many people in America even when of the second or third native-born generation. Although many have achieved positions of prestige and leadership in business, politics, and the professions, yet many others encounter strong barriers of race prejudice when seeking an opportunity with non-Jewish concerns. Feldman writes:

Innumerable business organizations, employing thousands of workers, are closed to Jews. Some employers, who themselves have no objection to employing or promoting Jews, fear the possible prejudices of customers or associates. Indeed, Jewish concerns themselves, in deference to the prevailing prejudice, sometimes find it expedient to bar fellow racials from positions involving contact with the general public.[21]

Another matter that peculiarly affects the second-generation Japanese is that of citizenship. According to the laws of the United States, any child born in this country is an American citizen, no matter if his parents are aliens, no matter even if they are ineligible to citizenship. But this is not the law of many countries, including Japan. In the latter case, the child of a citizen is a subject of his parent's country, regardless of where he is born. Because of these two different views of citizenship, the second generation has held a dual citizenship, both of the United States and of

---

[20] Kay Yasui, "Jap!" "Jap!" "Jap!" from the *Japanese-American News* and reprinted in *Pacific Citizen,* January 15, 1931.

[21] H. Feldman, *op. cit.,* p. 164; quoted by permission of Harper & Brothers, publishers.

Japan. In 1925 Japan materially changed her law so that a second-generation Japanese must declare his wish to remain a Japanese citizen, otherwise he is an American citizen. In the nine southern counties of California under the Japanese consulate of Los Angeles, the Consul reports 20,354 second generation in 1930, of whom 9,123 hold dual citizenship and 11,231 hold only United States citizenship (Table 12, p. 143). The status of the dual citizen has not been definitely established. Apparently he can vote here and can also have the protection of the Japanese government.

The matter of citizenship has apparently made relatively little difference to the Japanese. But what has been of great importance was whether they were brought up essentially as Japanese or as Americans. Many have been sent to Japan for their education, some remaining and others returning here. These are Japanese in most respects, frequently speaking little or no English upon their return, but are American citizens, at least dual citizens, by birth. In contrast are those second-generation Japanese who have been brought up in this country and know little or no Japanese. In between are many who have had some education in Japan or who have attended the Japanese-language schools and so have acquired some mastery of both languages.[22] The evidence we have accumulated (see chapter vii) raises the query as to the possibility of the second generation mastering both English and Japanese under existing conditions. Whether the trouble is due to their being naturally poor linguists or to their not getting proper instruction in Japanese and their having no adequate social environment in which to develop a mastery of English is not known. But it would seem that they are seldom successful in attempting to be both Japanese and American. This means that they must early decide to be one or the other, which adds one more element to all the others that cause bewilderment and indecision. Their future occupational career is thus determined to a considerable degree by the decision they make.

SOCIAL RELATIONSHIPS

Social contacts between whites and Japanese have been largely restricted to those in school. The California school segregation law was intended to eliminate even this, but the law has never been put into operation except in four small school systems, namely, in the towns of Courtland, Florin, Isleton, and Walnut Grove in Sacramento County.

---

[22] See pp. 186 and 187–89 for data regarding residence and education in Japan, Hawaii, and the United States.

Certain legal restrictions have prevented the first generation from entering into the life of the community. Their ineligibility to citizenship removed all possibility of their taking part in political matters. The anti-alien land laws prevented them from taking root in rural communities. The miscegenation law in nine states forbids intermarriage.[23] This probably has had little effect, for there was slight tendency in this direction anyway. Only the last one of these three legal restrictions affects the second generation. The anti-alien land laws are now practically inoperative. Our evidence is that they are not enforced, and the recent decisions of the courts make it possible for the first generation to hold land in the names of their minor children who are born here.[24]

Elimination of all legal restrictions would have little effect upon social relations. It is race prejudice that keeps the two groups apart. Observation of the behavior of school children indicates that they have far less of this feeling than adults. It is not innate, but develops as a result of specific or unconscious instruction by adults and of personal experience. (See chapter iv for further discussion of race prejudice.)

Manifestations of ill-will have forced the Japanese community apart from the white, and neither race knows the other. Each leads its distinct social life. Even churches and Y.M.C.A.'s will not welcome the influx of any considerable number of Japanese, though they are hospitable to a few individuals.[25]

Mr. E. W. Field of our staff made a particularly careful study of the social life of the Japanese in the Hawthorne district, outside of Los Angeles. He found that comparatively little contact had been made between Japanese and whites, and that it is not essential. The Japanese do not seek the whites in this district, for "they are not worthy of attention," according to a Japanese leader. The self-sufficiency of the Japanese is apparent on every hand. They are amply supplied with their own stores, professional people, publications,[26] and cultural and recreational activities for everyone—so much so that the situation invites ex-

---

[23] See footnote 3, p. 255.

[24] For further discussion see pp. 44–46.

[25] In a typical Y.M.C.A. the Japanese are given certain privileges but not that of the pool. Race prejudice is an amazing thing. The Japanese who bathe every day are excluded, and Mexicans are accepted!

[26] The Japanese are well served by the two large Los Angeles Japanese dailies, *Rafu Shimpo* (*Los Angeles-Japanese Daily News*) and *Rafu Michi-bei* (*Japanese-American News*). One seldom sees American newspapers, magazines, or books around the Japanese homes, even those of the better class.

clusion of American activities. The Japanese get the balance of trade, for more whites patronize their stores than the other way around.

Socially, the Japanese hold many meetings, gatherings, picnics, camping trips, *gakuen* (Japanese-language school) entertainments, etc. In sports they show a growing independence of the white race. Their seriousness about their sports is very significant. Tennis is played a great deal, mostly among themselves. Then there are classes in *judo* (wrestling), *kendo* or *gekken* (fencing), *kyujutsu* (archery), and *sumo* (wrestling). *Kendo* has a very deep religious significance. *Sumo* is the oldest of the traditional Japanese sports and is very ritualistic in procedure but has the least religious significance, possibly owing to its antiquity. American culture is conspicuous by its absence, except in matters of dress, automobiles, and slang.

There is an active Baptist Church in the community which runs a bus to bring the children to its Sunday School. A Buddhist Church has recently been built, and the morale of the congregation is distinctly on the up-grade. Parent-Teacher Associations reach few Japanese mothers, one reason at least being that these mothers are too busy. The Japanese-language schools are growing and their effect is more powerful and potent than ever before.

The whites find the Japanese on the whole honest, industrious, well-ordered, and therefore not undesirable. No discrimination is reported within the district. None is shown in neighboring movie houses or restaurants, but some plunges and dance halls at neighboring beaches have refused them admittance. But, as Mr. Field points out, there may have been many cases of "dodging." For example, while interviewing a Japanese newspaper man the writer noticed a golf bag in the corner of his office and inquired if he played. From his answer it was evident that he enjoyed golf very much. When asked if he had ever experienced any unpleasantness while playing on the municipal course, because of his race, he said "No." Later on, when we were better acquainted, he admitted he and his friends always played early in the morning, which was a convenient time for them, and never on Sundays or holidays. He did not suffer from discrimination because he "dodged" the possibilities of its being shown. This "dodging" may be a more important factor in the life of the Japanese than the actual mortification that occasionally occurs from overt discrimination.

Social contacts, as far as the first generation is concerned, are practically nil, in Mr. Field's district. The most significant contacts have been made by the second generation through the schools, some few churches other than those mentioned above, night schools, and opportunity classes. There is in this district apparently more of a tendency for the whites to seek the Japanese than the other way about. The Japanese fêtes, athletic events, etc., are not as a rule attended by white people. Mr. Field believes that if the matter were properly handled much could be done to bring the two peoples together by giving Japanese sports some tactful publicity, as was done at the Orange County Fair by having a "Japan Day" and interspersing the rodeo with different Japanese sports.

Mr. R. B. McKeown found much the same situation in the city of Fresno. He reports there is neither much opportunity nor much desire for increased contacts. The Fresno Chamber of Commerce has from ten to twenty members from the Japanese section, but these men feel that the Chamber is anxious only to get their membership dues and doesn't care for their company and is unwilling to do anything for their section of town. When Mr. McKeown first arrived in Fresno he went to the Chamber of Commerce to get information about the Japanese section and its leaders and found dense ignorance of and lack of interest in the subject. The writer found the same situation at San Diego.

The Fresno Y.M.C.A. allows Japanese boys to use the game and reading rooms but not the gymnasium or the swimming pool, though Armenians, Greeks, and others have these privileges. In fact, none of the town pools admit Japanese, so far as could be discovered. They are served in restaurants but do not receive as good service as whites—at least, so they claim. The Hotel Californian, perhaps the largest and best in Fresno, is an exception, and Japanese are courteously treated there. Most of the stores treat them well, although some clerks are more or less rude to them. The children use the main town library a great deal, as well as their own west-side branch, and are not only welcomed but well liked there.

There seem to be no zoning restrictions against them at present, and a few Japanese live on the east side (the socially preferred district). The Board of Education has no segregation policy. Most of the children attend on the west side, but those going on to college usually attend the larger east-side high schools, where they seem to be well liked and are successful.

What shall be done about all this? Are the second generation to grow up a distinct racial group as far as all social contacts are concerned? Is it actually possible to amalgamate the two races? May they not be happier developing by themselves, even though this may hamper their economic advancement? Does it necessarily follow that segregation will hamper their economic development?

There is one phase of this subject of social relations which is not ordinarily considered but which has been brought to the writer's attention by several Japanese. It is that the second generation are still too inexperienced to want to make the effort to overcome a social disability. They point out that the Chinese, who have been here a generation longer, are much more at ease and can laugh and jest about themselves before the whites but that to the Japanese the situation is no laughing matter. Possibly time is the only solvent here. Possibly those who are discussing this subject are too impatient and are demanding too much, just as parents proverbially expect too much from the first-born, not yet perceiving that increasing maturity takes care of many deficiencies.

Twenty years from now there will be from forty to fifty thousand Japanese voters in California. This will be a small minority, but small minorities sometimes have considerable influence with politicians. It is reasonable to expect as time goes on that there will be amelioration of the present Japanese-American situation because both the first generation and the old-time agitators will have largely passed on and the typical Japanese will be an Americanized voter, having personal acquaintanceship with a number of whites dating back to school days.

Co-operation in altruistic activities has immeasurably strengthened the Service Clubs. Similarly, better social relationships between whites and Japanese can be established if the two will join together in furthering religious, social, and political programs.[27]

CAN JAPANESE BE ASSIMILATED?

That the Japanese cannot be assimilated has been maintained by many during the days of agitation for restriction of immigration and is now being repeated by those opposing the granting of a quota to the Japanese. What does the term "assimilation" mean? David Starr Jordan told us that

> The word "assimilation" has two meanings—interbreeding and comprehension of political and social conditions. In the latter sense, the young Japanese are more readily assimilated than people of several European races; in the former, fortunately, scarcely at all, for a certain pride of ancestry makes Japanese, as a whole, averse to "mixed marriages."[28]

---

[27] In this connection see H. Feldman, *op. cit.,* particularly Part II.

[28] David Starr Jordan, in a statement presented to a Congressional committee and reported in *Hearings before the Committee on Immigration* (United States Senate, 68th Congress, First Session, March 1924), p. 60.

The Los Angeles editor, Boddy, quoting the dictionary, says "assimilation" means "the act of appropriating so as to incorporate into itself, or that process by which one is brought into resemblance, harmony, conformity or identity with regard to the others." He believes that,

> Politically speaking, assimilation means that process by which an alien people are taught to adopt the customs, practices and mode of living prevalent in the country in which they reside.[29] . . . . The whole question simmers down to whether or not the Japanese mental outlook and thought processes can be changed in conformity with the prevailing mental attitude of those around them. Assimilation, therefore, becomes a matter of culture rather than a matter of physical difference.[30]

Perusal of the literature indicates that few recognized authorities on either side would deny that second- and certainly third-generation Japanese lack the mental qualities necessary for cultural assimilation. The question does not apply to the first generation, for cultural assimilation is never accomplished by any first generation. The evidence in the preceding section goes to prove that the Japanese are not acquiring the culture of the whites, and that they are perpetuating to a large degree that of Japan. But this evidence is not conclusive, first, because this is still a first-generation community, the second generation being still almost entirely minors; and, second, because they have had little opportunity to show their powers of cultural assimilation. The writer agrees with most authorities that the Japanese have the necessary capacity. His question is, will they have the necessary opportunity?

Boddy goes farther and states:

> Assimilation is not and never will be a biological matter. It is purely a question of the individual alien adapting himself to his environment . . . . We have in the United States some ten million negroes today. The author has never heard of anyone contending that the negro could not be or has not been assimilated.[31]

Boddy must have in mind the same view as was expressed by Booker T. Washington when he said:

> In all things that are purely social we [the Negroes] can be as separate [from the whites] as the fingers of the hand, yet one as the hand in all things essential to mutual progress.[32]

It seems difficult to reconcile Boddy's views with his definition of assimilation—"that process by which one is brought into resemblance, harmony, conformity or identity with regard to the others." Whites

---

[29] E. M. Boddy, *Japanese in America* (1921), p. 121.

[30] *Ibid.*, p. 124.

[31] *Ibid.*, p. 122.

[32] E. R. Embree, *op. cit.*, p. 120.

and Negroes are not identical, nor are whites and Japanese. The question is whether or not they are in harmony and conformity with each other. To many, assimilation means not merely the living of two regulated groups in the same community but the fusing of the two into one. So far this has not been accomplished except through intermarriage.

Intermarriage.—Both those for and those against the Japanese agree that intermarriage between them and the whites is undesirable. Thus Boddy writes:

> Those Japanese who have married into the white race have been severely criticized for so doing, both by the whites and their own people. . . . . Intermarriage is not advocated by either the whites or the Japanese. Irrespective of any other consideration the difference in color makes it impractical. The white race has never laid aside its color prejudice and the Japanese, on the contrary, feel that they have equal grounds for prejudice.[33]

And McClatchy added in 1929:

> Intermarriage being frowned upon by both races and even forbidden by California law, the races drift apart socially, meeting only occasionally at public functions. Inevitably the Japanese become race conscious, American citizens by rights, but a group apart with separate interests. Thus is produced an unfortunate situation, detrimental alike to Japanese and whites, and most serious from the national point of view, since the country must look to a homogeneous citizenry for permanent stability and progress.[34]

The fact is that there have been a few intermarriages. In the Hawaiian Islands where such marriages are legally possible it has been the Japanese who have refrained, not the whites. Between July 1, 1920, and June 3, 1924, 98.6 per cent of Japanese grooms and 98.3 per cent of Japanese brides married within their own race. But only 75.4 per cent of Caucasian grooms and 92.2 per cent of Caucasian brides married within their group, including here Portuguese, Spaniards, and Puerto Ricans. Nearly 20 per cent of the white grooms married Hawaiians, Caucasian-Hawaiians, or Asiatic-Hawaiians, and nearly 2 per cent married Chinese, Japanese, Koreans, or Filipinos.[35] The Japanese are comparative newcomers to the Islands. Their strong family ties and their custom of marrying as the elders of the family direct have militated

---

[33] E. M. Boddy, *op. cit.*, p. 132.

[34] V. S. McClatchy, *The Japanese Problem* (California Joint Immigration Committee, 1929), pp. 8–9.

[35] Romanzo Adams, T. M. Livesey, E. H. Van Wimble, *A Statistical Study of the Races in Hawaii* (1925), p. 17.

against intermarriage. If the old customs are gradually abandoned, as many expect, it may be that intermarriages will be more common. In fact, Professor Adams told the writer that there were indications of an increasing marriage rate between Japanese and Chinese.

Whites have cohabited with all races, but few have married Negroes. Yet some sociologists believe the Negro question will ultimately be solved by elimination of the blacks. And the fact is that considerable progress has been made in this direction, unpleasant as are its implications.

> While accurate records of ancestry are impossible to obtain, such facts as are available indicate that well above half of the Negroes in America have some white or Indian blood, the extreme estimates on either side being the twenty per cent "mulattoes" reported by the census and the eighty per cent of mixed blood found by students of race . . . . The greatest amount of the mixture in years past came because of the helpless condition of the colored women. As the Negro gains better status, there is a tendency on his part and on that of the white man to avoid further interbreeding. No races in history have lived side by side over long periods of time without almost completely mixing their bloods; and in the future, this course may prove to be inevitable in the United States. Those who regard miscegenation with dread should realize that so far throughout the New World the chief offender against "race purity" has been the white man, that the degraded position of the Negro has made possible the enormous amount of race mixture that has already taken place, and that improved standing and self-respect for the Negro is the only thing that is likely to retard the interbreeding of the white and colored groups.[36]

Apparently we face the plain dilemma: intermarriage and in time complete assimilation, or no intermarriage and great restriction of social contacts. Regardless of law and custom, will the Japanese and whites keep apart? Will it be possible for those who defy the law to be happy and to bring up children who will be normal and accepted by others? Will laws against intermarriage do more good than harm? They will undoubtedly check some unions, but those who are pioneers in any movement are not easily deterred.

There are too few cases of intermarriage between these two races to warrant any conclusion as to the biological aspects of such unions. The evidence is conflicting at best. Personally the writer feels that such unions cannot be condemned on biological grounds. The real objection is social consideration. Both whites and Japanese oppose such marriages and both will make it exceedingly disagreeable for those who defy their point of view. If this were France, with its easy attitude toward color,

---

[36] E. R. Embree, *op. cit.,* pp. 9 and 47; quoted by permission of the Viking Press, publishers.

the problem would be simplified. But it is not. The American feels very strongly on the subject.

If whites and Japanese could be sure there would be neither intermarriages nor illegitimate relations, fear could be eliminated in time and social relations, at least on a limited basis, be established. But as Galen Fisher, who was for many years secretary of the Y.M.C.A. in Japan, says:

> The fear of intermarriages, and the constant possibility that "the lightning may strike our house next," will continue to act like a wet blanket on all efforts to bring about close and equal friendship and co-operation between the races.[37]

Since there are such cases in existence, this haunting fear can hardly be allayed within a generation, if then. The tragedy is that this fear keeps the two groups apart during the adolescent period as far as social affairs are concerned. Even at the University of Hawaii, where students of all races may be seen dancing on the same floor, it is seldom that Japanese or Chinese dance with whites, although the latter associate with Hawaiians. Fisher agrees that while there is "danger of marriage resulting from unrestrained association between the youth of two races" there is "practically no such danger in normal social contacts and co-operation between mature and cultivated adults of the two races."[38] But who can be sure when his son or daughter is participating in "normal" and not "unrestrained association"? What is the dividing line between them? Also, how much real social contact can be engendered if it must be limited to "mature and cultivated adults of the two races"? In fairness it must be pointed out that both Fisher and Akagi[39] have presented quite extensive programs for the development of social contact, but most of their activities are to be carried on by the church, the Y.M.C.A., and similar bodies. Much could be done in this way, possibly enough to give the whole movement the start that is needed. But can these agencies do that which so far they have not accomplished, namely, make the Japanese feel at home?

CONFLICT OF STANDARDS

Without minimizing in the slightest the seriousness of race prejudice and its resulting accompaniment of social segregation, it seems to a

[37] G. M. Fisher, *op. cit.*, p. 11.

[38] *Ibid.*, p. 12.

[39] R. H. Akagi, *The Second Generation Problem* (Japanese Students' Christian Association in North America, 1926).

psychologist that after all the most serious handicap confronting the second generation is the chaotic state of mind being induced in it. A well-ordered mind makes possible definite, clean-cut decisions and purposeful behavior. A mind full of conflicting ideas, ideals, and aspirations results in all manner of starts and stops, with the expenditure of much energy and with little or no progress in any direction. That this condition is not peculiar to the Japanese is indicated in the following quotation from an English writer concerning "the importance in good morale of adequate self-knowledge and the possession of purposes and ambitions appropriate to one's abilities":

> The question of the elimination of conflicting and irrelevant ambitions is perhaps particularly important for the rising generation. I have heard both teachers and employers constantly complain of the irresponsibility, purposelessness and lack of persistence of modern youth. I think this complaint has more behind it than the traditional adult tendency to overestimate the virtues of their own youth. I think it is a genuine observation of a sociological change that is intimately connected with the mechanisms of morale. It seems probable that it is an effect of three social changes that are going on in our times: first, the gradual breakdown of rigid social barriers between the classes; secondly, the multiplication of occupational openings due to increased specialization of functioning; and thirdly, the spread of conflicting standards of achievement and behavior that has resulted from modern developments in mechanical communication. The result of these changes is that the adolescent who in earlier generations had a limited number of vocational choices before him—limited both by industrial conditions and by social class, family standards and traditions—is now faced with a welter of half-understood possibilities, a miscellaneous collection of ideals and standards often picked up haphazard from different social groups and sometimes even from a different continent: as, for example, through the American films. Such a chaos is the inevitable result of a changing social order. Its effect on the morale of the adolescent, causing conflicting purposes and hence doubt and dissipation of energy, is only to be counteracted by the widespread understanding of the nature of the mechanisms involved.[40]

The second generation are confronted by a welter of dilemmas. Shall they be essentially Japanese or American? shall they stay here or go to Japan or some other place, as Brazil? shall they attend college or not? shall they marry as their parents direct or as they themselves please? shall they be Buddhists, Christians, non-believers? and, above all else, what shall they do to earn a living? The white child is confused enough by all that he encounters, but the second-generation Japanese child has many additional causes for bewilderment.

It is not surprising that we have examples of the dynamically opti-

---

[40] A. Macrae and M. Milnor, "Interest and Ability," *Journal of the National Institute of Industrial Psychology*, Vol. V, No. 3 (July 1930), p. 153.

mistic, who are determined to overcome all obstacles, and of the feebly pessimistic, who have given up the conflict. It is not surprising to hear such expressions as, "All right, if that's the way you feel about us, why I'll ——" without any really clear idea of what is to be done. Another "gets even" by declaring he would like to "break into Westwood," the home of the University of California at Los Angeles, where citizens of Japanese ancestry may not reside. They want the "undisputed keys to the city." Who would not like to have them? But it is only too evident that those who speak thus have no clear idea as to what they would do if successful. They are forced to "dodge" whites to avoid a display of racial discrimination; they are equally forced to dodge many an issue because they cannot grapple with its consequences.

It is plain that injured dignity must be forgotten, that vague fears and poorly founded conceptions must be put aside. A sound solution can be reached only by dispassionate accumulation and evaluation of facts.

II. HISTORICAL DEVELOPMENT OF THE IMMIGRATION PROBLEM

The value of historical research lies in the fact that the conditions of the present may be more fittingly met if they can be evaluated in the light of past experiences with similar conditions. Unfortunately, the proper application is not always made and the same "trial and error" method of handling a difficulty is repeated again and again.

After the middle of the nineteenth century the United States had to deal with the problem of rapidly increasing Chinese immigration. It solved this by the Exclusion Act of 1882. Three years later Japanese immigration began. California, remembering the recent Chinese situation, was early aroused to protest. But there is little evidence, so far as the writer has found, that the United States had profited by its past experience. Action was delayed until finally in 1924 Congress was virtually stampeded into a rather tactless enactment of restrictive measures.[1] Filipino immigration[2] has since commenced, and apparently we have had to have mob action and the killing of a Filipino to make us perceive that past experiences should again be taken into account.

The historical events incident to Japanese immigration have been given in great detail by many writers. There is no thought here of adding to what has already been presented or even of summarizing all that has been recorded. Certain happenings of the past are reported, however, in order to remind the reader of facts which have a bearing upon the Japanese problem. As the earlier Chinese immigration undoubtedly had an effect upon the events incidental to the later Japanese immigration, the chapter reviews the former before coming to the latter.

IMMIGRATION OF CHINESE

The evidence from early California history is clear that efforts were made to restrict the coming of the Chinese almost from the beginning

---

[1] Of course there is a simple explanation as to why the past is disregarded; the country is very large, and local conditions must assume gigantic proportions before they are noticed elsewhere. The Atlantic Coast is still unaware of a Filipino problem, and the Pacific Coast is wholly unaware of the problem occasioned by the influx of some 150,000 Puerto Ricans.

[2] See *Facts about Filipino Immigration into California* (Department of Industrial Relations, State of California, 1930); and Bruno Lasker, *Filipino Immigration* (1931). In 1930 there were about 75,000 Filipinos in the Hawaiian Islands and about 60,000 on the mainland of the United States.

of the immigration. The lure of gold in 1849 brought Chinese as well as other nationalities to California. In the *Annual Reports of the Commissioner-General of Immigration,* 42 Chinese are recorded as entering the United States prior to 1853, 42 more during 1853, and 13,100 in 1854. Thereafter until 1869 the number did not exceed 7,518 in any one year and averaged 4,567 for the years 1855–68 (see Table 36, p. 274, for United States census figures). Many more than reported prior to 1854 must have arrived,[3] for "as early as 1852, even before the larger movement began, the governor of California advised that Chinese coolie immigration be restricted and that Congress be urged to prohibit coolie labor in the mines, giving as his arguments that the Chinese were unassimilable, that they lowered the standards of living of labor, that they came here merely for money which they would take out of the country, and that unless checked they would soon be coming in such overwhelming numbers as to endanger the public tranquillity and injure the interests of the people.[4] In 1855 the State Legislature enacted a law imposing a head tax of $55 on every immigrant Chinese. This was followed in 1858 by a law forbidding Chinese or Mongolians to enter the state, and later by other restrictive enactments; but all such legislation was declared unconstitutional by the California Supreme Court, and, finally, in 1876, by the Supreme Court of the United States."[5]

In this question, as in any other, the economic factor was a vital one. Conditions of employment and unemployment largely determined the attitude toward the Chinese. It was when there was shortage of work that the cry arose, "The Chinese must go." When there was shortage of labor, as during the Civil War and while the Central Pacific Railroad was being built, Chinese coolies were readily employed and agitation against them ceased.

The railroad was completed in 1869. Two years earlier the Pacific Mail established the first direct service to the Orient.

> These two great systems of transportation opened up a new route for trade and travel between Europe and Asia. As a result of this great development of

---

[3] By February 1849 there were 54 Chinese in California; in January 1850 the numbers had increased to 789, and a year later to 4,025. See H. H. Bancroft, *History of California* (1890), XXIV, 336.

[4] *Journal of the Senate* (Third Session, 1852), pp. 669–75.

[5] *Annual Report of the Commissioner-General of Immigration* (1919), pp. 53–54.

communication a spirit of optimism prevailed. Visionaries saw tremendous trade possibilities between the United States and China. Accordingly, an outburst of sentiment and consideration for the feelings of the Chinese paved the way for the passage of the Burlingame Treaty of 1868, a treaty which granted to both countries the mutual advantage of free migration and emigration of their citizens and subjects respectively, from the one country to the other for the purpose of curiosity, or trade, or as permanent residents.[6]

During the next twenty-one years (1869–83) the immigration of Chinese averaged 14,087 a year, so that they constituted about 9 per cent of the population of California during that period (Table 36, p. 274).

Instead of the expected trade expansion, economic depression followed the completion of the railroad. Thereupon arose agitation to be rid of the Chinese, who were real competitors for the few jobs available. For a time, local restrictive measures were employed. But after the United States Supreme Court decision of 1876, "the people of the Pacific Coast states turned earnestly to Congress for relief. A congressional inquiry took place in 1876–77; the California legislature appealed to the national government in 1877 and 1878, and Pacific Coast members made a vigorous effort for exclusion legislation."[7] Evidence of the unanimity of feeling in California is shown by the fact that all but 4,000 registered voters went to the polls in September 1879 and all but 883 out of 155,521 votes cast were for exclusion.[8] In 1879 Congress passed a bill limiting the number of Chinese who could come to the United States in any one vessel to fifteen, and repealed the favored-nation clause in the Burlingame Treaty of 1868 which provided for free immigration and emigration between China and the United States. President Hayes vetoed the measure.

In 1880 was concluded another treaty with China which gave the United States the right to "regulate, limit, or suspend" the immigration of Chinese laborers but not to "absolutely prohibit it." In 1882 Congress sought to take advantage of the new treaty's provisions and passed a bill suspending the immigration of Chinese laborers for ten years but giving the right of re-entry to Chinese lawfully in the United States. In 1884 another law was enacted which strengthened the law of

---

[6] R. D. McKenzie, *Oriental Exclusion* (American Group, Institute of Pacific Relations, 1927), pp. 26–27.

[7] *Annual Report of the Commissioner-General of Immigration* (1919), pp. 53–54.

[8] E. G. Mears, "California's Attitude towards the Oriental," *Annals, American Academy of Political and Social Science* (1925), p. 3.

1882 in some particulars.[9] The Act of 1882 was the first national restrictive immigration measure.

The passage of the 1884 immigration law occurred at a time of great stress with regard to the Chinese. In 1883 the Northern Pacific Railway was completed. In 1885 the Canadian Pacific was finished. In both cases large numbers of Chinese laborers were thrown out of work. Lack of employment forced them into competition with whites over a wide area. It was at this time that some of the more serious race riots occurred. "During the autumn of 1885 a great orgy of anti-Chinese behavior swept across the Northwest. The most serious attack upon the Chinese took place at Rock Springs, Wyoming, where in one evening twenty-eight Chinese were murdered, many wounded, and hundreds were driven from their homes."[10] Owing to lack of employment and to persecution the Chinese scattered widely over the country. Many returned home, and there were few new arrivals. The number in any community was too small to arouse antagonism. Since 1890 there has been little or no agitation against the Chinese.

Several facts were established during this period of Chinese immigration that should have been more widely taken into account during the days when the matter of Japanese immigration was the great problem. First, California did not want immigration of Chinese.[11] The same was true of other localities where Chinese congregated in considerable number.[12] Second, it was not within the power of the state of California to restrict entry of Chinese into the state. Third, practically all forms of local legislation of a discriminatory nature against the Chinese were

---

[9] *Annual Report of the Commissioner-General of Immigration* (1919), pp. 53–54.

[10] R. D. McKenzie, *op. cit.*, p. 29. There had been other attacks; for example, the Los Angeles massacre occurred in 1871, when twenty-two Chinese were hanged by a mob following the death of one officer and the wounding of two others who had attempted to break up a tong war. See R. G. Cleland, *A History of California, The American Period* (1922), p. 418.

[11] In 1879 California incorporated into her Constitution these words: "The presence of foreigners who may not become citizens of the United States is dangerous to the well-being of the State, and the legislature shall discourage the immigration of all such aliens by all means within its powers."

[12] "Canada's experience in restricting Chinese immigration reveals a similar trend toward increasing national assertiveness. Starting in 1886 by the imposition of a small head tax, $50 on each Chinese immigrant, the Dominion Government gradually raised the amount to $100 in 1901 and then to $500 in 1904. Even this tax, however, did not seem to accomplish the end desired. Consequently, Orders in

unconstitutional. Fourth, the only way to prevent entry of Chinese into California was through national legislation. And, finally, large numbers of Chinese immigrants returned to their country within a few years.[13] Consequently, data based on entry alone give a distorted picture of how many are in the country.

IMMIGRATION OF JAPANESE

The visit of Commodore Perry to Japan in 1853, followed by the first treaty with Japan five years later, opened up that country to foreign trade. Previously foreigners had not been permitted entry to Japan and her own citizens had been forbidden to leave the country on pain of death. It was not until 1885 that the Japanese government legalized emigration. Thus Japanese immigration began just after the close of Chinese immigration.

In the following year an agreement was entered into between the governments of Hawaii and Japan providing for the importation of Japanese laborers. The need of cheap labor both in the Islands and on the mainland was one of the main causes of the resulting Japanese influx. A second cause was the very low wage scale in Japan. A third cause, one which greatly facilitated the movement, was the opportunity of profit afforded steamship lines and emigration societies which were organized to recruit laborers and furnish them jobs in Hawaii or on the mainland.[14]

Council were resorted to in order to prevent the landing of Chinese laborers. Finally, the Chinese Immigration Act of 1923 completely shut off the flow of Chinese immigrants to Canada" (R. D. McKenzie, *op. cit.*, p. 16).

"The Chinese Immigration Act of 1923 restricts the entry to or landing in Canada of persons of Chinese origin or descent, irrespective of allegiance or citizenship, other than government representatives, Chinese children born in Canada, merchants, and students—the last two classes to possess passports issued by the Government of China and endorsed by a Canadian immigration officer" (*The Canada Year Book* [1924], p. 176).

[13] This has been true of immigrants from many European countries as well as those from China and, later, those from Japan. As for the Chinese, 228,899 arrived between 1853 and 1880. But the United States Census for 1880 gives only 105,465 in the country. Something like 120,000 must have returned. During 1880–90, 61,711 are reported entering. About 60,000 must have returned in order to leave but 107,488 in the country in 1890. (Of the 61,711, the great bulk, i.e., 39,579, came in 1882 just before the restrictive measure of 1882 went into effect.)

[14] See R. L. Buell, "Development of the Anti-Japanese Agitation in the United States," *Political Science Quarterly*, Vol. XXXVII, No. 4 (December 1922) and Vol. XXXVIII, No. 1 (March 1923).

Within five years (1890) there were 12,360 Japanese in the Hawaiian Islands and 2,039 in the United States.[15] During the next ten years these figures had increased, respectively, to 61,111 and 24,326 (Table 34, p. 270). It was during this period that the Hawaiian Islands were annexed to the United States (1898). Beginning with July 1899 the Japanese immigration to the mainland increased greatly, having averaged 1,645 a year from 1890 to 1899 and increasing to 7,146 a year for the period from 1899 to June 1907. In addition to those who came direct from Japan, there were many more who were leaving Hawaii for the United States. Apparently this country could absorb 25,000[16] without awakening opposition. When that number was surpassed and the increase per year was mounting rapidly, antagonism developed. As soon as this became overt it was easy for the blaze to burst into a great conflagration; for with the people on the Pacific Coast there was still a smoldering recollection of their recent experience respecting the Chinese.

Early opposition was first of a local nature, each locality desiring such restrictions as promised to be effective. McKenzie[17] points out that because the Japanese came into competition with organized labor and organized retail services in cities there resulted city ordinances, land laws, and trade restrictions rather than the direct action in labor camps which so characterized antagonism to the Chinese.

The first real protest came from a mass meeting in San Francisco in 1900, under the auspices of the San Francisco Labor Council, which urged extension of the Chinese exclusion laws to the Japanese. In the same year the State Labor Commissioner referred to the sudden increase of Japanese laborers and the Governor called attention to the "Japanese Problem" in his message. In 1904 the American Federation of Labor met in San Francisco and memorialized Congress to extend the Chinese exclusion laws to Koreans and Japanese.[18] The next out-

---

[15] United States Census, 1890.

[16] The total Japanese population in continental United States in 1900 was 24,326 (see Table 34, p. 270).

[17] R. D. McKenzie, *op. cit.*, p. 31.

[18] It should be recognized that the opposition of organized labor to Oriental immigration has continued for nearly seventy years. From 1866 to 1872 the National Labor Union included in its platform exclusion of Oriental immigration. In 1881 the Federation of Organized Trades and Labor Unions of the United States and Canada, out of which developed the American Federation of Labor, had a similar plank in its platform. More recently the Federation "has been

standing event was the appearance of a nine-column article in the *San Francisco Chronicle* on February 23, 1905, calling attention to the dangers of Japanese immigration. This was quickly followed by the organization of the Asiatic Exclusion League and by a resolution unanimously passed in the state senate against unrestricted immigration of Japanese and asking the federal government for immediate protection.

If the experiences incident to Chinese immigration had been taken into account, the federal government, as well as the Japanese government, could easily have foreseen that Japanese immigration could not be continued and steps might have been taken to work out a satisfactory arrangement before heated agitation arose. But instead of this the federal government postponed action and the state of California, joined with other Western states, had to force the issue. This view was expressed in the *Argonaut* (San Francisco) in the words:

> We shall not be able at the present time to impose our beliefs about Japanese exclusion upon the people of the nation—80,000,000 of them—who have been carefully educated to believe the Jap a charming little fellow.[19]

At about this same time, a writer in the *San Francisco Bulletin* remarked:

> We have learned a lesson from the experience of the Southern States. Their race problem is an ancient inheritance; a condition with which they must struggle. What amount of foreign commerce would the South not gladly sacrifice if by the sacrifice the blacks would be persuaded of their own free will to migrate to Africa or some other congenial clime? Our race problem is still in the future. We can prevent it from developing further if we act firmly and sanely now and put aside the counsels of doctrinaires and academicians.

No one can assess how much of the disturbance that followed was

---

growing continuously more exclusionist . . . . In 1919 it advocated the prohibition of all immigration for four years. Between 1919 and 1923 it demanded the abrogation of the 'gentlemen's agreement' with Japan and the total exclusion of all Japanese. During those same years it also opposed the admission of Mexican laborers to the United States and the importation of Chinese workers into Hawaii." Still more recently it has opposed efforts to put the Japanese under the quota law. It is interesting to note that the first use of the label was made in 1874 by the cigar makers in San Francisco "in their fight against sweatshops employing Chinese." See L. L. Lorwin, *The American Federation of Labor* (1933), pp. 7, 12, 23, 272, 402.

[19] See *Literary Digest,* March 25, 1905.

fomented in order to arouse the nation, how much was caused by agitators who wanted to have a hand in getting rid of the Japanese, and how much was engineered by politicians in order to win votes. But as we look back upon this period it seems as though almost everything was tried—with one important exception. Direct action had been used against the Chinese, resulting in many deaths from mob action. Nothing of this sort was attempted with the Japanese. Kawakami, writing in 1921, testified that "no Japanese has suffered physical attack at the hands of 'hoodlums'."[20]

From 1905 until 1924, when restriction of Japanese immigration was enacted by Congress, many discriminatory measures were advocated and a few passed by the California legislature. In addition, many local activities of a discriminatory nature were put into effect, such as boycotts against the Japanese and even against white merchants and manufacturers who employed Japanese.

It was the action of the San Francisco School Board (October 11, 1906) requiring all Japanese in the public schools to attend the Oriental school in Chinatown[21] which forced the issue upon the nation. Even though the Japanese people had shown their good-will by contributing $244,960 through the Red Cross to the relief of San Francisco after its great earthquake and fire of April 1906, a contribution that exceeded the combined contributions from all other foreign nations,[22] the agitation against the Japanese continued. Subsequent investigation has made clear that there were almost no rational grounds for the seg-

---

[20] K. K. Kawakami, *The Real Japanese Question* (1921), p. 132. Will J. French, director of the Department of Industrial Relations, in a letter of June 30, 1932, to the writer states that there was no record in his department of Japanese having been "killed or injured in California as an outcome of immigration problems. . . . . I have checked up the foregoing with Dr. Louis Bloch, and he agrees." The writer has, however, run across two or three references to assaults upon Japanese, one in connection with the boycott of the Cooks' and Waiters' Union against Japanese restaurants, and another in connection with a street-car strike in San Francisco. No definite proof of either has been discovered.

[21] Established in 1885, in accordance with state legislation of various dates from 1866 on. See R. H. Thomson, "Events Leading to the Order to Segregate Japanese Pupils in the San Francisco Public Schools" (unpublished Ph.D. thesis, Stanford University, 1931), pp. 70–73.

[22] P. J. Treat, *Japan and the United States* (1921), p. 254. In referring to the action of the School Board, Treat says: "Although various explanations of this resolution were given at the time, the real reason was to start the process of discrimination which would eventually lead to the enactment of an exclusion law."

regation of Japanese school children,[23] but the measure was passed by a school board under the domination of the labor party,[24] and the corrupt city government of Schmitz and Ruef. The violent outbursts of Japanese opinion which viewed the measure as a treaty violation and a national insult forced the President to intervene in the matter. In his message to Congress of December 4, 1906, he denounced the segregation measure as a "wicked absurdity" and went so far as to recommend the enactment of a law providing for the naturalization of the Japanese.[25] In return for an understanding that the President would bring Japanese immigration to an end, the School Board rescinded its action.[26]

GENTLEMEN'S AGREEMENT

On March 14, 1907, the President issued a proclamation ordering that "Japanese or Korean laborers, skilled or unskilled, who have received passports to go to Mexico, Canada, or Hawaii, and come therefrom, be refused permission to enter the continental territory of the United States."[27] But this action did not stop direct immigration from Japan to the mainland. Some time in the latter part of 1907 or early in 1908 the Japanese government itself agreed to restrict such immigra-

[23] According to Miss Ruth H. Thomson there were only 93 Japanese pupils in a school population of nearly 29,000. "Of these 93 Japanese, moreover, 28 were girls and 25 were American-born. Of the 65 boys, 26 were under 15 years of age, 7 were 15, 7 were 16, 13 were 17, 6 were 18, 4 were 19, and 2 were 20. . . . . President Altmann of the San Francisco Board of Education in an interview with a *Chronicle* reporter admitted that 'nothing can be said against the general character and deportment of Japanese scholars.'"

Miss Thomson concludes that "there was nothing in the school situation per se to demand the passage of a Japanese segregation order." The real explanation is to be found in the agitation of labor for fifty years against Oriental labor, an issue that had been capitalized by politicians for years in order to win votes. See R. H. Thomson, *op. cit.,* pp. 80, 83, 89, chapters v, vi.

[24] Agitation against the Japanese originated largely with the labor unions, which were opposed to any immigration increasing the number of workers, and much of this agitation was due to politicians who seized upon the issue to advance their own purposes. Later on protests arose from the country districts which developed into enactments to drive Japanese off the land.

[25] *Congressional Record,* Vol. 41, Part 1 (1906), p. 31; also J. D. Richardson, *Messages and Papers of the President* (1911), pp. 7434–36.

[26] R. L. Buell, *Japanese Immigration,* World Peace Foundation Pamphlets, Vol. VII, Nos. 5–6 (1924), p. 287.

[27] Department of Commerce and Labor, Bureau of Immigration and Naturalization, *Immigration Laws and Regulations of July 1, 1907,* Rule 21, p. 44.

tion. The exact details of this "Gentlemen's Agreement" have never been made known. The first official announcement of the agreement appears in the *Annual Report of the Commissioner-General of Immigration* for 1908 (p. 221), where it is stated that

an understanding was reached with Japan that the existing policy of discouraging the emigration of its subjects of the laboring classes to continental United States should be continued and should, by co-operation of the governments, be made as effective as possible. This understanding contemplates that the Japanese Government shall issue passports to continental United States only to such of its subjects as are non-laborers or are laborers who, in coming to the continent, seek to resume a formerly-acquired domicile, to join a parent, wife or child residing there, or to assume active control of an already possessed interest in farming enterprise in this country . . . . With respect to Hawaii, the Japanese Government of its own volition stated that, experimentally at least, the issuance of passports to laboring classes proceeding thence would be limited to former residents and parents, wives, or children of residents.

A similar agreement was entered into between Japan and Canada at the same time. Immigration to Mexico was also limited by Japan.[28] The country, as a whole, accepted the Gentlemen's Agreement as settling the California problem. For the most part, the American attitude was friendly and desirous of maintaining Japanese friendship, though there were some jingoists whose war talk was alarming.

In California at this time many favored limited Oriental immigration. These were farmers of large tracts, merchants, lumbermen, housewives, and included in fact nearly all except labor unions, small ranch owners, politicians, and jingoes. The former found cheap and plentiful labor an advantage; the workingman found it of great disadvantage. In addition, many business interests and their allies did not want Japan to be offended, as such a condition might threaten favorable commercial relations. In fact, practically all, including the unions, desired to avoid force or violence and sought co-operation and friendliness. Many investigators, from within and without the state, emphasized that race prejudice was not the predominant factor involved. The objection to Japanese labor was that it tended to lower the standard of living of the workingman.

The Gentlemen's Agreement checked the immigration of 6,686 a year and cut it to only 2,689 per year (1908–13). From then on it

[28] There were 3,945 passports issued by the Japanese government to Mexico in 1907. The following year only 18 were issued. In 1913, 106 were issued, the largest number since 1908. See H. A. Millis, *The Japanese Problem in the United States* (1915), p. 16.

increased until it averaged 5,879 from 1917 to 1924 (Table 3, p. 85; see also Fig. 1, p. 87). Those Japanese coming in after 1907 were largely women and children. Some of the women were wives in the American sense, but the majority were married to Japanese in this country by proxy. Entry of these "picture brides" did not appeal to Californians as playing the game. They felt that through this evasion of the Gentlemen's Agreement they had been tricked. Moreover, what they wanted—namely, restriction of Japanese immigration—had not been obtained. It was felt that, if anything, it was worse to have Japanese born in this country and so become future citizens than to have merely male Japanese who would eventually return to Japan or die here childless.

Neither the Exclusion League nor the state legislature considered the matter settled by the Gentlemen's Agreement. The first agreement of Japan in 1900 to restrict immigration had accomplished very little and that only temporarily, and there was no reason to expect better things from the second pact. In addition, there were the Japanese already in the state. Although there was no legal way of forcing them to leave, conditions could be made so disagreeable as to cause them to leave "voluntarily." Agitation was continued, and many bills designed to cause unpleasantness were introduced in the legislature. These were all dropped at the 1909 session, owing to the intervention of President Roosevelt and Governor Gillett.

The Treaty of 1911 with Japan added further cause for alarm. The former treaty (1894) had provided that citizens of each country "shall have full liberty to enter, travel or reside in any part of the territories of the other Contracting Party, and shall enjoy full and perfect protection for their persons and property." The new treaty appears to have authorized such admissions only for purposes of trade, as pointed out by Buell,[29] for it provided that

> The citizens or subjects of each of the high contracting parties shall have liberty to enter, travel, and reside in the territories of the other to carry on trade, wholesale and retail, to own or lease and occupy houses, manufactories, warehouses and shops, to employ agents of their own choice, to lease land for residential and commercial purposes, and generally to do anything incident to or necessary for trade upon the same terms as native citizens or subjects, submitting themselves to the laws and regulations.

So far the 1911 treaty restricted more than the 1894 treaty. But the latter had a clause that "the provisions of the treaty should not in any

---

[29] R. L. Buell, *Japanese Immigration* (1924), p. 290.

way affect the laws, ordinances and regulations with regard to the immigration of laborers, or which may hereafter be enacted in either country," and the new treaty had no such limitation in terms of present or future immigration laws. It had, instead, a signed statement from the Japanese Ambassador attached to it, guaranteeing that Japan would keep the Gentlemen's Agreement in force. Whereas the old treaty gave the United States full control of Japanese immigration, the new treaty gave this power into the hands of the Japanese government. Revocation of this principle was one of the objectives agitators kept ever in mind until the Immigration Act of 1924 was passed. The outbursts against this treaty by the 1911 California legislature resulting from the absence of the clause of the 1894 treaty were calmed by the intervention of President Taft.

ANTI-ALIEN LAND LAWS

By 1913 it was well known in California that the Japanese immigration was continuing and that, in addition, there was a rapidly increasing Japanese population due to birth. Attention had also by this time been called to the increasing acreage owned or controlled by Japanese. This fact afforded a new purpose in attacking the Japanese, namely, to take the use of agricultural land away from them. Despite a strong protest from President Wilson, the Webb-Heney Bill was enacted in 1913. This bill left to aliens ineligible to citizenship all rights to real property granted by treaty, but no other—except the right to lease land for three years. As the Treaty of 1911 did not grant Japanese the right to acquire land, they now had no rights in regard to the acquisition of agricultural land. Certain weaknesses appearing in this law were eliminated in 1920 by an initiative measure that was carried by a vote of 668,483 to 222,086. In 1923 the third anti-alien land law was passed. By these laws Japanese can neither own nor lease land, since tenancy is a recognized legal interest in the land. Cropping, an agreement whereby the tenant works the land on agreement that a fixed percentage will be his and a fixed percentage will go to the landowner, is specifically, by law and by interpretation, forbidden, and a cropping agreement cannot be camouflaged by calling it a contract of employment or a bonus contract.[30]

---

[30] The United States Supreme Court upheld, in 1923, the California land laws in two cases, saying in part that, "in the absence of a treaty to the contrary, a state has power to deny aliens the right to own land within its borders," and that, "in forbidding such [cropping] contracts, the state law violates no right of the land-

Recent decisions of the California Supreme Court now permit croppage contracts between Japanese and whites and provide that a Japanese alien may act as guardian for a minor born in the United States.[31] In these two ways the anti-alien land laws may be evaded. The Japanese can lease land for commercial or residential purposes, since this right is set forth in the Japanese-American commercial treaty.

Mears, writing in 1927, states:

> It cannot be denied that over the state there is a general lack of enforcement of the combined acts of 1913, 1920 and 1923. The law . . . . is plain, the Supreme Court of the United States has affirmed its constitutionality. The Attorney General of the State . . . . is strict in his rulings and his position has been made clear . . . . What has happened is that, acting upon the advice of able counsel, prior to the operation of the 1920 act, a good many land corporations were formed in which Orientals have a substantial but minor interest; also, title is sometimes taken out in the name of an American-born child; sometimes, straight wages are supplemented by gifts or special arrangements; or regular wages may be scaled to the desired level, while the ineligible alien occupies a position in fact but not in theory equivalent to that of tenant or operator. . . . . Under the system of county politics, the local district attorney is responsible for initiating actions in alleged violation of these statutes. The farmer—rancher, as he is usually called in California—has great influence in state affairs.[32]

Consequently, when it is to the advantage of the whites to lease their land to Japanese, they find a way to do it. In the survey conducted by the writer, ample evidence that this is common practice was found, but in order to protect the Japanese who were willing to supply the facts our interviewers did not attempt to gather data on this subject.

The claim has repeatedly been made by pro-Japanese writers that there was little need for the land laws. Because the report of the Labor Commissioner, J. D. MacKenzie, supported this view, it was suppressed by the state legislature. Among other things he is quoted as having said:

> The Japanese land owners are of the best class; they are steady and industrious, and from their earnings purchase land of low value and poor quality. The care lavished upon this land is remarkable, and frequently its acreage has increased several hundred per cent in a year's time. . . . . Most of the proprietors indicate

---

owner or the alien under the Federal constitution" (*Porterfield* v. *Webb,* and *Webb* v. *O'Brien,* U.S. Reports, Vol. 263 [October term, 1923], pp. 232, 321–24; see also pp. 225, 313).

[31] *Yano, Estate of,* 188 Cal. 645.

[32] E. G. Mears, *Resident Orientals,* pp. 253–54.

an intention to make the section in which they have located a permanent home, and to adopt American customs and manners. . . . . Some form of labor such as is now represented by the Japanese is essential for the continuance and development of the specialized agricultural industry of California.[33]

Since the exclusion of the Japanese, California has witnessed a great immigration of Mexicans and a lesser one of Filipinos and Negroes. It is interesting to speculate upon the possibility that if California had not had Chinese and Japanese for common laborers she might have had a great influx of Negroes in early days. Millis[34] states there was "no real problem," for, according to assessment rolls, the Japanese owned in 1912 only 331 farms in California, aggregating 12,726 acres and valued at $609,605. Even the figures gathered by the Board of Control in 1919 were not alarming, showing 74,769 acres owned or bought on contract and 383,287 acres under lease or crop contract, out of a total of 11,389,894 acres of improved land.[35] Such writers have missed the real significance of the land laws, which were designed primarily to stop Japanese immigration. Every year of such immigration only made matters worse. These measures were framed to discourage Japanese from coming to California or even from staying here and also to force the federal government to enact restrictive measures. It was fear of what might happen, together with fresh memories of mob action against the Chinese and consideration of the unsolved race problem in the South, that governed the thinking of the better element and led to the almost unanimous conclusion that a large number of Japanese could not live in harmony with the whites in California.

Several writers, particularly those friendly to the Japanese, have pointed out that many who voted in 1920 for the anti-alien land measure did not really understand the issue and that they voted so because of general antagonism to the Japanese, part of this antagonism being due to Japan's Shantung demands on China and her reported military aggressions in Manchuria, Korea, and Siberia. Treat[36] traces the development of the surprisingly sudden change in attitude of the peoples of Japan and the United States from genuine friendliness up to the close of the Japanese-Russian War (1904–5) to suspicion and criticism.

---

[33] J. T. Bramhall, "The Orient in California," *World Today,* April 1911, p. 469.

[34] H. A. Millis, *op. cit.,* p. 215.

[35] *California and the Oriental,* Report of State Board of Control to the Governor (1920, revised in 1922), p. 47.

[36] P. J. Treat, *op. cit.,* chapter x.

This was intensified by extensive propaganda, some of it most outrageous, which without question influenced the whole situation. Diplomatic relations, however, remained friendly and the official correspondence repeatedly expressed high regard each for the other.

During the two decades following the close of the Russo-Japanese War (1905) the fact that war with Japan was a possibility was almost constantly kept before the American public, many maintaining it to be inevitable. Americans sided with Japan in her conflict with Russia, for they believed her statement that she was only endeavoring to keep Korea and Manchuria free from Russia. But when it was revealed that Japan intended to keep these areas for herself, antagonism immediately appeared. Self-interest was involved when the suspicion arose that Japan was not seriously supporting the Open Door policy. A friendlier feeling resulted from the Root-Takahira Agreement (1908), which upheld the Hay doctrine of equal opportunity and the preservation of China's integrity. Many other events have occurred, alternately arousing antagonism and allaying it, such as the necessity of fortifications in the Pacific to safeguard the Philippines, Hawaii, and the Pacific Coast, the world cruise of our battleships and Taft's visit to Japan, the annexation of Korea by Japan in 1910, the Magdalena Bay furore in 1912, the Twenty-one Demands upon China and the rigorous suppression of the uprising in Korea in 1919. Following the World War were other events, such as the refusal of the United States and Great Britain to grant Japan's demand for racial equality at the Peace Conference, the Washington Conference for limitation of armament in 1921, the Four-Power Pact, and the Nine-Power Agreement, resulting in Shantung's being returned to China and some of the Twenty-one Demands being withdrawn. All these and many others that might be mentioned have kept Japan ever in the limelight. There is no doubt that they have affected the immigration question greatly. Many citizens have voted against Japanese interests because of antagonism to Japan arising from one or more such events. Many, on the other hand, have espoused her cause because of certain other events very creditable to her. And this applies not only to Californians and to the action of their state but also to citizens of the whole country and to federal legislation.

THE 1924 EXCLUSION ACT

The Japanese immigration question has been before Congress from time to time since 1905, when Mr. McKinlay and Mr. Hayes, representatives from California, introduced bills to exclude Japanese and

Koreans.[37] Other bills were introduced in 1907 and 1908, prior to the signing of the Gentlemen's Agreement. The Burnett-Dillingham Bill including illiteracy tests was vetoed by the President on February 1, 1913. At the next session practically the same bill was reintroduced, with an added clause to restrict those "who cannot become eligible to become citizens."[38] This clause was voted down, showing Congress was not yet ready for such a measure. Veto of the remainder of the bill, in January 1913, brought an end to discussion of immigration for the time. Finally, the Immigration Act of 1924 was passed (effective July 1, 1924), giving California what she wanted, namely, exclusion of Japanese. This act abrogated without notice the Gentlemen's Agreement and provided for the exclusion of all aliens ineligible to citizenship. Table 3 (p. 85) and Figure 1 (p. 87) show the immediate and drastic drop in immigration following the passage of this act.

A number of issues were involved in this Japanese immigration question. Restriction of Japanese immigration through the Gentlemen's Agreement for sixteen years had led to general acceptance of the belief that restriction was essential. It was also fairly generally accepted that this agreement had failed to exclude Japanese as the West had desired. But men differed as to the degree of desirable restrictions and the method of accomplishment. Those friendly to Japan believed that Japan would be ready to modify further the Gentlemen's Agreement so as to give the United States a workable solution. Others favored putting Japan, like the European nations, upon a quota basis. This group were particularly anxious not to offend Japan, not to discriminate against her. A difficulty with putting Japan upon a quota basis was that the United States was not ready to put all Asiatic nations on such a basis. To grant such a concession to Japan meant to discriminate in her favor, which apparently many were not willing to do, particularly against China. On the other hand, there were those who believed that control of immigration should be in the hands of the United States, not of Japan. They were thus opposed to the Gentlemen's Agreement, since it gave Japan control. Furthermore, members of Congress believed that control of immigration was a prerogative of Congress, whereas the President was in control through his Gentlemen's Agreement, with the possibility of further developments in this direction if

[37] *United States Document, Serial Number 4903, House Journal* (59th Congress, First Session), p. 182.

[38] *Congressional Record*, Vol. 51, Part 3 (63d Congress, Second Session), p. 2596.

he were permitted to reopen the question with Japan. Interjected into all these ramifications of the subject was the insistent demand of California and other Western states for complete exclusion.

It seems impossible to guess what might have happened in 1924 if it had not been for an unfortunate note from Ambassador Hanihara to the Secretary of State which was printed in the *Congressional Record* of April 11. The significant sentence is:

> Relying upon the confidence you have been good enough to show me at all times, I have stated or rather repeated all this to you very candidly and in a most friendly spirit, for I realize, as I believe you do, the grave consequences which the enactment of the measure retaining that particular position would inevitably bring upon the otherwise happy and mutually advantageous relations between our two countries.[39]

Three days later Senator Lodge called attention to the phrase "grave consequences" as "improper" and a "veiled threat" against the United States. Though Hanihara assured Congress no such meaning was intended, many Congressmen changed their vote because of Lodge's interpretation, and the exclusion bill was passed. The significant clause in the exclusion bill is as follows:

> No alien ineligible to citizenship shall be admitted to the United States unless such an alien (1) is admissible as a non-quota immigrant under the provision of subdivision (*b*),[40] (*d*),[41] or (*e*)[42] of section 4, or (2) is the wife, or the unmarried child under 18 years of age of an immigrant admissible under such subdivision (*d*) and is accompanying or following to join him, or (3) is not an immigrant as defined in section 3.

Ichihashi gives the impression that there was no need for abrogation of the Gentlemen's Agreement when he writes:

> In response to the agitation, unwarranted though it appeared to be, the Japanese Government took the initiative in 1921 to stop female immigration to this country. During the next four years (1921–1924), the total number of alien Japanese admitted to this country was 39,237, while that of departures was 40,452, a loss of 1,210.[43]

---

[39] *Congressional Record,* Vol. 65, Part 6 (68th Congress, First Session), p. 6074.

[40] Immigrants "previously lawfully admitted to the United States" and "returning from a temporary visit abroad."

[41] Bona fide ministers of religious denominations, and professors with their wives and unmarried children under eighteen years of age.

[42] Bona fide students over fifteen years of age.

[43] Y. Ichihashi, *Japanese in the United States* (1932), p. 63. (See also Table 40, p. 278.)

This implies that the restriction of women was accomplished. Actually there was only a slight decrease in the immigration of women between 1921 and 1924 as compared with the years 1916–20 (see Fig. 1, p. 87). Departures of Japanese males, however, greatly exceeded arrivals, which accounted for the total net decrease.

The 1924 act was viewed by Japan as a "deliberate insult"; "a gross insult to Japan"; "harsh, cruel, and unjust"; "selfish and arrogant."[44] In America, the majority of newspapers, magazines, and organizations of all types condemned the method employed, although many supported the idea of exclusion itself. The *Hartford Times,* for example, declared:

> The Japanese protest is the understandable act of a proud nation. It is not based upon any theory that Japan has a right to dictate our domestic policies. It is a plea for fair treatment.[45]

The *New York Times* said that there was

> no justification for the Senate's shocking disregard of the feeling of the Japanese. The proper way to solve the problem was through diplomatic channels. In wilfully ignoring this the Senate inflamed Japanese hatred of the United States and totally misrepresented the true attitude of the people of this country.[46]

Would Japan have materially altered the Gentlemen's Agreement in the direction of the restriction desired by California? Two actions on her part suggest that she might have done so. Following the reports of various investigations which showed that the Gentlemen's Agreement had not stopped immigration, particularly of women, Japan on February 25, 1920, voluntarily stopped granting passports to "picture brides." As the passports were good for six months, immigration of "picture brides" did not actually cease until August 1920. Even this action did not have any noticeable effect upon the number of Japanese entering the country, for unmarried Japanese returned to Japan and married their brides before bringing them to the United States[47] (see Table 3, p. 85, and Fig. 1, p. 87). The second action of Japan pertained to naturalization. On December 1, 1924, the Japanese Diet amended the Law of Na-

---

[44] See R. L. Buell, *Japanese Immigration* (1924), pp. 314–35.

[45] From *Literary Digest,* June 14, 1924, pp. 8–10.

[46] *New York Times,* May 27, 1924.

[47] These brides were referred to as *kankodan.* In the year September 1, 1920, to August 31, 1921, 2,197 such brides arrived (*Hearihgs before the Committee on Immigration. Hearings . . . . on S. 2576, March 11–15, 1924* [68th Congress, First Session], p. 27).

tionality. By this amendment a child born of Japanese parents, regardless of where they are living, is not to be classed as a Japanese subject unless the parents declare, within fourteen days after birth, their intention of retaining Japanese nationality. Persons may also abandon their Japanese citizenship at any time by making a simple notification. The law was made retroactive. This change eliminated the necessity of dual citizenship for those of Japanese ancestry born in Hawaii or on the mainland; hitherto they had been citizens of the United States by birth and of Japan by Japanese law. (See p. 140 for further discussion.)

Did Japan perform her part of the Gentlemen's Agreement? She claimed that she had done so "most scrupulously and faithfully."[48] As far as we know, the agreement specifically provided that laborers would be given passports provided they were "to resume a formerly-acquired domicile, to join a parent, wife or child residing there, or to assume active control of an already possessed interest in farming enterprise in this country."[49] Evidently this means that if there was a single member of a family already in the country all other members were free to join him. Moreover, if one purchased an interest in a farming enterprise he was also free to come. With such wide latitude it is no wonder that immigration increased while Japan claimed she was faithfully carrying out her agreement!

Was Theodore Roosevelt derelict to his duty when he promised California restriction of immigration and then accepted this agreement? We believe not. Up to 1907 very few Japanese women had come to America. The inclusion of the clauses cited appeared to be harmless not only to him but to California. It was only several years later that California woke up to their significance as the stream of Japanese female immigrants increased.

CONFLICTING VIEWS OF JAPANESE AND WHITES

The conflicting views of Japanese and whites can best be brought out by presenting each in turn. Consider first the views of the Japanese.

What do the Japanese want?—Apparently some desire freedom of entry and citizenship. Thus Yoshitomi has gone so far as to contrast the small population per square mile in the United States with the large number in Japan and to insist that any people have the right to settle on

---

[48] Letter of Ambassador Hanihara, *Congressional Record,* Vol. 65, Part 6 (68th Congress, First Session), p. 6073.

[49] See p. 42 for a more complete statement.

land not already taken up. He argues that immigration is not a domestic problem but an international one:

> D'après notre conception, tout dépend de la règle de droit émanant de la solidarité internationale. ... Un pays qui a trop de richesse naturelle pour sa capacité d'exploitation, a le devoir commandé par la règle de droit, d'ouvrir la porte aux autres peuples qui peuvent les exploiter d'une manière plus efficace.[50]

And the Japan-born journalist, Kawakami, who has lived in the United States since 1901, concludes his book as follows:

> It is obvious that a program to establish permanent peace with justice should contain one of two propositions, namely, a more equitable distribution of territory, or the removal of the exclusive policy adopted by Western colonial powers against Asiatic people. . . . . This, in short, is the fundamental question. It goes without saying that it cannot be solved by a "gentlemen's agreement," an exclusion law, a "percentage" plan, or such palliative measures. As the question is fundamental, its solution must also be fundamental. Can it be done? It must be done, if it takes centuries. The idea is chimerical in the sense that Christianity and all great doctrines are chimerical, no more or no less.[51]

These writers are, however, in conflict with the attitude of many nations who regard immigration as "an incontestably domestic question with which no international body could deal without express authority to do so."[52] It is inconceivable[53] that Japan would herself consent to an international agreement by which she would be unable to check unlimited immigration of Chinese, Filipinos, or Hindus into her own country.

Many Japanese both in Japan and in this country desire a continuance of immigration on about the basis of the Gentlemen's Agreement, that is, limited immigration. The 1932–34 program of the Japanese-American Citizens' League, an organization of second-generation Japanese, contains these items:

> That the national council exert every possible means and power on the following problems:

---

[50] M. Yoshitomi, *Les conflits Nippo-Américains* (1926), p. 329.

[51] K. K. Kawakami, *The Real Japanese Question* (1921), pp. 235–36; quoted by permission of the Macmillan Company, publishers.

[52] Statement of President Wilson, August 19, 1919, Treaty of Peace with Germany, *Hearings of the Senate Committee on Foreign Relations, Senate Document No. 106* (66th Congress, First Session), p. 501.

[53] We are considering here immigration for permanent settlement. Two or more countries could of course formulate rather easily an agreement respecting the back-and-forth flow of laborers in search of labor opportunities between different countries.

a) To straighten out any difficulties which may exist now or hereafter with reference to passports issued by the Department of State.
b) To have Congress grant citizenship to Japanese World War Veterans.
c) To have Congress admit alien wives, husbands and/or parents of American citizens of Japanese ancestry into the United States as non-quota immigrants.

McKenzie expresses the thought in this way:

Both China and Japan, according to the repeated utterances of their representative leaders, accept the principle of immigration restriction. They realize it is in the interests of all concerned to prevent a too rapid intermingling of the races.[54]

Whether or not McKenzie intended to emphasize the expression "too rapid intermingling," it appears to the writer that it should be stressed, for apparently there are Japanese who desire some immigration to the United States even if in relatively small numbers.

After analyzing the Japanese population problem Crocker concludes that emigration sufficient to solve the problem is unthinkable but that a relatively small emigration might mitigate the situation in Japan appreciably. He says:

It may be emphasized that the significance of emigration for Japan should not be exaggerated. Emigration by itself can be only a palliative at the best, and sometimes not even a palliative; and even in the case of a country like Japan, experiencing as it is a falling birth-rate, a rising conception of the standard of life, and an increasingly productive economic system, an outlet large enough to absorb all the men and women who may be redundant at home could never be found. Japanese officials and Japanese students are aware of all this. But the point is that to drain off only a portion of the unemployed might serve as a much needed safety valve for the hot social vaporings of the coming twenty or thirty years, and in so doing preserve the tranquillity of the country. By organizing streams to the four groups discussed (i.e., North Eastern Asia, East Indian Islands, particularly Borneo and New Guinea, South Pacific Islands, and Brazil), and by adding the flow of technical and professional men to Japan's own territories, it ought to be practicable to dispose of not less than 50,000 to 100,000 emigrants a year; and 50,000 to 100,000 a year may be "the little more or the little less" that will save the peace. It was the last straw that broke the camel's back.[55]

That the difficulties [of emigration] will be surmounted we can confidently expect from what we know of the Japanese attitude of mind. A glimpse of this is given in the handling of the only emigration of account that is now taking

---

[54] R. D. McKenzie, *op. cit.*, p. 180.

[55] W. R. Crocker, *The Japanese Population Problem* (1931), pp. 202–3; quoted by permission of the Macmillan Company, publishers. It is the college graduate who must become a clerk, mechanic, or manual laborer for lack of suitable employment who is the greatest "threat to social tranquillity," according to Crocker (p. 209).

place—that to Brazil.[56] Museums are established exhibiting the life and customs of the country, and regular courses are given the emigrants a few weeks before embarkation on the food, clothes, religion, and general habits of its natives so as to facilitate a ready adaptation. Subsidies are granted and loans extended to emigrating families, and their interests are carefully safeguarded all the way. The real difficulty will not come from the capacity of Japanese to manage the project, but from the prevailing attitude to territorial possession among the Powers.[57]

The *San Francisco Chronicle* of June 26, 1934, reports that Brazil has restricted Japanese immigration to "2 per cent of the total Japanese emigrants entering that country during the last 50 years . . . . The new quota means that only about 3,500 emigrants will be accepted yearly from now on instead of the 30,000 who have been entering annually from Japan for several years." Table 41 (p. 280) gives 64,191 Japanese in Brazil in 1925 and 160,387 in 1932, an annual gain of 13,742.

Many others claim that the Japanese are at least acquiescent with regard to exclusion but object strenuously to the method employed for accomplishing this. Thus McKenzie states that "Japanese of the official and commercial classes are unanimous in their insistence that their complaint is not against the *operation* of the present law, but rather against the *principle* of discrimination involved in the law itself."[58] A recent editorial in the *Japanese-American Courier* of Seattle supports this view:

"I do not think it was kind."

Such was Dr. Inazo Nitobe's comment on the exclusion law in an address he delivered on his recent visit to this city. In that single short sentence is contained the attitude of the intelligent Japanese citizen toward the exclusion law which was passed in this country in 1924.

The intelligent Japanese knows that it was the sovereign right of the United States to pass such a law, and recognizing this, does not deny that this nation did not go beyond its rights in the matter. Nevertheless, that does not vitiate the fact that many unkind things are done with the perpetrator acting perfectly within his rights.

There are two specific grounds on which the exclusion law might be termed unkind. The first is that immigration legislation passed since then has largely done away with the necessity for such an exclusion law and the second is that the law was aimed specifically at Japan.

The national origins act has been passed since 1924 by the United States government to limit immigration from all nations. Under the provisions of this

---

[56] See Table 41 (p. 280) for emigration data.

[57] W. R. Crocker, *op. cit.*, p. 196; quoted by permission of the Macmillan Company, publishers.

[58] R. D. McKenzie, *op. cit.*, p. 45.

act and if the exclusion law were not in force only 185 Japanese would be admitted to this country in the course of a year. Considerably more than that number return to Japan to take up their permanent residence there. As a result the exclusion law as it now stands bars but a nominal number of Japanese from this country. Under these conditions its repeal would be but a gracious gesture toward making amends for what was and still is an unkind act.

In the second place the law was directly aimed against the Japanese. Its proponents said that the law was designed to exclude all Orientals, but the fact of the matter was that long before, in 1882 to be specific, a law was passed barring Chinese from entering this country.[59] Consequently, the law through barring them from this country stigmatized the Japanese as being an inferior race. What could be more unkind than this act of international discourtesy?

What is the principle to which the Japanese so object? According to Buell it is that Japan "objects particularly to being classed with Chinese, Tartars, and Hindus — under the indiscriminate heading of 'aliens ineligible to citizenship.' Such a classification refuses to recognize, in her opinion, the extent to which Japan and the Japanese have outdistanced other peoples in the Orient in their readjustment to occidental civilization."[60] Buell points out in this connection that Japan put up a strong fight at the Paris Peace Conference for the adoption of "an amendment to the covenant of the League of Nations guaranteeing 'to all aliens, nationals of states, members of the League, equal and just treatment in every respect, making no distinctions, either in law or fact, on account of their race or nationality'." Eight[61] members, including the United States, Great Britain, and her possessions, voted against the measure, thus defeating it, as it had to be passed unanimously. Later on, "Baron Makino gave notice of the poignant regret of the Japanese Government and people at the failure of the Commission to approve of their just demand, and of their intention to insist upon the adoption of this principle by the League in the future." Treat believes that "in advocating this great principle the Japanese won a moral advantage in spite of their defeat."[62]

---

[59] Because the Chinese and all other Asiatics except Japanese had already been excluded, the 1924 act did not do more than include in the classification of Asiatic the one nationality previously omitted. Obviously Japanese object to this classification.

[60] R. L. Buell, *Japanese Immigration* (1924), p. 298.

[61] "Either 11 or 12 (out of 19) voted favorably. The exact number has been in doubt since this silent session" (P. Gallagher, *America's Aims and Asia's Aspirations* [1920], p. 322).

[62] P. J. Treat, *op. cit.*, p. 234.

Crocker, however, believes that the Japanese demand for equality included also the right of immigration. He writes:

> The point, however, is that the Japanese seem to have been seeking something more substantial than a humanitarian gesture: it seems that they desired their racial equality clause to include the right to immigrate. At least that is the deduction to be drawn from a statement made by Mr. Hughes, at that time Prime Minister of Australia, in the Commonwealth Parliament. According to Mr. Hughes, he offered the Japanese delegation at Paris to accept their motion provided that the equality be understood as equal treatment of aliens already living in a country, and that the right to immigrate be excluded. The Japanese declined the offer. "It was not enough for their purpose," said Mr. Hughes.[63] . . . . The records of the discussions at Paris in 1919 and at Geneva in 1924 suggest, then, that not only was Japan still interested in immigration and emigration, but was even contemplating the possibility of using belligerent action at some time or other on their account. We may be assuming too much from the records and may be investing their attitude with an interest and a purpose that were in fact not present; but in the light of what a close examination of the recent statements of Japanese statesmen on emigration reveals, namely, that no renunciation whatever to promote emigration has been made, our assumptions seem not unfounded and scarcely unreasonable.[64]

Japanese insist upon the principle of racial equality and consequently object to their countrymen being excluded because of race or nationality and particularly on the ground of "ineligibility to citizenship."[65] In other words, they really object to our naturalization law, but they express the principle in terms of political justice. Ichihashi expresses this latter view as follows:

> Japan's desire to enjoy equal privileges in respect to emigration in her relations with other powers has been misinterpreted and misunderstood as a desire to send large numbers of Japanese wherever Japan pleases. The fact of the matter is that Japan's stand on racial equality in her international relationships does not primarily concern itself with emigration as such; its underlying principle is political justice. No self-respecting nation can afford to be discriminated against on account of race. This is not difficult to understand; Japan is an important member of the family of nations and is treated as such except in a few countries, including

---

[63] W. R. Crocker, *op. cit.,* p. 199.

[64] *Ibid.,* p. 201; quoted by permission of Macmillan Company, publishers.

[65] So declared in 1922 by the Supreme Court of the United States. According to Section 2169 of the Revised Statutes, naturalization is limited to "free white persons and to aliens of African nativity and to persons of African descent." The decision was that Japanese are not "free white persons" and are not therefore eligible to citizenship.

Indians have the right of citizenship if they voluntarily leave their tribes and take up homesteads, under the provisions of the Dawes Act of 1887.

the United States. If Japan desires that its subjects be treated by America on the basis of equality with other nationals regardless of race, she desires it for political reasons. Suppose Japanese immigration is placed on the quota basis; that means the admission of 146 Japanese per annum; as a solution of her population problem, it will have no significance.[66]

Steiner insists on the right of naturalization much more openly:

The other serious grievance against America is our refusal to grant to the Japanese the rights of citizenship. . . . . The Japanese are right in demanding that steps be taken by our Federal Government to give the Orientals who can qualify the same rights of citizenship as are open to other foreigners. . . . .

It must be borne in mind that the Americans and Japanese are approaching the problem of racial contacts from fundamentally opposing points of view. To the Americans the proper solution seems to be the caste system which has been our traditional method of establishing a working relationship with the colored races. Under this system the Japanese are assigned a definite status and racial harmony prevails as long as this status is maintained.

The Japanese on the other hand insist that their association with us shall be on the basis of race equality. That they should be permanently made to occupy an inferior place or forced into a position where they do not have full enjoyment of economic and political opportunities is from their point of view unjust and therefore intolerable.

When the issue is stated in these terms, the significant nature of the controversy is apparent. It is very evident that America has allowed itself to be placed in an awkward position that is rapidly becoming untenable. Our treatment of the Orientals can not gain wide and continued support because it is economically unsound and contrary to our political ideals. In a dispute of this kind the Japanese have everything to gain by keeping in the foreground the issue of race discrimination. Their desire to remove the stigma of racial inequality must gain increasing support among thoughtful and high-minded people. Any determined and widespread opposition to them in this struggle will simply strengthen their national solidarity and make their leadership in the Orient more secure. Our future peaceful relations with the whole Orient depend upon our ability to develop a national policy that will diminish rather than increase race friction on the Pacific Coast.[67]

What are the views of whites regarding Japanese immigration?— The preceding quotation represents one extreme view; the opposite of it is that of the Exclusion League in affiliation with the American Legion, the State Federation of Labor, and the Native Sons and Daughters. In 1919 it definitely stood for (1) rigorous exclusion of all Japanese immigrants, (2) confirmation and legalization of the policy that

---

[66] Y. Ichihashi, *op. cit.*, p. 388.

[67] J. F. Steiner, "Some Factors Involved in Minimizing Race Friction on the Pacific Coast," *Annals, American Academy of Political and Social Science*, XCIII (January 1921), 119–20.

Asiatics be forever barred from American citizenship, and (3) amendment of the Federal Constitution providing that no child born in the United States shall be given the rights of American citizenship unless both parents are of a race eligible to citizenship.[68]

Many quotations are probably necessary in order to set forth adequately the views of Americans on this subject, but the writer feels that statements from former Governor Stephens of California, from the late Theodore Roosevelt, and from Chester Rowell are sufficient.[69] In Governor Stephens' letter to the Secretary of State, June 19, 1920, he expressed the view of California on this subject:

> California harbors no animosity against the Japanese people or their nation. California, however, does not wish the Japanese people to settle within her borders and to develop a Japanese population within her midst. California views with alarm the rapid growth of these people within the last decade in population as well as in land control, and foresees in the not distant future the gravest menace of serious conflict if this development is not immediately and effectively checked. Without disparaging these people of just sensibilities, we cannot look for intermarriage or that social interrelationship which must exist between the citizenry of a contented community.[70]

In his autobiography former President Roosevelt gives utterance to the same view:

> In the present state of the world's progress it is highly inadvisable that peoples in wholly different stages of civilization, or of wholly different type of civilization, even though both equally high, shall be thrown into intimate contact. This is especially undesirable when there is a difference in both race and standard of living. In California the question became acute in connection with the admission of the Japanese . . . .
>
> But the Japanese themselves would not tolerate the intrusion into their country of a mass of Americans who would displace Japanese in the business of the land. I think they are entirely right in this position. I would be the first to admit Japan has the absolute right to declare on what terms foreigners shall be admitted to work in her country, or to own land in her country, or to become citizens of her country. America has and must insist upon the same right. The people of California were right in insisting that the Japanese should not come thither in masses; that there should be no influx of laborers, of agricultural workers, or small tradesmen—in short, no mass settlement or immigration.[71]

---

[68] R. L. Buell, "Development of the Anti-Japanese Agitation in the United States," Part II, *Political Science Quarterly,* XXXVIII, 68–69.

[69] See chapter v for many other quotations expressing anti-Japanese views.

[70] W. D. Stephens in *California and the Oriental* (1920, revised in 1922), p. 10.

[71] Quoted from *Hearings before the Committee on Immigration. Hearings . . . . on S. 2576* (1924), p. 12.

Chester Rowell calls attention to the dangers that arise from the presence of two racial groups who do not amalgamate:

> If we were to continue to admit Asiatic immigration in even such numbers as we can readily and permanently accept from Europe, there would grow up among us still another large group distinguished from the main body of the population by the hereditary and ineffaceable marks of physical race. And that, ultimately, would mean either amalgamation by general intermarriage, or else its prevention by the social curse of caste. Even the present small group promises its difficulties, but, if it remains small, we can live with its problem whether we solve it right or wrong, or not at all. Its cruelties will be individual, and its social consequences limited. If we allowed it to grow large enough to be serious, our whole history teaches that we would solve it wrong.[72]

RECOMMENDATIONS

The writer believes the following five recommendations would go a long way toward alleviating the conflicting views of Japanese and Americans:

I. Restrict very greatly immigration from all countries into the United States.[73] The world has recently emerged from an era, extending back as far as history goes, in which underproduction was always present and meant want to most of the population. It will take the world some time to adjust itself to the new era of overproduction. No one can foretell what changes must occur, but the paradox of excess supplies of material goods with depression and unemployment must be mastered. At this time it is folly to add to the difficulties confronting the country by increasing unemployment through further immigration.

II. Rigorously exclude all Asiatic laborers from entry into the

---

[72] C. H. Rowell, "Western Windows to the East," in *Survey Graphic,* May 1926, pp. 174–75.

[73] Over eighteen million immigrants entered the United States between the years 1901 and 1929. Since July 1, 1929, immigration has been restricted very greatly under the National Origins quotas, which permit all told only 153,541 immigrants a year. Under this plan Great Britain and Northern Iceland have a quota of 65,721; Irish Free State, 17,853; Germany, 25,957; France, 3,086; etc. The minimum quota of 100 for each country does not mean that Asiatics are not actually excluded as heretofore, for, if other provisions of the law exclude a race, those who are acceptable from the particular jurisdiction are from a non-excluded race.

Because of the excessive unemployment in 1930 United States consuls in foreign countries were instructed by the State Department to refuse visas if it appears "that the applicant may probably be a public charge at any time, even during a considerable period subsequent to his arrival." This action has practically halted the immigration of laborers.

United States. In doing so, let us face the actual facts. The United States has one unsolved race problem because of the presence of twelve million Negroes. It has a multitude of lesser race problems because of the presence of millions of foreign-born whites from many countries. It cannot afford at this time further to increase its race problems by admitting Asiatics who cannot be amalgamated into the whole within several generations. It is not a question of superiority and inferiority; it is a psychological matter. Practically none of us are civilized enough to be free from race prejudice,[74] particularly when our daily livelihood is threatened, or we believe it to be threatened, by foreigners in our midst.

Such exclusion of Asiatic workers need not of course be one-sided. In this connection McClatchy indorses a plan of Theodore Roosevelt, as follows:

> President Roosevelt proposed a practical remedy, alike fair and affording any necessary salve to Japan's pride, a reciprocal arrangement which would keep out of Japan those Americans who wish to settle and become part of the resident working population, and keep out of the United States the Japanese who wish to adopt a similar policy. It is probable that any existing misunderstanding would disappear if those now encouraging Japan to demand a quota would, instead, devote time, influence, and energy to secure, here and in Japan, the approval of President Roosevelt's plan and to inaugurate the necessary steps to put it into operation.[75]

There seems to be no reason why the diplomats of the two countries could not agree upon the phrasing of a substitute to the objectionable clause in the 1924 exclusion act which would be agreeable to both countries, since both are desirous that laborers shall be excluded.

Quota for Japan.—Giving a quota to Japan like those assigned to European nations[76] was advocated at the time the 1924 exclusion act

---

[74] In the "Summary of Arguments for and against a Quota for Japanese Immigrants" of the Commonwealth Club (January 1933), there appears as the first argument against the quota the following: "It is not prejudice, but obvious and clear-cut racial, religious, economic, political, and cultural differences which make ineligible Asiatics unassimilable." These differences are important because they give rise to prejudice. Why not admit the prejudice when it is so self-evident?

[75] See V. S. McClatchy, *The Japanese Problem,* p. 10; the quotation from Roosevelt is in a letter from him to Congressman William Kent, February 4, 1909 (*Congressional Record,* Vol. 65, Part 6 [1924], p. 5804).

[76] The law reads as follows: "The annual quota of any nationality for the fiscal year beginning July 1, 1929, and for each fiscal year thereafter, shall be a number which bears the same ratio to 150,000 as the number of inhabitants in

was passed. The matter has recently been revived by the California Council on Oriental Relations as a good-will measure, as follows:

> Good-will among nations is very largely determined by a nice consideration for just such things as pride, national honor, and the like, and by careful adjustment of our relations with our neighbors in conformity with a spirit of justice and fair play. In the minds of all influential Orientals this wound to their national pride, so needlessly inflicted, still rankles, and there can be no true feeling of friendship, cordiality, and good-will established upon a sincere basis until this injustice has been rectified.

This Council has also emphasized the importance of good-will in trade, claiming that

> Many business men engaged in foreign trade believe that our trade with the Orient, and with Japan in particular, has suffered through the passage of this discriminatory law. While there is considerable evidence to support this view, such contentions are extremely difficult to prove by means of actual figures. However, everyone would admit that good-will is just as important an asset in the affairs of nations as it is in the lives of individuals and that in the conduct of business, all things being equal, price and quality acceptable, a business goes to our friends.[77]

Space will not permit the discussion of the many pros and cons concerning a quota for Japan. It is well to recognize, however, that the quota is being considered from at least three different points of view.

First of all is the distinctly immigration aspect—how will granting the quota to Japan affect the Japanese population in the United States? The addition of 185 a year to the Japanese population of 138,834 in

---

continental United States in 1920 having that national origin (ascertained as hereinafter provided in this section) bears to the number of inhabitants in continental United States, in 1920, but the minimum quota of any nationality shall be 100.—Section II-*b*." On this basis Japan would have a quota of 185; China, 105; and nine other Asiatic countries, 100 each. All but Japan are now excluded by laws passed prior to 1924.

[77] In this same brief appears the following: "In 1913 our entire Asiatic trade was only $125,000,000 while today it is over two billion, an expansion of over 1500 per cent in a little over fifteen years. Millions of our neighbors across the Pacific, through multiplying contacts with the Western world, are becoming each year in ever-increasing numbers, consumers of Western goods. In the comparatively short space of time since the World War, our trade with China has doubled, and our trade with Japan trebled. California's trade alone with the Orient has increased over 300 per cent" ("The Square Deal in the Pacific," presented before the Immigration Section of the Commonwealth Club, by S. J. Hume, secretary of the California Council on Oriental Relations, December 1932).

continental United States will not be noticed by Americans and so will not increase hostility toward Japanese already here. In fact, it is quite likely that more than that number are coming into the country annually.[78] Asiatics other than Japanese were excluded under the Barred Zone Act of 1917. Consequently a quota could be extended to Japan and not to any other Asiatic country by revision of the Immigration Act of 1924. Those in favor of a quota for Japan are mindful of this situation and argue that such a quota will admit only 185 Japanese a year. If, however, the principle respecting Asiatic immigration is to be changed and not merely an exception made with reference to Japan alone (and many feel that Japan should be given no better treatment in this respect than China), then revision must necessarily be made of both the 1917 and 1924 immigration acts. The many ifs, ands, and buts involved here cannot be considered for lack of space, except to point out that the extreme opposite to giving the quota to Japan alone involves giving the quota to Japan, China, and some other Asiatic countries, with the entry of 1,190 a year.[79]

A quota of 185 Japanese a year would make it possible, if the Japanese wished, to handle the problem of broken families[80] to some extent at least, by arranging to put members of such families upon a preferred list.

Second is the race prejudice aspect of the quota question—how will the status of the Japanese now in California be affected? If there is little or no opposition, the change in the immigration law will seemingly have little or no appreciable effect, but if opposition develops in California it will be extremely easy for those who object to fan the

---

[78] In an editorial in the *San Francisco Chronicle* of May 26, 1930, the statement is made that "it is estimated by the immigration authorities that more than 700 [from the 8,300 who entered in 1928–29] were out and out immigrants, entitled to stay if they choose. It is remembered, of course, that merchants and professional men are not excluded by the law of 1924." (See Table 38, p. 275, which shows that for 1928–29 there were 716 immigrants from a total of 8,278 entering Hawaii and continental United States.)

[79] Even this number would be restricted greatly if the present measures referred to in footnote 73, p. 59, remain in force. See also footnote 76, p. 60.

[80] See p. 163 for discussion of the number of children, on the one hand, and parents, on the other hand, now excluded from joining their families in the United States. It is important to recognize in this connection that regardless of the number admitted there will always be broken families, for new conditions are always arising whereby some relative should be included in the family group.

lingering embers of the recent agitation against the Japanese into a blaze. Increased animosity may do more harm to the Japanese in California than the quota can do good. A writer in the *San Francisco Chronicle* is evidently considering the quota from this standpoint when he says:

> The whole present question is one of timeliness. Even from that standpoint this would be an especially good occasion to do it, provided we can. At the very time when we are, of necessity, in sharp disagreement with Japan on one question, it would be highly desirable to make a gesture of friendliness on another. We are, in fact, friendly to the Japanese people, and we have only the most cordial attitude toward Japan—in Japan. Our difference is with the present actions outside of Japan. The quota question has nothing to do with that.
>
> The only risk is in Congress. If the opening of the question would start our jingoes to shouting, and defeat the measure besides, it would do more harm than good. Those who are promoting the measure should look into this aspect of it. In every other way they are right and timely.[81]

Third is the international aspect of the quota question—how will relations between Japan and the United States be affected by adoption of the quota? Many Americans are convinced that the Japanese are genuinely incensed over the present method of excluding them and that if the method were changed we should gain much in friendship, security, and opportunity abroad.[82] This is the view of the California Council on Oriental Relations, referred to above.

In politics it often happens that a shibboleth is played up to such an extent that the populace demands the mere form and forgets all about the real substance of the matter. Wilson was re-elected, among other causes, because he kept us out of war. The fact that he declared war immediately after his second inaugural was resented by few. It may be that the Japanese nation has concentrated upon the quota so long that they must have it to be contented. In that case granting it may satisfy them, although logically it would seem that the real crux of the dissatisfaction of the Japanese must lie in the expression "ineligible to citizenship," with its seeming implication of inferiority. If the present resentment in Japan because of the 1924 immigration act can be eliminated by placing them upon a quota, the admission of 185 Japanese a year might be a very cheap price to pay for improved international relations.

---

[81] *San Francisco Chronicle,* August 17, 1933.

[82] See earlier discussion, pp. 48 and 54.

III. Make naturalization available to all who are permitted to settle here permanently.[83] In a democracy all should be represented; certainly all capable of understanding what their votes mean should be represented. To force certain groups to live apart as far as all political matters are concerned is only to invite trouble. If we do not want certain peoples to become citizens we should not admit them.

All the evidence set forth in the following pages makes clear that the Japanese are far more worthy of naturalization than many racial groups who are now accepted without question.[84] The most determined exponent of exclusion of Japanese, Mr. McClatchy, recognizes that "mentally, morally, and physically the Japanese have shown themselves to be our equals. In some matters, notably in economic competition, they are our superiors, and that fact is sufficient justification taken in conjunction with high birth-rate and lower standards of living, for exclusion of those who could easily displace our race under favorable opportunity."[85]

It is very unlikely that a law could be passed today extending naturalization to Japanese. Let us hope that the matter will be handled satisfactorily at a later date.

IV. Extend such friendly treatment to the Japanese who do not intend to settle here permanently, such as students and tourists, and to those who come here for purposes of trade, as we should like to receive were we to visit Japan for similar purposes. Presumably the commercial treaty with Japan amply covers this situation.

V. Remove all discriminations against Japanese immigrants as such who are now here. They were admitted by our laws and have a legal right to remain.

---

[83] "It would be wise government to raise the standards of naturalization for all races and then to bury the old naturalization law which spoke of 'free white persons' and which was killed in 1868 and 1870 with the 'exception' enfranchising millions of negroes, and was given a further shove graveward in 1924 with the blanket of citizenship thrown over all native-born American Indians" (one of the pros in "Summary of Arguments for and against a Quota for Japanese Immigrants," Commonwealth Club of California, January 1, 1933).

[84] They are equal to whites in intelligence, amount of education, and ability to bear arms; they are superior as far as obeying the law, not becoming public charges, and in not provoking disturbances and riots (none have been killed and possibly none seriously injured despite all the agitation against them, which is not true of many other immigrant groups).

[85] V. S. McClatchy, *Brief in the Matter of Immigration Quota for Japan* (California Joint Immigration Committee, December 1931), p. 6.

In the past almost every possible kind of discrimination has been proposed and a few proposals have been enacted into law. State courts or the federal Supreme Court disposed of most of these laws as unconstitutional. It is very difficult to get around the broad, sweeping injunction of the Fourteenth Amendment to the Constitution—"nor shall any state deprive any person of life, liberty, or property without due process of law, nor deny to any person within its jurisdiction the equal protection of the laws." In addition, the courts have had to take into account the treaties between the United States and Japan, which afforded the newcomers many additional forms of protection. All in all, there were few loopholes by which the Japanese could be discriminated against in a legal manner. The school segregation law, the miscegenation laws of nine states,[86] and the anti-alien agricultural land laws were about all that proved legally possible. The former, as we have already stated, has been inoperative except in four small towns where there were about twice as many Oriental as white children.[87] The land laws are each year being more restricted in their operation by court decisions and, more important still, they are not being enforced, for whites as well as Japanese suffer from their effects. They may never be repealed, but they will affect the Japanese first generation less and less as time goes on. There is little or no desire today to discriminate against the Japanese in any legal way, and in almost every respect they have all the rights and privileges of anyone. Because they are not citizens they encounter certain restrictions which affect men of other races who are not citizens, as, for example, inability to practice law. The second generation, being citizens, are free from such discriminations. That difficulty, therefore, is one which time will inevitably resolve.

But both generations have suffered from many forms of social discrimination. This has been a natural result of an unpopular immigration. The great problem is how to eliminate as much of the social discrimination as possible.

All recognize that since the restriction of immigration, conditions have improved, and all fervently hope that they will continue to improve. But such improvement is unquestionably contingent upon continued restriction of immigration. Any apparent increase of Japanese population will stir up trouble.

---

[86] See footnote 3, p. 255.

[87] See also chapter viii.

Disgraceful as it is to admit it, one cannot overlook the fact that one racial group can treat another minority group very shamefully even today. Within a short period of time Filipinos have been killed in California, Chinese driven out of Mexico, the Jews treated abominably in Germany, and hundreds of Chinese living in China proper killed by Japanese. There has always been race prejudice and probably always will be. So long as there are in our midst racial groups such as the Japanese, we must find ways to adjust conditions so that this social malady of racial prejudice shall be minimized.

III. INCREASE OF JAPANESE POPULATION

How many Japanese there are in the country, where they live, and whether or not they are shifting their residence from one part of the country to another or from rural to urban localities, or vice versa, are questions which bear upon that of how the second generation will earn a living. If the Japanese are widely scattered, they will have to compete with the whites in every respect. If they are segregated in certain areas, many, at least, of their number will earn a living by serving their fellows in some capacity or other. The fact that the Japanese still form colonies is proof that, all told, they profit more from dealing with one another than with others. There is a real question as to whether they must continue to do so or will be able to enter into business relations with the general public on something like an equal footing. Consequently it is important to notice any tendencies toward spreading throughout the country, or throughout the state of California, or, on the other hand, toward concentrating in certain areas, rural or urban.

The first generation are a group selected from the standpoint of willingness to emigrate. Will their children follow their example and move on to some new place, as, for example, Brazil, and will those in Hawaii come here? Any large movement will affect the size of population and so the opportunities open to the coming generation. Any sudden influx to continental United States from Hawaii may also again stir up manifestations of race prejudice in certain quarters. The last section of this chapter considers the likelihood of Japanese coming to California from Hawaii.

Because increase in Japanese population aroused such a storm of protest and led to various restrictive measures it has seemed essential to present as a second section to this chapter the data regarding increase in population, i.e., the arrivals and departures and the births and deaths during the last three decades. It is important to know today what the facts are so that earlier statements may be checked. In the past there were many misunderstandings and misinterpretations by men who sought the truth, as well as many vicious misrepresentations by those who did not scruple about the means used to secure their end.

The effect of various restrictive measures upon Japanese immigration is also considered in this chapter. This is still a live question in various parts of the world, and the facts of our earlier experiences have a real bearing upon the movement to grant the quota basis of immigration to the Japanese.

JAPANESE POPULATION IN THE UNITED STATES

The Japanese numbered 138,834 in continental United States in 1930 (see Table 34, p. 270). According to the 1870 census there were at that time only 55 Japanese in the country. During the next twenty years the total increased to 2,039, an inconsequential number. But starting with 1890, the Japanese population increased rapidly, reaching 24,326 in 1900; 72,157 in 1910; 111,010 in 1920; and 138,834 in 1930. The increase of nearly 28,000 in the last decade is nearly equal to that of the preceding decade, but only slightly over half of the increase from 1900 to 1910, which was the period of greatest gain. The increase during the last decade has been due to births, whereas that in 1900 to 1910 was almost entirely the result of immigration.[1]

Concentration of Japanese in California.—Although there is at least one representative of the Japanese race in every state, except New Hampshire, there are seven states that report less than ten and only eight that report as many as one thousand. The great bulk of the Japanese population is in the single state of California, i.e., 97,456 out of 138,834, or 70.2 per cent. Not only have the majority of Japanese come to this state but they have increasingly preferred this state, for the percentage in California of the total has risen from 41.7 per cent in 1900 to 57.3 per cent in 1910, to 64.8 per cent in 1920, and to 70.2 per cent in 1930. Of the total increase of 66,677 from 1910 to 1930, that of 56,100, or 84 per cent, has been in California. In the state of Washington there has been an increase of 4,908, or 7½ per cent of the total increase, and in Oregon an increase of 1,540, leaving for the remaining forty-five states an increase of only 4,129, several hundred less than the increase in Washington alone. As far as continental United States is concerned, the Japanese problem is a Pacific Coast problem and primarily a California problem.

The figures for the last decade alone completely confirm this statement. Between 1920 and 1930, there was an increase in Japanese population in twenty-three states, a decrease in twenty-two states, and no change in three states. But in most cases the increases noted were very slight—less than 10 in six states, and less than 50 in eleven states. California showed an increase of 27,824; Oregon, 807; Colorado, 749; Pennsylvania, 458; Washington, 450; Utah, 333; Arizona, 329; and

[1] It is interesting to note that the total Japanese population in continental United States has approximated very closely that in the Hawaiian Islands during the years from 1910 to 1930 (see Table 34, p. 270).

New York, 244. These eight states are the only ones which had sufficient increase to suggest immigration into them. Increases in the others may be due to immigration but probably are due to birth. These figures do not suggest that there is any noticeable tendency for the Japanese to spread out through the country. A Japanese resident is quoted in the newspaper as saying that "there has been for some time a constant shift of my countrymen from Seattle to Los Angeles. Warnings of the leaders against poorer economic conditions in the latter city owing to overcrowding do not avail against the great difference in climate."

JAPANESE POPULATION IN CALIFORNIA

Japanese are to be found in all but nine counties of California (Table 35, p. 272). But they are far from evenly scattered in the remaining forty-nine counties, for over half are in the three counties of Los Angeles (with 35,390), Sacramento (with 8,114), and San Francisco (with 6,250). There has been a decrease in population during the last decade in nineteen counties, no change in eight counties (in which there are only three Japanese all told), and an increase in thirty-one counties. In the twenty-two counties containing less than 100 Japanese each, there are only four counties in which there has been an increase, and all of those increases are very slight. All told, the population in these twenty-two counties has dropped from 445 in 1920 to 300 in 1930. It is evident that the Japanese are not spreading out in this state but are rather concentrating in certain localities. The areas that are receiving the greatest increases are, first of all, Los Angeles County, with an increase of 15,479 (61 per cent of the increase in the entire state); second, the area about San Francisco Bay, including Santa Clara County (increase of 1,339), San Francisco County (increase of 912), San Mateo County (increase of 506), and Alameda County (increase of 494), a total increase of 3,251 (13 per cent of the increase in the entire state); third, Sacramento County, with an increase of 2,314; fourth, Santa Barbara County, with an increase of 959; fifth, Monterey County, with an increase of 657; and, sixth, San Luis Obispo County, with an increase of 567. Increases in these nine counties account for 23,227 (91 per cent) of the total increase of 25,504. When the natural increase due to the ratio of births and deaths is taken into account, it is evident that most of the counties have lost Japanese by emigration and that the Japanese are concentrating in a few favored areas. The Japanese problem not only is essentially a California problem but it is becoming more and more a Los Angeles County problem (0.8 per cent of the Japanese in continental

United States were in Los Angeles County in 1900; 11.7 per cent in 1910; 17.9 per cent in 1920; and 25.5 per cent in 1930).

This movement of the Japanese population is away from rural districts toward the larger cities. In 1920 there were 28,223 Japanese living in the nineteen cities of California each having a population in excess of 25,000 in 1930. Ten years later the number had risen to 42,228, an increase of 50 per cent. For the city of Los Angeles the gain was 81 per cent, for the remaining eighteen cities the gain was 27 per cent, and in the remainder of the state the gain was only 13 per cent.

Since almost all of the second generation are still minors, whatever the movements in Japanese population may be, they are still very largely the reactions of the first generation to their environment. Such movements may help in understanding the attitudes of the parents of the second generation and in this way acquaint us with some of the factors influencing the children, but they may also lead to faulty prophecies, since the second generation may react in a way very different from that of their parents. In fact, it is the belief that there will be such a difference, which is responsible for so much of what is unsolved in the second-generation problem.

Rate of increase.—From 1880 to 1890 the Japanese population in California increased 1,234 per cent (Table 36, p. 274), and from 1890 to 1900 it increased 785 per cent. No wonder people were alarmed when such figures were announced. These percentages have, however, dropped rapidly, so that during the last decade the percentage increase was but 35, about half of the percentage increase for the entire population. The latter was, however, phenomenal—66 per cent. There has been, nevertheless, a real increase in Japanese population, a percentage increase greater than that for the state as a whole during the last thirty years and equal to it during the last twenty years.

IMMIGRATION AND EMIGRATION OF JAPANESE

It has seemed necessary to analyze the data regarding immigration and emigration of the Japanese, since the answers both pro and con to many moot questions regarding them have been based upon the figures in the *Annual Reports of the Commissioner-General of Immigration.* It is important to know when the Japanese came to Hawaii and continental United States and in what numbers, also to determine the effect upon their immigration of the various restrictive measures that have been passed.

The writer undertook this section with naïve enthusiasm, only to discover that many years might elapse before all the ramifications of the subject could be run down (if they ever could). The *Reports* give data based on an ever changing classification of the Japanese, representing a steady improvement in analyzing the problems involved. But it is far from easy to trace any movement throughout the period because of these changes, some of which are far from clearly explained. There are many volumes on the subject, and frequently material in an earlier volume is not made clear until a later one has been studied. All in all, the writer is far from certain that he has uncovered the facts. At least the gaps and inconsistencies he must present should warn the reader not to rely too much on any set of figures on the subject until they have been carefully checked. According to our interpretation a surprising number of tables published by writers on this subject and based on these *Reports* have errors in them. A few of these errors are pointed out at the close of this chapter to illustrate how certain misconceptions have arisen.

In the next few pages are given the figures regarding increase in population of the Japanese, first in the Hawaiian Islands and then in continental United States.

INCREASE OF JAPANESE POPULATION IN HAWAII

Immigration to either Hawaii or continental United States was inconsequential until 1884. In that year a convention was signed by the Japanese government with the sugar planters in the Islands permitting the importation of Japanese laborers. This marks the beginning of the labor immigration of the Japanese. Six years later the 1890 census records 12,360 Japanese in the Hawaiian Islands. In 1900 the total had increased to 61,111. But during these years many returned to their homes, so that the total of those who came to the Islands was far in excess of these census figures. Ichihashi[2] has calculated that there were all told 82,555 arrivals between 1886 and 1899, an average of 5,503 annually. Consequently over one-fourth of those who came to the Islands had left by 1900, most of these returning to Japan, as few in those days came from Hawaii to the mainland.

The Hawaiian Islands were annexed by joint resolution approved July 7, 1898. It was provided that all laws of the Islands except the country-wide federal statutes in relation to the exclusion of Chinese should continue in force until Congress otherwise provided. A complete Territorial form of government for the Hawaiian Islands was estab-

[2] Y. Ichihashi, *Japanese in the United States* (1932), p. 28.

lished by the passage of the Act of April 30, 1900, which became effective June 14 of that year. The Commissioner of Immigration stated that the passage of this act "has resulted in the cessation of the importation thereto of the Japanese coolie labor described in the last annual report."[3] In anticipation of this restriction apparently, large numbers of Japanese came to the Islands during 1898–1900. In the *Reports of the Governor of Hawaii* for 1900 and 1901 it is stated that 9,434 Japanese arrived and 2,193 departed during the calendar year 1898; 26,103 arrived and 2,780 departed during 1899; 6,017 arrived and 983 departed between January 1 and June 14, 1900; and only 390[4] arrived in the year ending June 30, 1901. In another place it is stated that 589 Japanese arrived and 4,079 left the Territory between June 1900 and August 31, 1901.

What is of chief concern to us is the immigration after 1900, for it was at this time that the first steps were taken in California to stop Japanese immigration and it was after this date that large numbers of Japanese left the Islands for the mainland. The annual immigration figures give an idea of the effect of various restrictive measures.

The number of immigrant, non-immigrant, emigrant, and non-emigrant[5] Japanese coming to both the Territory of Hawaii and continental United States since 1900 are given in Table 38 (p. 275). In Tables 39 (p. 277) and 40 (p. 278) these figures are segregated according as the Japanese entered or departed from Hawaii and the United States respectively.[6] In Table 1 are given summaries by ten-year periods of arrivals at and departures from Hawaii, together with births and deaths, so that the effect of these factors upon increase in population may be noted. It is of importance to ascertain how closely the total population at the end of each decade, as based on these figures, agrees with the United States census figures, since the more nearly the two agree the more likely it is that the former are correct.

---

[3] *Annual Report of the Commissioner-General of Immigration* (1899–1900), p. 43.

[4] The figure 338 in Table 39 (p. 277) for the year 1900–1901 may therefore cover only a portion of that year. The date is not given as to when the office of the United States Immigration Commission was opened in the Islands. An officer was sent to the Islands during the last month of the year, presumably the fiscal year, i.e., in June 1900.

[5] These terms are explained on pp. 77–78.

[6] The writer fully appreciates that Hawaii is part of the United States. But the term "continental United States" is so unwieldy that for the purposes of this discussion the more convenient headings "United States" and "Hawaii" have frequently been used.

TABLE 1

ARRIVALS AND DEPARTURES, BIRTHS AND DEATHS
TERRITORY OF HAWAII

	1900–1910	1910–20	1920–30
Arrivals			
From Orient, mainly	77,421* (From Orient and from mainland)	36,531† (From Orient)	
Immigrants			9,538†
Non-immigrants			15,103†
Citizens** returning			6,764‡
From mainland			
Aliens		475§	1,393‖
Citizens		.....	976¶
Births, estimated††	10,640	34,248	55,011
Increase in population	88,061	71,254	88,785
Departures			
To Orient, mainly	36,754* (To Orient)	28,095† (To Orient)	
Emigrants			1,884†
Non-emigrants			27,276†
Citizens			14,311‡
To mainland			
Aliens	38,057*	1,030§	1,515‖
Citizens	.....	.....	1,949¶
Deaths, estimated	9,067	12,647	13,105
Decrease in population	83,878	41,772	60,040
Net increase, based on arrivals, departures, births, deaths, etc.	*4,183*	*29,482*	*28,745*
Census total at end of decade (1910, 1920, etc.)	79,675	109,274	139,631
Census total at beginning of decade (1900, 1910, etc.)	61,111	79,675	109,274
Net increase, based on census	*18,564*	*29,599*	*30,357*
Discrepancy in calculated net increase and that derived from census figures	−14,381	−117	−1,612

** Many such admitted as aliens prior to the enactment of the 1924 exclusion law.

* From *United States Immigration Commission, 1907–10, Abstracts of Reports,* I, 709. The figure for total arrivals differs by one from the summary of column 1 for 1900–1907 and column 3 for 1907–10 in our Table 39 (p. 277), viz., 77,420. Departures to the mainland are 38,057 (see Table 42, p. 281); this figure plus 375, who were Chinese and Koreans, subtracted from 75,186 (the number reported to have left the Islands) gives 36,754 to the Orient.

† Table 39.

‡ *Annual Report of the Commissioner-General of Immigration* (1929–30), Table 111, p. 249

§ Table 42.

‖ For 1920–24, Table 42; for 1924–30, Table 43, p. 283.

¶ Table 43.

†† From *Annual Reports of Board of Health of Hawaii* for 1900–1911 and from *Annual Reports of the Registrar-General* for 1911–30. Returns for 1908–11 are reported as incomplete, and are probably so for earlier years. The 1910 census gives 19,889 native-born. Some corrections were made of what appeared to be clerical errors.

According to the figures in Table 39 (p. 277), based on the *Annual Reports of the Commissioner-General of Immigration,* 77,420 Japanese immigrants and non-immigrants were admitted to the Islands during the period 1900–1910. During this period it is reported that 75,186 left the Islands. From records published by the Immigration Commissioner of Hawaii[7] it appears that 38,057 went to the mainland (not including the 375 who were Chinese and Koreans); presumably the remainder of the 75,186, i.e., 36,754, went to the Orient. The difference between the 77,420 arrivals and the 74,811 departures is 2,609 and, since the census shows a total increase in Japanese of 18,564, apparently there has been an increase of 15,955 through excess of births over deaths in the Territory. This increase is not corroborated by the figures in Table 1, which show an increase of only 1,573. The Hawaiian authorities mentioned that the birth figures were incomplete. And since the United States Census gives 19,889 native-born in 1910, most of whom must have been born in the decade, the discrepancy is probably due to inaccurate birth statistics. Another explanation may be found, according to one authority, in the fact that the United States census return for 1900 is less complete than that for 1910.

There is illustrated here one of the striking phenomena of the Japanese immigration to this country, namely, the large numbers that came and went and the relatively small number that remained permanently. To call attention to the 77,420 who came to the Islands in ten years is one thing, to emphasize the residual of 2,609 after departures are taken into account is quite another.

During the years 1910 to 1920, 36,531 arrived in the Islands from Japan and 28,095 departed, presumably for the Orient, leaving a net gain of 8,463 (Table 39, p. 277). During this period there were 34,248 births and 12,647 deaths, a gain of 21,601, which is two and a half times that due to immigration.[8] When account is taken of the slight movement between the Islands and the mainland (the figures for which we suspect are not very accurate) and of the gains from immigration and from births over deaths, we obtain a total increase of 29,482, which agrees almost exactly with the difference between the census figures for 1920 and 1910, viz., 29,599 (see Table 1).

---

[7] *First, Second, and Fourth Reports of the Board of Immigration to the Governor of the Territory of Hawaii* (1905, 1906, and 1912). Also see *United States Immigration Commission, 1907–10, Abstracts of Reports,* I, 699.

[8] The United States Census for 1920 reports 48,658 native-born; that for 1930 reports 91,185 native-born.

During the last decade, 1920–30, 24,641 alien Japanese arrived at the Islands from the Orient and 29,160 departed thence, leaving a net decrease of 4,519. There was also a net loss of 7,547 native-born Japanese going to Japan and of 1,095 going to the mainland, giving a total decrease in the Islands due to immigration and emigration of 13,161. To offset this there was an increase of 41,906 from excess of births over deaths, giving finally an increase for the decade of 28,745. This again agrees very closely with the increase according to the census figures of 1930 and 1920, viz., 30,357. It would appear that the figures in Table 1 are approximately correct except those regarding births for 1900–1910.

Between 1900 and 1930 there were, in addition, two other changes in population. At the beginning of this period there were very few native-born; in 1910 the percentage of native-born was 25, in 1920 it was 45, and in 1930 it was 65. Also during the period there was a steady interchange of women for men,[9] so that, whereas in 1900 the ratio of men to women was 3.5 to 1, at the end of the period it was 1.16 to 1.

INCREASE OF JAPANESE POPULATION IN CONTINENTAL UNITED STATES

Table 2 gives a summary of arrivals and departures and births and deaths of Japanese as they affected the Japanese population in continental United States between 1890 and 1930. At the beginning of the forty-year period there were 2,039 Japanese in continental United States, and at the close, 138,834.

From 1890 to 1900.—According to the *Annual Reports of the Commissioner-General of Immigration,* 27,984 were admitted during 1890–1900, of whom nearly half came in during the last year (see Table 37, p. 275). This very large increase in immigrants is attributed to the fact that "many were diverted to San Francisco from Honolulu because of the bubonic plague which had made its appearance."[10] There are no available statistics regarding the number who returned to Japan, nor are there data regarding births and deaths. Births must have been few, since there were only 111 women in the country in 1890 and only 553 in 1900. We have used here as an estimate of births the number of

[9] In 1890, 10,219 males and 2,391 females, a ratio of 4.3 to 1; in 1900, 47,508 males and 13,603 females, a ratio of 3.5 to 1; in 1910, 54,784 males and 24,891 females, a ratio of 2.2 to 1; in 1920, 62,644 males and 46,630 females, a ratio of 1.3 to 1; and in 1930, 75,008 males and 64,623 females, a ratio of 1.16 to 1.

[10] *United States Immigration Commission Reports* (1907–10), Vol. 23, p. 13.

TABLE 2

ARRIVALS AND DEPARTURES, BIRTHS AND DEATHS
CONTINENTAL UNITED STATES

	1890–1900	1900–1910	1910–20	1920–30
Arrivals: Immigrants**	27,984*	54,929	55,182	22,461
Arrivals: Non-immigrants**		4,154	32,394	48,629
From Hawaii		35,278†	1,030†	3,464‡
From Orient, citizens		?	?	?
From Mexico, surreptitiously		8,342§	.....	.....
From Canada		1,500	.....	.....
Births, estimated	269‖	4,233	44,555	57,505
Increase in population	28,253	108,436	133,161	132,059
Departures: Emigrants**	?	25,536¶	13,875	18,294
Departures: Non-emigrants**			56,529	68,153
To Hawaii		?	475†	2,369‡
To Orient, citizens		?	1,612°	3,834°
Deaths, estimated	730	5,727	12,303	13,104
Decrease in population	730	31,263	84,794	105,754
Net increase, based on arrivals, departures, births, deaths, etc.	*27,523*	*77,173*	*48,367*	*26,305*
Census total at end of decade (1900, 1910, etc.)	24,326	72,157	111,010	138,834
Census total at beginning of decade (1890, 1900, etc.)	2,039	24,326	72,157	111,010
Net increase, based on census	*22,287*	*47,831*	*38,853*	*27,824*
Discrepancy in calculated net increase and that derived from census figures	5,236	29,342	9,514	−1,519

** Table 40, p. 278.

* From *Annual Reports of the Commissioner-General of Immigration* for 1890–1900.

† Table 42, p. 281.

‡ For 1920–24, Table 42; for 1924–30, Table 43, p. 283.

§ Estimated at 9,000, but 658 entered with passports.

‖ The United States Census reports 269 native-born in 1900.

¶ Report of the Japanese government of those returning to Japan. See Y. Ichihashi, *Japanese in the United States* (1932), p. 60.

° *Annual Reports of the Commissioner-General of Immigration* (1917–30), "Native-Born Emigration." A total of 5,585 are reported, but 139 left Hawaii. The last figure does not agree with that given in Table 1.

native-born according to the 1900 census. Deaths are estimated on the basis of a death-rate of 8.5 per thousand,[11] i.e., 730. When immigra-

[11] The average death-rate per thousand of the six five-year periods for 15- to 45-year-old males in Japan for 1898–1903 was 8.37, and for 1908–13 it was 8.46. The corresponding figure for the United States for 1901 was 7.97. See *United*

tion, births, and deaths are taken into account, there appears to be a net increase of 27,523 for the decade, whereas the difference between the 1900 and the 1890 census figures is only 22,287. The discrepancy of 5,236 does not seem excessive considering that no account has been taken of those who returned to Japan and also that, in all probability, neither census figure was correct.

From 1900 to 1910. — Many have stated that 137,042 Japanese entered continental United States during this period, basing their figure upon the data in Table 38 (p. 275).[12] They have been misled by the headings of the tables in the *Reports of the Commissioner-General of Immigration,* believing that the phrase "United States" refers to the mainland only, whereas the term refers to all of the United States, including the Territory of Hawaii. The only way to obtain data concerning the mainland is to subtract the figures for entering Japanese entitled by the Commissioner-General of Immigration "Declared Destination Hawaii" (see column 1 of Table 39, p. 277) from those in column 1 of Table 38, giving the figures in column 1 of Table 40 (p. 278). There is reason to believe that some who declared Hawaii to be their destination actually went elsewhere, so that the figures are not entirely correct. The sum of Japanese immigrant and non-immigrant aliens coming to the mainland is given in the *Annual Reports of the Commissioner-General of Immigration,* but the two groups are not given separately. But if the figures entitled "Immigrant Aliens Admitted; Declared Destination Hawaii" are used at their face value, it is possible to obtain, as pointed out above, the "Immigrant Aliens Admitted" to continental United States.

Commencing with the year 1907–8 the *Annual Reports of the Commissioner-General of Immigration* classified incoming aliens as immigrant or non-immigrant depending upon whether or not they intended to reside permanently in the United States; also departing aliens were considered as emigrant or non-emigrant aliens. If they were considered to have had a permanent residence in the United States and were now leaving to establish a permanent residence elsewhere, they were classified as emigrant aliens. If they were making only a temporary visit

---

States Life Tables, 1890, 1901, 1910, and 1901–10; *United States Census,* pp. 64–75; and *United States Abridged Life Tables* (1919–20), pp. 12–15. As far as we can estimate, however, this ratio is somewhat low in terms of the death-rate statistics given in Table 15 (p. 165).

[12] For example, J. W. Jenks and W. J. Lauck, *The Immigration Problem* (1922), pp. 237 and 238, who refer to continental United States and then give figures for both the United States and Hawaii combined.

abroad, they were viewed as non-emigrant aliens.[13] Ordinarily one subtracts emigrants from immigrants to obtain net increase in population. But because many Japanese immigrants were classified as non-emigrants upon departure, the foregoing procedure gives a net increase much greater than the actual situation. It is consequently necessary to combine immigrant and non-immigrant on the one hand and emigrant and non-emigrant upon the other in order to obtain a correct idea of the net increase or decrease of Japanese population.[14]

During 1900–1910, 54,929 Japanese immigrant aliens were admitted to continental United States (column 1, Table 40, p. 278). For the three years 1907–10 there were 10,420 immigrant aliens admitted and, in addition, 4,154 non-immigrant aliens, a total of 14,574 (see Table 40). But during these three years 7,327 who were called "emigrant aliens" departed and 7,497 more who were called "non-emigrant aliens," a total of 14,824. All told, there was a net decrease of 250 for these three years. As this period of three years was one of agitation against the Japanese culminating in the Gentlemen's Agreement, one cannot safely draw any inference from these figures regarding the situation during the seven years just preceding, except that there must have been considerable emigration back to Japan. From Japanese sources it appears that 25,536 returned during the ten-year period.[15] If this number is deducted from 59,083 (54,929 immigrants plus 4,154 non-immigrants reported for 1907–10), we have an increase of 33,547 for the years 1900–1910. The net gain according to the census was 47,831. There is here a discrepancy of 14,284. How may this be accounted for?

During 1906–10 there were 3,070 Japanese deaths in the registration area of the United States (see Table 15, p. 165). During this period the registration area covered about 81 per cent of the Japanese population. On this basis we may estimate 3,816 deaths for all of the United States. There were approximately twice as many Japanese in the United States during 1905–10 as between 1900 and 1905. Hence the total deaths for 1900–1910 were approximately 5,727. There were 134 births reported in California in 1906, the number increasing each year to 719 in 1910 and totaling 2,211 for the five years. For the entire United

---

[13] This new system of recording does not seem to have worked perfectly until 1913, for the various tables do not check during the years 1907–13.

[14] See pp. 90–94 for further discussion.

[15] Y. Ichihashi, *op. cit.*, p. 60. Offhand, this figure seems low, since during the last three years of the decade the Japanese were returning at the rate of 5,000 a year.

States, for the ten years, we should estimate 3,700 births. The census, however, reports an increase of 4,233 native-born—from 269 (1900) to 4,502 (1910). We therefore conclude there must have been this number of births. For the decade then there was an excess of 1,494 deaths over births. This makes our discrepancy 15,778.

Certain estimates of the Commissioner of Immigration account for far more than 15,778 additional Japanese. His reports[16] indicate that about 9,000 had crossed over from Mexico, 1,000 to 2,000 from Canada, and 37,000 from Hawaii during the seven years between 1902 and 1909. These figures were not included in the immigration figures, for most of those coming from Mexico and Canada had entered surreptitiously and those from Hawaii were not enumerated,[17] as they were not coming from a foreign country. If all these are to be counted as coming in during this period, it gives an excess of about 31,000 in terms of the census figures.

With regard to those coming from Mexico, Inspector Brann is quoted as follows:

> With reference to the Japanese, he reported that within two years (1906–1907) more than 10,000 had been imported into Mexico as contract laborers, being sent out by the various emigration companies, but that most of them had left their employment, and that the entire number in the Republic at that time (June, 1907) was only about 1,000. Inasmuch as they had not left the country through the ports, it was concluded that they had immigrated to the United States, lawfully previous to the issue of the President's order of March 14, 1907, surreptitiously ever since . . . . Since that time the importation of contract laborers to Mexico has been discontinued and the large influx of that race across the border has ceased.[18] The investigation of Japanese employed in various places failed to discover more than a comparatively few who had entered the United States since the summer of 1907, other than those who had come directly from Japan.[19]

Only a few Japanese came from Canada. A reference to this movement by the United States Immigration Commission follows:

---

[16] *Annual Report of the Commissioner-General of Immigration* (1906–7), pp. 146–49. Also, *United States Immigration Commission Reports* (1907–10), Vol. 23, pp. 6, 14–15.

[17] *United States Immigration Commission, 1907–10, Abstracts of Reports,* I, 624.

[18] Millis reports 3,945 passports issued by the Japanese government to its subjects wishing to emigrate to Mexico in 1907, and only 18 in 1908, 13 in 1909, 37 in 1910, etc. (H. A. Millis, *The Japanese Problem in the United States* [1915], p. 16).

[19] *United States Immigration Commission Reports* (1907–10), Vol. 23, p. 15.

Japanese residents of Honolulu attempted to profit by a similar migration and transported 2,777 [elsewhere given as 2,779] laborers during [the first] ten months of 1907 to British Columbia, whence no doubt a large percentage entered the United States . . . . as in other races, there is no doubt that a fairly large number have come across the Canadian border. The problem presented there, however, has been solved by an agreement entered into in 1908 between the Canadian and Japanese governments limiting the number of passports which the latter shall issue to emigrants to Canada in any one year to 400.[20]

Whether or not the 10,000 who went to Mexico and "a large percentage" of the 2,779 who went to Canada finally reached continental United States will probably never be known. It would appear that most of them did so.

In addition to a wealth of discussion about Japanese leaving Hawaii for the United States, the four *Reports of the Board of Immigration of Hawaii,* 1905 to 1912, record 38,432 Orientals who went from the Islands to the mainland. At least 375 of these were Koreans and Chinese, and, of them all, 2,779 went to Canada, leaving 35,278 Japanese who came to the United States (see Tables 42 [p. 281] and 2). The sudden drop in this movement between 1907 and 1908 was occasioned by the President's order of March 14, 1907.[21]

If 8,342 entered from Mexico,[22] 1,500 from Canada, and 35,278 from Hawaii, it means there was a net increase between 1900 and 1910 of 77,173, whereas according to the two census reports there was a gain of only 47,831. Is there any way to account for the discrepancy of 29,342? If these figures are accepted, the census should have recorded 101,499 instead of 72,157. Millis, who believes the 1910 census was an understatement, estimated the population as 95,679 in 1913.[23] As there was a net loss of 542 in immigration during 1910–13 (see Table 40, p. 278), his estimate would apply about equally well to 1910. Senator Phelan explained how the census might be inaccurate, saying in 1924:

The low census enumeration is due to the fact that under our system ten cents is allowed for each name counted, and the enumerators actually rebelled, struck, if you please, against the Census Bureau when they were asked to go into the interior of the State and find the Japanese on the farms and in the mountains. They said they could not undertake that work for ten cents a name, so they enumerated only

---

[20] *United States Immigration Commission Reports* (1907–10), Vol. 40, pp. 66–71; also Vol. 23, p. 6.

[21] See above, p. 41.

[22] Estimated at 9,000, but 658 entered with passports and so are included in the 54,929 immigrants recorded in Table 40 (p. 278).

[23] H. A. Millis, *op. cit.,* pp. 1 and 24.

those who were close by in the cities. Therefore the census is confessedly in error. The department itself admitted its inability to enumerate the Japanese.[24]

The discrepancy may be explained in part, at least, on the suppositions that the number reported by the Japanese government as returning to Japan was too low, that the number coming from Mexico was an overstatement, that there were some who returned to Hawaii,[25] and that there were some native-born children who were sent to Japan for their education, of which we have no record, although at this time they presumably were included among non-emigrants.

From 1910 to 1920.—For this decade the Immigration Commissioner's *Reports* give a net increase of 17,172 (55,182 immigrants and 32,394 non-immigrants, totaling 87,576, and 13,875 emigrants and 56,529 non-emigrants, totaling 70,404 [see Table 40, p. 278]). Births in California for this decade amounted to 30,743, which gives 44,555 for the entire country on the basis that 69 per cent of all the Japanese women were in California.[26] Deaths for the entire country amounted to 12,303.[27] There was accordingly a net gain of 32,252 from the excess of births over deaths; also a gain of 555 (the difference between those who came from Hawaii[28] and those who departed to Hawaii). According to our Table 2 there is a loss of 1,612 due to citizens leaving for the Orient. This is more or less offset actually by citizens returning, but we have no record of such. The total gain according to these figures is 48,367, whereas that given by subtracting the 1910 census figure from the 1920 census is 38,853, leaving a discrepancy of 9,514.

---

[24] J. D. Phelan, *Hearings before the Committee on Immigration* (United States Senate, 68th Congress, First session, March 13, 1924), p. 108.

[25] It is reported that some Portuguese imported into Hawaii came to the mainland and then returned to the Islands after the crops had been gathered (see *United States Immigration Commission, 1907–10, Abstracts of Reports,* I, 711).

[26] This ratio agrees with that between the total births in California and in the United States for 1918–20 (see Table 15, p. 165). These are the first two years in which births of Japanese from most of the United States were reported. The figures seem high in terms of the increase in native-born reported for the census, i.e., 25,170. The discrepancy may possibly be explained on the basis that many children were sent to Japan at this time for their education.

[27] Deaths totaling 11,331 are reported for an area covering 91.7 per cent of the Japanese population.

[28] The California State Board of Control reports 506 came from Hawaii during 1910–19 (*California and the Oriental* [1922], p. 25), which does not agree with Table 42 (p. 281).

From 1920 to 1930.—The *Reports of the Commissioner-General of Immigration* give a net decrease in population for this decade of 15,357 (22,461 immigrants and 48,629 non-immigrants, totaling 71,090, and 18,294 emigrants and 68,153 non-emigrants, totaling 86,447 [see Table 40, p. 278]). Estimates of births and deaths give 57,505 and 13,104, respectively, a net increase of 44,401 (see Tables 15 [p. 165] and 2). There was a gain of 1,095 in population due to movement between the Islands and the mainland, but a reported loss in our table of 3,834 due to citizens going to Japan.[29] All in all there was a net gain according to these calculations of 26,305, to be compared with a gain of 27,824 based on census data. In this case the discrepancy of only 1,519 represents too small an increase in our calculations.

If there were no census figures since 1900 and the only available figures were those in Table 2, we should be forced to conclude that the Japanese population in 1910 was 101,499 (instead of 72,157), in 1920 was 149,780 (instead of 111,010), and in 1930 was 176,085 (instead of 138,834). Although it is likely that the census figures are somewhat low, particularly in 1910, yet no one would maintain the difference is as great as these figures suggest for 1920 and 1930. The best data available regarding Japanese population increase are not complete for the mainland. Consequently estimates based on these are apt to be misleading. It is to be emphasized in this connection that our calculations agree more nearly with the census figures as time goes on. It seems impossible to escape the conclusion that there is something radically wrong with the figures for 1900–1910.

This matter has been gone into in detail because much of the agitation against the Japanese was based upon calculations many of which we now can see were quite faulty. Some of the misunderstandings between the governments of Japan and the United States are due to similar causes, sometimes to the fact that Japan based her contentions on one set of figures and the United States upon another set. It is unfortunate that more complete information was not available from twenty to thirty years ago. For example, for the period 1910–20, the

[29] Between 1917 and 1930 the *Annual Reports of the Commissioner-General of Immigration* give 5,585 native-born going to Japan, of whom 139 departed from Hawaii. Of this number, 4,233 were under five years of age, 1,167 between five and ten years, and only 32 were twenty years of age and over. Two hundred thirty-four went to Japan in 1917–18, 363 in 1918–19, 1,138 in 1919–20, 745 in 1920–21, 877 in 1921–22, 842 in 1922–23, 542 in 1923–24, 147 in 1924–25. During 1925–30, 139 went on the average each year.

"admissions" to the mainland reported in the *Annual Reports of the Commissioner-General of Immigration* are 87,576 (see Table 40, p. 278) and the "embarkations" from Japan to the United States are 81,891, while the "embarkations" reported by Japan are 82,140. There is here a difference of only 249 between the corresponding figures of the two governments. In the case of "departures," Table 40 gives 70,404, the United States government figures for "debarkations to Japan" are 66,853, and the Japanese government reports 82,259. Here there is a discrepancy of 15,406 between two sets of figures presumably measuring the same thing and given side by side in the *Annual Reports of the Commissioner-General of Immigration.* If the figures of the Japanese government were used in Table 2, our calculated population at the end of each decade would be less than the census figures, instead of greater. Evidently many Japanese have left the country without any record in the United States of their going, or else the United States census figures are farther below the truth than anyone surmises.

Data from Japanese sources regarding Japanese population in Hawaii, North America, and South America are presented in Table 41 (p. 280). (See also Tables 11 [p. 142], 12 [p. 143], and 28 [p. 216].) They agree approximately with the figures from the United States Census in Tables 34–36 (pp. 270–74). On the whole, they are slightly higher. This is easily explained for California, since the Japanese figures for this state are the returns from the two consular districts of San Francisco and Los Angeles, which include not only California but also the adjoining states of Nevada, Colorado, Utah, New Mexico, and Arizona, as well as Lower California in Mexico.[30] This fact is often lost sight of by those who quote the figures pertaining to California from Japanese sources.

The increasing Japanese population in South America is significant. This immigration commenced at about the time the Gentlemen's Agreement was signed. It is quite likely that those who have gone to South America would have come to the United States had it not been for the restrictive measures against immigration. In 1927 there were 680,000 Japanese residing outside of Japan, 20.7 per cent in continental United States, 19.0 per cent in the Hawaiian Islands, 9.6 per cent in Brazil, and 36.9 per cent in China.[31]

---

[30] The San Francisco consular district includes Nevada, Colorado, and Utah and all but the nine southern counties of California.

[31] Japanese Department of Foreign Affairs, *Leaflet No. 2,* p. 19.

EFFECT OF RESTRICTIVE MEASURES UPON JAPANESE IMMIGRATION

What effect did the Gentlemen's Agreement and the 1924 immigration act have upon Japanese immigration to the United States? Is there justice in the claims of the Japanese government and of many persons in this country that the Gentlemen's Agreement was sufficient to control Japanese immigration to this country?

Effect of restrictive measures in Hawaii. — As has already been pointed out the annexation of the Islands "resulted in the cessation of the importation thereto of the Japanese coolie labor." In anticipation of this restriction, 41,554 arrived during the two and a half years prior to June 14, 1900 (an average of 16,621 a year), and only 390 during the year 1900–1901. This looks like a great drop. But it is apparent that most of the drop is due to the fact that those who would normally have come somewhat later hurried up and came a little earlier, for, during the years 1901–8, 74,521 arrived, an average of 10,646 a year. This first restrictive measure of eliminating coolie labor apparently had little or no effect upon the number coming to the Islands. In fact, the sugar planters would have welcomed more and, because they did not come, were forced to bring in Portuguese, Puerto Ricans, and, later, Filipinos.

The next restrictive measure was the Gentlemen's Agreement between Japan and the United States, going into effect in 1908. During the seven years before (i.e., 1901–8), 74,521 Japanese arrived, an average of 10,646 per year, and afterward (i.e., 1908–24) 40,463 arrived, an average of 2,529 per year.[32] The agreement cut down the average yearly arrival by three-fourths.

The final restrictive measure was the Immigration Act of 1924. The annual arrivals of 2,529 were cut to 92, if alien immigrants alone are considered (see Table 39, p. 277). When all four classes of immigrant, non-immigrant, emigrant, and non-emigrant are considered, it appears that there was a net annual increase of 536 per year during 1908–24 and a net annual decrease of 1,063 during 1924–30.

EFFECT OF GENTLEMEN'S AGREEMENT IN CONTINENTAL UNITED STATES

The Gentlemen's Agreement went into effect in 1908. In March of the preceding year the President ordered that Japanese with passports to Mexico, Canada, and Hawaii should not be admitted to continental United States. This order was supported by Japan, which

[32] See Table 39, p. 277.

practically ceased giving passports to Mexico and limited the number to Canada to 400 a year. The President's order, accordingly, stopped what would have been a large increase of immigrants regularly admitted by passport from Hawaii, Canada, and Mexico; and the voluntary action of Japan checked further surreptitious entries from Canada and Mexico, for at that time the United States Immigration Commission did not have inspectors enough to man the two borders.

The effect of these two restrictive measures upon immigration is shown in Table 3. Apparently there was a decided drop. But one must

TABLE 3

EFFECT OF GENTLEMEN'S AGREEMENT AND 1924 IMMIGRATION ACT UPON JAPANESE IMMIGRATION TO CONTINENTAL UNITED STATES*

(Figures are yearly averages for period given)

Date	Immigrants	Immigrants and Non-Immigrants	Emigrants and Non-Emigrants	Increase	Total Immigrants to Hawaii and Continental United States	
					Males	Females
	BEFORE THE GENTLEMEN'S AGREEMENT					
1890–95	1,419					
1895–99	2,066					
1899–1904	7,531				11,291	2,060
1904–08	6,686				15,667	2,460
	GENTLEMEN'S AGREEMENT					
1908–13	2,689	4,288	5,396	–1,108	1,775	3,250
1913–17	5,692	8,938	6,443	2,495	3,812	4,984
1917–20	7,375	11,805	9,227	2,578	4,267	5,567
	ENTRY OF "PICTURE BRIDES" STOPPED BY JAPANESE GOVERNMENT					
1920–24	4,759	9,809	10,113	–304	3,025	3,981
	1924 IMMIGRATION ACT					
1924–30	571	5,309	7,666	–2,537	441	221

* Based on Tables 37, 38, and 40 (pp. 275 and 278).

not overlook the fact that just before the enactment of any restrictive measure there is a rush to enter followed by a natural drop afterward. Comparisons based upon the few years before and after are misleading. So we see that in 1913–17 the number of immigrants had risen to 5,692 per year, and in 1917–20 the number (7,375) exceeded the annual arrivals during the four years before the two restrictive measures went into effect. Part of this increase was occasioned, however, by a new rush to get in before the 1924 act went into effect. These immigration figures do not indicate any great decrease attributable to the Gentlemen's Agreement.

There are no figures giving the number of male and female immigrants entering continental United States. But such figures for Hawaii and continental United States combined are given in the *Annual Reports of the Commissioner-General of Immigration,* and averages are presented in Table 3. Here it appears very clearly that there was a noticeable decrease in males (11,291 a year for 1899–1904, and only 3,812 for 1913–17) but a steady increase in females, for each three- or four-year period shows an increase over the preceding period. The Gentlemen's Agreement had no effect upon female immigration.[33]

The situation can be more clearly presented in terms of the data secured in our survey of 9,690 Japanese.[34] Figure 1 presents the number of males and females who arrived each year from 1887 to 1930. The graph for the males shows unmistakably that a large and increasing immigration was checked in 1908. The graph for the females shows just as clearly that female immigration had hardly started in 1908, continued, always increasing, until checked somewhat by Japan's refusal to give passports to "picture brides" (1920), and was finally cut short in 1924.

Many government officials at various times have declared that the Gentlemen's Agreement was a satisfactory arrangement. On the other hand, many, particularly in California, have denounced the agreement as a failure. Evidently there must have been two different standards by which the value of the agreement was measured. For example, in the memorial presented to the President by the Japanese Association, September 18, 1919, Professor P. J. Treat is quoted as follows:

> Since this agreement went into effect in 1907, it has met every need. No one has found ground for questioning the scrupulous good faith of the Japanese foreign office in the issue of passports. In fact, the admission of Japanese under the passport system has worked out with fewer abuses than the admission of Chinese under the exclusion laws which we administer ourselves.[35]

---

[33] Female immigration would undoubtedly have dropped very materially in a short time anyway. About twelve thousand more in 1925 would have supplied all the Japanese bachelors with wives.

[34] Discussed in chapter vi.

[35] *California and the Oriental* (1920, revised in 1922), p. 228.

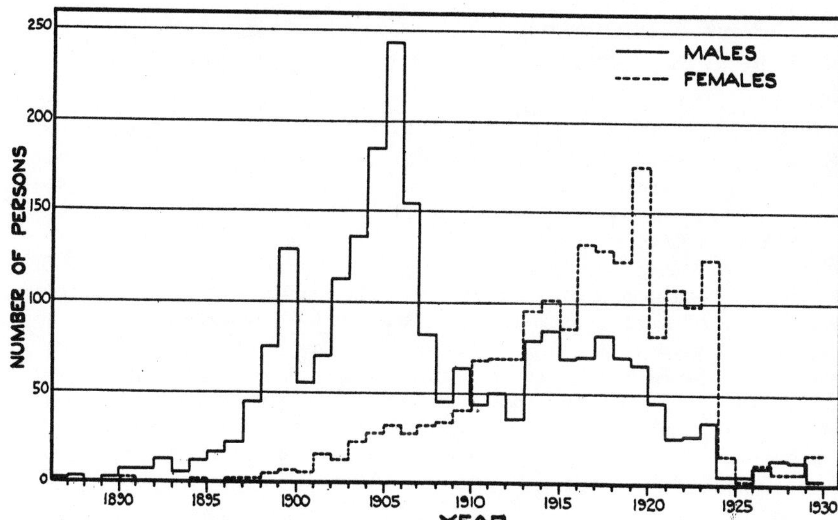

FIG. 1.—Numbers of Japanese arriving in continental United States, 1887–1930. Based on interviews with 2,298 males and 1,781 females.

And, immediately below, the Japanese give immigration figures showing a steady rise in number from 2,720 in 1910 to 10,213 in 1918!

The view of those who denounced the Gentlemen's Agreement is well expressed by the following, taken from the report of the House Committee on Immigration and Naturalization:

> The agreement was consummated under direction of Theodore Roosevelt while President. He makes it clear, through official correspondence (amounting to a compact) with the Legislature of California, and by statements in his autobiography, that the real intent agreed upon with Japan, was to be more restrictive under this plan. Japan was to prevent the coming of her people to continental United States so that the Japanese population therein would not increase; it being frankly explained by Roosevelt that an increase of Japanese in this country, with their advantages in economic competition and general unassimilability, would be certain to lead to racial strife and possible trouble between the two nations.
>
> There is no question that the purpose of the agreement as thus explained by Roosevelt has not been carried out. It is clearly established that the Japanese population of continental United States has very materially increased during the operation of the Agreement, partly by direct immigration and partly by birth, and doubtless also partly by surreptitious entry.[36]

---

[36] Report entitled "Restriction of Immigration" accompanying *H.R. 7995*, March 24, 1924. The reference to surreptitious entry was unfair, for it was Japan, not the United States, that really stopped such entries.

The view of those who upheld the Gentlemen's Agreement has been far more often implied than stated. Possibly the following from McKenzie expresses it as well as any statement:

Restrictive or selective immigration inevitably breaks up natural human groups. Human beings are not like grains of corn that can be sifted and sorted into classes without doing violence to sentiments and causing individual suffering. The most serious effect of exclusion upon Orientals domiciled here is that related to marriages and the family.

It is well known that the family is a more fundamental social institution in China and Japan than in Western countries. The familial behavior of Orientals is difficult for anyone to understand who is not at least somewhat familiar with their kinship attitudes and customs. In the first place, practically every normal Chinese or Japanese man expects to marry and rear a family. To fail in this is to fail in life. No matter what possessions a man may have, he is not a success unless he is married and has a family. More than this, his relations toward his parents are much more rigidly fixed by custom than is the case in Western civilization. Filial piety is stronger and the sense of obligation to parents keener.[37]

The Japanese view presupposed that a man would have his wife and children with him. If he did not have a wife, he most naturally would get one in due time. And all this was specifically granted to the Japanese by the provisions of the Gentlemen's Agreement, as far as those provisions have been given publicity. Looking back upon the matter now, it is easy to see how the provisions regarding admission of members of the family were accepted by Roosevelt. The Chinese had not brought their women folks to the United States and the Japanese had hardly started doing so in 1908. The provision appeared harmless at that time. But in 1924 even Gulick, one of the strongest spokesmen for the Japanese, conceded that,

through the admission of the parents, wives and children, there has come an amount of immigration which has caused serious conditions—serious psychological conditions. And it seems to me that we ought to say frankly to Japan that we believe the Gentlemen's Agreement is not satisfactory—"We believe you have observed it, but, nevertheless, it is not satisfactory, and we need a new adjustment of the matter."[38]

The conflict between the two views arose because the addition of wives for all the Japanese in the United States meant a doubling of population and then a future still greater increase from births. At the same time both sides to the controversy were right. Japan carried out her promises and made several changes in the direction of further

---

[37] R. D. McKenzie, *Oriental Exclusion* (1927), p. 79.

[38] S. L. Gulick, *Hearings before the Committee on Immigration* (United States Senate, 68th Congress, First Session, March 12, 1924), p. 72.

restriction. But the agreement itself was to blame. It made possible further increase of Japanese population, which California believed was unwise.

EFFECT OF 1924 IMMIGRATION ACT IN CONTINENTAL UNITED STATES

The data in Table 3 and the graphs in Figure 1 make unmistakably clear that the 1924 immigration act practically stopped Japanese immigration. The annual number of immigrants dropped from 4,759 in 1920–24 to 571 in 1924–30. The net gain of 2,578 per year in 1917–20 changed to a net loss of 304 during 1920–24 and of 2,537 in 1924–30.

Between 1890 and 1930, 160,556 Japanese immigrants arrived, and, between 1907 and 1930, 85,177 non-immigrants arrived, making a total of 245,733. Most of these returned to Japan within a few years. Between 1907 and 1930, 173,240 immigrants and non-immigrants arrived and 171,675 emigrants and non-emigrants departed, leaving a balance of only 1,565 for twenty-three years! If it had not been for the admission of women the Japanese population would be only a little more than a quarter of what it is today, since half are now native-born.

MISUNDERSTANDINGS AND EXAGGERATIONS

Some of the misstatements regarding Japanese immigration have been due to the manner in which the data have been presented by the Commissioner-General of Immigration. Many of his table headings are not clear and the terms are not defined in conjunction with them. Frequently the only clue to the meaning is given in another volume.[39]

One of the most serious misunderstandings of the situation arises from the fact that the data for the Territory of Hawaii following its annexation are included with those for continental United States, but without any warning to the reader of the fact. Only by noting that there is added the column "Declared Destination Hawaii" is one notified of this change. Beginning with the year 1907–8 there is included a special report on Japanese, giving combined immigrants and non-immigrants to continental United States and to Hawaii separately. But one is unlikely to get all these tables straightened out except after many hours of painstaking analysis. The result has been that many have quoted data pertaining to Hawaii and continental United States com-

[39] For example, in 1925–26 we learn how many arrived in 1890–91 and 1891–92 (see last footnote to Table 37, p. 275).

bined when they thought they referred only to the mainland. One writer, for example, gives the total immigration for the mainland between 1908 and 1926 as 136,052, the total emigration as 46,494, and the net increase as 89,558. Yet these figures pertain to both continental United States and Hawaii; if the correct figures had been used, the net increase for continental United States would have been found to be 50,080 (39,478 less).

McKenzie[40] gives in his "Table C, Immigration to and Emigration from the United States," data on Japanese beginning in 1861. This table refers only to the mainland, but beginning with 1900–1901 it includes data for Hawaii without reference to the fact. As his Tables A and B specifically mention continental United States and Hawaii, it is not likely that any ordinary reader would remember that the Territorial form of government was established for Hawaii in 1900 and, therefore, that data for Hawaii would be included in Table C beginning with 1900–1901. In his Table 2 he gives a total immigration between 1917 and 1926 of 123,790; for continental United States it was actually 91,685.

A second misunderstanding easily arising from the *Annual Reports* is that data based on "country of last residence—Japan" are interpreted to refer to Japanese. Of course, most of those coming from Japan were Japanese, but some Englishmen and Germans came to the United States from Japan and were included under this heading; also some Japanese came from other countries and so were classified under the country of entry and not as Japanese. The *Annual Reports* give immigration only by country until July 1, 1898, so that before that date this is all the information available. But after that date, figures based on "race or people" should be employed. McKenzie copies both sets of data in his Tables C and D. Mears[41] used only data based on country. The difference between the two is not large, so that error due to this misunderstanding is not a serious one.

A third and most natural misunderstanding arose from the attempt to determine the net increase of immigration by subtracting emigrants from immigrants. Seemingly non-immigrants and non-emigrants should cancel each other and they should not be considered. But non-emigrants have greatly exceeded non-immigrants. For example, during 1910–20

[40] R. D. McKenzie, *op. cit.* The material for this book was prepared for the Conference of the Institute of Pacific Relations in Honolulu, a connection in which Hawaii would naturally be thought of as an integral part of the United States.

[41] E. G. Mears, *Resident Orientals,* Table 2.

there were 56,529 non-emigrants and 32,394 non-immigrants, a difference of 24,135, and, during 1920–30, 68,153 and 48,629, respectively, with a net decrease of 19,524 (Table 40, p. 278). Evidently a large number of Japanese returned to Japan as non-emigrants who must have been classified as immigrants upon arrival.[42] To exclude these from the calculations as to net increase is a most serious mistake. Yet who would think of considering these two classes unless he had first made a careful study of what, offhand, would not appear to be a fruitful investigation?

In a statistical report of the Institute of Pacific Relations,[43] issued in 1931, it is stated on page 28 that 5,655 Japanese departed from the United States in the five years 1925–29, and on page 24 that 11,809 returned from the United States in one of these five years (i.e., 1928)—twice as many returning in one year as in five years! The Institute's data are apparently taken from sources other than those of the United States Commissioner of Immigration. Judging from such data in our Table 38 (p. 275), it would appear that 5,505 emigrants departed in the five-year period and that 1,055 emigrants and 9,614 non-emigrants, a total of 10,669, departed in the one year. This merely illustrates again the kind of conclusions that may be drawn from Japanese immigration statistics when only emigrant figures are used at one time and emigrant and non-emigrant figures combined are used at another time. The only way to ascertain total arrivals and departures is to use both immigrant and non-immigrant figures on the one hand and total emigrant and non-emigrant figures on the other hand.

As previously stated (p. 90) one writer not only included data for Hawaii unwittingly but he failed to add data concerning non-immigrants and non-emigrants, giving, as we have seen, a total net increase of 89,558 during 1908–26. If non-immigrants and non-emigrants are considered, the net increase turns out to be 8,565. His figure is 39,478 higher than it purports to be and ten times higher than the actual situation. McKenzie included these two classes and arrived at a net increase of 3,505 for 1917–26. As pointed out, this includes Hawaii and the mainland. The net increase for the latter alone is 1,955, so that his error happened to be slight.

---

[42] It would be most natural for Japanese to attempt to be classified as non-emigrant instead of emigrant, since the former classification would permit return to the United States.

[43] *Migration in the Pacific* (Institute of Pacific Relations, 1931).

The State Board of Control prepared a report regarding the Oriental situation[44] and in it estimated the Japanese population in California as of December 31, 1919, to be 87,279. They did not include non-immigrants and non-emigrants, which during the period showed a net loss to the mainland of 22,209. It would have been difficult to estimate what proportion of this loss should be allocated to California. Nevertheless an attempt should have been made, for many of these 22,209 left California and to that extent cut down the actual population. No wonder the estimate was found to be 15,327 greater than that reported by the United States Census of 1920.[45]

These examples taken from the work of men who were interested solely in presenting the facts are sufficient to show how misunderstandings of the *Annual Reports of the Commissioner-General of Immigration* gave credence to the belief that far more Japanese were coming to these shores than was the case, or, rather, to the belief that more were continuing to reside here than was the case. For the greatest cause of error lay in the fact that far more were returning to Japan than was realized.

One or two additional examples may be appended illustrating what hysteria added to the picture. Chambers, writing in the *Annals,*[46] claimed that there were 100,000 Japanese in California in 1921 (the United States Census for 1920 gave 71,952) and that, since the Japanese population at the time of signing the Gentlemen's Agreement was not quite 30,000 and the births, less deaths, added only 20,000, the remaining 50,000 had come in violation of the agreement. After referring to the Japanese as a "marvelously prolific race," he added that "at this rate in ten years there will be 150,000 Japanese born here, and by 1949 they will outnumber the white people."

Stoddard, writing in the same issue of the *Annals,*[47] pointed out the unsatisfactory nature of the Gentlemen's Agreement and as evidence

---

[44] *California and the Oriental* (1920, revised in 1922), p. 25.

[45] For other examples of the confusion arising from improper handling of these immigration figures, as pointed out by other writers, see: S. L. Gulick, "Japanese in California," *Annals, American Academy of Political and Social Science,* Vol. XCIII, No. 182 (January 1921), p. 55; R. C. Adams, "Japanese Migration Statistics," *Sociology and Social Research,* May–June 1929; Y. Ichihashi, *op. cit.,* p. 57.

[46] J. S. Chambers, "The Japanese Invasion," *Annals, American Academy of Political and Social Science,* XCIII (January 1921), 23.

[47] L. Stoddard, "The Japanese Question in California," *ibid.,* p. 44.

stated that "over sixteen thousand were admitted in 1919." This figure must have referred to the 16,174 (including 9,279 immigrants and 6,895 non-immigrants [Table 38, p. 275]) admitted to continental United States and Hawaii. But if he had, in fairness, given the corresponding emigrants and non-emigrants, totaling 15,653, his "evidence" would have lost most of its effect.

McClatchy[48] criticizes Gulick's claim that there was a net increase of only 10,959 due to immigration into continental United States in the sixteen years following 1908 (see last column of Table 40, p. 278, for 1908–24) on the ground that Gulick included non-immigrants and non-emigrants. We have already pointed out that since non-emigrants greatly exceeded non-immigrants the only way to determine net increase or decrease is to include these classifications; otherwise many who were classified as immigrants upon arrival and as non-emigrants[49] upon departure are not credited with having left the country. To claim that "we are concerned only with the immigrant class that comes for permanent settlement" is to hide behind a statement that sounds fine but does not fit the situation. But McClatchy misleads in even worse ways than this. After specifically stating that he is discussing the "Japanese population in continental United States," he quotes authorities who are using data for both continental United States and Hawaii and so "proves" that the net gain was 72,906 and not 10,959 as stated by Gulick. If non-immigrants and non-emigrants are taken into account, as they must be, the net gain is 20,042 for both Hawaii and continental United States and 10,959 for the latter alone, as Gulick gives it.[50]

In 1933 McClatchy replies to the argument of the San Francisco Chamber of Commerce and the California Council on Oriental Relations that "in the last nine years 20,000 more Japanese have departed from the United States than have arrived" by the following:

> The Report of the Secretary of Labor for 1923, p. 133, declares that between 1908 and 1923 Japanese total immigration into continental United States was 125,773 and emigration 41,781, a net gain of 83,992, during the period when the

[48] V. S. McClatchy, *America and Japan* (leaflet published by the California Joint Immigration Committee, 1925).

[49] Japanese who were classified as non-emigrants signified they expected to return. This gave them an opportunity to decide after arrival in Japan whether they would return or not.

[50] Calculations of R. L. Buell in *Japanese Immigration* (1924), p. 291, support Gulick.

Gentlemen's Agreement guaranteed practical exclusion of Japanese immigration. Regardless of feats of legerdemain that may be done with statistics of legal arrivals and departures (usually by adding "non-immigration" figures), the Japanese population of continental United States, and particularly California, has not decreased in the past nine years, while such population in Hawaii has materially increased.[51]

It will be noted that the reply refers to the years 1908–23 and not to "the last nine years" and is consequently not an answer at all. Second, the reply refers to "continental United States," whereas the data pertain to the entire United States including Hawaii (Table 38, p. 275, not Table 40, p. 278). Third, the reply refers to immigration after the Gentlemen's Agreement was in effect, namely, from 1908 to 1923, whereas the immigration data actually included by McClatchy begin with June 1907 (year 1907–8) and include many thousands of immigrants who arrived before the agreement went into effect. Fourth, data based on immigrants to continental United States and Hawaii for 1907–23 are alone used, whereas data on non-immigrants and non-emigrants must be used to record the true situation, as follows:

Immigrants	125,773	Non-immigrants	64,049
Emigrants	41,781	Non-emigrants	122,904
Gain	83,992	Loss	58,855

To emphasize the gain of 83,992 and to disregard the loss of 58,855 means that one is simply not facing facts. The net gain according to these figures is 25,137 during sixteen years. The data that should have been used by McClatchy in this connection, i.e., for continental United States alone and for the years 1908–24, are:

Immigrants	77,373	Non-immigrants	54,470
Emigrants	31,315	Non-emigrants	89,569
Gain	46,058	Loss	35,099

Here is a net gain of 10,959 during sixteen years, which is only about one-eighth that claimed by McClatchy for "continental United States" after the Gentlemen's Agreement had gone into effect. Finally, if one will check over the figures in Table 40 (p. 278), one will see that there was a net loss of 14,142 during the six years 1924–30, which is in agreement with the argument of the California Council on Oriental Relations,

[51] Statement issued by the California Joint Immigration Commission, November 13, 1933.

that 20,000 more have departed than have arrived during the last nine years (presumably 1924–33).[52]

Another source of misunderstanding is to be found in the discrepancy between the figures of the Japanese government and those of the Immigration Commission relative to embarkations and debarkations, both published in the *Annual Reports of the Commissioner-General of Immigration* for 1908–24. (Neither of these sets of figures agrees with entries and departures given in our Tables 38, 39, and 40, pp. 275–79.) There is fair agreement between the Japanese and the United States figures for embarkations to Hawaii or continental United States from Japan, but not in the reverse direction. For example, the Japanese government records 82,140 as having left Japan for continental United States between 1910 and 1920, and the United States government records 81,891. But the former gives 82,259 as arriving in Japan from the United States, and the latter states that 66,853 left the United States for Japan. Consequently there is a net decrease in Japanese population in the United States of 119 for the ten years according to the Japanese figures and a net increase of 15,038 according to the United States figures. (For Hawaii there is a net decrease of 1,905 and a net increase of 9,278, respectively.) The Japanese government could very well have believed that they had stopped increase in Japanese population in the United States, since their figures showed a net loss, and Americans could equally well believe the contrary, since their figures showed a decided increase.

IMMIGRATION OF JAPANESE FROM HAWAII TO THE MAINLAND

It has been stated that a very large number of the Japanese in the United States came via the Hawaiian Islands, and that those who immigrated to the Islands were a group inferior to those who came directly to the mainland. If the latter statement is correct it is important to know to what extent these inferior Japanese are present in the United States.

Another problem closely related to this one is that regarding the possibility of large numbers of Japanese immigrating to the mainland from the Hawaiian Islands during the next decade. In other words, has there been, in the recent past, a considerable immigration to the

---

[52] A net loss of 14,142 during 1924–30 has reference to immigration and emigration, not to net decrease in population. According to Table 15 (p. 165) there was during this period an excess of births over deaths of 23,452.

mainland from the Islands and is there likely to be a large influx in the future?

Number of Hawaiian Japanese in California.—Professor Mears[53] quotes Mr. T. Takimoto, secretary of the Japanese Association of America, and Mr. Tsutomu Obana, a young Japanese specialist in agricultural economics (June 1927), as follows:

> The Japanese who came to America directly from Japan were generally of good character, but these only represented approximately 20 per cent of the total; the other 80 per cent—the peasant class—came from Hawaii, where they worked upon sugar plantations and lived monotonous lives exposed to the wilderness. As certain classes of Japanese migrated to the United States in quest of fortune, large numbers of the peasant class left the sugar plantations and followed them, the majority of whom entered into contract labor in California and Utah upon arriving in America.

Mears comments on the statement above as follows:

> Thus, practically 80 per cent of the Japanese born in America have parents who came from Hawaii, the other 20 per cent, from Japan directly. The differences in heredity are often noticeable in the children. Because of their preponderance, the Japanese who have migrated from the Hawaiian sugar plantations to the mainland are the *point d'appui* which the Coast residents have for their knowledge of the Nipponese.

From the reports of the Board of Immigration of the Territory of Hawaii and of the Governor of the Territory it appears that 35,278 steerage passengers went to continental United States from Hawaii between 1902 and 1910 (see Table 42, p. 281). It is possible that as many as 5,000 more went to Canada or Mexico and later entered the United States. But it is quite likely that many of these had spent very little time in the Islands but had merely stopped off in Honolulu and then moved on to the mainland. Between 1910 and 1929, 2,462 more came in steerage to the United States from Hawaii. If all these are considered as having lived for a time in the Islands, they still constitute but 24 per cent of the immigrant aliens arriving between 1900 and 1930. The estimate of 80 per cent is excessive unless a very much larger percentage of those coming from Hawaii than of those coming direct from Japan have remained in the United States, and data from our survey flatly contradict this supposition.

From among 9,690 Japanese interviewed in our survey there were 335 Japan-born men and 65 Japan-born women who have visited Ha-

---

[53] E. G. Mears, *Resident Orientals,* p. 14. See also *United States Immigration Commission, 1907–10, Abstracts of Reports,* I, 660.

waii at some time or other, presumably on their way to California. (Eighty-two per cent of them came between 1900 and 1907.) These constitute but 14.6 per cent of the men and 3.7 per cent of the women born in Japan who were interviewed. These few men averaged 4.1 years in the Islands (the women, 5.1 years). There is no way of reconciling our figures with the estimate of Obana unless the Japanese who have come from Hawaii are segregated in parts of the country other than those covered in our survey. Whether the Japanese who originally went to Hawaii and later came here are inferior to those who came direct to the United States is a matter of relatively little importance, since they constitute such a small proportion of the total first generation.[54]

Are the Japanese who came by way of Hawaii inferior to those who came direct, as Mears implies? The data from our survey uphold this view. Their education is somewhat less, as is also that of their parents, than the education of those who came direct. But the difference is not great.

Likelihood of Japanese coming to California from Hawaii.—According to Table 42 (p. 281) there has been very little travel of Japanese steerage passengers between the Islands and the mainland. All told, 1,582 went to the Islands and 2,472 came to the mainland from Hawaii between the years 1910–30. Professor Romanzo Adams has very kindly supplied the data in Table 43 (p. 283), giving not only steerage passengers but also cabin passengers and segregating the Japanese into aliens and citizens. According to these figures there is a slight tendency for first-generation Japanese to leave the mainland for Hawaii (net loss to the mainland of 205 in the six years, 1924–30) and the reverse tendency for second-generation Japanese to leave the Islands for the mainland (net gain to the mainland of 973 in the six years). The data in Table 43 indicate that travel is increasing slightly toward Hawaii and more pronouncedly toward the United States,[55] also that about three-fourths of those who are traveling are men.

---

[54] From our survey we estimate that 6.5 per cent of the 97,456 Japanese in California spent some time in the Hawaiian Islands before coming to the mainland, or were born there and subsequently moved here. On this basis there are 6,346 Japanese in California and 9,037 in continental United States who have spent some time in Hawaii.

[55] Adams emphasizes that these net gains and losses cannot be taken at their face value. If a Japanese from Japan stops off a boat at Honolulu on his way to the mainland and later returns direct to Japan, his departure from Honolulu to the

Whether or not the Japanese in the Islands will tend to remove to California is an important aspect of the situation. If any considerable number should do so it would intensify many phases of the problem considerably. The writer spent some time investigating this matter when in the Islands and came to the conclusion that there was not any real likelihood of an influx of Japanese from Hawaii. The Japanese there seemed to be unanimously of the opinion that they were better off than they would be here. Many perceived that there was a stronger sentiment of race prejudice in California than in Hawaii, and some reported that the Japanese in California did not like the Hawaiian Japanese except in the case of the girls. On the other hand, if the economic conditions in the Islands should be badly affected by further importation of cheap labor or by curtailment of sugar, pineapple, and other crops, or by failure of the plantation managers to attract Japanese labor, then a decided immigration to California may occur. Quite probably some of the better educated of the second generation may come to the mainland in the hope of a wider scope of vocational endeavor than is possible in the geographically limited field of the Islands. The numbers of these will for some years at least be hardly sufficient to complicate the present situation.

---

mainland would be counted in the tables given but no credit would be given for a departure from the mainland back to Honolulu when he returned to Japan direct. If an equal number of Japanese travelers stop off at Honolulu going both ways, the net gains and losses mean what they purport to, but if there is any tendency to stop off in traveling one way more often than the other way then the net figures are misleading to that extent. The facts are not known.

IV. RACE PREJUDICE

That the white citizens of the United States should exhibit a feeling of race prejudice against the Chinese, Japanese, and Filipinos in their midst is possibly regarded by those peoples as strange and deplorable. Actually it is only an example of a social phenomenon which commonly attends the intimate meetings of two races. Race prejudice is widespread. It is not at all peculiar to Caucasians. Stratton, for example, writes:

> It is found among peoples ancient and modern; great and small; savage, barbarian, and civilized. A survey might disclose peoples who have never felt it, who feel only sympathy with all aliens or at least no aversion; but this seems improbable.[1]

Although we must conclude that under appropriate conditions any race will exhibit race prejudice toward any other racial group, yet it has appeared that some nationalities are less prone to do so than are others. Thus, it is frequently asserted that the French accept Negroes much more readily than Americans do. In the absence of exact information based on scientific investigation of the subject, the writer feels extremely doubtful as to any fundamental difference among various nationalities in this respect. Apparent differences in attitude may often be explained in terms of actual differences in conditions affecting the relationship of the races.

FACTORS THAT CAUSE RACE PREJUDICE

What then are the factors that cause race prejudice? Race prejudice is based first of all upon the fact that differences exist between two races. Differences, in and of themselves, are psychologically significant. To a sudden noise, to a moving object, to any pronounced change, man usually responds with reflex movements primarily defensive in nature. Under certain conditions he may not do more than pay attention to the stimulus, but the paying attention is essentially a being ready to act defensively if necessary. The varied reactions to an automobile horn according to its intensity and location illustrate the principle. Under certain conditions differences occasion curiosity, not fear. A familiar object occasions no alarm; in fact, it hardly attracts any notice at all. A strange object, if noticed, causes a feeling of uncertainty, which is akin to unpleasantness or strain. There is, then, a fundamental con-

---

[1] G. M. Stratton, *Social Psychology of International Conduct* (1929), p. 43; quoted by permission of D. Appleton-Century Company, publishers.

nection between strange objects or differences and uncertainty, unpleasantness, and being on one's guard.

Man rapidly adapts himself to the strange and new and ceases to pay particular attention to it; strangeness alone is not sufficient to explain race prejudice. Under certain conditions, strangeness accounts for the initiation of a series of responses out of which emerges the habit-formed way of reacting known as race prejudice. Let us see how all this develops.

Differences between individuals of one's own race are noted early in life and become automatically accepted. With members of another race the primary racial difference is so pronounced that it overshadows all others, so that the Caucasian first coming into contact with Japanese feels that all Japanese look alike. Just so the Japanese doubtless feel about Caucasians.

This general similarity among the members of a different race has an important bearing upon our subject. For man tends to judge any new experience in terms of similar past experiences. A white, to whom all whites look different, is able to meet strange whites with an open mind. A man he met yesterday may have cheated him, but the man he meets today has no features in common with that man and arouses no distrust. On the other hand, all Filipinos resemble each other decidedly to the white man's eye. The one met yesterday aroused an unfavorable impression. The physical stimulus presented by the sight of the one met today is so similar that the same unfavorable reaction is immediately produced. Herein lies one of the fundamental bases of race preference or prejudice. We react to all of the new race on the basis of one or very few experiences; we do not distinguish among them as we do in the case of members of our own race, because we cannot.

How we meet the first representatives of a race new to us is crucial to the attitude we shall take. If, from our point of view, they are dressed poorly, if they are performing menial tasks, if their use of our language is pitifully inadequate, if they differ from us in any way denoting inferiority, we are most prone to consider not only themselves but all of their race as inferior. This has been the reaction Americans have made to every new race that has immigrated. Only after a racial group has established itself and raised its whole status have we been ready to receive it on an equal basis. Usually this has been impossible for the first generation, and so the second and sometimes even the third generation have had to fight for recognition of their true characteristics.

The psychology of liking and disliking has never been satisfactorily worked out. To some objects we react immediately by liking, for example, as to sugar, or by disliking, as to quinine. Most objects and people we come to like or dislike in terms of our experience with them. Apparently it is extremely easy to attach this feeling aspect to objects or people. And apparently also, once attached, the feeling remains fairly permanent. In an individual there is relatively slight change from twenty-five to fifty-five years of age. During the decade from fifteen to twenty-five years of age there is proportionately greater change. Probably the first fifteen years of life constitute the chief period in which our likes and dislikes are established. Consequently, once an adult becomes possessed of a race preference or prejudice he is apt to maintain it throughout life.[2]

One of the causes for such permanency is the tendency to seek "reasons" which explain our reactions. If we have mistreated a person, we naturally do not like him. But we cannot give others this explanation. So we find something about the person which will appear to others as a good explanation of our dislike. If the disliked individual belongs to another race that fact affords a very ready defense (rationalization) for our attitude. Most of the propaganda against the Japanese has been of this nature. The agitators did not like the Japanese and looked for the most plausible explanations as to why they were undesirable. When men are so motivated it is almost impossible to influence them with facts, since they will ignore them or distort them for their own purposes.

Habits are formed throughout life. In early life they are few in number and not well established. In adult life habits become stable. Sometimes we refer to this phenomenon by saying, "He has got into a rut." Actually all persons become more and more addicted to their own ways of doing things, and the older they become the less they want to change. Herein is one of the characteristic differences between older men and younger ones.

> Doing new things necessitates the developing of new habits, usually at the expense of old ones. This is easy in youth because the existing habits are not too strongly established and there is surplus energy for the purpose. But later in life the reverse is the case, for old habits are well established and can be broken only with genuine effort, and there is less energy available for this.[3]

A foreigner, with ways differing from one's own, usually forces one to new adjustments, and each such change is disliked particularly by

---

[2] E. K. Strong, Jr., *Change of Interests with Age* (1931).

[3] *Ibid.*, p. 74.

adults. The consequence is that the dislike of the forced adjustment is carried over to the foreigner.

Race prejudice is furthermore due to the tendency to develop stereotypes or generalizations on insufficient evidence, and from the personal standpoint. The unfamiliar and new is interpreted by each individual in terms of his own experience. Thus the reaction to the unknown is partly an expression of the unknown itself and partly, often mostly, an expression of the individual's background. One of the ways of analyzing the character of individuals is to note their reactions to similar incidents. The honest, upright man will interpret the incidents on the basis of honest behavior; the dishonest man sees crookedness even where none exists.

> For the most part we do not first see, and then define. We define first and then see. In the great blooming, buzzing confusion of the outer world we pick out what our culture has already defined for us, and we tend to perceive that which we have picked out in the form stereotyped for us by our culture.[4]

Thus, the strange is interpreted in terms of the familiar but also it is usually so interpreted in terms of *one* experience with it, and thereafter it is most likely reacted to in the same way. One sales manager, for example, would not hire men with red hair. The first one he employed had been a failure. Therefore, as far as he was concerned, all red-headed applicants would be failures. It is this tendency to form a generalization upon insufficient evidence that makes stereotypes such dangerous elements in social relations.

When a generalization is based on many experiences it is much more likely to be true. One such is this editorial from the *San Francisco Chronicle,* entitled "Californians Cannot Believe Chinese Servant the Killer":

> The Grand Jury revoking its indictment of Liu Fook as the murderer of his aged employer is only one of the surprising motions in this strange case. This new trend arises, we believe, from the profound conviction of the public mind that the crime is one entirely out of tune with the character of an old Chinese servant.
>
> We believe the records will support a statement that never in all the years in which California has been used to this old type of Chinese servant has there been a single case of murder with robbery or of a crime of passion against an employer.
>
> A Chinese may kill a white person but in insanity or to "save face," that strange Oriental requirement for re-establishing lost dignity. But never is robbery a motive or even an incident. If Liu Fook had killed his employer it would have been utterly

---

[4] Walter Lippmann, *Public Opinion* (1922), p. 81; quoted by permission of the Macmillan Company, publishers.

out of character for him to have touched the jewels or the money found secreted on the premises and offered as evidence against him. . . . .

The developments in the Liu Fook case are an interesting demonstration of the understanding and tradition that have grown up in many years of contact with the loyalty of old Chinese servants. California public opinion cannot believe that it was Liu Fook who killed and robbed Mrs. Baker.[5]

When a generalization is based not only on many experiences but on experiences which have been carefully controlled and measured, then there results a scientific law. The unfortunate aspect of human behavior in this connection is its willingness to believe implictly a generalization based on a single personal experience and to accept with misgivings the promulgations of scientific work.

Stereotyped reactions are made to certain signs or symbols. Our language is filled with just such cues which set off elaborate sentiments, beliefs, judgments, or trains of thought. It is in this way that stock phrases, shibboleths, slogans, and the like become so effective in gaining the desired response through advertising, propaganda, and the utterances of political spellbinders. An example of how easily one may respond unfavorably to a term which actually characterizes oneself but without appreciating this fact is given by Katz and Allport in their measurement of snobbishness at Syracuse University. In Table 4 are given the percentages of students willing to admit certain groups to their fraternities or rooming-houses. Very few state they would admit "loafers" or "students low in intelligence." Such terms are "unpopular stereotypes, notwithstanding the fact that loafing itself may be fairly popular. Although many students indeed must have been of only mediocre intelligence, and though many were idlers, many of these very students refused to recognize dullards or loafers as belonging in 'their set.' The prejudice is thus against an abstract *name* rather than against individuals in the concrete. It is a standard upheld by lip service, though unreal in fact, which is asserted in order to preserve one's personal pride or self-respect."[6]

Once prejudice has been established toward a single Japanese, for example, the differences in his appearance or manner become signs not merely of membership in the Japanese race but, more important still, of the stereotyped reactions. When any other Japanese is encountered, the peculiarities of his race set off the stereotyped reaction. The second Japanese is not an individual first and incidentally a member of the

---

[5] *San Francisco Chronicle,* December 20, 1930.

[6] D. Katz and F. H. Allport, *Students' Attitudes* (1931), p. 145.

TABLE 4

PERCENTAGE OF STUDENTS WILLING TO ADMIT CERTAIN GROUPS TO FRATERNITIES AND ROOMING-HOUSES

(After Katz and Allport)

Group	Home Economics	Graduate School	Entire University
Protestants	88.6	90.7	86.7
Working-class students	56.4	81.5	68.1
Nordics	40.6	79.6	56.2
Catholics	36.1	79.6	53.4
Gentiles	31.7	72.2	43.9
Conservatives	17.8	63.0	38.0
Students of low social standing	13.9	40.7	28.8
Shabbily dressed students	19.3	29.6	26.9
Grinds	18.8	29.6	26.7
Students having relatives with jail records	8.4	37.0	22.6
Socialists	6.9	53.7	22.4
Jews	10.3	40.7	20.7*
Queer-looking students	13.4	38.9	19.5
Atheists	7.4	40.7	18.6
Italians	5.0	51.9	17.5
Reactionaries	3.0	40.7	17.5
American Indians	4.0	31.5	16.7
Agnostics	3.5	37.0	14.2
Slavs	1.0	42.6	12.7
Armenians	8.9	42.6	12.1
Greeks	3.5	40.7	10.6
Students of unconventional morals	0.5	16.7	8.9
Orientals	5.0	37.0	8.9
Turks	0.5	33.3	8.2
Hindus	1.0	33.3	8.0
Students low in intelligence	4.0	5.5	7.5
Bolshevists	0.5	22.2	7.3
Loafers	2.0	11.1	7.0
Anarchists	0.5	14.8	6.5
Negroes	1.0	14.8	5.4†
Average	23.4	41.8	23.4
Total number of students	208	56	3,515

* "Since about 12 per cent of the students were Jews, the 21 per cent including Jews does not indicate a very widespread tolerance in social contacts extended toward members of this race."

† "Since 5 per cent probably includes the Negroes' on the campus, it follows that only a very small fraction of white students are willing to live with Negro students."

Japanese race; he is a "Jap" first, endowed with all the undesirable attributes of the stereotype, and only incidentally a particular individual.[7]

Prejudice is just what the word implies, the result of pre-judging a person or group.[8] The general meaning of the term is that of opinion, favorable or hostile, based on prepossessions, and therefore biased or unreasonable.

There is still another factor which contributes to race prejudice. Each individual prefers to be himself rather than anyone else. The world radiates out from each of us. Our views, standards, beliefs are the true ones; what others hold to are strange, illogical, wrong. As each of us grows older he extends his ego out to include more or less his own family, his friends, his acquaintances, his own social group. Similarly he comes to view their attitudes and generalizations as more or less his own. And he views with distaste or antagonism those who fall without his own group, in so far as they differ from him. It is in this way that each race comes to believe itself superior. As Young[9] expresses it:

> The white race has for centuries taken this attitude toward the colored races. And of all the white groups the Anglo-Americans have carried this attitude of superiority to the extreme. Impressed by the material progress of the past two hundred years, in ignorance of the factors which produced it, one writer seriously remarks:
>
> "All we can do is to ask for the evidence that other races are our equals. All the evidence in hand seems to indicate the superiority of the whites. . . . . The maximum good of the world lies in the continued prosperity of the white race. . . . . Does it not seem that the race which has extended its sway over the world, politically, militarily, and industrially, is a superior race?"[10]
>
> In contrast to this, the Orientals consider themselves the equals of, if not superior to, the whites. Before China had been opened up to Western contact, one of the emperors wrote to a Western ruler advising him and his people that true wisdom was to be found only in the Middle Kingdom.
>
> Yat-Sen Sun expresses the present attitude:
>
> "Our Chinese civilization has already advanced two thousand years beyond yours (the whites). We are willing to wait for you to progress and catch up with us, but we cannot recede and let you pull us down. Two thousand years ago we discarded imperialism and advocated a policy of peace. . . . . We have got rid of the old savage, pugnacious sentiments and have attained to a true idea of peace."[11]

---

[7] G. M. Stratton, *op. cit.*, chapter v; also K. Young, *The Social Psychology of Oriental-Occidental Prejudices* (American Council, Institute of Pacific Relations, 1929). [8] K. Young, *op. cit.*, p. 4. [9] *Ibid.*, pp. 7–8.

[10] C. C. Josey, *Race and National Solidarity* (1923), pp. 152, 224.

[11] Yat-Sen Sun, *San Min Chu I* (1927), pp. 94, 96.

And Taraknath Das remarks:

"The Whites are in the habit of taking a narrow view of the white world. They have not always been a superior race. They learned religion from the Hebrews, astronomy, chemistry, and mathematics from the Arabs, and the invention of the compass and gunpowder from the Chinese. They are the pupils of those whom they call the colored races. They are, however, forgetful of these facts, and look down upon the Orientals as belonging to inferior races."[12]

Both sets of quotations represent the secondary, elaborated rationalizations of academically trained men in the Occident and the Orient. They are but an intellectualization of notions already found in the common folk of both groups. The Americans are well filled with the idea of the superiority of the whites to all colored races. The domination of the Negroes by the whites in this country is one clue to this view. Yet it extends for the common man from Negroes to the other colored races.

Any manifestation of equality or superiority from one we view as inferior, personally or as a member of a group or nation other than our own, is immediately resented. It is a challenge to our whole conception of life. It is all wrong and cannot be overlooked. Chester Rowell, writing in the *San Francisco Chronicle,* expresses this point very well:

What irritates nations, writes Gilbert K. Chesterton in the *Forum,* is the anger of each nation at the pride of another. Pride is obviously the prerogative of the superior. That is ourselves. Why should other peoples, who are self-evident inferiors, have the impudence to hold up their heads in pride in the presence of us, their superiors? Especially, why should they have the arrogance to discover any faults in us? We may have them, but it is our business, not that of underlings, to point them out. Rather let us, with the privilege of manifest superiority, point out their faults to them.

Try it on yourself. Why don't you like an Englishman? Certainly, not because he is an inferior person. In fact, you do like Englishmen of that sort. The only ones you don't like are the ones who "swell around." What is a "good nigger"? Ask any Southerner. The answer is easy. A "good nigger" may be ignorant and slovenly; he may steal chickens and get drunk and loaf on his job and lie out of scrapes. Those are venal faults. His redeeming virtue is that he is humble; he knows that he is your inferior, and shows it. What is a "bad nigger"? Easy, also. He may be a college graduate, a leading physician, a philanthropist and a reformer, but he is "impudent." He doesn't "know his place." He acts as if he thought he was as good as the lowest white man, or even as good as you are. What is the worst fault of the Japanese? They are "cocky"; that is, they think they are as good as we are. What was the most hateful quality of the pre-war Prussian Junker? His "arrogance." That is always the supreme fault—in the other fellow.

Embree carries this thought one step farther when he asserts that there is "a great need for every man, however humble or stupid, to

[12] Taraknath Das, *Is Japan a Menace to Asia?* (1917), p. 123.

feel that there is someone or some group still lower than he is. Thus only can the craving for a sense of superiority be fed."[13] Psychologists have not worked out the principles and elements that are involved here. There is no doubt, however, that much in life can be plausibly explained on such a basis. Enjoyment of many jokes, newspaper "funnies," and gossip results from the fact that they enable us to feel superior at the expense of others. The enthusiasm with which many receive belittling stories of great men is another example. They cannot cope with such men personally, but they can gloat over them imaginatively and in company with their cronies. On this basis we should expect to find, as we actually do, that the lowest social classes exhibit the most intense forms of race prejudice.

These conceptions of the superiority of ourselves and our group and of the inferiority of those outside our group have led to the sociologists' terms of "we-group" and "other-group" (or "in-group" and "out-group"). J. Merle Davis[14] found that it was the politician, the legionnaire, the native son, the workingman, the small farmer, and the shopkeeper who were usually opposed to the Japanese. These were the people who came into personal contact and very often into personal conflict with the Japanese. Their standards and privileges were threatened by a race which they felt should be inferior. On the other hand, the president of the Chamber of Commerce, the financier and banker, the importer and exporter, the absentee landowner, the large rancher, the mission secretary and the church worker, the social worker, and many school teachers and university professors were friendly to the Asiatic. These people were securely established. They had no feeling of threatened supremacy. The different reactions of these two economic groups may be due not only to the presence and absence of competition but also to the fact that the latter group is much more likely to encounter superior representatives of the Japanese than is the group of workingmen.

By those who feel themselves in direct competition with the out-group, race prejudice is exhibited by open hostility and more or less direct action; by those who are free from competition it is exhibited by a patronizing attitude, by paternal solicitude, or by quiet amusement at the behavior of the out-group; they may sometimes appear to show

---

[13] E. R. Embree, *Brown America* (1931), p. 201; quoted by permission of the Viking Press, publishers.

[14] J. Merle Davis, "We Said: 'Let's Find the Facts'," *Survey,* LVI, 140.

liking for the out-group, nursing neither grievance nor contempt.[15] The children of both classes of the in-group soon sense the situation and develop the same attitudes as their parents. It is a real question which attitude does the greater harm—the open expression of hatred which is easily understood and reacted to, or the quiet feeling of complete superiority, toward which the out-group has no satisfactory response. Clearly some of the second generation have reacted to race prejudice by the development of a strong determination to succeed; others by more or less surrender to what they feel are overwhelming odds. Writing on this subject Miller states:

> An oppressed group is abnormally subjective. Its inability to realize itself freely has turned back attention to itself until its self-consciousness becomes entirely out of focus. In other words, an oppressed group is hyperaesthetic to itself. There is a complete incapacity to view its own problems objectively. Women have through long history belonged to an oppressed group and a prevailing psychosis is illustrated by the reply of the woman whose husband said to her, "The trouble with women is that they take everything personally." "That isn't so," she said, "I don't." Any one who has known Irish, Jews, Poles or any other people who have long been dominated is familiar with this tendency to personal interpretation. There is always a chip on the shoulder to which the slightest jar calls attention. Closely related to this subjectivity is the tendency to be suspicious, which is nothing but a method of being on guard. Social workers have often remarked that certain immigrant nationalities are suspicious. In the group experience a suspicious attitude has been necessary as a protective device. In the effort to resist absorption which used all sorts of subterfuges, the dominated group learned to meet any overture with suspicion.[16]

---

[15] There are three relationships, according to McKenzie, that may arise between two racial groups, namely, competition, parasitism, and mutualism. The former produces friction, conflict, and individual or group consciousness. The second "seems to occasion less trouble, and the attitudes arising from the relationship may be those of indifference or even tolerance." When the third is present, "an attitude of cordiality and good-will tends to develop and to give rise to good-will organizations of various sorts" (see R. D. McKenzie, "The Oriental Invasion," *Journal of Applied Sociology* [1925–26], X, 120–30).

McKenzie's "mutualism" pertains to the relationship between racial groups where race prejudice is absent—the goal of social endeavor. In connection with his second relationship of parasitism one wonders if McKenzie has not overlooked the fact that there is inevitably a patronizing attitude on the part of the superior group which is just as much race prejudice although expressed in a different form from that where competition is felt. Although parasitism may not occasion serious trouble, it fosters a caste system which is distinctly not desirable.

[16] H. A. Miller, "The Oppression Psychosis and the Immigrant," *Annals, American Academy of Political and Social Science,* Vol. XCIII, No. 182 (January 1921), p. 139.

Prejudice toward an individual reveals concern, jealousy, and fear because of actual or threatened competition. This is well illustrated by a clipping from the "Forum" of a daily paper:

I am a native American, have no independence, have never had any, and want none; I want a job. I sympathized with the Filipinos in their homeland, but have lost it all in the competition with them for the job. How I wish the Government would send them all home, and keep them there. If it takes a million soldiers to do it, that will make more jobs for the poor men here.

The contrary of prejudice is good-will. This involves respect for, confidence in, and co-operation with the other person or group. The greater the social distance between two individuals, or two groups, the less the chance for good-will between them. Clearly, race prejudice is best overthrown by bringing both groups together in some enterprise so that they will collectively become an in-group with reference to some other out-group and in their co-operative activities have an opportunity to develop respect for and confidence in each other.[17]

MEASUREMENTS OF ATTITUDE TOWARD JAPANESE

From the concepts of in- and out-groups has come another, namely, "social distance" between two racial groups. Bogardus[18] has measured this in the following manner.

Several hundred people on the coast were asked to rate the Japanese, Chinese, Hindus, Mexicans, Armenians, and thirty-five other races according to the primary reactions that they experienced toward each race. For example, would they willingly intermarry with the Japanese; would they like to have Japanese as chums in their fraternal groups; would they like to have Japanese live as their neighbors on their street; would they like to have Japanese in their occupation (as possible competitors); in this country as citizens; in this country simply as visitors; or would they exclude Japanese from the country altogether? This arrangement of choices is one of decreasing intimacy and understanding—from intermarriage to total exclusion—as determined by fifty judges.

The arithmetical means of the ratings of 110 Americans are given in Table 5.

The Chinese are put 4.28 groups, and the Japanese 4.30 groups, away from complete intimacy and understanding, whereas the English are put only 0.27 of a group away.

---

[17] See K. Young, *Source Book for Social Psychology* (1927), chapters iv, xviii, xix.

[18] E. S. Bogardus, "Social Distance: A Measuring Stick," *Survey,* LVI, 169 ff.; see also "Social Distance and Its Origins" and "Measuring Social Distance," *Journal of Applied Sociology,* IX (1925), 216–26 and 299–308.

TABLE 5

Social Distance between Americans and Other Racial Groups
(After Bogardus)

Race	Social Distance Index	Race	Social Distance Index
English	0.27	Armenians	3.51
Canadians	0.30	Bulgarians	3.97
French	1.04	Negroes	4.10
Danes	1.48	Chinese	4.28
Germans	1.89	Japanese	4.30
Czech-Slovaks	3.46	Turks	4.80

The 110 Americans report that in a five year period they have undergone changes in their opinions of (and attitudes toward) immigrants. Table 6 gives a record of these changes with reference to sample races. The relatively large figures in the third column indicate that changes in opinion regarding races take place slowly—more so than would be anticipated. Through personal interviews "no changes" are the result either of no racial contacts and experiences, or else of having settled convictions for or against various races.

Bogardus adds that the changes are due largely to personal experiences, either pleasant or unpleasant.

TABLE 6

Changes in Opinion and Distance (110 Persons) in Five Years
(After Bogardus)

Race	More Favorable	Less Favorable	No Change
Armenians	23	9	79
Chinese	19	10	81
Germans	6	34	70
Hindus	3	11	96
Japanese	23	19	68
Mexicans	15	22	73
Scotch	0	0	110
Turks	1	16	93

Thurstone,[19] using the method of paired comparisons, obtained from 239 undergraduates at the University of Chicago their preferences toward 21 nationalities. The preferences are given in Table 7 in terms of a scale where preference for Americans is adopted as a point of

[19] L. L. Thurstone, "An Experimental Study of Nationality Preferences," *Journal of General Psychology,* I (1928), 405 f.

origin. Young people in Chicago evidently prefer Chinese and Japanese to Negroes, whereas those on the Pacific Coast, who encounter more Orientals and fewer Negroes, reverse the order of preference. In both cases, the Orientals are placed near the bottom of the list. Evidently there has been built up in the minds of Americans a very unpleasant stereotype regarding Turks, a race with which few of these raters have ever had any contact.

TABLE 7

NATIONALITY PREFERENCES

(After Thurstone)

Race	Scale Value	Race	Scale Value
American	0.0	Russian	−4.1
Englishman	−1.3	Pole	−4.4
Scotchman	−2.1	Greek	−4.6
Irishman	−2.2	Armenian	−4.7
Frenchman	−2.5	Japanese	−4.9
German	−2.6	Mexican	−5.1
Swede	−2.9	Chinaman	−5.3
South American	−3.6	Hindu	−5.4
Italian	−3.7	Turk	−5.8
Spaniard	−3.8	Negro	−5.9
Jew	−3.9		

Katz and Allport[20] have measured social distance or attitude toward nationalities in a different way. They asked members of fraternities and societies to indicate their preferences as follows:

> Provided they are otherwise good fraternity material, I feel personally that the following types of students should be admitted to my fraternity. Check at the left of each of the following groups [see Table 4, p. 104] whom you think should be admitted.

Students not members of these organizations were asked a somewhat similar question.

> Assume that you are living in a student rooming- and boarding-house and are brought into daily social contact with the other students living in the house. The policy as to who should be admitted is to be determined by the roomers already present. Check at the left of each of the following groups whom you would be willing to vote to admit, provided that otherwise they would be desirable tenants in every way. It is to be understood that you would be willing to become a roommate of members of any of the groups which you check.

---

[20] D. Katz and F. H. Allport, *op. cit.*, pp. 142 f.

The groups referred to in the two questions are listed in Table 4 (p. 104), together with the percentages of students who checked them. Data from the College of Home Economics, which was the least tolerant, and from the Graduate School, which was the most tolerant, as well as data from the entire University are reported.

Orientals are preferred to Turks, Hindus, students of low intelligence, bolshevists, loafers, anarchists, and Negroes; but they are less preferred than Greeks, Armenians, Slavs, agnostics, American Indians, etc.

> The wide extent of exclusiveness in students' attitudes is revealed by the fact that, out of the thirty listed types, only four were checked as admissible by as many as half the students in the University. These types were Protestants, students from the working classes, Nordics and Catholics.

It is refreshing to note that the superior students who have gone on for graduate work are much more liberal in their attitudes toward all the racial groups than the undergraduates. But even they rate Orientals below all racial groups except Turks, Hindus, American Indians, and Negroes. They, however, consider shabbily dressed people, grinds, bolshevists, students with unconventional manners, anarchists, loafers, and students of low intelligence inferior to the Oriental.

According to these experiments Japanese are rated very low. Certain data collected by the writer under entirely different conditions raise the query as to what these "very low" ratings actually mean. In Table 8 are given the percentages of 604 twenty-five-year-old men and of 396 fifty-five-year-old men who like and dislike twenty peculiarities of people.[21] Of both these groups, 84 per cent like "progressive people" and only 2 per cent like "men who use perfume." "Foreigners" are liked by about 32 per cent and "Negroes" by about 20 per cent. As Japanese are rated in the preceding tables in about the same manner as Negroes, it is probably safe to say that Japanese are liked better than the items appearing below that of Negroes in Table 8. Although this means that Japanese are not particularly liked by adult men, nevertheless there are many types of people that are liked less by them. As an actual fact, the attitude toward Japanese falls about midway between the two extremes which are given in this table, i.e., an attitude index of +80 for "progressive people" and an attitude index of —78 for "people who talk very

---

[21] E. K. Strong, Jr., *Change of Interests with Age* (1931), Table 55. Liking and disliking refer, of course, to reactions somewhat different from those involved in prejudice. Thus a white woman might like Negroes and yet not wish to marry one and might dislike men who chew tobacco and yet marry such a man in preference to a Negro.

loudly." It is also interesting to note that fifty-five-year-old men like "foreigners" and "Negroes" 5.5 per cent better and dislike them 9.0 per cent less than do twenty-five-year-old men, whereas the average change for fifty-three such items is an increase in liking of 1.8 per cent and an increase of disliking of 2.0 per cent.

TABLE 8

PERCENTAGES OF LIKES AND DISLIKES OF ADULT MEN TOWARD PECULIARITIES OF PEOPLE

(After Strong)

Peculiarities of People	Likes, at Age		Dislikes, at Age		Attitudes (Likes-Dislikes) at Age	
	25	55	25	55	25	55
Progressive people	84	84	5	4	79	80
Athletic men	75	71	2	1	73	70
Optimists	70	77	9	5	61	72
Conservative people	44	52	15	14	29	38
Foreigners	30	35	16	7	14	28
Religious people	35	47	25	16	10	31
Teetotalers	25	48	22	13	3	35
Negroes	17	23	29	17	–12	6
Socialists	15	8	29	42	–14	–34
Irreligious people	14	11	34	47	–20	–46
Men who chew tobacco	9	7	38	48	–29	–41
Spendthrifts	10	5	51	69	–41	–64
Quick-tempered people	10	10	59	68	–49	–58
Bolshevists	8	4	55	70	–47	–66
Pessimists	5	6	62	72	–57	–66
People who talk about themselves	3	2	72	77	–69	–75
Men who use perfume	2	2	73	75	–71	–73
Side-show freaks	5	2	73	79	–68	–77
People who borrow things	3	2	74	86	–71	–84
People who talk very loudly	2	3	79	81	–77	–78

Goodwin B. Watson[22] has reported on the attitudes of over 3,000 persons regarding five Pacific Ocean problems. Over half of his subjects were students, the remainder being drawn from widely different groups. The questionnaire called for replies on fifty-seven items as to "how you feel" and eighty-one items as to "what you think." The instructions and several samples follow:

[22] G. B. Watson, *Orient and Occident* (American Group of the Institute of Pacific Relations, 1927).

A. How You Feel

Directions: Read each word listed in CAPITAL LETTERS in the column below and think quickly how you feel about it. Notice your own immediate reaction to it before you read further. Then read the words or phrases suggested about it, noticing which comes nearest to agreeing with your own reaction. Write the number of that word or phrase in the parentheses in the right-hand margin. If none seems just right, choose the one which comes nearest to expressing your feeling. If several appeal to you, choose the one truest to your first quick response. Do not try to reason out the logically best one.

1. JAPANESE: (1) Alert and progressive; (2) Untrustworthy; (3) Courteous; (4) Ingenious; (5) Conceited; (6) Politically ambitious ( )
2. CHINESE: (1) Laundry; (2) Cruel; (3) Strange; (4) Highly cultured; (5) Beauty-loving; (6) Dependable ( )
3. SOVIET GOVERNMENT: (1) Spreading confusion in China; (2) Plots; (3) Won't work; (4) Helping China; (5) Bold idealistic experiment; (6) Good and bad, fifty-fifty ( )
4. YELLOW PERIL: (1) Jingo press; (2) Real danger; (3) Caused by white imperialism; (4) Over-stressed; (5) Eventual; (6) No longer used even in propaganda ( )

B. What You Think

Directions: Please indicate your opinion about each of the statements below by drawing a circle around the letter or letters in the margin which express your judgment. This is what the letters mean:

T = True (absolutely)
PT = Probably or Partly True
D = In Doubt, Divided, Open Question
PF = Probably or Partly False
F = False (absolutely)

If you do not know enough about an item to express any opinion about it, cross it out.

T PT D PF F 1. Japan's growing population problem cannot be solved unless white peoples allow free Japanese immigration into their countries.

T PT D PF F 2. The property of American missions in China should be turned over to the Chinese Christians.

T PT D PF F 3. America can render greater service to the Filipino people by developing their economic resources than by granting them independence.

In addition, the subjects were asked questions regarding their geographical location, the extent of their travel, and their nationality, education, religion, membership in societies, reading, etc.

Watson stresses quite properly that the replies furnished in this investigation are not necessarily indicative of the attitudes of the people in the United States and that furthermore, since only about one-third of those to whom questionnaires were mailed replied, the results may not properly represent the groups mentioned, as answers are more apt to come from those interested than from those not interested.

In order to summarize the large number of items, Watson combined many of them under five headings: namely, Attitude toward Chinese, toward Chinese Nationalism, toward Japanese Problems, toward Philippine Independence, and toward United States Policies. The material included under these headings is grouped according to its favorable or unfavorable character, as two pertinent sections indicate:

Attitude toward Chinese

Favorable. The extent to which the group recorded any agreement with such ideas as—

That the Chinese are dependable, cultured and equal to Americans in intelligence; that there can be mutual understanding between the races; that we have a great deal to learn from the Chinese; that Chinese immigrants should be treated as are other immigrants; that Chinese history should have a place in our schools.

Unfavorable. The extent to which the group recorded any agreement with such ideas as—

That the Chinese are of inferior intelligence, unclean, cruel, and that we have little to learn from them; that there can be no mutual understanding between Chinese and Americans; that the Chinese should not have the privileges accorded to European immigrants.

Attitude toward Japanese Problems

Favorable.

That the Japanese are alert and progressive, and have maintained a fine attitude toward the United States; that mutual understanding between the two races is possible; that the Japanese are not plotting war against us, and are not waiting to seize the Philippines; that missionaries should go to Japan only if requested; that Japanese in this country should be treated as are other immigrants; that Japan should be put on the quota basis.

Unfavorable.

That the Japanese are untrustworthy, and that there can be no mutual understanding between Orientals and Americans; that exclusion of the Japanese is desirable, and that our immigration policies should be made without regard to their feelings; that Orientals are to be treated differently from other immigrants; that the Japanese are planning for war with the United States, and will seize the Philippines if we relinquish them; that the Japanese are crowding us out of California.

A few of Watson's summaries are included in Table 9. The American students residing at the International House, Columbia University, are very "favorably" disposed toward these five problems, whereas the

TABLE 9

"FAVORABLE"* ATTITUDE TOWARD FIVE PACIFIC OCEAN PROBLEMS BY CERTAIN GROUPS

(After G. B. Watson)

Group	Percentages of the Group Favorable				
	Chinese	Chinese Nationalism	Japanese Problems	Philippine Independence	United States Policies
American students residing at International House, Columbia University	79	85	78	69	76
Women	67	56	47	41	51
American members of the 1927 Conference of the Institute of Pacific Relations	63	59	71	45	54
Three thousand people†	62	52	48	41	46
Business men	57	43	46	28	25
High-school students	55	42	38	25	37
Labor groups	47	57	28	46	57
Employed	44	43	34	32	40
Prisoners, Bridewell Jail, Chicago	39	37	23	21	31
Farmers	38	32	37	26	32

* The term "favorable" has reference to the items of which two groups are given in the text in contrast to the "unfavorable" items.

† These figures are practically identical with those from students and teachers.

relatively few farmers included in the study are distinctly "unfavorable." In between are the other groups, with laboring men tending toward "unfavorable" attitudes and women and students tending in the opposite direction. Business men are about equally divided on the first three problems and "unfavorably" disposed on the last two, that is, they are opposed to Philippine independence and they support an imperialistic policy for the United States.

It is difficult to compare these results with those obtained by Bogardus, Thurstone, and Katz and Allport. But it would appear that Chinese are rated higher here than in those other studies. It is, however, the votes of students and teachers that are responsible for the favorable average attitude toward the Chinese. Business men are slightly favorable, and laboring men unfavorable. The groups are about equally divided toward Chinese and Japanese problems, being slightly more favorable toward the Chinese than the Japanese.

On the specific items regarding the Japanese, 92 per cent of the groups gave the largest vote for "alert and progressive," 4 per cent gave a plurality to "untrustworthy," 3 per cent to "politically ambitious," and 1 per cent to "courteous." Among California housewives 80 per cent voted for "alert and progressive." Of 97 trade unionists in California 31 per cent were for this characterization and 11 per cent affirmed that the Japanese were "conceited." Few, however, among the 3,000 voted for this last.

The labor groups showed an unusual number of objections to the Chinese, a high degree of interest in Chinese nationalism, the largest amount of opposition to the Japanese, the strongest expression of the desire to make the Philippine Islands independent, the greatest opposition to foreign missions, the least antagonism to the Soviet, and a somewhat lower information score on the fact items involved. The women's clubs and housewives showed a small amount of objection and a large amount of favor for the Chinese, little objection to Chinese nationalism, or to the Japanese. The group of farmers was too small to permit valid generalization. This particular group seemed to be very cautious, seldom expressing opinions for or against the issues involved. Partly because of this general tendency they showed the least favor for China, the least interest in Chinese nationalism, the smallest degree of opposition to, or interest in, foreign missions. In spite of this generally low per cent of response, they were distinctly on the side of the imperialists so far as the policies of the United States are concerned.[23]

Geographical differences among the groups seemed to have no significant effect upon their attitudes. But economic differences were important. "California labor is more like Ohio labor than it is like the business men of California."[24]

The tendency is fairly clear for those with Oriental friends to be more favorable to the Chinese, more interested in Chinese nationalism, more favorable to the Japanese, to Philippine independence, more opposed to imperialism, less interested in missions, and better informed on the Orient.[25]

The effect of travel abroad upon attitude toward these problems is rather uncertain, possibly because most of the travelers had visited Europe and not the Orient. The effect of reading is also not clear because of the variety of reading that is indulged in. On the whole, it appears that "the best informed were most likely to have a favorable attitude toward the Japanese and toward Chinese nationalism."[26]

---

[23] G. B. Watson, *op. cit.*, p. 42.

[24] *Ibid.*, p. 45.

[25] *Ibid.*, p. 46.

[26] *Ibid.*, p. 48.

HOW RACE PREJUDICE DEVELOPS

Among children.—It is pretty well agreed among authorities that small children show little or no evidence of race prejudice, that they are "born democrats." Stratton bases part of his argument against considering race prejudice as instinctive on this ground.[27] There is equal agreement that a more exclusive attitude is exhibited by many children by the time they have reached adolescence.[28] Miss Gretchen Tuthill gives this example:

> In many cases the Japanese children feel no difference whatever between themselves and their classmates until they hear some expression of it on the lips of their elders or the American children, as was true of a Japanese girl. She had reached the second year of high school without being the least conscious or sensitive because of her race. She was very fond of public speaking and dramatics, and elected all such courses as she could until one day one of the American boys in the public speaking class said as she finished reciting, "why do you talk so much?" This set her thinking, she said, and she then realized for the first time the feeling that Americans have for Japanese people. After this she lost all interest in elocution, for she felt that she must make herself as inconspicuous as possible, having become oversensitive of the racial difference and feeling regarding it.[29]

If our preceding analysis of the factors involving race prejudice are correct, it is only natural to expect that race prejudice will gradually develop as children grow older, provided they are associated with adults who exhibit such attitudes. A stereotype must be learned like any other habit. Moreover, it is an outgrowth of a considerable number of habitual ways of viewing the world. Chief among them is the development of the ego to the point where it includes within it not only the family but the little group to which the family belongs. Once this stage is reached, the foundation is ready for the building up of in- and out-

---

[27] G. M. Stratton, *op. cit.*, p. 45.

[28] "Children of school age in Wales (*a*) readily state a preference for one people over another [Negroes were preferred to Chinese in the proportion of approximately 3 to 1; British were preferred to Americans in the proportion of about 19 to 1], and (*b*) willingly ascribe virtues and vices to whole groups, as distinguished from individual members of those groups. It does not appear that racial prejudice diminishes with increasing age through the years of school life (i.e., from eight to seventeen years)." The questionnaires in this study were so framed, however, that the children were more likely to reply as indicated in (*b*) above than in any other manner. (G. H. Green and Sydney Herbert, "Racial Prejudice in Children of School Age," *Kwartalnik Psychologiczny,* Vol. I, No. 2 [1930], pp. 145–55.)

[29] G. T. Tuthill, "Japanese in the City of Los Angeles" (unpublished Master's thesis, University of Southern California, 1924), p. 25.

group attitudes. Remarks of adults are then seized upon and incorporated into the developing stereotypes, whereas at an earlier period they would probably have been ignored.[30]

It is true that evidence of race prejudice is relatively slight in children until they begin to develop adult reactions. It would seem to be adult training which is responsible for keeping race prejudice alive. Yet the writer is convinced that were children brought up entirely free of adult influence, some aspects of race prejudice would develop among them as they advanced in years.[31] On the other hand, if adults freed themselves of these attitudes there would be a correspondingly greater freedom from prejudice on the part of their children.

Goldenweiser[32] argues that because race prejudice is not a "natural antipathy" it is the problem of the educator "not to impart to the child an attitude foreign to his nature and contradicted by his spontaneous inclination, but to keep the child from learning something which, if unlearned, it will never possess, namely prejudice." We are in hearty sympathy with this program for the educator, but we disagree most emphatically with the statement that race prejudice is foreign to the nature of the child. It is foreign only in the sense that walking or growing a mustache or making love is foreign to the nature of the newborn babe or, more accurately, that dancing or learning to read and write or yelling for our football team is foreign to infants born in the United States. They do not possess these qualities at birth, but they have the kind of organism that will most surely acquire these activities as they grow up under existing conditions. To fear and hate those who interfere with our activities is a natural reaction of all. Jealousy and prejudice arise "naturally"; the aim of sound educational policy is to minimize them as much as possible.

Among adults.—The three words "welcome," "antagonism," "exclusion," have been freely used to express the three stages of American attitudes toward the Chinese, Japanese, and Filipinos. When these races

---

30 See L. L. Thurstone, "The Measurement of Changes in Attitude," *Journal of Social Psychology,* II (1931), 230–35, for one method of measuring the effect of such factors upon attitude. There is great need for careful research in this field.

31 Proof of this is amply afforded by the exhibitions of the strong feelings developed among college students toward other groups of all sorts and kinds made up of their own nationality. The more striking differences due to race would be similarly seized upon as the basis for other in- and out-groupings.

32 A. Goldenweiser, *Race and Race Relations* (American Council, Institute of Pacific Relations, 1931), p. 19.

were few in number and widely scattered they were viewed as interesting curiosities and certainly with no alarm. Increase in their numbers, particularly when it became economically significant, quickly developed irritation, animosity, and desire to be rid of them. Stratton believes that the size of the foreign group,[33] its solidarity, the support it is conceived to receive from the rear, and the important interests endangered by its presence are the significant factors that precipitate race prejudice. In the case of the Chinese since 1890 and that of the Japanese since 1924, antagonism has waned because there is no longer fear of increasing numbers to contend with, there are no new conditions to face, and the whites are becoming accustomed to those already settled here.

One may well ask why there has been such strong race prejudice against these Orientals on the Pacific Coast and so little manifested in the Hawaiian Islands. Authorities seem to agree upon the difference. For example, Littler writes:

> . . . . with the possible exception of the French in their relation to the negroes, the people of Hawaii have gone farther toward breaking down race barriers than any other civilized people in the world have done. In the Islands no race is regarded as grossly inferior, as are the negroes in the Southern states, and there is no racial animosity such as pervades certain districts in California against the Japanese. Those who speak with unrestrained antagonism toward the Japanese and the Filipinos do so in the manner of politicians attacking opponents of whom they have only read. To walk down the streets of the Oriental districts and to behold fathers who have donned clean kimonos to take well-behaved children out for a walk before the evening meal quiets considerably the agitated feeling of Oriental hatred. . . . .
>
> The truth is that in Hawaii there is racial consciousness but not racial antagonism. The intermixture of nationalities is a problem but not a danger. Indications are that the problem is being met. While calm logic would dictate that there is little probability of Oriental domination, still there is some possibility of it. Founded or unfounded, anxiety lest this come about is so widespread that Hawaii will not furnish the forty-ninth star in the American flag, for at least some time to come.[34]

Stratton emphasizes that this difference in race attitude on the mainland and in the Islands is due largely to the absence of serious economic threats against the whites. He writes:

---

[33] G. M. Stratton, *op. cit.*, p. 52. See also C. N. Reynolds, "Newspaper Treatment of Oriental-White Race Relations," *Publications, American Sociological Society*, Vol. XXIV, No. 2 (1930), pp. 151–52; and p. 149 of this volume.

[34] R. M. C. Littler, *The Governance of Hawaii* (1929), pp. 221–22.

In the Hawaiian Islands . . . . it has seemed to some that racial prejudice does not exist. And indeed a remarkable softening of its effects has been attained. Yet it would be idle to deny its presence; an anxiety, a tension, cannot but be noticed, with here and there some actual occurrence which reveals the forces which are so nearly overcome.[35] . . . . Economic interest, if great and if the alien brings clear gain and only gain, may—as in Hawaii—prevent racial prejudice from displaying itself in violence. But the ebb and flow of emotion is not to be understood as due to monetary gain alone.[36] . . . . The Americans in Hawaii, having felt no menace from the weak and unaggressive Polynesians there, have intermarried with them and have not lost caste; indeed in the "first families" of the Caucasians in Hawaii a racial mixture may be found. Feeling thus waxes and wanes with the circumstances which touch and awaken group anxiety.[37] . . . . The antipathies in Hawaii are eased by the thought that the alien races are needed by those in power. Over them all, furthermore, is a system of law and government; the more important interests of the several groups are assured by a strong common government of them all, without need of their own private alarms and violence. And although social distinctions are made, yet the Caucasians still confront no strong and dangerous rivals. There is no inner urging to paint the opposite party black and one's own party white, for mere purposes of group protection. The difficulties foreseen in the near future appear to the leading men there not to be beyond their powers of adjustment, provided only, as I was told in Honolulu, that America has no war with a nation whose immigrants are in a large number in the Islands. As things now stand, we see in Hawaii how inert is racial prejudice when not influenced by the seeming need of protecting large interests imperiled.[38]

Galen Fisher sums up his discussion in these words:

But in a community like Hawaii, which has an abnormal economic basis, there is no danger of serious friction so long as the immigrants are willing to stay in humble occupations. The tendency to friction appears as soon as the children of the immigrants begin to compete with their white contemporaries. In Hawaii there are signs that this stage has been entered, but the friction has been to a large extent prevented or allayed by the powerful missionary tradition among the Americans, and by the friendly, restrained attitude of the Orientals, due in part to wise local leadership, in part to pressure from Japan, and in part to the *force majeure* of American authority.[39]

HOW RACE PREJUDICE MAY BE LESSENED

As has been pointed out above, race prejudice is not an instinctive reaction but is an outgrowth of the peculiarities of human beings, so

---

[35] G. M. Stratton, *op. cit.*, p. 40. [36] *Ibid.*, p. 50. [37] *Ibid.*, p. 52.

[38] *Ibid.*, p. 54; quoted by permission of D. Appleton-Century Company, publishers.

[39] G. M. Fisher, *Relations between the Occidental and Oriental Peoples on the Pacific Coast of North America* (1928), p. 14; quoted by permission of the International Missionary Council, publishers.

that for practical purposes it may be viewed as a type of behavior that will arise when two different groups are brought together under ordinary conditions.

We have shown that this type of behavior arises for the following reasons: (*a*) The first reaction to an observation of difference is a feeling of strain and uncertainty; (*b*) the readjustment to a new situation involved in contacting a race different in looks and customs is unpleasant to those with established habits; (*c*) because our own status is affected economically or our feeling of superiority threatened by the presence of another race, we dislike that race and seize upon every positive objection to it as a rationalization of our dislike; (*d*) our first unfavorable reaction to the member of another group tends to become the stereotyped reaction to all members of that group.

"Eliminate the cause and cure the disease" is a sound precept in medicine. It may well be applied to the state of mind we are considering.

Already the fact that Japanese immigration has ceased and that consequently the fear of economic rivalry has been removed from California has eliminated much of the hard feeling in that state toward the Oriental. Agitation is practically a thing of the past. The Japanese can now be judged on their merits, not as a growing menace.

The second-generation Japanese may remain Oriental in face and figure. But in dress, speech, and manner they are more and more like the American type. The degree of difference, while probably never wholly changing, will become less with each generation. Similarity in ethical standards and ideals is the great common denominator.

The stereotyped reaction can be broken down only by greater experience. Because stereotypes are often gross exaggerations of the real situation there may be a strong reaction against them when the facts are known. Usually they are so engrained in one's emotional life that a single favorable impression is not sufficient to offset the earlier unfavorable attitude; but the latter may be outweighed by ten favorable impressions.

Sir Henry Thornton tells us that "the first factor in improved international relations to which all others are subordinate, must be an understanding of each people with respect to other peoples." This is to be accomplished by education through "study, travel and instruction from those who are competent to teach." "A nation," he says, "is more than fields, workshops and mines; its reaction will be determined by the spirit and mentality of its citizens. And if we are to understand the peoples of other nations, we must understand the spirit that moves within them, that living spark, intangible and ethereal, which is the self-starter of all national activities. There is an old proverb, 'know thyself,' but far more important it is to know thy neighbor."[40]

The conclusions of Watson, given above, together with those of Reynolds[41] and others, raise doubts as to the effectiveness of study, reading, and travel in eliminating race prejudice. Apparently these have an ameliorating effect, but it is clear that college graduates may be as strongly possessed of a given stereotype as anyone else. There is a challenge here to our educational institutions that instruction shall not only involve facts but that it shall be applied to practical problems involving prejudice. Race prejudice and all other forms will not be minimized until the educational forces of the world are directed to this end. The study of history introduces us to other peoples, but the gain from added acquaintanceship may be more than offset by the inculcation and fostering of unfortunate stereotypes. Did not the English stir up the Indians to massacre our forefathers? How much of the suspiciousness of England in the minds of Americans today is due to the implanting of such emotional bits of dynamite in us when we went to school?

The present forms of education are helpful in combating race prejudice; they could be made far more so. But seemingly the best way to combat the prejudices which are so easily inculcated about an unknown group is to increase acquaintanceship with representative members of that group.

---

[40] H. W. Thornton, *Men and Industry* (a Brackett Lecture at Princeton University, 1931), p. 12.

[41] C. N. Reynolds, "Oriental-White Race Relations in Santa Clara County, California" (unpublished Ph.D. thesis, Stanford University, 1927).

V. SPECIFIC COMPLAINTS AGAINST JAPANESE

Previous to the time when the Japanese problem developed, California had already experienced the whole gamut of events leading up to the Chinese exclusion act. During this time "popular feeling developed to such a pitch that many unfortunate incidents occurred of grave wrong done to individual Chinese as the result of mob and other illegal violence."[1] The exclusion of Chinese had had most salutary effects in that it saved the state from the evils of race prejudice and agitation.

When the Japanese immigration reached such size as to arouse similar race prejudice and agitation against them, the most obvious solution was exclusion. But here the state was confronted, as before, with certain difficulties. First, the state could not bring about exclusion. That was a matter for the federal government. Second, the state was divided in its attitude: some citizens had felt the menace of increasing Japanese immigration and desired exclusion immediately, some were profiting from Japanese labor, and many did not belong in either of these groups and were indifferent to the whole question. Those who wanted immediate exclusion were sure they were right, were certain exclusion would have to come, and argued that it had better come before affairs became too serious. They had before them the task of convincing their fellow-citizens of the state and of arousing sentiment sufficient to induce the federal government to pass an exclusion act.

On the opposite side were the Japanese themselves, newcomers, ignorant of the country and its customs, relatively few in numbers, and without a vote. Favoring them were many of the large landowners who needed cheap farm labor. As the Japanese increased in numbers this group felt less and less need for admitting more of them. There were also some business men who appreciated the trade between Japan and the United States and did not want it jeopardized. There were finally many public-spirited people whose primary concern was that individual Japanese already here should be treated properly and that relations with Japan and the Orient should be continued on a friendly basis. All of these stood for the status quo. But procrastination is a poor program against positive action supported by a militant group. It is almost surely foredoomed to failure.

---

[1] W. D. Stephens, governor of California, in letter transmitting to Secretary of State, Bainbridge Colby, the Report of the State Board of Control, *California and the Oriental* (1922), p. 7.

During the period of agitation leading up to the exclusion of Japanese in 1924 none of them, as far as the writer can determine, suffered serious physical injury.[2] Respect for the prowess of the Japanese government was partially responsible for this. A second explanation is that the Japanese were never as great a menace as the Chinese, for at only one census report did the former exceed 2 per cent (2.1 per cent) of the population of the state, whereas the Chinese constituted approximately 9 per cent of the population in 1860, 1870, and 1880 (see Table 36, p. 274). Another reason that the Japanese were treated much better than the Chinese in earlier years was that the frontier days had largely passed and there was a stronger public opinion opposed to violence in any form. The groups friendly to the Japanese helped keep this better public opinion to the fore.

Determined to stop the Japanese immigration, the agitators proceeded to convince a majority of the voters of the Pacific Coast of this necessity and to annoy the Japanese already here so much that they would voluntarily depart for Japan. When one believes he has been injured by another he naturally strikes back in whatever way is feasible. And so the agitators struck at the Japanese in every possible way. Many of the political leaders among these agitators were experienced in such matters. The result was that few stones were left unturned or unthrown. Every significant thing about the Japanese, whether favorable or unfavorable, was seized upon and twisted about until it made a suitable weapon for injuring the newcomers. Hence, if they asked less than the going wage, they were threatening the American standard of living; if they demanded better wages, they were avaricious; if they were successful in farming and saved enough to buy their own ranch, they were driving the whites out; if they were unsuccessful, they were "wearing out the land."

As an actual fact, the specific charges made against the Japanese have little significance in themselves. They were merely the smoke pouring up from a bonfire; they gave evidence of a fire and that was about all. This the Japanese and their friends discovered when they attempted to answer the charges with facts. It was as useless to answer the charges as to pour water on smoke. Only direct elimination of the cause of the agitation could stop it. This could be done only by excluding the Japanese. Eventually the country perceived this, and the Immigration Act of 1924 was passed.

---

[2] See footnote 20 in chapter ii (p. 40).

Now that peace has been restored and the ill-feeling is dying down, it is a good time to note what these charges were and to consider what truth there was in them. For it is only at a time when emotion is not aroused that cold facts can influence most men. The truth should be established in fairness to the Japanese. It should be told in order that existing prejudices may be allayed and both whites and Japanese may come to live together on a better basis of understanding.

The writer early came to the conclusion that the most serious obstacle to the success of second-generation Japanese in this country is the existence of race prejudice. In order to understand it he gathered expressions of this feeling from all available sources. The remainder of the chapter gives samples of his findings. There is no particular attempt to answer these criticisms in this chapter, since the remainder of the volume is largely an answer to them.

There is real need today for a careful evaluation of these charges against the Japanese, for they are being repeated in British Columbia[3] and are being broadcast by organizations even today which oppose extension of the quota system to Japanese immigration. False statements, and particularly distorted statements, do incalculable harm in the consideration of any question, as they confuse the main issue and indirectly discolor many others.

TREATMENT OF JAPANESE TYPICAL OF THAT EXTENDED ALL IMMIGRANTS

There is a very natural tendency in reading about the Japanese situation to come to believe that their experiences and the attitudes shown toward them are peculiar to the Japanese themselves. Yet similar studies of other immigrant groups would show very similar treatment.[4] Such differences as might be noted would be found to be more largely expressions of peculiarities of the period or locality than of the racial group. The material which follows constitutes the reactions of whites

[3] *Report on Oriental Activities,* prepared for the Legislative Assembly of British Columbia in 1927. One example of many where the reader is given a distorted conception is this: "In three years the number of Japanese children in the public schools has increased 74 per cent, while in the same time the number of white children has increased by 6 per cent." On the next page it appears that only 2,072 Japanese children were born in the Province during these three years. The *Canada Year Book* gives a total of 30,462 births in British Columbia for these three years, i.e., 1923–25.

[4] See, for example, Bruno Lasker, *Filipino Immigration* (1931); and H. Feldman, *Racial Factors in American Industry* (1931).

toward a racial group that offered real competition. It is an interesting chapter in social psychology. True appreciation of the Japanese situation, or that of any other immigrant group, will be possible only when we understand the general psychological principles that apply to such situations.

OBJECTIONS TO JAPANESE BY GOVERNOR STEPHENS IN 1920

Governor Stephens pointed out that the Japanese had many "admirable qualities" and that "California harbors no animosity against the Japanese people or their nation. California, however, does not wish the Japanese people to settle within her borders and to develop a Japanese population within her midst." The reasons given in support of this view are:

1. "California wants peace." Mob and illegal violence resulted from increasing Chinese immigration. Such are likely to occur if the Japanese immigration is not stopped.
2. Control of many of California's important agricultural industries has passed into Japanese hands and they are increasing their holdings very rapidly.
3. Their economic standards are "impossible to our white ideals."
4. Their fecundity "far exceeds that of any other people that we have in our midst."
5. "Their children outnumber our own in many country schools. The deep seated and often outspoken resentment of our white mothers at this situation can only be appreciated by those people who have struggled with similar problems."
6. The two races are too dissimilar. Racial superiorities or inferiorities are not implied, merely differences too great for assimilability.
7. The prevalent attitude toward the Japanese is "too deep-seated to remove. And with this attitude goes the necessity of Japanese isolation and that inevitable feeling which socially a proscribed race always develops."[5]

This letter of Governor Stephens was unquestionably written with due regard to the susceptibilities of American citizens in the eastern part of the country and of the Japanese nation. Let us note next the attitudes of students given in personal interviews where there was little thought of the necessity of catering to the judgment of those at a distance or of considering the politics of the situation. The attitudes of

---

[5] W. D. Stephens, *op. cit.*, p. 10.

these students were obtained three years after the exclusion act was passed and so were probably less extreme than those which might have been expressed during the excitement of the agitation period.

OBJECTIONS BY STUDENTS[6] IN 1927

Reynolds found among ninety students only fourteen who felt the Japanese were more desirable than the Chinese.[7] This group expressed 151 favorable reactions regarding the Chinese and an equal number of unfavorable reactions, whereas they gave 251 adverse characterizations of the Japanese and 150 that were favorable (see Table 10).

TABLE 10

ATTITUDE TOWARD JAPANESE BY STUDENTS IN 1927 (Based on Tables X and XI of Reynolds)

Unfavorable Traits	Number Times Mentioned	Favorable Traits	Number Times Mentioned
Take unfair advantage: dishonest, tricky, treacherous (55); ruinous, hard, or unfair competitors (19); greedy, grasping, avaricious (3); selfish (2); wear out land (7); acquire all the best land (7)	93	Honest: frank, loyal, law abiding (6); honest, trustworthy (4); courteous, kind, etc. (17)	27
Low standards of living (21); low wages, long hours (9); make their women work (7); make their children work (5); bad living conditions, unsanitary (15)	57	Industrious: good workers, industrious (22); capable, skilled (16); thrifty, economical, frugal (9); ambitious (5); persistent (2); aggressive, purposive (2)	56
Send money back to Japan	10		
Hard to assimilate	10	Easily Americanized	2
Prolific, high birth-rate	7		
Low morals	7	Good people, good morals	2
Lower intelligence	4	High intelligence	39
Dirty	4	Clean, fine-looking, immaculate	11
Conceited (3); quick-tempered (2); repulsive (2); cruel, ferocious, dangerous (3)	10	Artistic	2
		Keeps his place	3
Miscellaneous	49	Miscellaneous	8
	251		150

[6] Based upon the reactions of ninety high-school seniors and college freshmen, all residents of Santa Clara County.

[7] C. N. Reynolds, "Oriental-White Race Relations in Santa Clara County, California" (unpublished Ph.D. thesis, Stanford University, 1927), chapter xiii.

The hostile or unpleasant qualifications are, also, more bitter and prejudiced. All but a small number of them appear in the stereotyped charges made against the Japanese during the anti-Japanese agitation of the Alien Land Law campaigns. . . . . The leading good quality listed was keenness of intellect or high intelligence. This trait was sometimes mentioned by individuals who were hostile to the Japanese and the same is true of the classification in second place, good workers, industriousness, etc.

Comparison of the two lists for the Japanese with those of the Chinese show plainly the effect of a keenly felt economic competition in the case of the former and its absence in the case of the latter. . . . .

The most frequently mentioned source of the feeling, expressed in the interviews, was the record of events as read from newspapers. Experience with Japanese, as children, was the second source in frequency of mention. . . . .

Reynolds continues:

The first of the two following interview statements shows an attempt to be fair to the Japanese in the face of an unconquerable dislike of their inability to keep in their place, while the second indicates some success in "living down" a dislike formed by early experience:

"I have known more Japanese than Chinese. In my school I have noticed that the Japanese are very bright and very conscientious in preparing their studies. They are very independent and also rather quick tempered. I heard one Japanese who was washing windows tell a woman 'Some day you do same for me.' This is one race which seems to be rather dangerous. They are almost too independent. Unlike the Chinese, the Japanese would love to put over something dishonest on a white man. They seem to hate the white because they are made to obey him. If they work for one, one has to be very careful in telling them what to do for if one bosses them too much they leave, usually without saying so; that is, if they have received their pay. On the other hand, I have known some very kind Japanese. One was especially kind and treated his wife and child as kindly as anyone. Of course, individuals vary, but I think I would trust a Chinaman farther than a Japanese. It seems to me that those born in their mother country are better than those who are born in our country. I have no special reason for this but I have noted it to be true."

"In California no matter what part of the state one goes, I believe one will always come into contact with the Japanese. When I was a small child I first learned to fear and detest these people, because of one who tried to approach me. Since then my opinions have been more or less moderated from this intense horror and hatred, to a more tolerant position. The Japanese have always impressed me as being a dirty sneaky race, and even now, that is my opinion. We have a Japanese gardener who, even though he is not of an educated class, seems more intelligent than most white gardeners. I cannot say why my hatred for Japanese has changed to tolerance unless it is just because I am getting older and am beginning to see things through a larger glass. Perhaps this gardener, who is around the house so much of the time, in an unconscious way, by his quaint manners which fascinate me, has taught me not to dislike the Japanese."

Two additional quotations are significant in showing how intensely strong the attitudes of these students were and at the same time how little they understood the cause of their attitudes:

"It has befallen me in my experience that several Japanese have been my schoolmates at various times, and I have observed others—truck farmers for the most part. All of them have impressed me as particularly hard workers, and, although an uncomfortable state of uncleanliness is prevalent among the farmers, upon considering the reasons for such conditions, they are excusable. These men lack opportunity. Can we expect them to reach our standards? As for the school fellows, I have never seen anyone, even among my friends, who kept themselves any cleaner, or who were of any higher mental calibre than they."[8]

"I don't know why I should have the feeling that they [the Japanese] are tricky, self centered and would cut a man's throat for fifty cents; unless it is their appearance as they quick-step down the street. Straw shoes, black or blue caps, close cropped hair, grim unsmiling expressions, enough to make a saint suspicious, especially on a dark night."[9]

Table 10 very briefly summarizes the attitudes expressed toward the Japanese by the ninety students of Santa Clara County. It is surprising to note that the great majority of both unfavorable and favorable remarks center around the idea of industriousness. Some admire them for the trait; others condemn them because they are too successful, and suspect them of being dishonest, tricky, greedy, grasping, and the like. As to intelligence, thirty-nine report that they have high intelligence and only four report low intelligence. Aside from these two items the judgments are scattered among many attributes. It is significant that only seven report low morals (two report good morals). Evidently morality is not an issue. Four find them dirty, and eleven state that they are clean, fine looking, immaculate.

OBJECTIONS ON ECONOMIC GROUNDS

Tasuka Harada obtained answers to a questionnaire regarding attitude toward the Japanese in 1920.[10] Mears[11] tabulated the replies from twenty-eight leading men on the Pacific Coast and classified 45 per cent of the replies as objections on economic grounds, 25 per cent on political grounds, 22 per cent on racial grounds, and 8 per cent on social grounds. On this basis, objections on economic grounds are of greatest importance and those on social grounds of least significance.

[8] C. N. Reynolds, *Oriental-White Race Relations,* p. 382.

[9] *Ibid.,* p. 384.

[10] T. Harada, *The Japanese Problem in California* (1922).

[11] E. G. Mears, *Resident Orientals,* p. 39.

The writer has found it far from easy to classify objections, as many pertain to two or more of these classifications. Only in a rough way has this system of classification been followed here.

Chester Rowell has presented the economic objections to Japanese as follows:

Because discriminations based on physical race touch human pride at its most sensitive point, there has been a tendency to protest that these exclusions are based on economic and not on racial grounds. In part, this is true. All the pressure for migration from the Orient is economic. The oriental peoples do not come to us because they like us, but because their lands are crowded and ours have room; because we are rich and they are poor. We, in turn, object to them because their standard of living is low; because they can overwork and underlive us, and by that defeat us in economic competition. The workingmen objected to the Chinese, and then to the Japanese, when they were competitors. The small farmers objected when the Japanese began buying land. The large landowners, who want cheap labor, do not object even now, but would prefer Chinese to Japanese. The merchants' objection was that "they send their money home." Now that the alien land laws are driving the Japanese back to the cities, the workingmen talk of relaxing those laws. Wherever in the world there is an oriental working population, there is no room for a white one. And even where orientals are fewer, they monopolize whatever occupations they enter. No one else can compete with them. All these motives are expressly economic. And economic causes doubtless also underlie much of the feeling which is more consciously racial.[12]

Representative Hayes is quoted as follows:

As is well known, no white man can compete with the Japanese laborers. They are satisfied to be housed in such cramped and squalid quarters as few white men in any part of the world could live in, and the food that keeps them in condition would be too cheap and poor to satisfy the most common labor in this country. Besides, the large percentage of Japanese immigrants have no families to provide for and no children to educate.

When the laborer with American ideals—with a home to maintain, a family to support, and children to educate—sees his job taken by a man wholly alien in race, with no family ties or responsibilities, and who, by the laws of our country, can never be admitted to the responsibilities of citizenship, he would not be worthy of the name of freeman if he did not fight for his home, his wife, and his children with every weapon at his command. He would be far from the intelligent laborer that he is reputed to be if he did not organize and join with his fellows to more effectually fight the common enemy. And every lover of his kind and every patriot should help him in this fight. The very existence of the Republic depends upon it. As the proportion of our citizens who work for wages increases it is becoming more and more important that the child of the laborer should be educated to understand and to bear properly responsibilities that will devolve upon him as a freeman, as one of the sovereigns of this great country. It is also more and more important

[12] Chester Rowell, "Western Windows to the East," *Survey,* LVI (1926), 174.

with the passage of each year that the laborer should be made to feel that the Government of this country will deal justly, yea, generously with him, and that it will assist him to maintain every equitable right and protect him from every enemy who would destroy his home and his American standard of living. From every consideration this House should hear this protest of the laborers of the Pacific Coast against Mongolian invasion. We should at least not deny their petition before it is heard or considered. The danger that threatens them is great and immediate. The spirit of immigration is rapidly taking possession of the Japanese mind, and in the immediate future the number coming to the Pacific Coast will greatly increase.[13]

According to Reynolds,[14]

The vision of the Japanese cheap labor driving out the American worker is the one which was most repeatedly called up in the propaganda against the Japanese and the one which left the most lasting impression. Consistency was not necessary in the campaign. One issue of the *San Francisco Chronicle* carried a long article devoted to the "absolute evidence" extant showing that the competition of Japanese had driven thousands of white workers out of employment and created myriads of hoboes, while the following issue presented an editorial stating: "The root of the trouble lies in the fact that there is real scarcity of effective unskilled labor in the United States owing to the fact that abundant opportunity has drawn the most effective native Americans to other avocations. This makes the opening which the Chinese first and now the Japanese are filling."[15] . . . .

There was a continuous display of news of economic competition of one sort or another in the daily press. All of this rested upon the belief that the Japanese standard of living gave him an unfair advantage and tended to force the white man to his level. This low standard of living included cheap housing, cheap foods, poor clothing, a whittling down of leisure time by working interminable hours, the forced labor of the women folk and the children, the foregoing of amusement and recreation. The extent to which this was a just appraisal of the Japanese immigrants' manner of living and working has never been determined but the reiteration of the charges in the daily news convinced large numbers of Californians of its truth.[16]

Another way of expressing the foregoing is to characterize the Japanese as "too successful." This is the way in which Lasker[17] refers to them after discussing the losses falling upon a community due to the presence of itinerant Mexican workers. Mears quotes the general manager of a large distributing firm, in referring to the Japanese as

---

[13] E. A. Hayes, "Japanese Exclusion," *Congressional Record,* Vol. 40, Part 4, p. 3753.

[14] C. N. Reynolds, *Oriental-White Race Relations,* p. 109.

[15] Quoted by Reynolds from the *San Francisco Chronicle,* February 25, 1905, p. 6.

[16] C. N. Reynolds, *Oriental-White Race Relations,* p. 314.

[17] B. Lasker, *op. cit.,* p. 330.

the most industrious people you ever saw. They can make money in a place where a white man would starve to death, because they generally have large families, and their wives and all the children go into the fields and work.[18]

James D. Phelan, United States Senator from California, expressed the same thought in these words:

The Japanese also lease lands and work for a share of the crop, and when thus working for themselves are impossible competitors, and drive the white settlers, whose standards of living are different, from their farms. The white farmer is not free from cupidity when tempted by Japanese to sell out at high prices, and they do sell out and disappear. The state, therefore, is obliged as a simple matter of self preservation to prevent the Japanese from absorbing the soil, because the future of the white race, American institutions, and western civilization are put in peril. . . . . We admire their industry and cleverness, but for that very reason, being a masterful people, they are more dangerous.[19]

That these statements about Japanese acquiring control of land were not mere propaganda is shown by the report of the State Board of Control of California.[20] Of 3,893,500 acres of irrigated land, "which comprise, very largely, the best lands in the state," in 1919 the Orientals occupied 623,752 acres, approximately 16 per cent. Basing the figures for 1909 on data compiled by the State Bureau of Labor Statistics and those for 1919 on data furnished by the Japanese Agricultural Association of California, the lands occupied by Japanese increased in ten years from 83,253 to 427,029 acres (413 per cent) and the value of the crops from $6,236,000 to $67,146,000 (977 per cent).

If the Japanese had been evenly scattered through the state, the effect would not have been so great as it was. Congregated as they were, in certain sections, they made a much greater impression of numbers.

In some of the richest counties in the state, Orientals occupy a total acreage ranging from fifty to seventy-five per cent of the total irrigated land, notably San Joaquin County with a total of 130,000 irrigated acres with Orientals occupying 95,829 acres; Colusa County with a total of 70,000 with Orientals occupying 51,105; Placer County with 19,000 total, Orientals occupying 16,321; and Sacramento County with 80,000 total, Orientals occupying 64,860.[21]

---

[18] E. G. Mears, "The Land, the Crops, and the Orient," *Survey,* LVI (1926), 149.

[19] J. D. Phelan, "Why California Objects to the Japanese Invasion," *Annals, American Academy of Political and Social Science,* XCIII (January 1921), 17.

[20] Report of State Board of Control of California, *California and the Oriental* (1920, revised in 1922), pp. 45 f. See also Elwood Mead, "The Japanese Land Problem in California," *Annals, American Academy of Political and Social Science,* XCIII (January 1921), 51.

[21] Report of State Board of Control of California, *op. cit.,* p. 50. These figures are not quite fair to the Orientals since their total holdings are contrasted with only

It was this very great concentration of Japanese in certain sections that intensified opposition to them before they had had opportunity to secure control of a larger total of the state's irrigated land.

The Japanese concentration took also another form. They quite naturally specialized in the raising of certain crops. According to data furnished in March 1921 by the Japanese Agricultural Association, they raised 91 per cent of the berries in the state, 81 per cent of the onions, 65 per cent of the asparagus, 59 per cent of the green vegetables, 53 per cent of the celery, etc.[22] The fact that these crops required "a stooping posture, great manual dexterity and painstaking methods of work which other laborers with long legs unsuitable for stooping cannot endure"[23] did not appear to be an extenuating factor in the minds of many opponents to the Japanese.

According to Mears,

> The essence of the economic factor is that nothing shall be done, domestically or internationally, to lower the American standard of living. To compete successfully with any peoples of so-called inferior standards of living, work and pleasure, the American must sacrifice his standard or go out of business. A cultured, well-educated, thoroughly Christian woman of San Jose remarked recently:
>
> "Please don't misunderstand me. I have absolutely nothing against the Japanese and I admire their thrift and patience and skill, but oh! I am so jealous of our land and our young men. The Japanese have come in and worked for such small wages and under such conditions that our boys haven't the slightest chance to compete with them. It isn't fair that our own boys are being driven away from the country because of cheap labor and poor working conditions."[24]

The first-generation Japanese were pioneers, probably a superior selection as regards initiative and industry. Economic necessity forced them to utilize every possible opportunity, which, for most of them, meant every possible hour of the day. One cannot but be impressed with the terrible toll which hard work on the farms, railroads, and other places has taken from these men and women. Farm wives of thirty-four and thirty-five often appear to be women of forty-five or fifty. One man, a Mr. M——, will serve as an example of the labor history of such men. Starting at the age of ten years he worked in

---

the total irrigated lands in the counties. But Oriental farming is almost entirely devoted to raising crops on irrigated land.

22 E. G. Mears, *Resident Orientals,* p. 241.

23 Report of State Board of Control of California, *op. cit.,* p. 52.

24 E. G. Mears, "California's Attitude towards the Oriental," *Annals, American Academy of Political and Social Science,* CXXII (November 1925), 9.

the rice fields ot Japan for twelve years, until he was twenty-two years old. Then followed six years in the sugar-cane fields of Hawaii. Thus, at the age of twenty-eight, after eighteen years of hard labor, he came to the United States, where he spent ten years "following the seasons" until at thirty-eight he married, and he has been "making vegetables" until today. Now, at fifty-five, after forty-five years of the hardest labor, he is a gnarled, broken old man, sick in bed most of the time, and with only a short time to live. His case is typical of many we interviewed.

OBJECTIONS ON RACIAL GROUNDS

Objections to Japanese were primarily economic in nature in the early days. But as the number of women and children increased there was a shift in emphasis to objections on racial grounds, i.e., that they were unassimilable. The Japanese, it was claimed, could not become amalgamated with the citizenship of the country. Intermarriage was unthinkable, and without it there could be no real social intercourse or the gradual elimination of those racial characteristics of size and facial appearance which mark them out as a people apart.

Chester Rowell presents this angle of the problem as follows:

> But there is also an impulse which is more than economic, and is expressly and biologically racial. Not in all the occupations into which Asiatics go do they displace workers of European race. In California the Chinese largely did work which there were no white workers to do, and the Japanese have improved land which we left waste, and developed products which we overlooked. There is no economic conflict here, but there is still hostility. Into the places vacated by departing Orientals now flow, not Americans, but Mexicans. Nobody objects, because nobody else wants those jobs. Tropical Australia is retarded in its development because it needs labor which British immigrants will not do; yet it refuses, on racial grounds alone and to its economic loss, to admit Chinese immigrants eager to do it. When Japanese move into a city neighborhood, in California, Americans move out, not because there is any economic competition, but because they will not live where persons of a different physical race live. American farmers sell out, when Japanese buy their neighbors' farms, because they will not have their children in a school where the other children are mostly Japanese. There is nothing else against these children. They are just as bright as American children, speak as good English, and have the same manners and impulses; they are American citizens; and of course there is nothing economic in which to compete. It is sheer racial caste. But it makes the American farmer move out, even at an economic loss.
>
> "Temporary prejudice, based on ignorance," the idealists say. But is that all? Consider what would happen if this situation, now confessedly within manageable limits, were allowed to increase by any extended mass migration. Unlimited immigration would, of course, simply annex our western states to the Orient. Just the

annual increase in Japan's population, exported to California, would in five years duplicate the present white population. One per cent of China would swamp the western half of America. And neither of these quantities would be sufficient to affect the situation in the oriental homelands at all. The resultant decrease in the death rate would leave the remaining population unchanged. The Orient is a limitless human ocean. No pumping process could change its level; but it might easily flood the lands on which it was discharged.[25]

How racial prejudice lowers rentals is described by Gates:

To get into a district they [the Japanese] will offer very high rent until some avaricious landlord gives them a lease. The house is then packed full of tenants. Even the bath tub goes into the backyard and the bathroom is used as a bedroom .... A shoe repair shop goes into the basement of the house and a laundry in the rear end, and a sign for house cleaners on a front window. The families next door on either side get tired of their neighbors and move out. The owners can get no new tenants except Japanese, for no white family will move into a house next to a Japanese. He must take a Japanese tenant at a reduced rent. Then the first tenants refuse to pay the former rent, and, in fact, after sufficient haggling, rent at their own terms. After the fire in San Francisco, they got a foothold in this manner in a choice residence district at a high rent. This now covers many blocks and rents have gone down 75 per cent. The owners of these houses have been compelled to sacrifice on the value of their property by a means that is as successful as it is merciless.[26]

A realtor in Los Angeles stated in 1930 that the ordinary American landlord will not rent to Japanese if an American tenant is available. His explanation is that the value of the property is reduced and rentals are at least $5 a month less. Japanese succeeded in renting property in the Tenth Street district because the buildings were from twenty-five to thirty years old and Americans were not interested in them. Now that the Japanese are located there the landlords are well satisfied, for the Japanese pay their rent promptly, are orderly, take an interest in the upkeep of the house and yard, are neat and clean, do not move often, and tend to their own businesses.

Phelan points out that "the Japanese do not assimilate with our people and make a homogeneous population, and hence they cannot be naturalized and admitted to citizenship."[27] But their American-born children are citizens, and the question is before California how far this second generation can be welded into the citizenry of the country.

---

[25] Chester Rowell, *op. cit.*, p. 174.

[26] W. A. Gates, "Oriental Immigration on the Pacific Coast," *National Conference of Charities and Correction* (Buffalo, 1909).

[27] J. D. Phelan, *op. cit.*, p. 16.

One aspect of the criticism of Japanese on racial grounds was the claim of their inferiority. Mears "believes that it is very unusual when a fellow resident regards the Japanese as inferior."[28] A perusal of the propaganda makes clear that although such claims were sometimes given they were seldom made with genuine enthusiasm. One such characterization is reported by Reynolds,[29] quoted from the *San Francisco Chronicle* of February 23, 1905:

> "We have already drawn attention to the deterioration in the character of the general immigration that now reaches our shores. That deterioration is even more marked in the case of the Japanese than it is elsewhere. Japan does not send us her best, but her worst. Her immigrants are not from those classes from which has come the clear call to Asiatic awakening, nor to any marked degree are they drawn from these sections of her people who have directed her progress into the paths of civilization. In other words, the Japanese immigrant is in no way representative of Japan as she is today but rather of Japan as she was before her cycle of advancement had arrived. Japanese immigration is made up of those who are unable to keep pace with their own people, who have been pushed upon one side by the rush of national advance and who have not the education nor the intelligence to readjust themselves to changed conditions, or to find for themselves new positions in their own country in place of the ruts from which they have been pushed. Japan has sent us, not her fittest but her unfittest; she has sent us the scum that has collected upon the surface of the boiling waters of her new national life, the human waste waterial for which she herself can find no use."

There are two aspects of this matter of racial inferiority: first, whether or not the Japanese are biologically inferior to the whites, i.e., are innately inferior in intelligence, ability, and the like,[30] and, second, whether or not they are socially inferior. There is no question that they were inferior in the latter sense when they came to this country. They were of the laboring class and all such immigrants have been socially inferior. The real question is, will their children be socially inferior to any greater degree than the second-generation Swede, German, Pole, Russian, Italian, Armenian, or Mexican?

OBJECTIONS ON POLITICAL GROUNDS

Under this heading are presented certain objections to the Japanese that concern his loyalty to the Mikado on a religious basis or to the Japanese government on a patriotic basis, either of which might cause

---

[28] E. G. Mears, "California's Attitude towards the Oriental," *Annals, American Academy of Political and Social Science,* CXXII, 12.

[29] C. N. Reynolds, *Oriental-White Race Relations,* p. 106.

[30] Evidence on this point is presented in chapter vii.

him to fight against our government in time of war or, in the case of the second generation, to vote as a Japanese and not as an American.

McClatchy[31] urged that the Japanese are unassimilable because of the reverence held for the Mikado, as "the one living God to whom they owe their very existence, and therefore all loyalty," and maintained that those inoculated with such sentiments "cannot be transmuted into good American citizens." A second objection to them is that "their government claims all Japanese, no matter where born, as its citizens. . . . . Every Japanese born here, even if his forebears for generations were born here, but had not been permitted to expatriate, is subject to orders from Japan, is kept track of through the Japanese Consulate[32] and other organizations, and is subject to call for military duty. Authorities on international law agree that since the United States confers its citizenship on the Japanese born here, unasked and with full knowledge of Japan's claims, we must, in the event of war, recognize those Japanese as the citizens of Japan." A third reason for unassimilability is that "in the mass, with opportunity offered, and even when born here, they have shown no disposition to do so [become citizens], but on the contrary, pronounced antagonism." McClatchy closes his article with this quotation from Benjamin Ide Wheeler, president emeritus of the University of California:

> "The two civilizations cannot mingle, and the leaders in Japan agree that it is not well to attempt to amalgamate them. They cannot and will not understand our civilization, and no matter in what part of the world he is, a Japanese always feels himself a subject of the Emperor, with the Imperial Government backing him, much as a feudal retainer had the support of his overlord in exchange for an undivided loyalty."

The point was also made that large numbers of Japanese children were sent back to Japan for their education only to return at a later date loyal and ideal Japanese citizens. (See p. 160 for further discussion.)

Considerable antagonism has been felt toward the Japanese-language schools on the grounds that the Japanese youth were being taught not only the Japanese language but also loyalty to the Mikado. In 1921 the California legislature passed a bill by which these supplementary schools

---

[31] V. S. McClatchy, "Japanese in the Melting-Pot: Can They Assimilate and Make Good Citizens?" *Annals, American Academy of Political and Social Science,* XCIII (January 1921), 29.

[32] Even in 1930 the Japanese government was still continuing its occasional enumeration of all Japanese in the United States and Hawaii.

came under the control of the Superintendent of Public Instruction.[33] With the decision of the Supreme Court of California in the case of *Farrington* v. *Tokushige,* the Attorney-General ruled in 1927 that the California Foreign Language School Law is unconstitutional, and all legal requirements are now waived. In the "Memorial Presented to the President while at San Francisco on September 18, 1919," by the Japanese Association of America[33] there appears the following:

> Aside from the schools for instructing Japanese in English, there are seventy-five so-called "supplementary" schools for teaching children the Japanese language. These are attended by the Japanese pupils after the public schools close for the day. They are primarily for the study of the Japanese language and are not intended to perpetuate the traditions and moral concepts of Japan. Of course, these are criticized by hostile Americans. But says Professor Millis, "They are supplementary schools, and at the worst, there is much less in them to be adversely criticized than in the parochial schools attended by so many children of the South and European immigrants. No real problem is yet evident connected with Japanese children on American soil."

One of the hysterical utterances along these lines is this of Gates:

> At the close of the Russo-Japanese war, the returned Japanese soldier found his former place filled, and thus became the emigrant. The large increase in emigration from Japan was of the discharged soldier. He came in numbers to Hawaii and the United States. It would be easy to marshal an army of fifty thousand Japanese veterans at any point in California in forty-eight hours. The same thing could probably be done in Hawaii. These ex-soldiers of Japan did not surrender their allegiance to their emperor. They are today as truly his subjects as though they lived in Japan, and he counts them as such. When the last war broke out, many a Japanese went home at the call of the emperor and entered the army. When the next call to war comes he will as quickly respond. If it is against Russia, home he will go to enlist in the service of his native country; but if it is against this country, then what?[34]

California has never seriously contemplated the possibility of the Japanese being organized into an army against her, since the Japanese have never constituted more than 2.1 per cent of the total population (Table 36, p. 274), but those who foresaw a large immigration ahead occasionally raised the issue. In the Hawaiian Islands the situation is quite different. For example, in 1930, the Japanese population there numbered 139,631 out of a total of 368,336 (see Table 34, p. 270). What the Japanese will eventually do as voters is really a far more significant question than what they might do as soldiers. At the present

---

[33] See *California and the Oriental* (1920, revised in 1922), pp. 232–33.

[34] W. A. Gates, *op. cit.* The United States Census gave a total of 41,356 Japanese in California in 1910, one year after Gates wrote this!

time most of those in the Islands cannot vote, being of the first generation and hence ineligible to citizenship, or being under age. But eventually those of the second generation over twenty-one years of age will constitute a considerable proportion of the voting citizenry. Adams estimates that by 1940 the Japanese vote will be not over 37 per cent, and probably about 22 per cent.[35] But their vote will be greater than that of the whites. There is no doubt that the latter experience some uneasiness over the situation. Sanford B. Dole is quoted by Littler as saying, "Hawaii will not be a state because some day we might have a Japanese governor," and Littler adds:

> The situation could not be put better. Men fear that if Hawaii should become independent of the restraint of federal domination the time would come when citizens of Oriental ancestry, and particularly citizens of Japanese ancestry, would gain numerical supremacy and would push into the background the *haoles* [whites] and the Hawaiians. While Hawaii remains a territory, the federal government can always step in to veto acts of a supposedly hostile electorate. Whether such fears are well grounded calls for consideration of the whole question of race relations in the Islands.[36]

Citizenship.—The propagandists had good grounds for the charge that Japanese would retain their loyalty to the Japanese government. When Japan first permitted immigration to Hawaii she stipulated that these immigrants should always remain citizens of Japan.[37] The Japanese laws of nationality were similar to those of France and certain other countries. "A child is a Japanese if his or her father is a Japanese at the time of his or her birth."[38] In conflict with this *jus sanguinis* law of Japan is that of the *jus soli* law of the United States under the Fourteenth Amendment to the Constitution, which provides that those born in this country are citizens of the United States.[39] The dual citizenship of the second-generation Japanese results from the conflict be-

---

[35] Romanzo Adams, "Some Racial Statistics on Hawaii," *Foreign Affairs,* II (1923), 316. Professor Andrew Lind predicted that in 1940 the total male voters of Japanese ancestry in Hawaii will be 29 per cent of the total registered voters (*Fourth Annual Conference of New Americans, Honolulu,* 1930). It should be realized in this connection that the Hawaiian vote has always exceeded that of the *haole.* An earlier estimate was 47 per cent for 1940 (see "A Survey of Education in Hawaii," *United States Bureau of Education, Bulletin No. 16* [1920], p. 20).

[36] R. M. C. Littler, *The Governance of Hawaii* (1929), p. 218.

[37] R. L. Buell, *Japanese Immigration* (1924), p. 281.

[38] Law No. 66 (March 16, 1899), Japanese Civil Code, Vol. III.

[39] The United States applies the principle of *jus sanguinis* in claiming as its citizens children of American citizens born on foreign soil.

tween these two principles of citizenship. Under what conditions, then, can a second-generation Japanese renounce his Japanese citizenship and become only an American citizen?

The 1916 Law of Nationality of Japan provided that a native citizen of the United States might expatriate himself either through a legal representative before the age of fifteen or by himself between the ages of fifteen and seventeen, but that after the age of seventeen he could not do so unless he had presented himself for military duty; moreover, the permission of the Japanese government was necessary before the renunciation was complete. Japanese Vice-Consul Ishii at San Francisco was quoted in 1920 as saying "that not to exceed a dozen such American born children have signed the 'Declaration of Losing Nationality,' provided for that purpose by the Japanese Law. So far as could be learned, none of these have been accepted by the Japanese government, in accordance with the provisions of the Civil Code of Japan."[40] The Japanese law further provides that, should a Japanese return to Japan and establish his residence there, repatriatism would follow, residence of one day being sufficient.

The Japanese American Associations on the Pacific Coast and in Hawaii memorialized the Japanese government several times in 1919–21 for further changes in the law, thus showing a genuine interest in this problem.[41] A new law was passed in 1924, effective December 1, 1925, providing that a Japanese born thereafter in any one of certain designated countries wherein he shall thereby have acquired nationality shall lose Japanese nationality from birth unless he declares intention to retain that nationality; and that a Japanese born in Japan, or born prior to operation of the amendment in a country conferring citizenship by birth, may renounce Japanese nationality at will if he retains the nationality of the foreign country and has domicile therein. In this manner has Japan met the dual-citizenship problem.

But what about those who are dual citizens? Have they shown a real desire to be American citizens only or have they merely followed the line of least resistance? Ichihashi writes:

> Under the circumstances it may be taken for granted that virtually all American-born Japanese choose American citizenship, for the one reason that, if they wish, they can repatriate or naturalize in Japan at any time and enjoy the privileges of Japanese citizenship in full standing.[42]

---

[40] See *California and the Oriental* (1920, revised in 1922), p. 199.

[41] K. K. Kawakami, *The Real Japanese Question* (1921), chapter i.

[42] Y. Ichihashi, *Japanese in the United States* (1932), p. 324.

The facts do not seem entirely to bear out this statement. In 1930 under the auspices of the Japanese government a census was taken of the Japanese in the United States (Table 11). This census reports

TABLE 11

JAPANESE POPULATION IN CALIFORNIA IN 1930 ACCORDING TO JAPANESE CONSULAR REPORTS*

	Total for Los Angeles and San Francisco Consular Districts	Outside of California†	In California
Citizens of Japan (first generation)	51,252	5,152	46,100
Dual citizens (second generation)	24,729	2,702‡	22,027
Citizens of United States only (second generation)	25,862	1,599§	24,263
Total	101,843	9,453	92,390

* It is reported that the totals are not complete, as some failed to reply. The United States Census gives 97,456 for California. The two censuses were taken at about the same time.

† Includes the states of Arizona (870), New Mexico (276), Colorado (3,065), Nevada (264), and Utah (367), and Lower California, Mexico (1,511).

‡ Includes 179 dual citizens of Japan and Mexico living in Lower California.

§ Includes 66 Mexican citizens only and 2 United States citizens only living in Lower California.

92,390 Japanese in California,[43] of whom 46,100 are of the first generation and 46,290 are of the second generation. Of the latter, 24,263 hold American citizenship only and 22,027 hold dual citizenship. Age distribution for the three types of citizenship is given in Table 12 for all but the nine southern counties of the state. Apparently 40 per cent of the second generation seven years of age and over have preferred United States citizenship (alone), for these could have reached this status only by definite renunciation of Japanese citizenship. During the five years 1925–30 the situation has been reversed and definite action is necessary if Japanese citizenship is to be retained by those born here since December 1, 1925. This change seemingly accounts for the increase in percentage of those with United States citizenship only. But it is also apparent that even today about a third of the Japanese children born in California are registered as citizens of Japan. Are these to be given all the rights and privileges of citizens in this country and also in Japan when they go there, or are they to be construed as citizens of Japan only?

[43] This is for the state of California only and not the additional area included in the two consular districts of San Francisco and Los Angeles.

TABLE 12

DISTRIBUTION OF JAPANESE POPULATION IN CALIFORNIA BY CITIZENSHIP AND AGE

(From Los Angeles and San Francisco Japanese Consular Reports of 1930)

Age Group	Nine Southern Counties of State		Remaining Northern Counties of State				
	Citizens of Japan*	Second Generation†	Age Group	Citizens of Japan	Age Group	Dual Citizens	Citizens of the United States Only
1-10.....	6,675	12,473	1-7	78	1-6	3,544	6,626
11-20.....	4,317	6,634	8-20.....	568	7-15.....	6,993	4,679
21-30.....	4,240	1,087	21-25.....	8,035	16-20.....	1,700	1,141
31-40.....	5,771	123	36-50.....	10,513	21-	667	586
41-50.....	5,816	24	51-.......	5,689			
51-.......	3,453	13					
Unknown	68						
Total..	30,340	20,354		24,883		12,904	13,032

* Includes dual citizens.
† Includes dual and United States citizens.

A similar situation obtains in Hawaii. In the Japanese census of 1930, 72,370 from among 139,903 were reported as having dual citizenship. Of the remainder, 49,000 are Japanese citizens (first generation), 17,215 were born since 1925 and have lost Japanese citizenship since their parents did not declare it, and 1,318 are American citizens by expatriation on their own initiative. Only 20 per cent of the second generation are thus American citizens, as distinct from dual citizens. Comment on this situation by a Japanese newspaper in Hawaii follows:

Though the primary object of the census was merely "to count noses," it has served to draw attention to a serious laxity on the part of a majority of the younger generation who were born in Hawaii and are thus American citizens by right of birth. The number of these has been roughly estimated at 80,000 of whom only 18,500 have ceased to be also citizens of Japan. That means that over 60,000 young American citizens, born in Hawaii of Japanese parentage, still owe allegiance to the Emperor of Japan! It means that dual citizenship is still the rule among the younger generation, and that they owe a divided loyalty to two nations!

Can they expect the complete trust and confidence of those who are *all American?* Can they blame other citizens whose allegiance is not divided if they look upon these dual citizens with suspicion? They are in the no-man's-land between two countries, neither wholly of the one nor wholly of the other.

There is an imperative necessity of taking prompt action in this matter if the younger generation of Japanese wishes to avoid a serious loss of prestige and open suspicion. When it becomes known in Washington that more than three-fourths of the Hawaiian-born Japanese have not thought highly enough of their American citizenship to free themselves from a divided allegiance and are still actually citizens of Japan, there will be plenty of suspicion and distrust. The jingoes will point their fingers at Hawaii and say—"Americanized? Oh, yeah! Now you tell one!"

And a fat chance Hawaii will ever have for *statehood!*[44]

Another phase of the objection to Japanese on political grounds had to do with opposition to the policies of the Japanese government itself. Prior to the close of the Russo-Japanese War the relation between the United States and Japan had been very friendly. But immediately afterward propaganda appeared in each country against the other, and from that time on there have been some in each country who see the other preparing for war or at least planning to win some advantage.[45] There is no doubt that, as Americans came to question many of the policies of Japan, the feeling of irritation and resentment was directed in large part against the Japanese immigrants to this country. And, no doubt, all this magnified particularly the significance of the political objections against them, namely, that they were soldiers of the Mikado and that the second generation at best were only dual citizens, retaining a loyalty to Japan. (See chapter ii, pp. 46–47, for earlier discussion of this point.)

OBJECTIONS RELATING TO PERSONAL CHARACTER

There remain several other objections to the Japanese which might have been considered under the headings listed above but which are grouped here since they seem to the writer more personal in nature than definitely racial or social.

"Cocky."—In discussing the question why Americans are hostile to the Japanese, Yoshitomi gives first of all this trait, writing:

> Les Américains ne peuvent pas supporter qu'une race de couleur (don't keep his place), qu'elle ne se tienne pas à l'écart, et qu'elle s'élève en face des Yankees.[46]

As we have pointed out in the preceding chapter, this characteristic is most damning in anyone classified as inferior. As Millis has said, "the Japanese have pride in their race and are anxious to be regarded as equal to any other race. They are neither cringing nor servile."[47] The

---

44 *Hawaii Hochi,* January 23, 1931.

45 P. J. Treat, *Japan and the United States* (1921), chapter x.

46 M. Yoshitomi, *Les conflits Nippo-Américains* (1926), p. 273.

47 H. A. Millis, *The Japanese Problem in the United States* (1915), p. 247.

whites cannot tolerate this attitude from those engaged in menial tasks. It will be interesting to see how the educated second generation will be received when they have achieved the success the writer believes will come to them. (Chapter vii presents facts supporting the conclusion that they are the equal of whites mentally and morally.)

Dishonesty.—This is one of the most frequently reported objections to the Japanese. It stands first of all according to figures gathered by Reynolds (see Table 10, p. 128). Several quotations on the subject follow, the first from a speech of Hayes in the House of Representatives:

> A close acquaintance shows one that unblushing lying is so universal among the Japanese as to be one of the leading national traits; that commercial honor, even among her commercial classes, is so rare as to be only the exception that proves the reverse rule.[48]

Hayes quotes a distinguished writer in the *Contemporary Review* for May 1905, as follows:

> "The Japanese traders, as a class, have, according to the universal verdict of those who deal with them, to this day the unsavory reputation of absolute unreliability in the fulfillment of any obligation; of having failed to acquire in their commercial transactions even the most elementary principles of common honesty."

Gates has this to say:

> The Japanese who come to this country cannot be trusted. They are intelligent and smart, but, with them, smartness means ability to beat the white man. They will not keep an agreement when it is for their interest to break it, and will not pay their obligations if they can avoid doing so. The Japanese, from the business standpoint, is as detested as the Chinese is respected. If we must have the yellow race, let it be the Chinese, for he is honest and only competes in the fields of common labor.[49]

Young writes:

> It is common opinion among thousands of people, especially on our Pacific Coast, that the Japanese are fundamentally dishonest in their business dealings." I have heard from intelligent men stories of how Japanese business men attempt to cheat American firms, just as one hears from the lips of the common workman how shrewd the "Jap" is in worming his way into better economic status.[50]

The Japanese who came to this country were very largely laborers, particularly farm laborers, together with some who had had a little

---

[48] E. A. Hayes, *op. cit.*

[49] W. A. Gates, *op. cit.*

[50] K. Young, *The Social Psychology of Oriental-Occidental Prejudices* (American Council, Institute of Pacific Relations, 1929), p. 10.

retail experience. Almost none came from the larger cities of Japan.[51] Their contacts had been peculiarly personal; they were not used to contracts as employed in this country. The breaking of a contract is regarded by whites as a serious matter, a form of dishonesty; to some extent at least it was regarded by the Japanese as merely a failure to observe a foreign custom. There is no doubt that the Japanese gave offense in this regard. How much they should be charged with dishonesty, and how much they should be excused because they did not comprehend the nature of a contract nor understand the exact terms of the contract, is an unsolved problem. There is no doubt that they encountered "dishonest whites" and felt justified in getting even when opportunity arose. It seems to be generally agreed that the Japanese have improved greatly in this regard since early days. Chapter vii recounts certain investigations in which Japanese are compared with whites regarding this trait.[52]

---

[51] E. K. Strong, Jr., *Japanese in California,* Table 14.

[52] One cannot help wondering whether or not there is any connection between the American complaint that Japanese immigrants did not live up to their contracts and that the Japanese government is failing in the same respect. Several editorials in the *San Francisco Chronicle* during 1933 have focused attention on the latter aspect. Consider this editorial of March 22, 1933, entitled "It Cannot Be Denied":

"Yosuke Matsuoka says the people of the United States have condoned the faults of Chinese misgovernment and magnified those of Japanese good government. The Japanese statesman speaks truth. The American people have done just that, and it really does Japan an injustice.

"However, it is necessary to look a little farther and ask why the American people should be backing Chinese disorder against Japanese order. Why do the American people overlook completely the immense provocation the Chinese have given Japan, the vast nuisance China has made itself to Japan, and to peace and order in the Far East?

"Japan itself has supplied the reason. Japan agreed with the United States and with most other countries not to use war as an instrument of national policy. Japan, under great provocation, it is true, has broken that solemn agreement and used war to carry out her national policy in Chinese territory. So we forget the provocation under which Japan labored and see only her broken pledge.

"Japan agreed with the United States and other countries to take no advantage of China's chaotic condition. She has broken that agreement and has taken two great provinces away from China. So we forget how sore a trial Chinese chaos has been to Japan and see only the flouted treaty.

"Japan's civil government has repeatedly given our Government, and other governments at the same time, solemn assurances that certain things would not be done, and while these assurances were being given, or the next day, Japan's military rulers did those very things. Perhaps we should admire the efficiency of the

Crime.—Reynolds reports that in his study of newspaper items

there is practically no news of Japanese connected with gambling, two items and six inches of space being the total for the ten years. Liquor law violations for the two races [Japanese and Chinese] are, however, practically identical. This news is frequently handled in a semi-humorous way, perhaps indicating the attitude of the public toward such violations. In minor crime commissions, again, the Japanese and Chinese are on a common level. The Japanese news in this field, however, is more apt than in the case of the Chinese, to concern deception in trade.[53]

Evidently the Japanese have had a very clean record as far as commission of crimes is concerned, or the agitators would have stressed their criminality. The fact that in such lame indictments as the following, quoted in this connection by Reynolds, they attribute to the Japanese responsibility for increase in crime among the whites is really proof that they can find no facts against them:

"Japanese influence on crime is shown in unmistakable statistics, the American laborer being forced into hoboism and criminality by the fierce competition with the degraded Asiatic laborer. It is proved by the records of courts and observations of students of political economy that the crime rate on the Pacific Coast is double that of similar populations in the East, while the number of tramps on the roads of California is greater than in any other part of the United States. These two effects are directly traceable to the competition of the Asiatic laborer for a cause. . . . ."[54]

Chapter vii (pp. 167–84) considers the Japanese record as to delinquency and crime. So far as this factor is concerned the Japanese have proved themselves most desirable for American citizenship.

Prostitution.—The following quotation is sufficient to show what charges were made under this heading:

The vast majority of the Japanese people do not understand the meaning of the word "morality," but are given up to practice of licentiousness more generally than any nation in the world justly making any pretense to civilization. I am told by those who have lived in Japan and understand its language that there is no

---

Japanese army except that our eyes are occupied with the spectacle of a nation promising one thing while at that moment it is performing the opposite.

"Our psychology may be all wrong in favoring the disorderly, troublesome, graft-ridden Chinese against the orderly, efficient and patriotic Japanese, but it is our own psychology and it is evident that Japanese do not understand it. It happens also to be the psychology of the rest of the world."

[53] C. N. Reynolds, *Oriental-White Race Relations*, p. 338.

[54] Quoted by Reynolds, *op. cit.*, pp. 107–8, from *House Documents*, Vol. 78, No. 184 (57th Congress, First Session), *Industrial Commission Reports*, Vol. 15 (1901), "Immigration," p. 758.

word in Japanese corresponding to "sin," because there is in the ordinary Japanese mind no conception of its meaning. There is no word corresponding to our word "home," because there is nothing in the Japanese domestic life corresponding to the home as we know it. The Japanese language has no term for "privacy." They lack the term and the clear idea because they lack the practice.[55]

Sidney L. Gulick, in the *Evolution of Japan,* published in 1903, says:

"The distressing state of the family life may also be gathered from the large numbers of public and secret prostitutes that are to be found in all the large cities and the singing girls in nearly every town. According to popular opinion their number is rapidly increasing . . . . Public as well as secret prostitution has enormously increased during the last thirty or forty years . . . . Although the sale of daughters for immoral purposes is theoretically illegal, yet, in fact, it is of frequent occurrence."[56]

It is only fair to remind the reader that a Japanese visiting the Barbary Coast in San Francisco at this same time could have uttered equally damning things about Americans.

Millis writes:

It can be said truthfully that the Japanese have never compared unfavorably with other races similarly circumstanced in that most of the men were leading the lives of single men in a foreign country, and that the evil among them has never been as great as among certain other races, as, for example, the Chinese and the Greeks. It can be said, also, that an equal organized effort to end it all has not been witnessed in the case of any other race. The Japanese associations in Fresno and various other places have fought the evil with much success and frequently without more than a reluctant co-operation on the part of the police and courts.[57]

Our own investigation in another locality has demonstrated that the Japanese section was singularly free from vice, while the Chinese section was seemingly almost entirely given over to gambling, drinking, and so on, with the police utterly indifferent to the whole matter.

Cleanliness.—The writer has noted frequent allusions to the uncleanliness of the Japanese. The belief seems to be widespread. Even in the city Y.M.C.A.'s on the Coast there is a feeling against the Japanese (whether on general grounds or on the specific one of cleanliness is not clear) such that Japanese are refused the use of the swimming pools. Our survey brought out the fact in one city that the younger Japanese were very bitter at this discrimination, since Mexicans were

[55] E. A. Hayes, *op. cit.,* p. 3749.

[56] Quoted by E. A. Hayes, *op. cit.,* p. 3749.

[57] H. A. Millis, *op. cit.,* p. 234; quoted by permission of the Macmillan Company, publishers.

permitted to use the pool, and the Japanese have little respect for the "cleanliness" of the latter. In discussing this point Galen Fisher writes:

> They [Y.M.C.A. secretaries] have, therefore, found a solution either by establishing Oriental branches or by admitting English-speaking Orientals to full privileges with the exception of the swimming pool and, in some places, the gymnasium. In Los Angeles, groups of Orientals, as well as of Negroes, are allowed to use the general Y.M.C.A. building only when they come in groups.[58]

In contrast to these views held by the average American, it appears that all investigators have been impressed by the frequent bathing of Japanese. "At every camp where Japanese are employed, a bath is provided. The Japanese are very clean about their persons."[59] "The day's work is usually followed by a hot bath."[60] But investigators did find much to complain of regarding their living quarters. It must be remembered, however, that the Japanese here studied were day laborers living in camps and had little or no incentive to spend money on improvements. Their living conditions were no worse than others which existed in some parts of the United States, but they did not measure up to the sanitary requirements of California. In other words, their standard of living was low but their personal cleanliness was high.

CHIEF OBJECTION TO THE JAPANESE

All of the preceding might have been true and yet there would have been little or no agitation against the Japanese provided there had been only a few Japanese in the state and few or none coming in. It was the comparatively large number of Japanese in the state, emphasized particularly by their concentration in certain localities, together with a steady immigration constantly augmenting the total, that made every other charge against them so significant.

Consequently much of the propaganda against the Japanese called public attention to how many were here and how rapidly they were increasing in numbers. Estimates were submitted as to how many would be in the state on given dates. Since the Japanese have congregated largely in certain sections, it was easy to obtain figures showing that they made up a considerable percentage of the total population in given

---

58 G. M. Fisher, *Relations between the Occidental and Oriental Peoples on the Pacific Coast of North America* (1928), p. 26; quoted by permission of the International Missionary Council, publishers.

59 E. A. Brown (Chief Sanitary Engineer, State Commission of Immigration and Housing) in *California and the Oriental* (1920, revised in 1922), p. 122.

60 H. A. Millis, *op. cit.*, p. 233.

localities and to present surprising percentage gains in population within a decade.

A great deal of emphasis was put upon birth-rate, and amazing tales were concocted as to the future increase of Japanese. The following, quoted by Reynolds,[61] is illustrative:

"Senator James D. Phelan discussing reservations to the treaty and League of Nations in the United States Senate on the subject of mandatories thoroughly aroused the spectators by the following statement with reference to the alarming increase of the Japanese population in California. He said:

" 'I have a chart prepared by Health officers in California containing tables that show, in the most approved and scientific methods used by the makers of charts, the relative birth statistics and the percentage of white babies born in the state of California.

" 'The chart shows that in the year 2010 at the same progress which is being made now, the white population will have been submerged by the Japanese native population. This is but 90 years from now.

" 'Unless some legislative action is taken,' said Senator Phelan, 'by the state of California, and the Federal government, the Japanese if allowed their way will have submerged, I repeat, the great state of California by an inundation of a permanently alien population'."[62]

American newspapers sometimes gave facts which were not in harmony with the usual propaganda against the Japanese. For example, the newspaper quoted above stated a year and a half later:

". . . . The Japanese are not, as has been supposed, the most prolific race in the Islands, but are surpassed in this regard by the Portuguese, Porto Ricans, part Hawaiians and Spanish. Of American women more than one in every six living in the Islands marry Hawaiians, part-Hawaiians, and others of blood strange to their ancestry.

"While the women of Korea lead all others, male and female, in the Islands in marrying with their race, there are other groups which are a close second in this respect. Only 0.3 to 1 per cent of Japanese women contract out-marriages, or unions with men of other races, while 0.7 to 1 per cent of Japanese men so pick their mates. The percentage for the Chinese is 6 per cent for the women and 41.5 per cent for the men; Americans 17.9 for the women and 51.7 for the men; Portuguese 32.3 for the women, 13.0 men; Hawaiian 40.5 women, 19.5 men."[63]

---

[61] C. N. Reynolds, *Oriental-White Race Relations*, p. 327.

[62] From the *San Jose Mercury Herald*, November 23, 1919. Two years later the Controller of the State of California, J. S. Chambers, estimated the Japanese would exceed the whites by 1949 ("The Japanese Invasion," *Annals, American Academy of Political and Social Science*, XCIII [January 1921], 26).

[63] From the *San Jose Mercury Herald*, May 8, 1921; quoted by Reynolds, *Oriental-White Race Relations*, pp. 337–38.

While the threat of a great Japanese immigration hung over California, these various objections, whether true or false, had an effective appeal because they fitted into the general atmosphere of apprehensiveness. Now that the immigration has stopped, they are no longer bitterly urged. In all probability, however, they have had their effect in an unconscious bias of the whites against the Japanese.

It seems most fitting to close this section with an editorial from the *Town Crier* of Seattle of May 30, 1931, entitled "An Admirable Race":

Frequently we are moved to reflect on the surprisingly numerous merits of the Japanese people. Here in Seattle the number of Japanese residents is sufficiently high for us to observe them in the mass. And what do we find? Intelligence, modesty, thrift, honesty, self sufficiency, a love of art, family loyalty, cheerfulness—indeed, the number of virtues one could enumerate grows so long as to look like an aggregation.

There seems to be no race so consistently industrious as the Japanese; you will see men of every other nationality idling about street corners and in bread lines, but somehow the Japanese manage to keep busy. That they will work for less money and at jobs requiring more patience than the white man has on tap is true, and for this they are always being belittled by their "superior" white brothers.

The behavior of Japanese market proprietors in comparison with that of their white neighbors in other stalls is illuminating. They attend to their business with quiet diligence, wrapping parcels and making change, always courteous and efficient. A pleasant relief from the loud mouthed bawling and smart-alecky antics of many of the others.

You don't hear of Japanese getting mixed up in brawls, scandals, shootings, divorces, and all those things that constantly adorn the pages of the press—or if you do the cases are few and far between.

The Japanese have always been lovers of the beautiful. Here in Seattle there are more Japanese artists probably than any other one nationality. For the last several years about ten or twelve have had paintings accepted at Northwest art exhibitions. Virtually all the members of the Seattle Camera Club are Japanese; the work of this organization is familiar to all who have seen Christmas annuals of THE TOWN CRIER.

It might not be such a bad idea if we did a little less caterwauling about our own troubles—economic, domestic and otherwise—and started emulating some of the virtues of the Japanese, one of the finest of which is the ability to mind their own business.

VI. VITAL STATISTICS

The preceding five chapters have outlined problems concerning the Japanese residents of the United States. There it has been shown that the greatest single obstacle confronting the second-generation Japanese in earning a living is race prejudice. This subject has been considered in some detail both as to its psychological nature and as to the specific charges that have been made against the Japanese.

This and the next two chapters present a great variety of facts designed to throw light on the whole subject. It is hoped that these facts will remove many misconceptions which have resulted from the propaganda of interested agitators. One objective of these chapters is to answer the charges which have been outlined in chapter v. A second objective is to give both whites and Japanese a better idea of how second-generation Japanese differ from the first generation. This is essential in that otherwise many of the prejudices already engendered will be continued. In order to accomplish this, it is important to show the background from which the second generation are emerging and to depict as far as possible the educational and vocational aspirations and capacities of the second generation, since these indicate the direction in which they desire to go.

Whenever possible, information concerning the Japanese in California has been based upon government statistics. But unfortunately these statistics do not differentiate between first- and second-generation Japanese in many matters of considerable importance. And on certain phases of the subject there are no government statistics at all. In these cases, data are supplied from a survey of approximately 10 per cent of the Japanese population in California.

Before considering these findings it is well to note the nature and scope of the survey itself, for the significance of the findings is dependent upon the accuracy with which the data represent the actual situation.

THE SURVEY[1]

The object of the survey was to obtain as accurate a picture as possible of the Japanese population in California. Personal interviews were held with 9,416 individuals.[2]

---

[1] For detailed description of the nature and scope of the survey, see E. K. Strong, Jr., *Japanese in California* (1933).

[2] In the interviewing, the family was made the unit. Because of this, data were

In order to include in the survey a proper sampling of children, women, old people, the sick, etc., it was decided that the interviewing should be based upon certain definite geographical districts so selected as to contain about one thousand persons each, and that an interviewer should be held responsible for interviewing everyone in his district. As the survey was undertaken in order to throw light upon the second generation, it was decided furthermore that the family should be made the unit of interviewing and that if one member of a family was interviewed every effort was to be made to secure complete information on all the remaining members of the family, regardless of where they were living at the time. In this way, data on individuals in other parts of the country and in Japan were included.

In selecting the districts, great care was exercised to include as nearly as possible proper representation of city, town, and country dwellers and to provide that the various occupations typical of the Japanese should be properly sampled. The districts about Livingston and Florin have frequently been surveyed as typical of some of the best and of the poorest features of Japanese life in this country. Such extremes were deliberately excluded, as we were primarily interested in obtaining a picture of the entire population and not merely the average of the best and the poorest.

As the survey was conducted to throw light upon the second-generation problem, it was considered not necessary to secure an equal representation of each occupational group among the Japanese but rather to secure sufficient information about each in order to discuss it intelligently. As the greatest variety of occupational activities is to be found in the cities, the greatest effort was made to have residents in them well represented. Efforts were also made to secure a good representation of those engaged in fishing and the different agricultural pursuits. This, we believe, has been achieved.

The specific districts selected were determined upon after conferences with a number of representative Japanese. Thus, Japanese living in cities were represented in the survey by 3,654 men, women, and children (1,290 from San Francisco, 620 from Fresno, and 1,744 from Los Angeles); those living in the country or small villages by 4,311 (857 from the Walnut Grove district of Sacramento County, 449 from the vicinity of Fresno, 1,006 from Santa Clara County, and 1,999 from

---

obtained concerning 257 individuals living in Japan and 17 living in the Hawaiian Islands. These bring the grand total up to 9,690.

the Gardena and Hawthorne districts of Los Angeles County); fishermen and their families were represented by 1,634 (436 from Monterey and 1,198 from San Pedro); and data were secured in addition from 91 University of California students. The grand total of 9,690 is 9.94 per cent of the entire Japanese population of California.

Eleven interviewers were employed for approximately three months each. About an equal number of Japanese and whites were employed, so that the influence of racial bias of the one would probably be offset by that of the other. Three of the six white interviewers employed regularly a Japanese interpreter, the others using interpreters from time to time as occasion demanded. As each interviewer was expected to fill out only thirteen questionnaires a day, and as many of these related to young children and could be completed in a few minutes, there was ample time to secure extensive information about the adults and to check up their statements in many ways.

Effort was made to standardize the interviewing, particularly the recording of information, by conferences before and during the three months of interviewing. The blanks were then all edited by Mr. R. B. McKeown with the help of several assistants. Many items that were not clear were taken up with the interviewers and in that way straightened out. As all the blanks for an entire family were handled together by the editor, it was possible to correct many obvious mistakes and to fill in items that had been obtained in one interview but not in another. In many cases items which were obvious errors were altered so as to fit the entire set of facts regarding the family. For example, if on the record of a married woman there is no indication that she has lived anywhere except in Japan and California but her first child was born in Colorado and the husband reports several months' work in that state, it is evident that she also spent time there, probably coterminous with his residence. There is no doubt that certain errors were added to the records by this process of editing, but it is believed that many more errors were eliminated. In addition, the editor established standard terminology for answering many questions and these were written in red ink in place of the wording of the interviewer. This made the coding of the blanks a much simpler matter and provided that interpretations of the peculiar wording of an interviewer should be made by one familiar with all the facts of the entire family instead of by the coding clerk, who merely considered the item itself.

The same assistants who had edited the blanks coded them and punched the Hollerith cards for tabulation. Each card was verified by a second person in order to eliminate errors. Once the cards were punched, the compilation of results followed with machine accuracy.

The Japanese population co-operated splendidly. At the beginning many of the leading Japanese were personally acquainted with the purposes of the survey directly and many others through newspaper publicity. The result was that very few individuals refused to co-operate and many inconvenienced themselves considerably to make the study a success.

One way of checking our survey data as to its adequacy in sampling the Japanese population in California is to compare our distribution by age and sex with that reported in the 1930 census. From the figures in Table 13 it appears that the survey includes 10.5 per cent of the women

TABLE 13

JAPANESE POPULATION OF CALIFORNIA, DISTRIBUTED BY SEX AND AGE PERIODS, SHOWING RELATIONSHIP OF SURVEY DATA TO 1930 CENSUS*

Age Group	Males			Females			Total		
	1930 Census	Survey	Percentage (Survey to Census)	1930 Census	Survey	Percentage (Survey to Census)	1930 Census	Survey	Percentage (Survey to Census)
0– 4	6,448	547	8.5	6,153	488	7.9	12,601	1,035	8.2
5– 9	8,474	846	10.0	8,273	871	10.5	16,747	1,717	10.3
10–14	5,528	676	12.2	5,212	625	12.0	10,740	1,301	12.1
15–19	3,157	441	14.0	2,536	370	14.6	5,693	811	14.2
20–24	2,293	268	11.7	1,805	256	14.2	4,098	524	12.8
25–29	3,387	299	8.8	3,154	316	10.0	6,541	615	9.4
30–34	3,415	293	8.6	4,280	417	9.7	7,695	710	9.2
35–44	8,272	596	7.2	6,306	629	10.0	14,578	1,225	8.4
45–54	11,262	838	7.4	2,581	284	11.0	13,843	1,122	8.1
55–64	3,696	275	7.4	604	59	9.8	4,300	334	7.8
65–74	408	19	4.7	73	3	4.1	481	22	4.6
75 up.....	31	...	...	8	...	...	39	...	...
Unknown	69	...	...	31	...	...	100	...	...
Total ..	56,440	5,098	9.0	41,016	4,318	10.5	97,456	9,416	9.7

* Whereas, in the survey, data concerning all members of a family were secured, individuals not living in continental United States are excluded from this table; of such there were 117 males and 140 females in Japan and 11 males and 6 females in Hawaii.

reported by the census and 9.0 per cent of the men. This smaller representation of males can probably be accounted for on the ground that there are proportionately more men to be found in the many counties of the state containing less than 2,000 Japanese all told, counties which were not covered in the survey. If this is the case, then our percentage of married male Japanese, reported on page 162, is proportionately high.

Another check upon our sampling is afforded by comparison with the occupational census made by the Japanese government in 1930. The percentages of the first generation by occupations according to this census are given in Table 27 (p. 209), together with corresponding figures from our survey. The latter reports 16 per cent fewer in agricultural pursuits and 10 per cent more in fishing than the Japanese official census. Aside from these two striking differences, there is good agreement between the two; our survey gives slightly more in professional work, business, and skilled work, and slightly fewer in common labor. These differences are to be expected, since there was no attempt on our part to obtain a random sampling of the entire Japanese population but rather to obtain representation from every occupation in which Japanese are engaged. As a greater variety of occupations are to be found in the cities, this necessitated a more extensive survey in urban than in rural communities. The excessive representation from the fishing industry is due to the fact that one of our interviewers devoted all of his time to Japanese fishermen and their families. In all that follows it should be remembered that the urban occupations and particularly the fishing industry are stressed proportionately more than agricultural and common labor occupations in our survey.

After working with this material for three years the writer believes the survey data are quite accurate. Each set of figures agrees surprisingly well, as far as it is possible to check the matter, with other related data. And when it has been possible to compare the information with tabular material from other sources, the agreement is highly satisfactory.

AGE OF JAPANESE POPULATION

Inspection of the total number of males, or females, or both, by age groups in Table 13 discloses a bimodal distribution. There is one mode at 5–9 years and another at 34–44 years (at 45–54 for the males). At 20–24 years of age there are only one-third to one-fourth as many as at these two modal points, and yet it is at this point in the distribution that the average falls, i.e., 23 years. We have here one of those relatively rare examples in which an average is a very poor measure of the group. What is the cause of this bimodality?

The Japanese population is composed of three groups: those born in Japan, in the Hawaiian Islands, and in continental United States. The first group constitute the first generation; the second and third groups constitute the second generation, who are citizens of the United States by birth. From a cultural standpoint, the three groups are not so clearly differentiated as the foregoing would suggest, for there are some Japan-born Japanese who have spent nearly all their lives in this country and are essentially second generation in every respect except citizenship, and there are some Hawaii- and United States–born who have been educated in Japan and know little of the language or customs of the country of their birth.

The age distribution obtained by our survey of the three groups of Japanese is given in Table 14 and in Figures 2 and 3. There are relatively few first generation under twenty-four years of age. This phenomenon is traceable to the Immigration Act of 1924, which stopped the influx of young people who might otherwise have come. Undoubt-

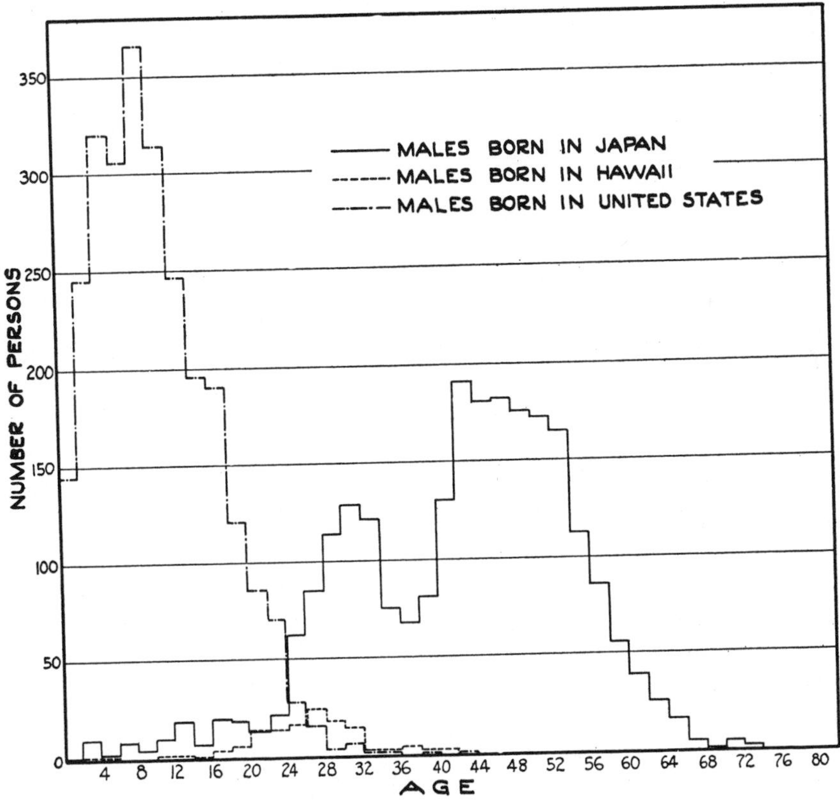

FIG. 2.—Age distribution of Japanese males according to birthplace.

TABLE 14

SEX AND AGE DISTRIBUTION, ACCORDING TO 1930 SURVEY DATA

Age Group	Males								Females								Total	
	Born in Japan		Born in Hawaii		Born in United States		Total		Born in Japan		Born in Hawaii		Born in United States		Total			
	Number	Percentage	Number	Percentage	Number	Percentage	Number	Percentage	Number	Percentage	Number	Percentage	Number	Percentage	Number	Percentage	Number	Percentage
0– 6	15	0.6	4	2.8	878	33.0	897	17.1	19	1.0	2	2.6	862	35.2	883	19.7	1,780	18.3
7–13	40	1.7	6	4.2	1,066	40.0	1,112	21.3	47	2.5	4	5.2	992	40.0	1,043	23.4	2,155	22.2
14–20	52	2.1	16	11.1	552	20.7	620	11.9	57	3.0	18	23.4	477	19.2	552	12.3	1,172	12.2
21–27	185	7.7	69	47.8	155	5.8	409	7.8	253	13.2	28	36.4	137	5.5	418	9.4	827	8.5
28–34	403	16.7	36	25.0	10	0.4	449	8.6	551	28.8	22	28.6	8	0.3	581	13.0	1,030	10.6
35–41	314	12.9	13	9.0	2	0.1	329	6.3	503	26.3	3	3.9	...	...	506	11.3	835	8.6
42–48	640	26.5	..	...	1	...	641	12.2	274	14.3	..	...	1	...	275	6.2	916	9.4
49–55	537	22.2	..	...	...	...	537	10.3	161	8.4	..	...	...	...	161	3.6	698	7.2
56–62	193	8.0	..	...	...	...	193	3.7	38	2.0	..	...	...	...	38	0.9	231	2.8
63–69	33	1.4	..	...	...	...	33	0.6	7	0.4	..	...	...	...	7	0.2	40	0.4
70 up	6	0.2	..	...	...	...	6	0.1	...	...	..	...	...	...	...	...	6	0.1
Total	2,418	...	144	...	2,664	...	5,226	...	1,910	...	77	...	2,477	...	4,464	...	9,690	...
Average age	41.7		25.1		10.0		24.9		35.2		24.1		9.7		20.9		23.0	

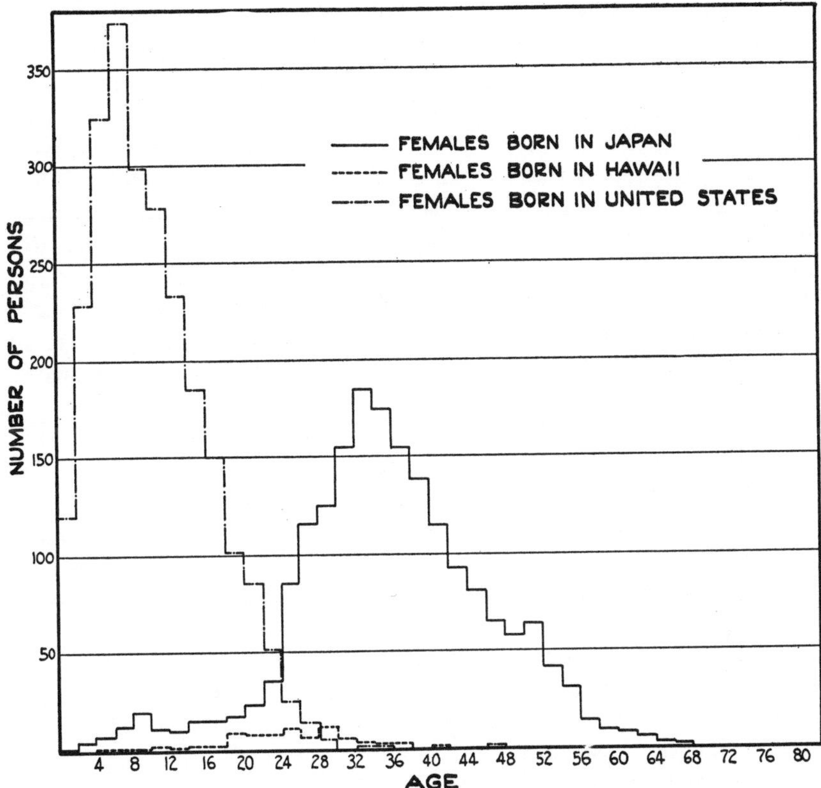

FIG. 3.—Age distribution of Japanese females according to birthplace.

edly the Gentlemen's Agreement is similarly responsible for the smaller number of men between the ages of twenty-four and forty than of men between forty and fifty-four. The immigration of women was not stopped by that agreement, and consequently their age distribution is not affected in this manner (see Fig. 1, p. 87).

The first generation as a group are younger than is commonly supposed—the males average forty-two years of age, the females thirty-five years.[3] The males have spent half their lives in continental United States, the females one-third of their lives.

[3] Based on our survey. Even if the untenable assumption were made that all males under 24 years of age were second generation and all over 24 years were first generation, the United States census figures would then give an average age of only 44.3 years.

In the literature much has been made of the supposed fact that the Japanese who first went to the Hawaiian Islands and later came to California were markedly inferior to those who came direct.[4] Such immigrants did have less education,[5] but whether or not they were inferior in other respects we have been unable to determine. In any case, they now represent only a small fraction of the total here. Of the 2,418 Japan-born males interviewed, only 335 report that they have lived in the Hawaiian Islands (for an average of 4.1 years); and of the 1,910 Japan-born females only 65 have lived in the Islands (for an average of 5.1 years). On this basis we should estimate that only 4,123 Japanese now in California came by way of Hawaii. If large numbers came by way of the Islands, as some claim, they have for the most part left California.

Native-born.—Of chief concern to this whole report are the data on the native-born, the second generation. According to the census there were 4,502 in continental United States in 1910, 29,672 in 1920, and 68,357[6] in 1930. Obviously this group are very young today. In Hawaii the native-born numbered 19,889 in 1910, 48,586 in 1920, and 91,185 in 1930, a much larger number than on the mainland and containing four to five times as many of voting age.

The relative unimportance of Hawaii-born Japanese is graphically shown by the fact that only 144 males and 77 females were encountered in our survey. On this basis there are but 2,278 such in California. This group average about twenty-five years of age (see Table 14, p. 158).

Males and females born in the United States have similar age distributions, having been born and brought up under similar conditions. Both groups average nearly ten years of age in 1930 and both include individuals up to thirty-six years. But only 6.3 per cent of the males and 5.8 per cent of the females are of age. The distributions indicate clearly that the number born each year is now rapidly decreasing, the maximum having occurred in 1921 (see also Table 15, p. 165).

Among the United States–born, 564 males have visited Japan for an average of 5.6 years and 487 females have visited there for 5.2 years. But 2,091 males and 1,985 females have not made the trip. Only 4 of these 5,127 young people have spent any time in the Hawaiian Islands.

---

[4] See pp. 95–97.

[5] One to two years less than those who came direct. See E. K. Strong, Jr., *Japanese in California*, p. 87.

[6] Of these, 48,979 were in California.

Number of second generation twenty-one years of age and over.—According to the census taken by the Japanese consulates in San Francisco and Los Angeles 2,500 of the second generation were twenty-one years of age and over in the state of California in 1930 (see Table 12, p. 143). The figure is somewhat too low, since this census did not include all the Japanese in the state (it reports 5,066 less than the United States Census). According to our survey data (Table 14) 118 males and 53 females born in Hawaii and 168 males and 146 females born in the United States were of age in the 9.7 per cent sampling of the state. This would give 5,000 second-generation Japanese twenty-one years of age and over. As pointed out previously, our survey gives too many young people as compared with the United States Census. If allowance is made for this, the 5,000 is reduced to 3,567.[7]

According to the Japanese census figures (Table 12, p. 143), there are 4,997 between the ages of sixteen and twenty. On this basis we can estimate the number of second generation of voting age in 1935 to be 7,497. From our survey data it appears there would be 10,959 additional in 1937, or, if allowance is made as above, the number would be 7,722. The total second-generation Japanese of voting age in 1937 would then be 11,289. Our adjusted estimates of increase for seven years and that based on the Japanese census for five years agree very closely. Neither of these estimates takes into account, however, future losses from deaths and departures from the state or increases due to arrivals. Because of the impossibility of estimating future arrivals and departures it appears to be impossible to make any valid estimate as to how many Japanese voters there will be in the state in future years. Half of those in the state are native-born and in 1951, if they all live, there will be 50,000 of them who can vote. Many may go elsewhere to live, cutting down this number, or many may come here from Japan (native-born now there) and from Hawaii. The biggest "if" in all such calculations has to do with the possible migration of native-born Japanese in Hawaii to California.

The status of Japanese, American, and dual citizenship has been considered in chapter v (see pp. 140–44).

MARITAL STATUS

The index of males to females is an important one to bear in mind in considering many sociological questions. It is abnormal for an adult

[7] In 1929 Mr. T. Takimoto, secretary of the Japanese Association in California, estimated there would be 1,650 of age in 1930 and 5,196 in 1934.

male not to be married, and when he is deprived of the opportunity through absence of women of his own race the situation is most likely to lead to unfortunate results.

As with most immigrant groups, the Japanese men came first and the women later. The Chinese have never shown any great tendency to bring their women to this country, and even today there are three Chinese men for every Chinese woman. The Japanese, on the other hand, commenced to bring their women after they had become established here. This is shown by the totals in Table 36 (p. 274) and by the ratios of males to females. For every female there were 17.4 males in California in 1900, 5.6 males in 1910, 1.7 males in 1920, and 1.4 males in 1930. It will not be many years before the ratio will be typical of that for populations in general. This is shown by comparing the number of males and females at various age levels in Table 14 (p. 158), or in Table 13 (p. 155). The numbers are approximately equal under fourteen years of age, and even up to forty-five years of age the difference between number of males and females is only 3,255, giving a ratio of 1.1 males to 1 female.

Out of a total of 2,205 males born in Japan, fourteen years of age or over, all but 335 are or have been married. Among the first-generation women, fourteen years and over, 98 per cent are or have been married. Among the 5,041 second-generation United States–born, only 19 males and 69 females are married, which emphasizes again the extreme youth of the second generation. Japanese men of the first generation have traditionally experienced difficulty in obtaining wives, yet their average age of first marriage is but 29.6 years, whereas the corresponding figure for Japanese in Japan is 28.4 years and that for all males in California in 1920–21 was 30.4 years.

The numbers of Japanese men and women in California according to the 1930 census (Table 13, p. 155) are:

Age Group	Men	Women	Difference
15–24 years	5,450	4,341	1,109
25–44 years	15,074	13,740	1,334
45 years and up	15,397	3,266	12,131
Total	35,921	21,347	14,574

From this it appears that 14,574 women are needed in order to supply every Japanese male fifteen years and older with a wife; in other words, only 59 per cent can possibly have wives living in California with them. The discrepancy between the census and our survey is probably to be explained on the basis that there are proportionately more men than women in the counties of the state containing less than 2,000 Japanese, which were not sampled in the survey, also that many of the men have, or have had, wives in Japan.

Size of family.—The average first-generation Japanese male who has married has had 3.1 children and the average Japanese female has had 3.3 children. If married women under forty-two years of age are excluded the average is raised to 3.4 children, of whom 0.5 are dead. The Japanese, like all immigrant groups, have had larger families than Americans, but there is no evidence that they have had on the average families of the size that popular opinion assumes.

Broken families.—The present immigration law prevents the union of certain Japanese families, some of whose members are in California and some in Japan. On the basis of our survey it appears that there are about 4,300 children living in Japan who cannot join one or both of their parents living in the state. Similarly, there are about 700 parents in Japan who cannot join their United States–born children, under twenty-one years of age, now in California. Seventy per cent of those parents are mothers. It should be recognized in this connection that many of these children and parents have had in the past very good reasons for staying in Japan and would not come here if they could. On the other hand, there are others who would jump at the opportunity to come.

BIRTHS AND DEATHS

One of the chief arguments against the Japanese has been that their birth-rate is so high that it endangers white supremacy. In 1920 the State Board of Control of California[8] presented these facts on the subject:

> In 1910, Japanese births represent one out of every 44 children born in the state. In 1919, Japanese births represent one out of every 13 children born in the state.[9]
>
> In 18 selected agricultural counties of the state, the average births of Japanese have risen from 3.2 per cent of the total births in 1910 to 12.3 per cent in 1919.
>
> In the rural parts of Sacramento County, 49.7 per cent of all births in 1919 were Japanese . . . .
>
> In 1910, 313,281 married white women had 30,893 births (9.9 per cent of births to mothers) while in 1919, 15,211 Japanese women had 4,378 births (28.8

---

[8] *California and the Oriental* (1920, revised in 1922), p. 37.

[9] See Table 15 (p. 165), which lists for the years 1910–19 the figures given by the Board of Control.

per cent). On this basis, the fecundity of the Japanese is nearly three times that of the Whites. If it were possible to select, for more accurate comparison, those white married women who were of a social, economic, and intellectual status similar to that of the Japanese, the disparity in birth rates would undoubtedly be less marked.

There are approximately three times as many Japanese men as there are Japanese women in California. Considering the high birth rate, under present conditions, what would it be, were there Japanese women in California sufficient for each Japanese man to establish a household?

The first three paragraphs above were printed in bold type. Directly below them appeared the following in ordinary type:

While the Japanese birth rate is far in excess of that of all other nationalities in the state, this is not infrequently true of a new people immigrating into a new land. Also among the Japanese, which is a new race here, most of the adults are comparatively young and of the family raising ages, while among the whites, a race long resident in California, there is necessarily the usual proportion of elderly persons.

Figures such as presented in the opening paragraphs of the passage cited lent themselves readily to the exaggerations of the agitator. Even as they stand, they are damning enough from the standpoint of those who wanted no further increase of Japanese population. The percentages were accepted at their face value by many readers of the report.

How have the facts of the ten years which have passed since this was written borne out the point of view it presents?

The numbers of Japanese births in California for each year from 1906 to 1930 are given in Table 15 and shown graphically in Figure 4. There is an increase from 134 births in 1906 to 5,275 in 1921 and then a decrease to 2,220 in 1930 (2,040 in 1931). One would judge from these figures that the number of births will continue to decline for about ten years, since the first generation have about completed their families and the second generation are not old enough to marry. There will then follow a decade or two in which the number of Japanese-American births will increase noticeably, since by that time the present second-generation children will average twenty years of age. The birth-rate, however calculated, will not reach the heights recorded in 1915 and 1920 (i.e., 59 and 69, respectively, per 1,000 Japanese population), for never again will the Japanese population be composed almost exclusively of adults of child-bearing age.

The number of Japanese deaths in California and for the registration area of the United States are given in the second half of Table 15 (see also Fig. 4). If the large increase in deaths occasioned by the flu

TABLE 15

BIRTHS AND DEATHS OF JAPANESE IN CALIFORNIA AND THE UNITED STATES*

Year	Births					Deaths				
	In California	In United States	Percentage of Japanese Population Included in Registration Area	Estimated Births in United States	Percentage Japanese Births of All Births in California	In California	In United States	Percentage of Japanese Population Included in Registration Area	Estimated Deaths in United States	Percentage Japanese Deaths of Total Deaths in California
	(1)	(2)	(3)	(4)	(5)	(6)	(7)	(8)	(9)	(10)
1906....	134	.....	....	.....	0.6	384	478	70.7	676	1.3
1907....	221	.....	....	.....	0.9	517	683	70.7	966	1.7
1908....	455	.....	....	.....	1.6	431	609	86.4	705	1.4
1909....	682	.....	....	.....	2.2	450	636	86.6	734	1.5
1910....	719	.....	....	.....	2.2	444	664	90.3	735	1.4
1911....	995	.....	....	.....	2.6	472	664	90.3	735	1.4
1912....	1,467	.....	....	.....	3.7	524	752	90.3	832	1.4
1913....	2,215	.....	....	.....	5.0	613	896	90.4	991	1.6
1914....	2,874	.....	....	.....	6.2	628	904	90.4	1,000	1.7
1915....	3,342	74	3.3	.....	7.0	663	987	90.4	1,091	1.7
1916....	3,721	51	3.3	.....	7.3	739	1,037	90.4	1,147	1.9
1917....	4,108	939	22.0	.....	7.9	910	1,246	90.4	1,378	2.2
1918....	4,218	1,040	22.0	.....	7.6	1,545	2,110	94.6	2,230	2.7
1919....	4,458	5,979	90.7	6,592	8.0	1,113	1,648	94.8	1,738	2.4
1920....	4,971	6,271	91.3	6,868	7.4	1,002	1,511	95.2	1,587	2.1
1921....	5,275	7,209	91.7	7,861	7.3	896	1,335	95.2	1,402	1.9
1922....	5,066	6,941	94.1	7,376	6.9	991†	1,439	97.5	1,475	1.9
1923....	5,010	6,972	94.1	7,409	6.2	979†	1,422	97.5	1,458	1.8
1924....	4,481	6,115	94.3	6,484	5.2	913	1,360	97.5	1,394	1.6
1925....	4,016	6,135	94.3	6,505	5.4	856	1,277	97.5	1,309	1.5
1926....	3,597	4,952	96.2	5,147	4.4	814	1,224	98.3	1,245	1.4
1927....	3,241	4,304	96.3	4,469	3.8	787	1,196	98.3	1,216	1.3
1928....	2,833	3,917	98.6	3,972	3.4	808	1,097	98.3	1,115	1.2
1929....	2,353	3,371	99.6	3,384	2.9	769	1,139	99.6	1,145	1.2
1930....	2,220	3,060	99.6	3,072	...	754‡	1,109	99.6	1,113	...

* California data from *Biennial Reports of California State Board of Health;* United States data on births from *Birth, Stillbirth, and Infant Mortality Statistics for the Birth Registration Area of the United States,* Table 2, Births, exclusive of stillbirths. Data in columns 3, 4, 8, 9, 10, are our calculations.

† Not given by Board of Health; taken from United States Census.

‡ Estimated.

epidemic during 1918–19 is disregarded, it appears that deaths have increased steadily until about 1922 and then more slowly decreased. Two factors explain this phenomenon: First, deaths increase in number with increase in population, which was occurring throughout the entire period; second, death-rate is proportionately very high for babies, and the subsequent drop in death-rate since 1922 is due to the decreasing birth-rate.

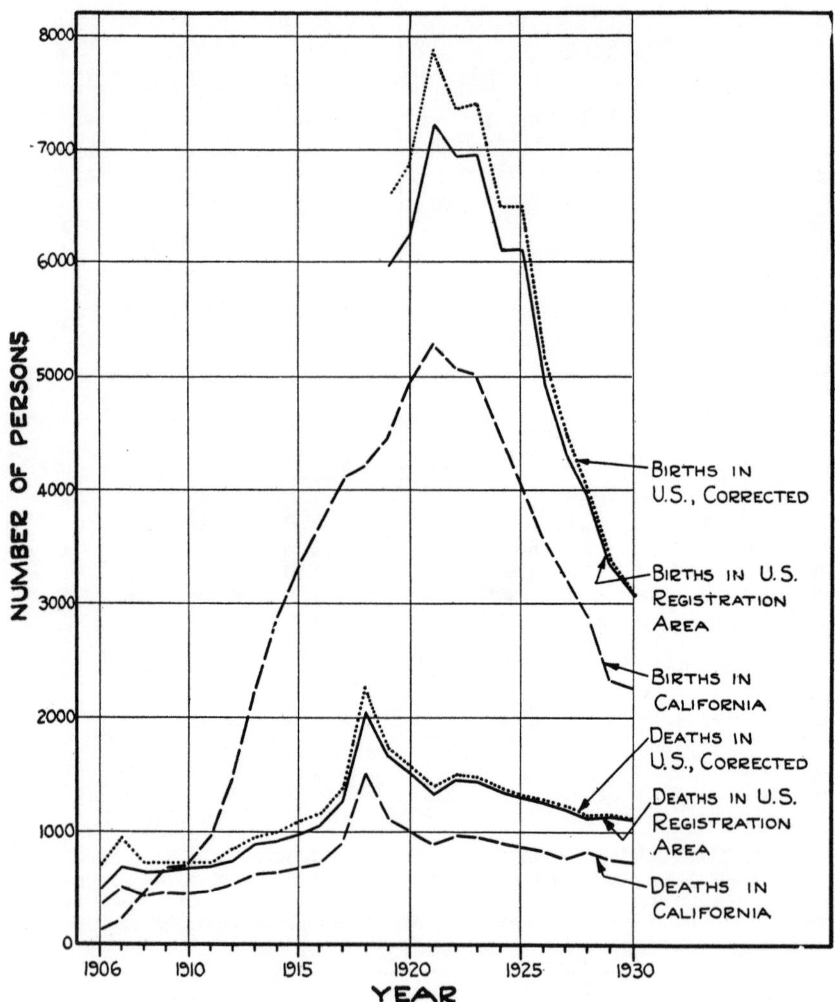

FIG. 4.—Births and deaths of Japanese in California and the United States

VII. PHYSICAL AND MENTAL ABILITY

How Japanese-Americans compare with whites in physical and mental ability is considered in some detail in the monograph *Vocational Aptitudes of Second-Generation Japanese in the United States.*[1] The objective of this study was to ascertain whether or not second-generation Japanese differ significantly from whites and particularly, if there are such differences, what bearing they have upon choice of occupation. In other words, is there any indication that Japanese should enter certain occupations and not other occupations because of their peculiar physical, mental, and moral make-up?

The general conclusion is that the differences between Japanese and whites, both born in the United States and educated in the same schools of California, are slight. In fact, they are so slight that there is no warrant for supposing that Japanese and whites should enter different occupations because of any differences in their physical or mental capacities. It must be emphasized immediately, however, that neither Japanese nor whites are able to select their life work solely on the basis of ability or inclination. All manner of environmental factors are important, and vocational selection must usually involve a certain amount of compromise between what one wants to do and what one has an opportunity to do. In this chapter there is no attempt to consider the environmental factors, so that the conclusions given here are based solely upon relative measurements of representatives of the two racial groups.

INTELLIGENCE

The most important single measure of an individual is his general intelligence score. This is the best standardized of all psychological tests and its significance is best established. Review of the literature of Japanese intelligence by Reginald Bell[2] makes clear that the two racial groups are about equal in this respect. He summarizes the literature as follows:

1. It is highly probable that the innate mental capacity of Japanese and Chinese children is greater than their Binet IQ's ascertained on scales administered in

[1] E. K. Strong, Jr., *Vocational Aptitudes of Second-Generation Japanese in the United States.*

[2] See *ibid.,* chapter iii, also Reginald Bell, *Public School Education of Second-Generation Japanese in California,* chapter iii.

English would indicate. There is reason to believe that mental ages so derived are at least 2 to 4 months too low.

2. Japanese and Chinese children seem definitely inferior to American white children in mental processes involving memory and abstract thinking based on meanings or concepts represented by the verbal symbols of the English language. There is some reason to believe that this is not due solely to language handicap.[3]

3. Japanese and Chinese children are probably at least equal and possibly superior to American whites in mental processes involving memory and thinking based upon concrete, visually presented situations of a non-verbal character. There is definite superiority of Japanese in performance-test situations.

4. Japanese children seem to be superior to American whites in mental processes involving acuity of visual perception and recall, and tenacity of attention.

Educational achievement, particularly when determined by achievement tests, measures very largely the same abilities as the intelligence test. The comparative studies so far made, with one exception, indicate that Chinese and Japanese are retarded somewhat in school with respect to subjects of a linguistic nature but in arithmetic and spelling seem to be superior to whites. However, one extensive study shows equality of performance in reading tests as well as in arithmetic. All studies show actual retardation in age-grade placement for Japanese, which varies from four to six months. (See also pp. 189–91 for further discussion.)

ABILITY TO USE ENGLISH AND JAPANESE

Second-generation Japanese, both in Hawaii and on the mainland, were rated for their ability to speak English and Japanese. All the data make clear that under existing conditions Japanese-Americans are mastering neither language.

Is this because the two languages are peculiarly unlike and more difficult to acquire than certain other pairs of languages? The writer, for example, has met several Chinese who speak beautiful English, but has never met a Japanese who was free from accent, always used the article correctly, and did not occasionally employ the Japanese order of words in a sentence. Is the failure of Japanese to master these two languages due to the methods of instruction? Or is it due to their lack of practice at home? Many of their parents know little English, especially the mothers, and few have a scholarly grasp of their own language. Or is it because the Japanese are deficient in linguistic ability?[4]

---

[3] See below for further discussion of linguistic ability.

[4] All the data pertaining to linguistic ability support the hypothesis that the Japanese are deficient in this regard. The matter should be investigated further, as it has an important bearing on the proper interpretation of intelligence-test scores.

An editorial in *The Oriental Outlook* supports this view that Japanese do not speak English as well as Chinese:

> Without being aware of it, perhaps, Japan has prejudiced public opinion in America against herself by what may seem to be a trivial thing. But none the less it has been a potent factor in the determination of our foreign policy in Oriental affairs. It is the atrocious manner in which, with few exceptions, the spokesmen for Japan have handled the English language. Add to this the further offense committed by the Japanese in the crudely worded and ungrammatical printed documents with which the country has been flooded, and you have the answer to why the United States is not more sympathetic to her next-door neighbor across the Pacific. The average American is prone to look upon one who speaks English haltingly as an ignorant and uncouth foreigner. The facility with which Chinese diplomats express themselves in flawless English, together with the fluency of practically all Chinese leaders who have appeared in this country, has without question helped to mould public opinion in China's favor.[5]

One way of measuring the relative ability in using English or Japanese is to ascertain preference for these two languages. Presumably that language will be preferred in which the individual is most proficient.

Only a handful of Japan-born men and women prefer English to Japanese, except in the age-group 14–20 years, where half prefer English. These young people have averaged 4.5 years in the United States and about 3.5 years in schools in the country. In contrast to these, 68 per cent of the Hawaii-born men and 46 per cent of the women prefer English to Japanese. Naturally a still larger percentage of preference for English is to be found among the United States–born. It is rather surprising, however, that only three out of four of this last group prefer English to Japanese.

Among those living in the cities there is a somewhat greater preference for English than among those living in country districts, which is only natural, since city life would force upon the Japanese greater use of the English language. This statement holds true of the Japan- and Hawaii-born Japanese but not of the United States–born. Among the latter no difference was found between the city and country groups respecting preference for the two languages.

There appears to be little or no relationship between preference for English and length of residence in this country. No Japanese who has been in this country thirty-five or more years prefers English to Japanese; all such were adults when they immigrated here. Apparently if

---

[5] *The Oriental Outlook,* I (March 1933), 4.

English is not well learned in youth it never really takes the place of the native tongue.

Additional data from high-school students indicate that 73 per cent of those born in Hawaii and 82 per cent of those born in the United States prefer English to Japanese. It is quite likely that many of those preferring the Japanese language, if not all, received their early education in Japan. Practically all college men (96 per cent), whether born in Hawaii or in the United States, prefer English to Japanese.

MOTOR SKILL

On the physical side, the Japanese are shorter in stature and do not weigh as much as whites. They are inferior in strength tests, according to Porteus,[6] but, on the other hand, they are quicker in the majority of twelve reaction and co-ordination tests.[7] The low correlation that exists between different motor performances warns against attempting any summarization here. Because Japanese, or whites, are superior in one performance does not mean that they will be superior in the next one. Nevertheless, the demonstrated speed and accuracy of muscular co-ordination of the Japanese, together with their recognized ability to work long hours, leads one to the conclusion that their physical abilities will not be found insufficient for almost any type of work they may wish to undertake in competition with whites except possibly that requiring very heavy lifting.

ARTISTIC APTITUDES

The fact that Japan has produced many exquisite works of art, coupled with the fact that most school teachers claim Japanese children are superior in art work, led us to expect that the second generation would surpass the whites in this respect. When scientifically tested, however, upon a variety of performances requiring recognition of proportions and colors, appreciation of perspective and of good forms, and the like, they proved, on the whole, to be only very slightly superior to whites.[8] They were particularly good in recognition of proportion and

[6] S. D. Porteus, *The Psychology of a Primitive People* (1931), chapter xx.

[7] Japanese high-school and college students were tested by Malcolm Campbell. Norms for corresponding white students were supplied by R. H. Seashore and W. R. Miles.

[8] Miss Gladys Bond gave the tests to 353 Japanese children in the schools of Los Angeles under the direction of Alfred S. Lewerenz, author of *Tests in Fundamental Abilities of Visual Art,* published by Research Service Company, Los

color[9] and visual memory of form, but correspondingly poor in originality of line drawing (except in the senior high school) and in the three tests of perspective.

The art treasures of a nation are not to be explained, however, in terms of the average ability of its citizens. It is the performance of exceptional individuals that accounts for the great in art. Only a very extensive study could determine whether there are more children exceptional along artistic lines among the Japanese than among the whites.

Apparently very few of either group are interested in this field. From one to two per cent more Japanese high-school boys than white high-school boys report they are interested in art work and plan to specialize in it, but in college no Japanese are interested in it, as compared with about half of one per cent of whites. Only about one per cent of both groups are interested in, or planning to specialize in, the related field of architecture.[10]

VOCATIONAL INTERESTS

Japanese and whites are again very similar as regards their occupational interests; see Table 16 for comparison of data from high-school boys.[11] This similarity is expressed in Table 17 by coefficients of correlation ranging between .63 and .95, depending upon the educational status of the two groups and upon the method of measuring the similarity.

Certain differences in vocational interests between Japanese and whites appear, however, to be fairly significant. When the differences, expressed by critical ratios,[12] are averaged, it appears that the interests

---

Angeles. Norms are based on approximately one thousand unselected cases from the same school system, grades 2–12. The conclusion cited is based upon an analysis of the results from the nine parts of the test and the eleven school grades.

[9] This conclusion should be rechecked, as the Japanese were apparently tested for recognition of color under more favorable conditions than the whites. If this is so, total scores probably average about the same for both groups.

[10] See pp. 218–22 and Table 30 (p. 221); also E. K. Strong, Jr., *Japanese in California,* Table 55.

[11] The Vocational Interest Blank, published by Stanford University Press, was used in this connection.

[12] Critical ratios are from Table 16 (column 7) and three other tables not reproduced here. Critical ratio is the quotient obtained by dividing a difference between two means by the standard error of that difference. A critical ratio of 3.0 or greater indicates that the difference is significant statistically.

TABLE 16

PERCENTAGE OF JAPANESE AND WHITE HIGH-SCHOOL BOYS WHO OBTAIN RATINGS OF A FOR INTEREST IN NINETEEN OCCUPATIONS; ALSO PERCENTAGE OF A AND B+ RATINGS AND OF A, B+, B, AND B— RATINGS COMBINED*

Occupational Interests	A Ratings			A and B+ Ratings				A, B+, B, and B— Ratings‡		
	Japanese	Whites	Differences	Japanese	Whites	Differences	Critical Ratio†	Japanese	Whites	Differences
	(1)	(2)	(3)	(4)	(5)	(6)	(7)	(8)	(9)	(10)
Farmer	14.8	13.4	1.4	39.4	32.2	7.2	3.1	75.1	67.9	7.2
Physician	13.8	8.9	4.9	29.5	23.6	5.9	2.7	59.5	54.1	5.4
Teacher	4.1	2.0	2.1	10.5	5.6	4.9	3.6	40.5	25.1	15.4
Architect	0.7	0.9	0.2	4.1	3.4	0.7	0.7	21.7	18.8	2.9
Chemist	4.6	5.8	—1.2	13.2	12.5	0.7	0.4	34.5	31.2	3.3
Engineer	13.3	13.6	—0.3	32.4	29.9	2.5	1.1	70.1	61.8	8.3
Minister	0.3	0.6	—0.3	2.5	2.1	0.4	0.5	17.2	10.4	6.8
C.P.A.	0.1	0.2	—0.1	0.5	0.6	— 0.1	0.3	4.1	6.8	— 2.7
Artist	0	0.1	—0.1	0	0.2	— 0.2	1.4	2.7	3.2	— 0.5
Advertiser	0	0.2	—0.2	0	1.2	— 1.2	3.6	7.2	11.6	— 4.4
Psychologist	0.1	0.6	—0.5	0.4	1.4	— 1.0	2.3	5.6	6.3	— 0.7
Y.M.C.A. secretary	0.7	3.7	—3.0	4.1	4.0	0.1	0.1	23.2	14.1	9.1
Life insurance salesman	0.6	1.0	—0.4	1.2	4.1	— 2.9	3.9	12.1	22.4	—10.3
Vacuum-cleaner salesman	3.4	3.8	—0.4	11.8	9.8	2.0	1.3	40.5	34.3	6.2
Personnel manager	0.3	0.6	—0.3	3.9	5.5	— 1.6	1.6	22.2	23.0	— 0.8
Journalist	8.1	9.3	—1.2	21.4	24.2	— 2.8	1.4	47.1	58.6	—11.5
Real estate salesman	0.3	2.8	—2.5	3.7	12.0	— 8.3	6.8	21.7	43.0	—21.3
Lawyer	1.3	3.2	—1.9	9.3	15.3	— 6.0	3.8	43.2	54.5	—11.3
Purchasing agent	3.7	6.0	—2.3	22.0	34.5	—12.5	5.8	84.6	82.4	2.2
Average	3.7	4.0	—0.3	11.0	11.7	— 0.6	...	33.3	33.1	0.2

* Based on data from 676 Japanese born in the United States and 1,086 whites.

† Critical ratio is the quotient obtained by dividing a difference between two means by the standard error of that difference. A critical ratio of 3.0 or greater is assumed to indicate that the difference is significant statistically.

‡ Those desiring to use the data on Japanese or whites as norms may readily obtain the percentages rating A, B+, B and B— combined, and those rating C by subtracting the A ratings from A and B+ ratings combined, and by subtracting the A and B+ ratings from the A, B+, B, and B— ratings combined. The differences between the latter and 100 give the percentage of C ratings.

TABLE 17

AGREEMENT BETWEEN OCCUPATIONAL INTERESTS OF JAPANESE AND WHITES

(Expressed in terms of correlation coefficients)

Different Measures	High-School Boys	College Men	Eleventh-Grade Only
Average scores	0.95	0.87	0.91
Percentage of A ratings	0.94	0.63	0.84
Percentage of A and B+ ratings	0.93	0.77	0.89
Percentage of A, B+, B, B— ratings	0.94	0.83	0.91

of the former paralleled more closely than those of the latter the interests of the following occupational groups:

Occupational Groups	Critical Ratios* Highest	Critical Ratios* Lowest	Average Critical Ratio
Teacher	4.3	2.0	3.2
Farmer	3.1	2.2	2.6
Physician	3.8	0.7	2.2
Minister	5.4	0.5	2.1
Chemist	4.0	0.4	1.9
Architect	4.2	—0.5	1.6
Y.M.C.A. secretary	3.7	—0.8	1.5
Engineer	2.3	0.5	1.2
Vacuum cleaner salesman	1.3	—1.5	0.4

* A minus sign before a critical ratio means the whites are superior to the Japanese; otherwise the reverse is the case.

And the interests of whites parallel more closely than those of Japanese the interests of the following:

Occupational Groups	Critical Ratios* Highest	Critical Ratios* Lowest	Average Critical Ratio
Certified public accountant	0.3	—1.4	—0.3
Psychologist	5.0	—3.4	—0.4
Artist	3.4	—3.4	—0.7
Personnel director	0.7	—2.6	—0.8
Journalist	—1.4	—3.0	—2.3
Purchasing agent	1.4	—5.8	—2.6
Advertising man	—0.8	—5.0	—3.2
Life insurance salesman	—2.4	—3.9	—3.3
Lawyer	—3.6	—5.5	—4.2
Real estate salesman	—3.9	—7.5	—5.9

* A minus sign before a critical ratio means the whites are superior to the Japanese; otherwise the reverse is the case.

At the present time these nineteen occupations can be classified into five groups on the basis of inter-correlations between them,[13] as follows:

I. "Science"*	II. "Language"	III. "Uplift"
Farmer	Life insurance salesman	Minister
Engineer	Real estate salesman	Teacher
Chemist	Advertiser	Y.M.C.A. secretary
Physician	Journalist	Personnel director
Architect	Lawyer	
Psychologist		
Artist		

IV. "Business"	V. "C.P.A."
Vacuum cleaner salesman	Certified public accountant
Purchasing agent	

* The headings in quotes are to be viewed merely as handy designations. Far more research is necessary before headings can be selected with real accuracy. See E. K. Strong, Jr., "Classification of Occupations on Basis of Interests," *Personnel Journal,* XII (April 1934), 6, also "Vocational Interest Test," *Occupations,* XII (April 1934), 8.

Consideration of these five groups with respect to the occupational interests of Japanese and whites makes clear that it is in the "science" and "uplift" groups that the interests of Japanese exceed those of whites, while it is in the "language" group that the interests of whites exceed those of Japanese. This generalization is not quite true, for the interests of whites, not Japanese, are more in accord with those of psychologists and artists in the "science" group and more in accord with the interests of Y.M.C.A. secretaries and personnel directors in the "uplift" group. But these last two occupations partake considerably of the interests characterizing business activities for which whites show slightly more interest than do Japanese.[14]

[13] See *Manual for Vocational Interest Blank* (January 1933); also L. L. Thurstone, "Multiple Factor Analysis," *Psychological Review,* Vol. XXXVIII, No. 5 (September 1931), and "A Multiple Factor Study of Vocational Interests," *Personnel Journal,* Vol. X, No. 3 (October 1931). The classifications cited are based on data from six more occupations than those supplied to Thurstone.

[14] This similarity of interests between the two racial groups is due, undoubtedly, in part to similarity in educational environment. But sufficient evidence has been accumulated to indicate that environment cannot alone explain such similarity. Some men who specialize in engineering, for example, do not possess the interests of that occupational group, and some men who have never even considered that occupational career have the interests of engineers. The fact, also, that the interests of identical twins correlate 0.50 and those of fraternal twins only 0.28 supports the latter view; see H. D. Carter, "Twin Similarities in Occupational Interests," *Journal of Educational Psychology,* December 1932.

In so far as interests determine one's life career these findings support the conclusion that Japanese and whites should enter occupations in practically the same proportions. Possibly a few more Japanese might enter "scientific" and "uplift" occupations than whites and a few less Japanese enter law, advertising, and selling than whites; but the differences here are not great.

PERSONALITY TRAITS

Results from the Bernreuter Personality Inventory[15] are less favorable to the Japanese. In Hawaii the Japanese are clearly less self-sufficient and less dominant and more introverted than the whites. In California the same tendency is evident, but only in the case of dominance is the difference statistically significant. Just what such differences mean has not been established, although many theories are extant. From the author's personal contacts with Japanese in California and Hawaii and particularly from their own discussions regarding lack of leaders among themselves he is inclined to believe there is some real significance in the findings of the test that the Japanese are less dominant. Leadership is dependent, however, upon a complex relationship between the leader and his followers and the total environment in which they find themselves. It is quite possible that as the Japanese-Americans become better adapted to the American environment appropriate leaders will appear among them. The test results, to be sure, would not deny this possibility, for the Japanese differ sufficiently widely among themselves in such scores so that there is plenty of opportunity for the more dominant to forge to the front. The comparative scores between the two racial groups suggest, however, that there are more whites who would dominate both Japanese and whites than the other way around. Time alone can determine this point.

DELINQUENCY AND CRIME

No two peoples have exactly the same customs or standards of living and conduct. The Japanese who came here left a country that had only recently emerged from feudalism. Their religion differed in many essentials from Christianity. In many respects their ways were not our ways, and in many cases they had to accept our ways regardless of whether they were better or worse than theirs and regardless of what they thought about them. This process of adaptation, like all learning, requires time. Under favorable circumstances, such learning can pro-

[15] Published by Stanford University Press.

gress rapidly, as is often seen in the case of wealthy and educated tourists. But the Japanese immigrants were not wealthy, even if many were fairly well educated, and there was little opportunity for them to learn the complicated life of this country while engaged as laborers on ranches.

Although they have been arrested to about the same extent as other immigrants for minor offenses, owing in part at least to ignorance of our ordinances and laws, yet they have made an enviable record as far as serious offenses are concerned. Beach[16] has recently published a study of Oriental crime in California based upon records of arrests, which, of course, are not equivalent to convictions. He points out that race discrimination may have caused a larger number of arrests among certain groups than among the native whites. He writes:

> In this respect Oriental immigrants do not differ from other aliens in the United States. Their offenses, as indicated in this study of commitments and arrests, are the consequences primarily of failure to observe city ordinances and similar state enactments, an understanding of which their very newness to American life makes difficult. Probably the most obvious fact brought out in this study of Orientals is that their behavior, in so far as it has involved the breaking of legal enactments, has run in the same channels and exhibited the same characteristics as the behavior of other aliens, for the larger part of their offenses are not of major importance. They are offenses classed as misdemeanors, part of them, at least, probably resulting from ignorance of the existence of such laws or from a lack of understanding of what is meant by them.

Our interpretation of the data furnished by Beach is somewhat less favorable to the Chinese and more favorable to the Japanese than is his own.[17] We would summarize his data as follows: During the entire period of 1900 to 1927 there was a total of 2,037,794 arrests in California for every sort of offense, serious or slight, running from murder to parking an automobile overtime, and by all manner of persons. The Chinese furnished 71,626 arrests, or 3.5 per cent of the total, and the Japanese, 17,727 arrests, or 0.9 per cent of the total. During this period the Chinese constituted 1.5 per cent of the total population of the state and the Japanese 1.7 per cent.[18] The Chinese accordingly furnished proportionately about twice as many arrests and the Japanese

---

[16] W. G. Beach, *Oriental Crime in California* (Stanford University Publications, University Series, History, Economics, and Political Science, Vol. III, No. 3 [1932]).

[17] *Ibid.*, pp. 92–93.

[18] These two percentages of 1.5 and 1.7 are based, respectively, on the percentages of Chinese and Japanese in California according to the last four United States census reports. See E. K. Strong, Jr., *Japanese in California,* chapter ii.

about half as many as the total population. During this period there were 65,919 commitments to the two state prisons of San Quentin and Folsom. The Chinese furnished 1,028, or 1.6 per cent, and the Japanese, 382, or 0.2 per cent. The Chinese, then, furnished their proportionate share of serious offenders and the Japanese only about one-seventh of their share.[19] Even if we take into account that during this period the Japanese have had a larger proportion of their population under fourteen years of age than is typical and discount the findings by half (41 per cent of the Japanese population in 1930 was under fourteen years of age), the results are still very favorable to them.

Under the direction of the writer, H. K. Misaki ascertained the extent of juvenile delinquency of the Chinese and Japanese between 1920 and 1930 in Alameda, Fresno, Los Angeles, San Francisco, and Santa Clara counties; also, in Honolulu County, Territory of Hawaii. Three of his tables, i.e., Tables 18, 19, and 20, make clear that Japanese-Americans have thus far made an admirable record as far as juvenile delinquency is concerned. Table 21, from Lind, supports this conclusion.

It would seem that there should be no particular difference between the Japanese and other racial groups relative to juvenile delinquency. The residential districts of the Japanese are close to, if not intermingled with, those of other immigrant groups. The children play with, and go to school with, these other children. The Japanese retail establishments are patronized by many recent comers to America. There is no apparent environmental difference. Yet there is a very real difference between the Japanese and many other racial groups with respect to juvenile delinquency. Why is this?

A number of reasons have been advanced for the small amount of Japanese delinquency, namely:

1. Close home control (10)[20]
2. General educational care by the parents (3)

---

[19] From a letter to the writer from the Director of Penology the following figures are appended: On November 30, 1930, there were 6,509 prisoners at San Quentin and Folsom. Of these, there were 102 white and 19 Negro women, leaving a total of 6,388 men. Whites constitute 89.1 per cent of this number; Negroes, 7.0 per cent; Chinese, 1.3 per cent; Filipinos, 1.0 per cent; Indians, 0.7 per cent; Japanese, 0.4 per cent; and Hawaiians and Hindus, 0.2 per cent. As the Japanese constituted 1.7 per cent of the population of the state in 1930, it is apparent that they are contributing not more than 23 per cent of their proportionate share of adult crime.

[20] The numbers in parentheses record the number of prominent Japanese who gave that explanation.

TABLE 18

CLASSIFICATION OF THE JAPANESE OFFENSES ACCORDING TO THEIR NATURE IN FIVE COUNTIES FOR THE TEN YEARS 1920–30

Offense	Los Angeles County	San Francisco County	Alameda County	Fresno County	Santa Clara County	Total	Percentage
Stealing	6	..	1	..	..	7	11
Truancy	3	..	..	..	..	3	5
Incorrigibility	5	..	..	..	..	5	8
Burglary	15	1	..	..	1	17	27
Larceny	3	..	1	1	..	5	8
Sexual immorality	4	..	..	1	1	6	9
"Sub. 11"*	1	..	..	..	..	1	1.6
Forgery	1	..	1	1	..	3	5
Vagrancy	1	..	..	..	..	1	1.6
Battery	1	..	..	..	..	1	1.6
Malicious mischief	1	..	..	..	..	1	1.6
Wright Act	1	..	..	..	..	1	1.6
"Sub. 13"†	9	..	1	..	1	11	17
Hold-up	..	1	..	..	..	1	1.6
Total	..	..	..	..	..	63	99.6
Dependents	21	..	20	..	..	41	....
Traffic violations	44	..	6	..	..	50	....
Investigation	1	..	1	..	..	2	....
Grand total	..	..	..	..	..	156	....

* "Sub. 11," "Who is leading, or from any cause is in danger of leading, an idle, dissolute, lewd, or immoral life" (*California Juvenile Court Law,* 1919).

† "Sub. 13," "Who violates any law of this state or any ordinance of any town, city, county, or city and county of this state defining crime" (*ibid.*).

3. Close supervision by adults in general over the second generation (2)
4. Moral influence of Japanese-language schools:[21] teaching of Japanese spirit (2)
5. Racial consciousness (4), racial pride (0), feeling of inferiority (4)
6. Social isolation from the American community (6)
7. So few children over fourteen years of age (15)
8. Many cases settled outside of court (1)

[21] See pp. 201–3 for evaluation of these schools.

TABLE 19

RATIO OF DELINQUENTS TO WHOLE SCHOOL POPULATION FOR VARIOUS RACIAL-NATIONAL GROUPS IN LOS ANGELES COUNTY

Groups	Number of Delin-quents	Census of 1929	School Enroll-ment for 1930	Ratio per Thousand	
				1929	1930
American	2,043	233,580	....	8.7	....
Negro	374	6,973	....	53.6	....
Chinese	2	1,031	783	1.9	2.5
Japanese	19	8,682	7,290	2.1	2.6
Italian	220	....	6,834	....	32.1
Mexican	963	40,646	....	23.6	....
Filipino	6	486	....	12.3	....
Russian	56	....	2,110	....	26.5
Spanish-speaking, including Mexican	1,055	....	39,099	....	26.9

TABLE 20

JUVENILE DELINQUENCY OF MALES IN HONOLULU COUNTY, HAWAII, 1913–28*

Year	All except Japanese			Japanese		
	Number of Delin-quents	Number of Boys 10 to 17 Years of Age	Ratio of Delin-quency to 10,000 Boys	Number of Delin-quents	Number of Boys 10 to 17 Years of Age	Ratio of Delin-quency to 10,000 Boys
1913	371	3,209	1,156	49	876	559
1914	286	3,368	849	20	962	208
1915	395	3,523	1,121	56	1,047	535
1916	371	3,688	1,006	29	1,132	256
1917	380	3,847	988	41	1,218	337
1917	274	3,847	712	41	1,218	337
1918	324	4,007	809	41	1,303	315
1919	140	4,167	336	21	1,388	151
1920	105	4,326	243	11	1,474	75
1921	217	4,583	473	30	1,757	171
1922	357	4,841	737	71	2,039	348
1923	260	5,098	510	30	2,322	129
1924	249	5,356	465	26	2,604	100
1925	250	5,613	445	30	2,887	104
1926	160	5,870	273	17	3,170	53
1927	228	6,128	372	25	3,452	72
1928	256	6,385	401	26	3,735	70
Total, 1917–28	2,820	60,221	468	369	27,349	135

* All cases between 1913 and 1917 are those brought before the court; these are not included in the totals.

TABLE 21

NUMBER OF JUVENILE COURT CASES AND RATIOS OF DELINQUENCY IN HONOLULU FOR THE YEARS 1926–28*

(After Lind)†

Racial Groups	Number of Juvenile Court Cases	Ratio of Delinquency per Thousand
Hawaiian	208	169.7
Part Hawaiian	176	46.9
Portuguese	173	65.1
Porto Rican	51	167.1
Spanish	7	46.3
Other Caucasian	26	10.7
Chinese	114	26.8
Japanese	109	12.1
Korean	43	72.8
Filipino	49	108.1
Total	960‡	38.3

* Ratio per thousand of public and private school population for the city of Honolulu.

† A. W. Lind, "Some Ecological Patterns of Community Disorganization in Honolulu," *American Journal of Sociology,* XXXVI (September 1930), 215.

‡ The total number of cases includes four causes classified as "All Others," which do not figure in the rates of any of the racial groups mentioned above.

Misaki believes that the infrequency of Japanese juvenile delinquency is due primarily to close supervision of the children by adults, coupled with their comparative isolation from other racial groups, which makes it relatively easy for the small Japanese communities to know what is happening. He quotes one official in the Los Angeles Juvenile Hall to the effect that "the more Japanese children are Americanized the more they tend to fall into delinquency." Many of the first-generation Japanese feel that their children will be demoralized if they associate with children of other racial groups.

The cases are too few so far to determine whether or not juvenile delinquency is increasing among the Japanese-Americans at a faster rate than the increase in their population. From the Japanese publications it appears that the Japanese themselves believe that delinquency is increasing among the second generation. For example, this clipping appeared in the official organ of the New American Citizens League of San Francisco.

Crime and immorality are increasing among the Japanese in the United States at a rate such as to render active repressive efforts an urgent necessity.

Murder, banditry, issuance of false checks, peeping toms, and the like.

The most deplorable feature of the whole situation is that this tide of crime is in great part due to the youth—boys and often girls of the bobbed-hair type.

This is unfortunate but preventable. If the Japanese people are to become members of this nation, they must be better and more respectable citizens than their Caucasian brethren. Legally speaking they are Americans by birth. But socially they are still Japanese. It is just as important to be accepted socially, since in America society comes before the law. If the second generation Japanese are to become an integral part of American society, they must be more law-abiding, more educated, more decent, and in every way above others.[22]

Beach points out that in the case of the Chinese there has been a decrease in the number of commitments to the prisons, "but the rate of decrease in commitments is smaller than the rate of population decrease." On the other hand, "the Japanese population in California increased greatly (over 600 per cent) between 1900 and 1920; but the rate of increase in the number of Japanese committed to San Quentin was very much less (33.6 per cent) than the rate of population increase."[23]

The Survey of Race Relations points out:

The Oriental, apparently, has been of very little expense to the American community. Such records of relief agencies as have been studied indicate that the amount of relief given is very small. The extent of poverty, delinquency, and crime—in so far as dealt with by American agencies—is slight.

It appears that the organization of the Oriental communities, in every case, has grown up out of the necessity of meeting the strains of life under American conditions. Their organized groups have rendered a service, not only in imposing a discipline upon the members of the Oriental community but in protecting them from conflict with the larger white community outside. This has been apparently, and in the first instance, the origin of both the Chinese Six Companies and the Japanese Associations.

All the more intelligent immigrant groups, when subjected to prejudice, have set up similar institutions and organizations. An investigation relative to pauperism among immigrants, made by the United States Immigration Commission in forty-three cities, covering the years 1850–1908 inclusive, showed that the proportion of native-born who received aid was very much greater than that of foreign-born. This was especially true of the more recent immigrants to the United States from southern and southeastern Europe, against whom there has been noticeable prejudice.

The Mexican, on the other hand, is one of the most disorderly of immigrant population and has only the most primitive organizations for mutual aid and protection. There is reason to believe that the rapid increase of the Mexican population is likely to increase vastly the amount of disease, crime, and poverty; and thus to enhance the cost to the community of this immigration over and above the economic value of the Mexican population as a source of labor.[24]

---

22 *Pacific Citizen,* August 1, 1931.

23 W. G. Beach, *op. cit.,* p. 94.

24 *Tentative Findings of the Survey of Race Relations* (1925), pp. 11 and 12.

The fine record so far established by the Japanese as regards crime and juvenile delinquency means either that their upbringing has been effective as far as law observance is concerned or that their capacity to adapt themselves to new laws is pronounced. In the early days the Japanese, in one district at least, were almost as great gamblers as the Filipinos are now, drank far more, and tolerated houses of prostitution in their section of town. Owing to the responsibilities of establishing homes and raising families as well as to the efforts of several individuals, the Japanese have become the most law-abiding members of the region. The long story of the struggle which finally led to a real cleaning up of their portion of this particular district is inspiring.

HONESTY

The evidence seems to be fairly conclusive that in earlier days the Japanese were not as honest as could be desired. Their apologists have maintained that this condition was caused in part by lack of experience with the Anglo-Saxon "contract." If so, the evidence seems to be that they have adapted themselves to this new custom for our results indicate they are trusted by housewives next to Scotch and Scandinavian servants and more so than German, Irish, English, Chinese, Negro, or native American servants[25] (Table 22). In the case of retail credit ratings they are not yet rated as high as whites or Chinese. Here, however, Japanese first generation, relatively new to business life in this country, are contrasted with second and third generations who have grown up in the country.

A careful check at several libraries revealed the fact that Japanese children are held in high esteem by librarians. One said:

> We find them punctual, neat, and very rarely having fines to pay because they bring their books back on time. But when they do have fines, they know it, and bring the money along to pay it without "crabbing." They are much better than the whites in this respect. They are obedient and obey the rules of the library. My reaction is very favorable.

The first-generation Japanese are apparently unable to co-operate among themselves to any considerable degree. For example, the inhabitants of two small towns a few miles apart could very well support a good Japanese-language school, employing a bus to bring the children to school. As it is, they maintain two schools of small size with poorly

[25] Native American servants are second generation, whereas the other groups, except Negro, are first generation.

paid instructors chiefly because the two groups belong to different ken and are always fighting each other. One of our interviewers who studied this situation reports that "partnerships are seldom lasting and generally Japanese are not trustful of one another, although there are some striking exceptions."

TABLE 22

EFFICIENCY AND TRUSTWORTHINESS OF INDOOR SERVANTS*

Nationality	Efficiency				Trustworthiness			
	Number	General Rating	Percentage Very Low	Percentage Rated Very High	Number	General Rating	Percentage Very Low	Percentage Rated Very High
Scotch	15	4.6	7	80	15	4.8	0	80
Danish, Norwegian, Swedish	66	4.5	0	64	65	4.6	3	72
Japanese	86	4.4	2	62	83	4.7	0	66
Finnish	35	4.3	6	63	35	4.7	3	74
German	59	4.1	8	54	59	4.5	3	70
Chinese	51	4.1	6	45	51	4.4	2	53
Colored	70	4.1	9	51	68	4.2	3	43
Irish	41	4.0	7	51	41	4.4	2	63
Filipino	25	3.9	0	28	26	4.0	4	19
English, Canadian	30	3.8	10	47	30	4.3	0	60
Miscellaneous†	42	3.7	7	31	40	4.2	0	40
American	147	3.6	12	41	143	4.3	2	57
Total	667	4.1	7	50	656	4.4	2	59

* Based on reports from 252 housewives who could have had no idea that the object of the investigation was concerned primarily with the Japanese. The ratings assigned were from 5 to 1, where 5 is the highest, meaning "Very satisfactory efficiency" and "Implicit trust in them."

† Miscellaneous group includes the following: Indian, Mexican, French, Hungarian, Russian, Swiss, Korean, Italian, Portuguese, Polish, Hawaiian, Russian, Belgian, Chilean, Spanish, Jugo-Slav.

Fisher[26] quotes an American university professor who is intimately and sympathetically acquainted with the situation, as follows:

"Among these various factions a local Christian Oriental may acquire a certain degree of leadership and may exercise a moderating influence, but no such leader commands a majority following. This should not be surprising in the case

[26] Galen M. Fisher, *Relations between the Occidental and Oriental Peoples on the Pacific Coast of North America* (March 1928), p. 12; quoted by permission of the International Missionary Council, publishers.

of a Christian, since the non-Christians greatly preponderate, but it is said that no non-Christian leader, either, has long been followed by a majority of his fellow nationals.

"It is well known that their meetings are honeycombed with petty politics. The first generation Japanese are interested in agriculture, hence the Japanese Associations. The second generation are interested in city callings, hence the chambers of commerce, and the clash between the two, with the consuls favoring one, then the other."

It is not clear what is the cause of this lack of co-operation. It may be due to genuine lack of integrity. It may be due to the fact that the Japanese are divided into cliques resulting from differences in religion, in the ken from which they come in Japan, and in their business activities. And it may be due to lack of real leaders. It is possible that early bringing up in a more or less feudal organization where those who immigrated were used to looking up to others for leadership has so inculcated this attitude in them that they have not been able to adjust themselves to an entirely new environment. The second generation often express themselves rather forcibly to the effect that when they grow up there will be better co-operation.

SUMMARY

One may take exception to this or that test procedure employed here, one may disagree with the particular interpretation of results in this section or that, but one must be impressed with the fact that in practically every section the same result is obtained, namely, that the second-generation Japanese and the whites obtain nearly equal scores. And where one group does surpass the other (whites are superior in strength), it is offset in the next measure (Japanese are quicker in reaction). The accumulation of evidence from a battery of widely different tests makes clear that the differences between the two groups are slight in comparison to their likenesses. One only has to call to mind the results of similar comparisons between whites and Negroes, or between whites and American Indians, or between northern and southern Europeans, to perceive how remarkable the similarity is.

VIII. EDUCATION[1]

The degree of education possessed is a fairly good index, today, of social position. Possibilities of advancement, for either an individual or a racial group, may be judged in terms of ability to assimilate educational advantages.

The preceding chapter has shown that Japanese-Americans do not differ particularly from whites in mental ability. Are they doing equally good work in school? Are they securing the same amount of education?

Scholastic work may be evaluated in three ways: first, by amount of education obtained by the individual; second, by scores on standard educational tests and measurements; and, third, by the grades or marks assigned by teachers. Comparisons between Japanese and whites on these bases are given below.

Two other related problems are also considered: first, the effect of segregation of Japanese pupils in special schools upon their progress in scholastic work, and, second, the effect of attendance at Japanese-language schools upon scholastic performance in the public schools.

Before considering these topics, we devote a section to the educational attainment of first-generation Japanese in California.

EDUCATION OF JAPANESE IMMIGRANTS

The average school grade reached or finished by the Japanese included in our survey,[2] according to sex, age, and place of birth, is given in Table 23. First-generation males, for example, between the ages of twenty-one and twenty-seven years, born in Japan, have reached or finished grade 11 (corresponding to the third year of high school). The older the males are today, the less education they have received, leaving out of account those under twenty-one years, who presumably have not finished their education. The same thing holds for the first-generation females, but they average fully a year less schooling.

The amount of education recorded here for the older Japanese born in Japan seems somewhat high. The information is based on the schooling these people claim they secured many years ago. It is not known to

---

[1] The material in this chapter is based very largely upon: (1) Reginald Bell, *Public School Education of Second-Generation Japanese in California,* and (2) E. K. Strong, Jr., *Japanese in California.*

[2] As the survey was taken in the summer, "reached or finished" means the grade just finished for the great majority; those halfway through a school grade were credited with the grade they were in.

TABLE 23

EDUCATION AS INDICATED BY SCHOOL GRADE REACHED OR FINISHED*

Age Group†	School Grade of Males			School Grade of Females		
	Born in Japan	Born in Hawaii	Born in United States	Born in Japan	Born in Hawaii	Born in United States
7–13	4.5	*5.8*	3.6	3.6	*3.8*	3.6
14–20	9.9	8.9	9.5	9.4	9.7	9.4
21–27	11.0	10.8	12.5	8.9	10.0	12.0
28–34	9.7	9.7	12.3	8.6	8.6	*11.3*
35–41	9.5	8.9	*16.5*	7.6	*9.3*	...
42–48	8.8	...	*8.0*	6.5	...	*12.0*
49–55	7.2	...	...	5.2	...	...
56–62	6.9	...	...	4.2	...	...
63–69	6.0	...	...	*1.9*	...	...
70 up	*3.3*	...	...	...	...	...
Average of all of school age	8.6	9.9	6.0	7.6	9.1	5.8
Average over 20 years	8.6	10.2	12.5	7.6	9.3	12.0
Average between 21 and 34	10.1	10.4	12.5	8.7	9.4	12.0
Total count	2,418	144	2,664	1,910	77	2,477
Report omitted	54	2	33	49	0	21
Too young	15	4	811	18	2	771
No schooling	26	0	5	42	0	1
Total considered	2,349	138	1,820	1,843	75	1,685

* Based on survey. Figures in italics are based on less than ten cases.

† Data for 0–6-year group are not reported, as the children under 6 years were included in the "too young" group in the interviewing and data based solely on 6-year-olds would be misleading here. The 6-year-olds are included in the averages, however.

what extent the figures are correct, and to what extent they are false because of forgetfulness, the tendency to magnify one's past performances, or the more likely possibility of confusing the educational opportunities of Japan in their day with those of their children today. It seems best to view these figures as overstatements of the actual facts. There is no way of estimating the size of the error, if such exists. It is possible, however, that the figures in Table 23 are essentially correct. The educational system was sufficiently developed in Japan for these immigrants to have received the amount of education they claim.[3] The

[3] United States government reports on illiteracy of the Japanese are conflicting and of doubtful value, as the percentages are based on who answers "no" to the simple questions "Can you read?" "Can you write?" For example, in one volume

amount of schooling credited to the Japanese immigrants is in excess of what the average person of similar age received in Japan. The immigrants who were early pioneers to this country were naturally an enterprising lot. If they had already shown this trait as regards getting an education, then the figures may be taken at face value.

Writers on this subject always point out that the Japanese who came here were representative of different groups. For example, Millis speaks first of young men "seeking opportunities to study or better opportunities to earn a living . . . . They were of course drawn largely from the most intelligent and ambitious of the middle class." Second, there were older men, fewer in number, "who had failed or had found farming or wage labor in Japan unattractive." Third, were those who came by way of Hawaii, "a large percentage of whom had been drawn from the poorest and most ignorant class."[4]

What concerns us today is not who came but who stayed. Between 1890 and 1930 a total of 245,733 immigrants and non-immigrants are reported to have arrived.[5] But today only about 50 per cent of the Japanese population are of the first generation, i.e., 70,477, which is but 28 per cent of the arrivals. No safe deductions from data based on those who arrived can be made regarding those now here, unless one knows that those who remained are a typical sampling of the whole. And it is just this that we doubt very much. All of our data indicate that there are few who came from Hawaii now in the United States.[6] And the census figures prove that there are few old men here. Consequently, it appears that the first generation is made up very largely of the young men of whom Millis speaks, plus their wives. If this is true, it is all the easier to accept the figures in Table 23.

EDUCATION OF SECOND GENERATION

Table 23 gives also the average amount of schooling obtained by Japanese born in Hawaii and in the United States. The average for males between the ages of twenty-one and twenty-seven years born in

---

the percentage of 24.6 who can neither read nor write is given on page 99, and on page 150 there appears for males the percentage of 97.8 "who are able to read and write their native language" (see *United States Immigration Commission Reports* [1907–10], Vol. 1, pp. 99 and 150). For more detailed consideration, see E. K. Strong, Jr., *Japanese in California*, pp. 91–93.

4 H. A. Millis, *The Japanese Problem in the United States* (1915), p. 5. See a similar quotation from Mears, p. 96, above.

5 See p. 89.

6 See pp. 96–97.

the United States is grade 12.5, or half a year in college, and for the females it is grade 12.0, or graduation from high school. Those born in Hawaii make a poorer showing—grade 10.8 for the males and grade 10.0 for the females. But even these figures represent a surprisingly high average amount of education.

From other data secured in our survey it is possible to express the amount of education obtained by the second generation in this way:

Category	Males (Percentage)	Females (Percentage)
Have done graduate work	0.2	0.2
Have graduated from college	0.8	0.5
Have been in college	4.3	2.9
Have graduated from high school	8.4	8.0
Have been in high school	19.1	17.3
Have graduated from grammar school	24.4	22.2

In evaluating these figures one must remember that the entire group averages 9.9 years of age and only 12.1 per cent are eighteen years of age and over (see Table 14, p. 158). The figures will be quite different ten years from now when there are proportionately fewer under ten years of age and more over eighteen years of age.

It is often asserted that the Japanese farming class is distinctly inferior to the Japanese living in the cities. Our data make clear that the children in the cities average only one grade more schooling than those in the country. Evidently the sons and daughters of the Japanese farmer are just as capable of getting an education as the children of the city dweller, for a difference of one year is easily accounted for by less opportunity to attend school.

The United States–born have received their education primarily in this country—only 665 out of 5,100 have had part or all of their schooling in Japan. Not a single United States–born child has attended a Hawaiian school. The fact that only 13 per cent of the second generation have received part or all of their schooling in Japan, coupled with the fact that this preference for Japanese culture is gradually dying out, tends to disprove the contention that "large numbers of Japanese children . . . . return [from Japan] at a later date loyal and ideal Japanese citizens" (see p. 138).

When the Japan-born youths were asked how much education they expected to obtain, their replies averaged grade 12.2 (slightly better than graduation from high school) for the boys and grade 11.6 for the girls. The United States–born boys are planning for two years in college (grade 14.0) and the girls for one year less (grade 13.1). These expectations are about a year to a year and a half beyond what the older second generation have so far actually obtained.

Evidently the Japanese immigrants have had far better education than that with which they have been credited, and their children are taking full advantage of the public schools of California. Such data as we have suggest that in this respect they average as well as whites.

SCHOLASTIC WORK MEASURED BY EDUCATIONAL TESTS

The most comprehensive study of the mental ability of Japanese children in the United States is that made by M. L. Darsie in 1922–24.[7] He tested by means of the Stanford-Binet, the Army Beta, and the Stanford Achievement tests nearly seven hundred American-born Japanese children from six cities and three counties of California, including practically all of the children from ten to fifteen years of age in the cities, and a representative sampling of the country children. Excluding the strictly rural children there were left more than five hundred with whom English was a more familiar tongue than Japanese and whose performance could be satisfactorily compared with that of American children.

The mean educational ages derived from the raw scores of the Stanford Achievement Test are given in Table 24. Japanese children as compared with American norms show a mean retardation of 14.25 months in reading, 12.5 months in language, 1.75 months in arithmetic, and 6.0 months in general information. In spelling they average 2.75 months above American children. In information based on knowledge of American history and literature they are 4.0 months behind the average American. Their retardation based on a composite educational score is 6.25 months. Darsie concludes:

1. In reading and language Japanese children are markedly inferior to Americans.
2. In informational subjects depending partly or largely upon reading, Japanese are slightly inferior to American children.
3. In arithmetic and spelling the differences are negligible.
4. In penmanship, drawing, and painting Japanese children are superior to Americans.

---

[7] M. L. Darsie, "The Mental Capacity of American-Born Children," *Comparative Psychology Monographs,* Vol. III, No. 15 (1926).

TABLE 24

EDUCATIONAL AGES OF JAPANESE-AMERICANS, AS BASED ON EDUCATIONAL TESTS

(After Darsie)

Test	Yrs. Mo. 10-6	Yrs. Mo. 11-6	Yrs. Mo. 12-6	Yrs. Mo. 13-6
Paragraph reading	9-8	10-5	11-0	12-1
Sentence reading	9-11	10-9	11-4	12-6
Word reading	9-5	10-1	10-6	11-7
Composite reading	9-8	10-5	11-0	12-0
Language	9-10	10-6	11-1	12-5
Spelling	10-7	11-9	12-9	13-10
Arithmetic computation	10-4	11-4	12-8	14-2
Arithmetic reasoning	10-1	11-1	12-2	12-9
Arithmetic composite	10-3	11-3	12-5	13-6
Science information	....	10-11	11-2	12-1
History information	....	11-5	12-3	12-10
Composite	....	11-2	11-8	12-6
Composite educational age	10-1	11-0	11-11	12-11
Mean Japanese retardation (months)	5	6	7	7

Bell analyzed the achievement-test results available from the Sacramento School Survey[8] of 1928 for the Japanese children in the Lincoln School, which had, at the time of testing, 632 Japanese pupils in a total enrollment of 1,272. Scores of these pupils were available on three tests: Monroe's Standardized Silent Reading Scale (revised 1926), Monroe's General Survey Scale in Arithmetic, and the Morrison-McCall Spelling Scale, List 1. In comparison with the medians for the city as a whole, he found that

1. The Japanese average significantly higher in arithmetic at all grades except the low third and the high fifth.
2. Neither inferiority nor superiority is shown by the spelling-test scores.

[8] J. B. Sears, *Sacramento School Survey* (1928), pp. 535–36; for supporting data see Reginald Bell, "A Study of Certain Phases of the Education of Japanese in Central California" (unpublished Master's thesis, Stanford University, 1928).

3. The Japanese average significantly lower in reading comprehension at all grades except the high third, when both point scores and achievement ages based on point scores are studied. Reading rate scores show less inferiority.

McAnulty[9] reports a study of achievement- and intelligence-test results of 1,236 Japanese children in the Los Angeles, California, elementary schools. This was approximately 10 per cent of the total Japanese enrollment in the city. Records from the group are compared with those of 1,074 white children selected by a sampling method similar to that used in selecting the Japanese children. Unfortunately the white group have an average intelligence quotient of 105, which is slightly above the average for whites. The Japanese average 100.8 IQ. The achievement tests employed by McAnulty were, for the most part, the primary and secondary forms of the Ingraham-Clark tests of reading and vocabulary, the Los Angeles Elementary Reading Test, the Los Angeles Sentence Vocabulary Test, and the Los Angeles Diagnostic Test of Fundamentals of Arithmetic. She concludes:

The average achievement of the children in the Japanese group is up to the city norms in both reading comprehension and reading vocabulary. The achievement of the Japanese group is far above expectation in arithmetic fundamentals.

It is to be noted that all three of these investigators find the Japanese children somewhat more retarded in school than white pupils; Darsie reports six and a quarter months, while McAnulty finds them "retarded chronologically on the average of approximately three months, as compared with city norms."

Although the data relating to educational achievement are somewhat conflicting, in general the Japanese-Americans approximate the scholastic work of the whites. The earlier studies of Darsie and Bell show lower performance in school subjects calling largely for linguistic ability. In arithmetic and spelling they hold their own. McAnulty's study indicates equality of performance in reading and superiority in arithmetic.

SCHOOL GRADES IN HIGH SCHOOL

Bell says regarding the use of school marks:

Though teachers' marks are notoriously open to criticism as being partially subjective, founded upon varying individual standards, and frequently unreliable,

[9] Ellen A. McAnulty, "Achievement and Intelligence Test Results for Japanese Children Attending Los Angeles City Schools," *Los Angeles Educational Research Bulletin,* Vol. XI, No. 5 (January 1932), pp. 65–69.

still they are the means by which in practice teachers register their opinion not only of the success or failure of their pupils, but also of the quality of pupil-performance. Their bearing upon pupil progress is thus immediate, and they form, at least for the present, the only record of quality of school performance which is in common usage.[10]

As a basis of comparison for school grades of Japanese pupils there was already available in published form a comprehensive study of teachers' marks given by teachers in the Los Angeles high schools in 1927–28.[11] These marks are descriptive of the entire junior and senior high school population of the city, and include all pupils—foreign-born, native-born of foreign parents, and native-born of native parents. No racial selection has been made, so that Negroes, Chinese, Japanese, and Mexicans, as well as Caucasian groups, are represented. To contrast with the grades of this heterogeneous group, representative of the city as a whole, Bell obtained twenty thousand grades of 985 Japanese pupils from corresponding schools of Los Angeles.

Table 25 gives the school grades from these two groups in the senior high schools. The data indicate:

1. The Japanese excel in securing scholastic grades of A at every level, a superiority that is statistically significant at all levels except A12, when the cases of Japanese pupils are so few as to make generalizations based on them entirely unsound.
2. This same superiority of statistical significance appears again in regard to securing B's at all levels except the last two.
3. Naturally, with marked superiority in the A and B categories, the Japanese have fewer C, D, and E marks, except at the erratic A12 level.

Although the Japanese are superior to the whites in securing A and B grades, yet this superiority decreases steadily from grade B9 to grade 12, as is shown in Figure 5. The same figure shows marked increase among the Japanese of D and E marks as they go higher in school and marked decrease in the same respect for the total population.

The school children in the Los Angeles city survey were divided into four ability groups—superior, average, slow, and undifferentiated. The Japanese show statistically significant superiority to all except the superior group, and practical equality to that.

---

[10] Reginald Bell, *Public School Education of Second-Generation Japanese in California,* chapter iv.

[11] C. H. Nettels, "Teachers' Marks," *Los Angeles Educational Research Bulletin,* Vol. VIII, No. 6 (February 1929), pp. 5 ff.

TABLE 25

COMPARISON OF MARKS RECEIVED BY LOS ANGELES SENIOR HIGH SCHOOL PUPILS OF JAPANESE PARENTAGE AT VARIOUS GRADE LEVELS WITH THOSE RECEIVED BY LOS ANGELES SENIOR HIGH SCHOOL POPULATION

(After Bell)

	Scholastic Grade A Percentage	Scholastic Grade B Percentage	Scholastic Grade C Percentage	Scholastic Grade D Percentage	Scholastic Grade E Percentage	Scholastic Grades A + B Percentage	Scholastic Grades D + E Percentage
Grade B9							
2,315 Japanese pupils..........	36	38	21	5	0	74	5
9,873 total school population..	13	28	34	15	10	41	25
Difference and P.E.D.*......	+23±0.7	+10±0.8	−13±0.7	−10±0.6	−10±0.2	+33±0.7	−20±0.4
Grade A9							
2,164 Japanese pupils	37	37	21	5	0	74	5
6,418 total school population..	11	26	32	19	12	37	31
Difference and P.E.D........	+26±0.7	+11±0.8	−11±0.7	−14±0.5	−12±0.3	+37±0.8	−26±0.5
Grade B10							
1,955 Japanese pupils	28	35	26	8	3	63	11
21,171 total school population..	15	32	29	14	10	47	24
Difference and P.E.D........	+13±0.7	+ 3±0.8	− 3±0.7	− 6±0.4	− 7±0.3	+16±0.8	−13±0.5
Grade A10							
1,457 Japanese pupils	28	36	24	9	3	64	12
11,200 total school population..	14	30	29	17	10	44	27
Difference and P.E.D........	+14±0.8	+ 6±0.9	− 5±0.8	− 8±0.6	− 7±0.4	+20±0.9	−15±0.6
Grade B11							
899 Japanese pupils	25	33	30	9	3	58	12
13,564 total school population..	15	34	30	14	7	49	21
Difference and P.E.D........	+10±1.0	− 1±1.1	0±1.1	− 5±0.7	− 4±0.4	+ 9±1.1	− 9±0.8
Grade A11							
521 Japanese pupils	28	34	26	10	2	62	12
13,105 total school population..	14	33	31	15	7	47	22
Difference and P.E.D........	+14±1.3	+ 1±1.4	− 5±1.3	− 5±0.9	− 5±0.4	+15±1.5	−10±1.0
Grade B12							
190 Japanese pupils	26	37	23	11	3	63	14
9,314 total school population...	17	39	27	12	5	56	17
Difference and P.E.D........	+ 9±2.4	− 2±2.4	− 4±2.1	− 1±1.5	− 2±0.8	+ 7±2.4	− 3±1.7
Grade A12							
25 Japanese pupils	20	32	28	16	4	52	20
4,629 total school population...	21	39	27	11	2	60	13
Difference and P.E.D........	− 1±5.4	− 7±6.3	+ 1±6.1	+ 5±5.0	+ 2±2.6	− 8±6.8	+ 7±5.4

* Probable error of the difference.

Table 26 gives the data for comparing the performance of pupils of Japanese parentage with the performance of the total Los Angeles

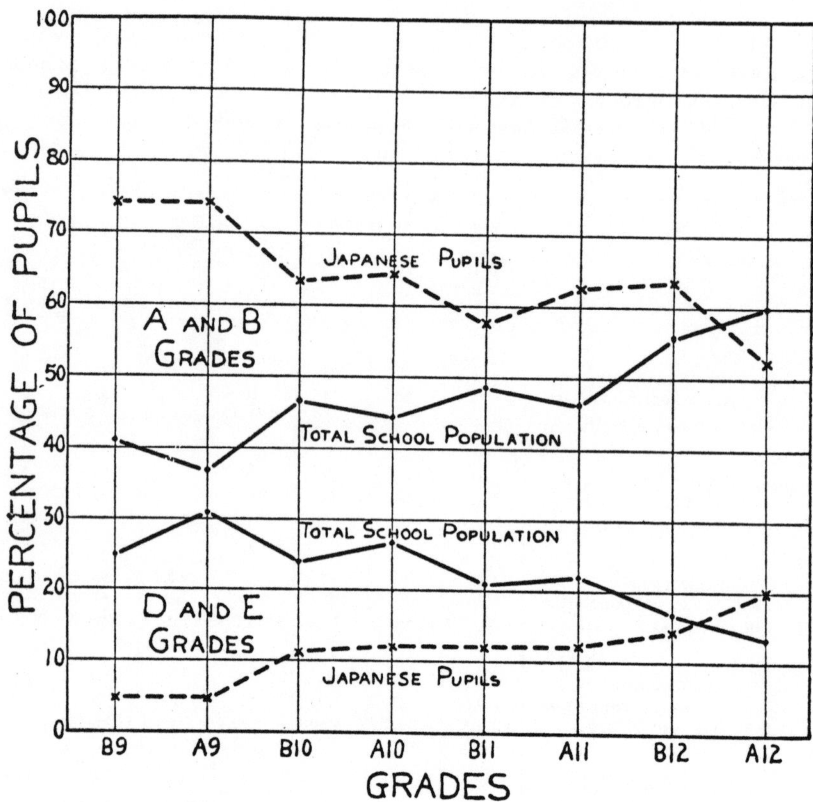

FIG. 5.—Comparison of grades received by Los Angeles senior high school pupils of Japanese parentage at various grade levels with those received by Los Angeles senior high school population as a whole.

group in the various divisions of subject-matter taught in the senior high schools. Bell concludes:

1. The Japanese have a larger percentage of A marks in all subjects except German where the difference is not statistically significant.
2. The largest differences in A marks in favor of the Japanese are in the subjects shorthand, clothing, foods, agriculture, and mechanical drawing, in that order.

It is of interest, and perhaps of vocational significance, to note that the Japanese-Americans are more strikingly superior to the heterogeneous group in the more distinctly non-academic school subjects. But it is to be emphasized that this does not mean Japanese inferiority in the academic subjects. As has been already stated, they are significantly superior in all subjects with the exception of German.

TABLE 26

COMPARISON OF MARKS RECEIVED BY LOS ANGELES SENIOR HIGH SCHOOL PUPILS OF JAPANESE PARENTAGE WITH THOSE RECEIVED BY THE LOS ANGELES SENIOR HIGH SCHOOL POPULATION IN THE VARIOUS SCHOOL SUBJECTS

(After Bell)

	Scholastic Grade A Percentage	Scholastic Grade B Percentage	Scholastic Grade C Percentage	Scholastic Grade D Percentage	Scholastic Grade E Percentage	Scholastic Grades A + B Percentage	Scholastic Grades D + E Percentage
Agriculture							
7 Japanese pupils	57	29	14	0	0	86	0
488 total school population	27	39	24	7	3	66	10
Difference and P.E.D.*	+30±12.7	—10±11.7	—10±8.9	— 7±0.8	— 3±0.5	+20±9.0	—10±0.9
Art and free-hand drawing							
465 Japanese pupils	49	33	14	3	1	82	4
5,857 total school population	25	40	24	7	4	65	11
Difference and P.E.D.	+24± 1.6	— 7± 1.5	—10±1.1	— 4±0.6	— 3±0.4	+17±1.3	— 7±0.7
Typing							
305 Japanese pupils	32	38	22	5	3	70	8
3,426 total school population	16	29	28	15	12	45	27
Difference and P.E.D.	+16± 1.9	+ 9± 1.9	— 6±1.7	—10±0.9	— 9±0.8	+25±1.9	—19±1.2
Junior business							
229 Japanese pupils	30	43	25	2	0	73	2
1,991 total school population	13	35	33	14	5	48	19
Difference and P.E.D.	+17± 2.1	+ 8± 2.3	— 8±2.1	—12±0.8	— 5±0.3	+25±2.1	—17±0.9
English							
1,724 Japanese pupils	19	36	31	12	2	55	14
20,968 total school population	12	33	31	14	10	45	24
Difference and P.E.D.	+ 7± 0.7	+ 3± 0.8	0±0.8	— 2±0.6	— 8±0.3	+10±0.8	—10±0.6
Practical arts: foods							
119 Japanese pupils	52	32	13	2	1	84	3
1,072 total school population	20	40	31	8	1	60	9
Difference and P.E.D.	+32± 4.0	— 8± 3.1	—18±2.3	— 6±1.0	0±0.6	+24±2.5	— 6±1.2
Practical arts: clothing							
220 Japanese pupils	59	28	10	2	1	87	3
1,667 total school population	19	41	31	7	2	60	9
Difference and P.E.D.	+40± 2.3	—13± 2.1	—21±1.6	— 5±0.8	— 1±0.5	+27±1.7	— 6±0.9
Latin							
165 Japanese pupils	42	30	21	5	2	72	7
2,434 total school population	22	32	24	11	11	54	22
Difference and P.E.D.	+20± 2.7	— 2± 2.5	— 3±2.2	— 6±1.2	— 9±0.9	+18±2.7	—15±1.5
Spanish							
724 Japanese pupils	27	34	26	11	2	61	13
6,114 total school population	13	27	29	18	13	40	31
Difference and P.E.D.	+14± 1.2	+ 7± 1.2	— 3±1.2	— 7±0.9	—11±0.5	+21±1.3	—18±0.9

* Probable error of the difference.

TABLE 26—*Continued*

	Scholastic Grade A Percentage	Scholastic Grade B Percentage	Scholastic Grade C Percentage	Scholastic Grade D Percentage	Scholastic Grade E Percentage	Scholastic Grades A + B Percentage	Scholastic Grades D + E Percentage
French							
107 Japanese pupils...........	29	32	29	7	3	61	10
1,849 total school population.	18	31	24	15	12	49	27
Difference and P.E.D.......	+11± 3.0	+ 1± 3.1	+ 5±3.0	− 8±1.8	− 9±1.2	+12±3.3	−17±2.1
German							
26 Japanese pupils............	12	46	35	0	7	58	7
247 total school population..	19	28	29	17	7	47	24
Difference and P.E.D.......	− 7± 5.7	+18± 8.6	+ 6±8.3	−17±1.6	0±4.4	+11±6.9	−17±3.8
Mathematics							
1,171 Japanese pupils.........	31	31	25	11	2	62	13
9,295 total school population.	13	28	28	18	13	41	31
Difference and P.E.D.......	+18± 0.9	+ 3± 1.0	− 3±0.9	− 7±0.7	−11±0.4	+21±1.0	−18±0.7
Mechanical drawing							
151 Japanese pupils...........	43	36	14	4	3	79	7
1,951 total school population.	16	33	30	14	7	49	21
Difference and P.E.D.......	+27± 2.8	+ 3± 2.7	−16±2.0	−10±1.2	− 4±1.0	+30±2.4	−14±1.5
Music							
256 Japanese pupils...........	40	37	19	4	0	77	4
7,352 total school population.	32	38	21	7	2	70	9
Difference and P.E.D.......	+ 8± 2.1	− 1± 2.1	− 2±1.7	− 3±0.9	− 2±0.1	+ 7±1.8	− 5±0.9
Physical education							
1,339 Japanese pupils.........	42	41	16	1	0	83	1
21,748 total school population	22	40	26	10	2	62	12
Difference and P.E.D.......	+20± 0.9	+ 1± 0.9	−10±0.7	− 9±0.2	− 2±0.1	+21±0.7	−11±0.2
Science							
919 Japanese pupils...........	27	36	28	8	1	63	9
11,735 total school population	11	30	33	18	8	41	26
Difference and P.E.D.......	+16± 1.0	+ 6± 1.1	− 5±1.0	−10±0.6	− 7±0.3	+22±1.1	−17±0.7
Practical arts: shop							
460 Japanese pupils...........	33	40	24	3	0	73	3
4,560 total school population.	15	40	33	10	2	55	12
Difference and P.E.D.......	+18± 1.5	0± 1.6	− 9±1.4	− 7±0.6	− 2±0.1	+18±1.5	− 9±0.6
Social studies							
947 Japanese pupils...........	26	38	27	8	1	64	9
15,505 total school population	14	33	31	15	7	47	22
Difference and P.E.D.......	+12± 1.0	+ 5± 1.1	− 4±1.0	− 7±0.6	− 6±0.3	+17±1.1	−13±0.7
Shorthand							
11 Japanese pupils............	73	18	9	0	0	91	0
1,804 total school population.	20	30	26	12	12	50	24
Difference and P.E.D.......	+53± 9.1	−12± 7.8	−17±5.9	−12±0.5	−12±0.5	+41±5.9	−24±0.7
Bookkeeping							
181 Japanese pupils...........	31	33	27	5	4	64	9
3,554 total school population.	17	33	30	11	9	50	20
Difference and P.E.D.......	+14± 2.4	0± 2.4	− 3±2.3	− 6±1.1	− 5±1.0	+14±2.5	−11±1.5

Comparison by Bell at the junior high school level shows almost the same results as for the senior high school level. There is the same tendency for Japanese to have decreasing success in getting A and B marks as they go from grade B7 to grade A9, and conversely the tendency to exhibit an increase in the number of D and E grades.

When a total of 36,014 marks for 1,823 Japanese pupils in forty-seven high schools in Los Angeles, San Diego, Fresno, Stockton, Sacramento, and San Francisco were similarly compared with the heterogeneous group from Los Angeles, substantially the same results were obtained.

How shall we explain the facts that Japanese pupils in Los Angeles have about the same IQ as the average pupil and score about the same on educational tests but obtain strikingly better grades? It may be that they possess to a greater degree than whites those qualities which endear pupils to a teacher; that is, they are more docile, occasion less disciplinary trouble, and give the appearance of being busy and striving to do their best. Such characteristics are in harmony with the results obtained on the Bernreuter Personality Test (see p. 175). Another explanation would be that they come from poorer homes than the average and early realize that they must make their own way in the world; in consequence, they are better motivated to do their best. This is the explanation advanced by several white high-school and college students, who added: "We don't have to work so hard, you know." In this connection, it would be most appropriate to ascertain how the school grades of other second-generation immigrant groups compare with those of the average pupil.

How also shall we explain the fact that the superiority in terms of school grades of Japanese-Americans steadily lessens from grade B7 to grade A12? One explanation would be in terms of a difference in type of mental growth of Japanese-Americans and Americans in general. That is, the former may mature more rapidly and then taper off in development, while the Americans in general continue their mental development throughout high-school days. This explanation should be investigated, but it seems unlikely to the writer that it will be substantiated.

A second explanation would be in terms of the assumption that a larger percentage of Japanese-Americans than of Americans in general continue in school through the senior high school, which would mean that the former are compared successively with better and better samplings of the abler ones in the American groups. This would explain the data given above. Unfortunately, so far, we have been unable to obtain the necessary data to check this assumption.[12]

In summary, four things stand out as clearly substantiated by the data:

1. The pupils of Japanese parentage in the junior and senior high schools of the cities of California are more successful than their fellow non-Japanese students if one judges on the basis of high (A and B) marks received.

2. The same superiority is noted if one judges by fewer low (D, E, or F) grades.

3. Pupils of Japanese parentage succeed relatively better in non-academic than in academic subjects.

4. The percentage advantage of Japanese pupils in getting A and B marks lessens or disappears as they move from grade B7 to grade A12, and their advantage in securing fewer D and E marks lessens even more strikingly.

SEGREGATION OF JAPANESE PUPILS

Racial segregation in the public schools raises two sets of questions. The first centers around the reason for segregation, as Bell has pointed out.[13]

> What led to segregation? Are there fundamental, valid causative factors, based on known mental and educational differences between the children of Chinese and Japanese immigrants on the one hand and those of Caucasian parents on the other? Are the social ideals and behavior of the one group so diverse from those of the other that school administrators have found it essential to separate them? Or is

---

[12] Of the total school population of the city of Los Angeles, 3.3 per cent are Japanese, and this group contributes but 0.7 per cent of those requesting work permits to attend continuation school and but 0.5 per cent to work outside school hours. The corresponding percentages for whites, not including Mexicans, are 78.8, 79.2, and 92.5. Commenting on these figures, Dr. Elizabeth L. Woods, superviser of educational research and guidance, writes: "These percentages seem to bear out your belief that the Japanese staying in school are a higher percentage of cases than are the white children."

The State Department of Education "regrets its inability to provide the information requested." The extent to which different groups are continuing in school should be investigated.

[13] Reginald Bell, "A Study of the Educational Effects of Segregation upon Japanese Children in American Schools" (unpublished Ph.D. thesis, Stanford University, 1933), p. 1.

the vastly important but propaganda-based fact of race prejudice the fundamental underlying cause?[14]

The second set of questions centers around the results of segregation. What are the effects upon the educational progress and social and civic attitudes of the children of Chinese and Japanese parentage of this segregation in American schools? Do either the one group or the other do better work in school because of the absence of the other in their classes and in their school associations? Do the children of the Asiatic immigrants progress more rapidly and more satisfactorily when they are regarded as a separated unit in the educational scheme, separately housed and taught? Do the children of Caucasian parentage in these school districts where there is such a large proportion of Chinese and Japanese families progress more satisfactorily when the children of the latter are separated from them in their educational and recreational activities? Or are the effects of segregation negligible one way or the other?

The only one of the many aspects of this problem selected by Bell for study was: "How, if at all, does segregation affect the educational status and progress of children of Japanese parentage who are attending American schools?"

The study was based upon "the school children of Japanese parentage in the third to the eighth grades in eight school districts in Sacramento and Placer Counties, California, namely, the Oriental schools at Courtland, Florin, Isleton, and Walnut Grove, and the non-segregated schools of Enterprise District, Loomis Union Grammar, Penryn, and Siena District." From the school population of these two sets of schools, two equivalent groups were selected whose progress over a period of eighteen months was measured by performance on reliable, comprehensive achievement tests (Stanford Achievement Test). In securing equivalence, the following factors were regarded: (1) general

---

[14] Undoubtedly one cause of segregation of school children by nationality or race is undue concentration in one district. No one particularly objects to the presence of a few foreigners, but when they outnumber your own children's group the matter is more serious. Although the Japanese constitute only 1.7 per cent of the population of California, yet nearly 50 per cent of the school enrollment of the Lincoln School in Sacramento is of that race. And in some country districts the situation is very much worse from this point of view. For example, in the Bouldin district near Stockton, 118 of the total minor population of 125 are Japanese. The really surprising aspect of this subject is that segregation has been established and since maintained in only four school districts (listed below) and in each case the total number of pupils was small and the Orientals constituted half or more. (The San Francisco segregation situation is discussed on pp. 40–41.)

See R. H. Thomson, "Events Leading to the Order to Segregate Japanese Pupils in the San Francisco Public Schools" (unpublished Ph.D. thesis, Stanford University, 1932), for the historical development of segregation.

intelligence, school ability or aptitude for scholastic success; (2) chronological age; (3) school grade; and (4) sex.[15]

When the two sets of pupils representative of segregated and non-segregated schools were first compared in October 1929, it was found that the latter were statistically superior to the former on all tests except arithmetic reasoning, history and literature, and language usage; and on the first and third of these the critical ratio[16] is so large as to be highly suggestive of statistical significance. When the two sets of pupils were similarly tested seven months later (May 1930), the differences in scores between them were quite considerably reduced. On only two tests were the differences then statistically significant. Eighteen months later (February 1931) the differences between the two groups had become still smaller. This decrease in superiority "goes so far that on two tests the advantage appears to swing from the non-segregated to the segregated group . . . . On all tests except arithmetic computation and history and literature the segregated group makes a larger gain than the non-segregated."

On the face of these returns Japanese children in segregated schools are better off than those in non-segregated schools, for on nearly every school subject they advanced more rapidly. But is this conclusion valid? Bell believes not. By a careful analysis of the individual items of the Binet Test he shows that the segregated children scored lower on the linguistic items, in proportion to the remaining items, than did the non-segregated children. He concludes that the segregated children at first obtained too low intelligence scores because of the linguistic handicap of not knowing the English language. Because of this situation the segregated children were actually superior to what their Binet intelligence scores indicated, and so were actually superior to the non-segregated children with whom they were compared. Because of this they advanced more rapidly in their school work than the non-segregated.

When all the details of this study are taken into account a good guess would be that the rate of progress in school subjects is affected

---

[15] Bell determined with great care that the two sets of schools were approximately equal as regards caliber of teachers and their interest in Japanese children, departmentalization of teaching, curriculum and time allotment, length of school year, and class size.

[16] Critical ratio, as used by Bell, is the quotient obtained by dividing a difference between two means by the probable error of that difference. A critical ratio of 3.0 or greater is assumed to indicate that the difference is significant statistically.

very little by whether the pupils are in segregated or non-segregated schools, such as are to be found in Sacramento County. At the same time it is quite clear that the Japanese children in segregated schools are more backward in the use of the English language than in the non-segregated schools. It is not clear whether or not this handicap is overcome as they progress through the segregated school. It seems difficult to believe that it is, for after all one presumably learns English more rapidly on the playground than in the schoolroom. There are still some knotty questions to be answered here.

One such question pertains to the white children. Do they gain or lose in mastery of the English language when they are in a school with few foreigners in contrast to a school where they are greatly outnumbered by foreigners?

Segregation as it affects Japanese in California is distinctly more an academic than a practical problem. For there are today only four schools in which Japanese are segregated. These are small schools; and there is no movement to increase their number.

EFFECT OF ATTENDANCE AT JAPANESE-LANGUAGE SCHOOLS

Many non-English-speaking peoples who have come to America have established private schools where their children may learn the parents' native language and some of the history, traditions, and customs of their native land. The Japanese have been no exception to this practice. Both in Hawaii and on the mainland they have established many Japanese-language schools. The writer has found widespread interest in them among the Japanese, but not all are favorably disposed to them. Many of the second generation feel that attendance at public schools should supply adequate schooling. But a number of the older second generation support their parents' views, maintaining that a Japanese should know how to read, write, and speak Japanese.

Judging from our survey of the Japanese in California, about 69 per cent of both sexes of the United States–born Japanese have attended Japanese-language schools for an average of 3.0 years for the entire group. If only those between the ages of fourteen and thirty-four years are considered, the average is raised to 4.4 years. Hawaii-born Japanese women now in California average 4.0 years and the men 5.5 years.[17] The foregoing figures make clear that about one-third have not

---

[17] E. K. Strong, Jr., *Vocational Aptitudes of Second-Generation Japanese in the United States,* p. 116.

attended these schools at all and the remainder have spent about six years in them.

What are the arguments in favor of the Japanese-language schools?[18] First, the common language binds the first and the second generations more closely together. This is important, since the tendency among all races that have come to America has been for the second generation to break away from the control of their parents, looking down upon them as ignorant of American ways. Miss Gretchen Tuthill expresses this point:

> The great gulf which exists between parents and children, since so few American-born Japanese children understand enough of the language of their fathers to use it freely, deprives both parents and children of the full benefits of family life as they should exist in normal home conditions. One of the children from a Japanese home where much English is spoken was heard saying, "My mother says she is jealous of us, that even in our dreams we speak English. She cannot always understand what we are saying." It is in this way that the young people slip out from under the guiding influence of the older minds.[19]

Reverend Mr. Kyogoku, chief priest at the Buddhist Church in Fresno, and superintendent of the largest Japanese-language school in the district, says:

> The language school is very important as a link between the first and second generation, so that parents and children can talk and understand each other's problems better; and so the parents can help keep the children straight on the moral side and give them advice. The second generation child who does not understand Japanese well is often misled. This is the most important function of the school.

A second reason for the language school is that it serves as a unifying social organization in the community. The Boy Scouts, Girl Re-

---

[18] The California State Law (effective June 30, 1921) did require that the teachers in these schools should pass an examination in American history and show ability to read, write, and speak English. Each school was required to secure a permit from the Superintendent of Public Instruction, which could be withdrawn at any time if the law was not complied with. Instruction for those under seventeen was limited to one hour a day after the close of public schools and to six hours all told per week. With the decision of the Supreme Court in the case of *Farrington* v. *Tokushige,* the California Attorney-General has ruled the California Foreign-Language School Law unconstitutional, and all legal requirements are waived. Ichihashi states that "the local school boards in the [Japanese language] association have so far retained the requirement that their teachers be able to speak both English and Japanese and must be graduates of at least the middle school in Japan" (Y. Ichihashi, *Japanese in the United States,* p. 330; see also R. M. C. Littler, *The Governance of Hawaii,* pp. 138–42; and Reginald Bell, *Public School Education of Second-Generation Japanese in California,* chapter iv).

[19] Master's thesis, University of Southern California, 1924.

serves, and religious groups and other similar organizations develop social and moral ideals and standards among Americans. In many Japanese communities the language school is the dominant factor in these respects. Here the children are taught, in addition to the Japanese language, the moral and cultural principles underlying Japanese civilization and the common practices of American life.

A third argument for the schools is that knowledge of the Japanese language is of help, in many cases a necessity, in securing vocational opportunities. This argument is valid only if the Japanese really master that language, which our evidence (see p. 168) would indicate is not the case.

Finally, the language schools raise the self-esteem of both generations of Japanese. In a country where they have been looked down upon and ill-treated it is natural for them to develop inferiority complexes. A study of what Japan stands for and has accomplished, a knowledge of its literature and art, an appreciation of its ancient culture and its recent advancement, all tend to increase the student's respect for his race and so for himself. Such study causes the young to appreciate their parents' background and point of view and so decreases the too numerous opportunities for misunderstanding and conflict.

All these advantages may be conceded and yet there may remain the practical objection to these schools on the ground that they are attempting the well-nigh impossible, as far as the majority of Japanese are concerned. There is no question but that the superior child can successfully carry the work required in the public school and the language school. But the evidence seems to be quite conclusive that the average and inferior child cannot do this. The data already presented indicate very clearly that few Japanese are mastering the English language to such an extent that they will not be handicapped in mingling with the white population, and the evidence seems to be equally clear that they are not obtaining a real mastery of the Japanese language. Ichihashi agrees:

> Generally speaking, these schools have been unsuccessful in their primary function—that of imparting a knowledge of the Japanese language to American-born children of Japanese descent—although they have done remarkably well in some other respects, in particular, in teaching proper conduct and behavior. . . . . The relative failure of the Japanese-language schools in this country to impart a knowledge of that tongue seems but natural; the achievement of real success by them is a hope beyond realization.[20]

---

[20] Y. Ichihashi, *op. cit.*, pp. 331–32.

Yoshioka, on the basis of rather scanty data, it is true, finds that children starting rather late in their study of Japanese catch up quite quickly to those of their own age who have studied much longer.[21] If this is true, the study of a second language could well be deferred to a later age. He finds further that

> the younger children were reacting in language study mainly on a mere sense-memory level, while the older ones were reacting on an ideational or meaning level. The second language for the younger ones seems to be just so much additional sense-memory to be associated with an object, while for the older it arouses an ideational content or meaning of its own associated with an object. The second language for the younger ones requires one more sound or form to be memorized, but for the older ones it may arouse a constellation of ideas in reference to an object distinct from that recalled by the first language. In other words, the younger are reacting unilingually while the older are reacting more truly bi-lingually.
>
> It is suggested that bilingualism in young children is a hardship and devoid of apparent advantage, because bilingualism appears to require a certain degree of mental maturation for its successful mastery.[22]

In endeavoring to determine the effect of segregation of Japanese-Americans in special schools Bell[23] noted that a larger percentage of segregated Japanese than of non-segregated Japanese attended Japanese-language schools. Mindful of the work of Yoshioka, he investigated the possible effect of attendance at the language schools upon performance in the public schools. Two methods were employed: first, a comparison of the scores on the Stanford Achievement Test of those attending language schools with those not attending, the two groups being carefully selected so that mental age, chronological age, school grade, and sex were held constant; second, partial correlation technique.

---

[21] Joseph G. Yoshioka, "A Study of Bilingualism," *Pedagogical Seminary and Journal of Genetic Psychology,* XXXVI (1929), 473–79.

[22] Smith finds that Oriental children attending foreign-language schools make lower scores on reading and general English tests even when paired with children of equal intelligence scores: "Intensive study of the errors made by Oriental children in reading seems to point toward a definite confusion of orientation among those children that attend two schools, which is probably a factor in their delayed progress in reading. Children may not be quite so disturbed by the different reading directions if they do not enter both schools at the same time" (M. E. Smith, "The Direction of Reading and the Effect of Foreign-Language School Attendance on Learning to Read," *Journal of Genetic Psychology,* Vol. XL, No. 2 [June 1932], p. 449).

[23] Reginald Bell, *Public School Education of Second-Generation Japanese in California,* chapter vii.

His results indicate no effect of language-school attendance upon achievement scores in the public schools.

RECOMMENDATIONS REGARDING ACQUISITION OF THE ENGLISH AND JAPANESE LANGUAGES

Some knowledge of Japanese appears desirable for all of the second generation. As has already been pointed out, such facility is needed in order to insure proper morale within the family and the Japanese group. It is this relationship which is seemingly so largely responsible for the low rate of juvenile delinquency reported in chapter vii. Furthermore, the second generation need to know of the achievements of their race, its history, literature, art, and recent economic development. They need this knowledge, among other reasons, in order to offset the feeling of inferiority which any second-generation individual is apt to acquire in a new environment.

The Japanese language is an exceedingly difficult one to acquire. For that reason, it would seem best to plan that the rank and file of the second generation should acquire real facility in English and only sufficient Japanese to meet the needs of ordinary family and group activity. The more intelligent and industrious should, in addition, acquire a far better grasp of this language. But this will necessitate more time than can be given to the subject during grammar-school days.

In the light of these considerations it seems to the writer that the best possible solution is to be obtained in some such way as this:

First, the work of the Japanese-language schools should be continued. In this way the Japanese language and culture will be transmitted to the second generation. But the conduct of these schools should be controlled in the light of developments to be brought about as soon as possible, as outlined below.

Second, study of Japanese should be introduced into certain junior and senior high schools, as a substitute for French or German. In the Palo Alto (California) schools those who are proficient in English may commence French in the seventh grade, otherwise in the ninth grade. Some such provision might be introduced regarding Japanese. This will provide instruction at the age when most of the second generation drop out of the language schools and would make possible more advanced instruction, which is badly needed. It will also give an opportunity for some whites to study the language, which from many angles seems to be desirable. (The writer knows of three white boys who have attended Japanese-language schools for this purpose, and one white high-school student asked for credit in the subject to meet entrance requirements at Stanford University.) As a matter of national policy there should be Americans who can understand Japanese. There is all the more need for this in connection with trade with Japan, unless we intend the Japanese to dominate there. At the present time "35.9 per cent of Japan's total export and import trade is with the United States" and this "trade, both export and import, has been increasing relatively to the total."[24] This trade with Japan constitutes 8.0 per cent of the entire foreign trade of the United States.[25] Trade with the Orient is destined to be much more important in the future.

Third, a course in the geography, history, and economic development of Japan and China, with proper consideration of their art and literature, should be given in certain high schools. Such a course is badly needed for the best development of American citizens of Japanese ancestry and it is equally desirable for other citizens growing up on the Pacific Coast. It is ridiculous to extol the usual courses about Greece and Rome as cultural and to classify a similar course about Japan as purely vocational. The latter can be made quite as cultural as the former; it will have the further advantage of being useful.[26]

Fourth, the present courses in American universities regarding the Japanese language and culture need to be strengthened materially. There are too few such courses all told.

Unless the development of commerce with Japan is to be left to the

---

[24] H. G. Moulton, *Japan, an Economic and Financial Appraisal* (1931), p. 257.

[25] Total exports to Japan in 1932 were $134,537,384, which was 8.3 per cent of the total export trade of the United States (6.4 per cent in 1931). Total imports from Japan in 1932 were $134,011,311, which was 10.1 per cent of the total import trade of the United States (9.9 per cent in 1931). Announced by the Department of Commerce, February 3, 1933.

[26] A letter from Mr. A. E. Holden, secretary of the Japan Society of Seattle, indicates that there has been some discussion in Seattle regarding the introduction into the high schools of courses in the Japanese language and also in Japanese history and literature.

See also E. C. Carter, *China and Japan in Our University Curricula* (1929), for a survey of what is offered by American universities in this field. Some 281 courses are reported, 66 of which are given in three Western institutions—Stanford University, the University of California, and the University of Washington. Of these courses, 152 are in the departments of history and political science and only 28 are language courses, one of which is at Stanford University, eleven are at the University of California, and four are at the University of Washington. For a brief survey of courses on China and Japan offered in secondary schools, see *Bulletin of the American Council, Institute of Pacific Relations,* November 3, 1933.

Japanese, many of whose leaders speak both Japanese and English, some attention must be given this subject, for at the present time Americans, aside from the second-generation Japanese and a very few others, mostly missionaries, know no Japanese and are not interested in the customs or culture of Japan.

Such recommendations appear, moreover, to be about as valuable as any which can be presented from the standpoint of aiding the Japanese to earn a satisfactory living in this country. Success in many occupations is dependent upon the minimization of difference in appearance. Mastery of good English is within the power of the Japanese-Americans, but the educational system of the country should be adapted so as to aid them in this respect.

SUMMARY

1. The first-generation Japanese immigrants claim to have had about eight years of schooling in Japan. This seems high in terms of the educational facilities in Japan at the time they were children and in terms of what the average American of their age has secured.

2. The second-generation Japanese who are between twenty-one and twenty-seven years of age report graduation from high school as their average school attainment. Japanese-American boys report they plan an average of two years in college, the girls one year less.

3. When compared with whites on standard educational tests, grammar-school Japanese-Americans score somewhat lower on the whole in school subjects calling largely for linguistic ability; in arithmetic and spelling they are equal to or superior to whites.

4. On the basis of school marks Japanese-Americans are distinctly superior to whites in junior and senior high schools.

5. Japanese pupils in the four segregated schools are inferior to other Japanese pupils in non-segregated schools in linguistic attainments. Progress in school as measured by educational tests is apparently little affected by segregation.

6. Attendance at Japanese-language schools has no effect upon achievement scores in the public schools.

7. Japanese-Americans from rural districts are obtaining only one year less of schooling than those from urban districts.

8. Only 665 out of 5,100 second-generation Japanese have received a part or all of their education in Japan. The evidence is fairly clear that the tendency to send young children to Japan for their education is waning.

IX. OCCUPATION[1]

Two sources are utilized here for occupational information. There is, first, the census taken by the Japanese government in 1930 (last column in Table 27), and, second, our own survey of the same year (columns 1–11 of Table 27). The latter represents 9.9 per cent of the Japanese in California, or more accurately 15.6 per cent of approximately two-thirds of the Japanese, i.e., those living in the counties of Fresno, Los Angeles, Monterey, Sacramento, San Francisco, and Santa Clara. Our survey places proportionately more emphasis upon the urban population and the fishing industry, and consequently reports a smaller percentage engaged in agriculture and a larger percentage in fishing than the Japanese census.

OCCUPATIONAL DISTRIBUTION

Fully half of the Japanese in California are engaged in agricultural pursuits (see Table 27). Not quite one-fifth operate small retail businesses. Five per cent are engaged in more general business activities. About one-seventh are common laborers, domestic servants, and fishermen, while only one per cent are skilled workmen. Two per cent are to be found in the professions and five per cent in miscellaneous activities. This distribution is quite unusual. It is, however, about what should be expected, for these immigrants started as common laborers on the farm or in the city and they have advanced themselves by becoming managers and owners of farms or of retail stores. It is to be noted that they have not entered the skilled trades nor are they found working in manufacturing concerns to any extent.

A Japanese is distinctly one who owns his business. These businesses are very small, requiring the services on the average of one-half of an employee, not counting members of the family. Today 14 per cent own their farms and 36 per cent are renters, so that there exists in farming as in business this same tendency to own the activity by which a livelihood is earned.

As the anti-alien land laws[2] prohibit first-generation Japanese from buying or even renting agricultural land, the query naturally arises as to the significance of the foregoing figures regarding ownership of land. Those reported as owners could legally be so if they acquired title

---

[1] The material in this chapter is based upon E. K. Strong, Jr., *Japanese in California,* chapter vi.

[2] See p. 44 for statement as to nature of these laws.

before the laws went into effect. Our interviewers succeeded in obtaining the confidence of the Japanese communities in which they worked and

TABLE 27

OCCUPATIONS OF MALE JAPANESE IN CALIFORNIA IN 1930*

Occupation	Born in Japan									Born in United States		Japanese Census 1930‡ Percentage
	Owner	Renter	Manager	Foreman	Skilled	Unskilled	Helper	Total Number†	Percentage	Total Number†	Percentage	
Agriculture	(1)	(2)	(3)	(4)	(5)	(6)	(7	(8)	(9)	(10)	(11)	(12)
Florist	52	31	1	..	..	20	4	108	...	5	...	...
Gardener	3	..	..	3	62	45	..	113	...	3	...	...
Nursery	14	5	..	6	..	10	..	35	...	2	...	...
Small fruits	6	44	4	2	..	9	1	66	...	5	...	...
Tree fruits	19	13	9	20	..	63	..	124	...	5	...	...
Truck	16	190	6	7	..	43	2	266	...	9	...	...
General	5	17	1	11	..	82	1	118	...	9	...	...
Total	115	300	21	49	62	272	8	830	38.3	38	6.3	54.3
Fishing	148	...	..	..	3	117	..	268	12.3	2	0.3	2.3
Domestic service	...	...	..	..	..	62	2	64	3.0	2	0.3	5.5
Business rendering service												
Barber shop	23	...	..	..	1	3	..	27	...	..	...	...
Bath house	6	...	..	..	..	..	..	6	...	..	...	...
Dry cleaning	33	...	..	..	..	..	1	34	...	..	...	...
Filling station	2	...	..	..	..	..	..	2	...	..	...	...
Hotel	53	...	5	..	..	1	..	59	...	1	...	...
Restaurant	64	...	1	..	1	4	1	71	...	4	...	...
Cook	...	...	..	..	20	..	..	20	...	..	...	...
Waiter	...	...	..	..	..	3	..	3	...	..	...	...
Laundry	9	...	..	..	..	13	..	22	...	3	...	...
Massage	8	1	..	..	..	..	..	9	...	..	...	...
Pool hall	17	1	..	..	..	1	..	19	...	..	...	...
Shoe repair	6	...	..	..	1	..	..	7	...	..	...	...
Tailor shop	13	...	..	..	3	1	..	17	...	1	...	...
Total	234	2	6	..	26	26	2	296	13.6	9	1.5	10.0

* Based on the writer's own survey. Totals include a few cases for which no rank was reported. If a man was engaged in several businesses, such as operating a barber shop, pool room, and candy store, he was assigned to the one that appeared to be the most important. Many such decisions were highly subjective. A man temporarily out of work or retired was assigned to the occupation he evidently considered to be his; the occupational rank was coded as "X" (not considered). Fortunately there were few such cases.

† Occupational rank was frequently not given. All such are included in the total for the occupation but do not appear in the subgroups.

‡ Includes California and also Colorado, Nevada, and Utah.

TABLE 27—*Continued*

Occupation	Born in Japan									Born in United States		Japanese Census 1930 Percentage
	Owner	Renter	Manager	Foreman	Skilled	Unskilled	Helper	Total Number	Percentage	Total Number	Percentage	
Retail stores	(1)	(2)	(3)	(4)	(5)	(6)	(7	(8)	(9)	(10)	(11)	(12)
Book store	6	...	2	..	..	2	..	10	...	..	...	...
Dry goods	18	...	1	..	..	9	..	28	...	4	...	...
Drug	15	...	..	..	..	1	..	16	...	..	...	...
Electrical	2	...	1	..	..	2	..	5	...	..	...	...
Fruit and vegetable	27	...	..	..	..	10	..	37	...	4	...	...
Grocery and market	47	...	3	..	1	20	..	71	...	14	...	...
Hardware	7	...	..	..	..	2	..	9	...	5	...	...
Jewelry	20	...	4	..	..	7	1	32	...	4	...	...
Soft drinks	19	...	..	..	..	3	..	23	...	1	...	...
Sporting goods	3	...	..	..	..	1	..	4	...	1	...	...
General	24	...	2	..	..	6	..	32	...	..	...	...
Total	188	...	13	..	1	63	1	267	12.3	33	5.5	7.8
Business employing common labor												
Packing and canning	1	...	3	3	1	10	..	18	...	4	...	...
Taxi	1	...	..	..	..	1	..	2	...	..	...	...
Trucking	16	...	..	..	..	11	..	27	...	6	...	...
General	3	...	1	1	..	11	..	16	...	2	...	...
Total	21	...	4	4	1	33	..	63	2.9	12	2.0	5.8
Business employing skilled labor												
Cabinet makers	9	...	..	..	..	4	..	13	...	1	...	...
Electricians	...	...	..	..	..	..	..	..	...	1	...	...
Moving-picture operators	2	...	..	..	1	..	..	3	...	..	...	...
Musicians	...	...	..	..	..	..	..	1	...	..	...	...
Photographers	7	...	..	..	..	..	..	7	...	1	...	...
Plumbers	1	...	..	..	..	..	..	1	...	..	...	...
Printers	...	...	..	..	11	3	..	14	...	2	...	...
Theatrical people	...	...	4	..	..	..	..	5	...	..	...	...
Miscellaneous	2	...	..	..	2	..	..	4	...	..	...	...
Mechanics, garage	14	...	1	..	6	3	..	25	...	4	...	...
Total	35	...	5	..	20	10	..	73	3.4	9	1.5	1.2
Manufacturing	16	...	..	..	..	..	..	16	0.7	0	0	0.8
Wholesale												
Import—export	13	...	4	..	1	2	..	23	...	1	...	...
Wholesale food	11	...	2	..	..	..	..	13	...	..	...	...
Wholesale non-food	...	...	..	..	..	1	..	1	...	..	...	...
Total	24	...	6	..	1	3	..	37	1.7	1	0.2	1.1

TABLE 27—*Concluded*

Occupation	Born in Japan									Born in United States		Japanese Census 1930 Percentage
	Owner	Renter	Manager	Foreman	Skilled	Unskilled	Helper	Total Number	Percentage	Total Number†	Percentage	
	(1)	(2)	(3)	(4)	(5)	(6)	(7)	(8)	(9)	(10)	(11)	(12)
Insurance, real estate, etc.§												
Insurance	5	...	..	..	10	..	..	15	...	..	...	...
Real estate	4	...	..	..	1	..	..	5	...	..	...	...
Stocks and bonds	1	...	..	..	1	..	..	2	...	..	...	...
Specialty salesman	...	...	..	..	4	..	..	4	...	1	...	...
Total	10	...	..	..	16	..	..	26	1.2	1	0.2	0.4
Professions												
Architect	...	...	..	..	..	..	..	1	...	1	...	...
Certified public accountant	1	...	..	..	..	..	..	1	...	..	...	...
Chemist	1	...	..	..	..	..	..	1	...	..	...	...
City, etc., official	...	...	9	..	..	..	..	10	...	..	...	...
Civil engineer	1	...	..	..	..	..	..	1	...	..	...	...
Dentist	...	...	..	..	..	..	..	14	...	2	...	...
Interpreter	4	...	..	..	..	..	..	4	...	..	...	...
Journalist, publisher	5	...	10	1	..	..	..	18	...	2	...	...
Laboratory worker	...	...	..	..	1	..	..	1	...	..	...	...
Lawyer	...	...	..	..	..	..	..	1	...	1	...	...
Minister	...	...	..	..	..	..	..	25	...	..	...	...
Optician	...	...	..	..	..	..	..	1	...	2	...	...
Pharmacist	...	...	..	..	..	..	..	4	...	..	...	...
Physician	...	...	..	..	..	..	..	25	...	..	...	...
School teacher	...	...	..	..	..	8	..	11	...	..	...	...
Social worker	...	...	..	..	..	..	..	2	...	..	...	...
Total	12	...	19	1	1	8	..	120	5.5	8	1.3	2.3
Miscellaneous	14	...	4	1	5	3	2	30	1.4	1	0.2	5.5
Student	...	...	..	..	..	..	..	52	2.4	478	79.7	...
Total	817	302	84	55	144	608	15	2,167	...	601	...	...
Total, not including students, agriculturists, and professions	690	2	44	5	81	328	7	1,165	...	77	...	...
Omitted, not considered	...	...	..	..	..	..	..	40	...	12	...	...

§ Salesmen were coded as "3" (skilled), but one who personally had an office was coded "1" (owner).

were given the figures quoted. Undoubtedly the actual percentage of owners and renters is greater than that recorded, as on many occasions men reported that they were managers or foremen, only to admit later that they were renting or had purchased the land. As far as could be discovered by our interviewers, the land law is non-operative in many sections of the state if not in all parts.[3] It makes it very difficult for the Japanese to obtain title, but for all practical purposes he can do so providing his go-between is honest. More recently, owing to California Supreme Court decisions, he can take title in the name of his native-born children.

One reason why the anti-alien land laws have been disregarded is that they worked hardship upon the white landowners as well as upon the Japanese. As long as the Japanese were working on share-leases, which was the most common arrangement, they had every incentive to work. By share-leases they divided profits and losses with the landowners, whereas outright leases might lead to carrying the total loss of a crop. The harder they worked, the larger would be the profit to the landowners and to themselves. It was an ideal arrangement, aside from the extension of Oriental power, in that the landowners had little responsibility. They needed to pay no great attention to their ranches, because it was certain that the Japanese would work them as efficiently as possible in their own best interest.[4]

---

[3] A prominent citizen and large landowner said to the writer that he had never heard of the law and that all about him white owners found it more advantageous to rent their land to Japanese than to farm it themselves.

[4] The effect of the anti-alien land laws in the state of Washington is reported by John A. Rademaker of the University of Washington:

"The proportion of farm land held by Japanese in the State has always been very low—less than 1.5 per cent of the number of farms, and less than one-fifth of one per cent of the acres in farm land in the State." The result of passage of the land laws in 1921 "has been a displacement of Japanese from some farms, and the abandonment of a very little land . . . . the total number of acres held in the State in January, 1925, was only 34 per cent of that held in January, 1921." There has been a slow increase in holdings since 1925, as ways have been found to circumvent the law, so that in 1930 the holdings amounted to 50 per cent of those in 1921.

"The defeated factions were penalized severely at first, insofar as they were directly concerned with the immediate effects of the Acts. The land owners lost income, and because of the pressure of taxes and the inability of other tenants to pay rents as high as those paid by Japanese, are in a precarious economic condition. The losses suffered by the Japanese farmers have in great part been passed on to the business men who benefited by their trade. The movement of Japanese farmers to the cities increased the competition between whites and Japanese there, and caused losses to the city merchants, who had supported the Acts. The effects of the passage of the Acts upon philanthropic organizations, importers and exporters trading with Japan, and other interested organizations, such as the Japan

Only here and there in continental United States is there to be found a Japanese earning his living in a skilled trade. This has raised the query as to whether or not the Japanese were competent for such work. The answer must be sought in the fact that they were not skilled when they came here and that organized labor afterward prevented their entry into such trades. In the Hawaiian Islands, where there has always been a scarcity of white skilled workmen, the Japanese have invaded this field. Today Japanese workmen, foremen, and contractors largely dominate the building trades there, and a prominent architect told the writer that he believed in time they would handle all such work. Whether or not the Japanese can effect an entry into these occupations on the mainland is a question no one can answer today. It would seem that many would do well in them and ought to be so engaged as far as their abilities and interests are concerned.[5]

There are so few of the second generation old enough to earn a living that no safe deduction can be drawn as to how they will do so. Of the 123 interviewed, 31 per cent are farming, 27 per cent are in retail stores, 24 per cent engage in business employing common and skilled labor, 6 per cent are doing clerical work, and the same number are in professional work.

Society, are for the most part indeterminable. The Japanese population of the State was reduced by about 25 per cent during the first two and one-half years following the first Act. The greatest reduction occurred in the farming population, farm operators and farm laborers gainfully employed decreasing by about 78 per cent (October 1, 1920 to October 1, 1924).

"The Acts have on the whole been a decided detriment to the population of the Region, in its competition with the populations of other regions, because they interfered with and delayed the development of an economically efficient division of labor in the agriculture of the Region. . . . . If the Japanese have brought added wealth, they have also brought in situations of competition, conflict, and accommodation which have strained the unity and solidarity of the Region. Yet from the stress and tumult of change a new equilibrium is emerging, defined ever more exactly by the growth of co-operation on the basis of an efficient division of labor in the agriculture of the Region. . . . . By granting the Japanese a chance to satisfy qualitative standards for citizenship, and abolishing the color line as a criterion of civic value, we should remove present injustice and benefit ourselves, economically, socially, and politically. The Japanese have demonstrated against odds that there is a place for them in the agriculture of the Region, mutually beneficial to themselves and to the rest of the population."—*Memorandum on Japanese Land Holding for Agricultural Purposes in the Puget Sound Region* (American Council, Institute of Pacific Relations, February 9, 1934).

[5] See chapter vii, above, for evidence of motor skill.

CHANGES IN OCCUPATIONAL STATUS

The story of how the Japanese entered the various sections of the state and how they shifted from one job to another has been recorded by many writers. It has not been the purpose of our survey to report these historical events but rather to describe the careers of the first generation in order to throw light upon what will probably be the life of the second generation.

There are two facts that stand out very clearly when the life history of the first generation is surveyed. The first is that the Japanese immigrant engaged in many different jobs. Ichihashi recorded this in 1915 in these words:

> The majority of Japanese farmers being tenants, share or contract, lack a permanent character. Independent farmers of today may become mere farm hands of tomorrow and vice versa. The majority of merchants are keepers of insignificantly small shops, they too come and go in quick order. Laborers are mostly unskilled; therefore, they shift from one occupation to another according to the seasons, and indeed, according to their whims and fancies. Clerks may become domestic servants at any moment. Domestic servants may take a fancy to farming or to railroad building. Farm hands may become gang hands, and vice versa; these again may work in canneries. They can shift about in these various occupations without any difficulty because none of these occupations requires any high degree of skill. A knowledge of English is necessary in certain occupations, but that too need not be more than elementary.[6]

But although there has been this remarkable shifting back and forth from one job to another there have been certain general trends toward some occupations and away from others. These trends have been carefully considered by studying a group of 1,457 Japanese who have lived in the United States twenty years or more and by noting (*a*) the occupations of their fathers in Japan, (*b*) their own occupations in Japan before emigrating to this country, and (*c*) their chief occupations for each successive five-year period since arrival. It is very evident that these Japanese have very largely followed the same occupations which they were engaged in in Japan and which their fathers had followed before them. Their absence from skilled pursuits is to be explained on this basis. During the years these men have been here they have shifted very little as regards types of occupation but have progressed noticeably from the station of common laborer toward that of ownership.

During the first five years in this country 80.7 per cent of these

[6] Y. Ichihashi, *Japanese Immigration* (1915), pp. 21–22.

1,457 men were engaged as common laborers in agriculture, domestic service, or various businesses, or were still going to school (7.2 per cent). At the present time only 46.1 per cent are engaged in these activities and most of them have graduated from common labor to ownership or managerial positions. On the other hand, the 19.3 per cent engaged in fishing, business, and professional work in the first five years' residence have increased to 54.2 per cent of the total today. In fishing the change has been from 1.9 to 11.7 per cent, in businesses rendering service from 9.7 to 16.6 per cent, in retailing from 3.1 to 11.6 per cent, in all other forms of business from 3.4 to 9.1 per cent, and in professional work from 1.2 to 5.2 per cent.

Even more noticeable than the change from more or less unskilled jobs to retailing and other business activities has been the change from common labor to ownership of farms and businesses. During the first five years of residence there were 13 owners and 78 renters of farms; today there are 87 owners and 241 renters. At the same time the number of unskilled laborers has decreased from 1,033 to 338.[7] In fishing, ownership has increased from 12 to 105, but here there has also been an increase in the number of common laborers, i.e., from 13 to 62. Ownership of retail stores has risen from 17 to 144 and of businesses rendering service from 45 to 199. In the first five years none were engaged in manufacturing, insurance, real estate, etc., and only 6 in wholesaling. Now there are 11 engaged in manufacturing, 9 in insurance, etc., and 20 in wholesaling. In businesses employing common labor there has been a slight increase in ownership (6 to 14) but a noticeable decline in those employed, i.e., from 183 to 13. The most noticeable weakness in the development of Japanese, occupationally speaking, is the very slight increase in the skilled trades. Here we find a shift from 4 to 19 in ownership of such businesses and an increase of from 17 to 31 in the number of skilled employees.

In agriculture there has been a decrease from 555 unskilled laborers to 169, the decrease occurring almost entirely in general farming in which the Japanese are seldom found as proprietors. It is this decrease which accounts for the total reduction from 46.6 to 40.4 per cent in agriculture. On the other hand, there have been increases in ownership and renting in all other forms of agriculture, except "tree fruits." Truck gardening easily leads in popularity, with steadily increasing numbers

[7] As previously pointed out, there are undoubtedly more owners and renters in this group than are recorded here, owing to natural reluctance to admit violation of the law.

becoming gardeners and raising flowers. In the San Francisco Bay area the Japanese have almost a monopoly of the growing of chrysanthemums, carnations, and roses.

The anti-alien land laws may have discouraged some from entering or continuing in agricultural work. There is, however, little to suggest this conclusion. It would appear to the writer that the drift to the cities is much more a movement of the common laborer who is getting too old for hard work and is looking for something easier to do in his latter days.

According to Japanese census figures it appears that the number of Japanese in gainful occupations in California has increased from 1910 to 1918 but that since that time the number of breadwinners has steadily decreased (see Table 28). Data based on the United States Census

TABLE 28

NUMBER OF JAPANESE IN GAINFUL OCCUPATIONS IN CALIFORNIA, CLASSIFIED BY FOUR MAJOR OCCUPATIONAL GROUPS, 1910, 1919, 1930*

(After Obana)†

	1910	1919	1930
Total number of Japanese	54,980	73,924	92,390
Number in gainful occupations	41,728	36,698	33,137
Agriculture	27,800	22,480	17,264
Commerce	6,244	6,657	4,341
Fishing	280	1,267	1,046
Miscellaneous	7,404	6,294	10,476

* Data for 1910 compiled from *Japanese American Year Book* of 1911; for 1919 from *Statistical Reports of the Japanese Association of America* (December 1919); for 1930 from *Statistical Reports of Consulate-General of Japan* (San Francisco, 1930), and *Consulate of Japan* (Los Angeles, 1930).

† T. Obana, "Japanese in California," *Pacific Affairs* (November 1932), p. 962.

indicate that the number of males, twenty years of age and over, has remained nearly constant at 32,000 from 1910 to 1930. Increase in Japanese population is due to increase in number of adult women and more strikingly to increase in number of children (Table 29). As the population figures from both these sources agree very well for 1920 and 1930 but differ greatly for 1910 (Japanese census reports 13,000 more), it depends upon which source is to be accepted whether one will conclude that there has been a decrease in breadwinners between 1910 and 1930 or not. The weight of evidence in chapter iii favors the view that the United States Census of 1910 was an understatement of the Japanese population. Accordingly it appears that the total number of Japanese in gainful occupations has decreased during these two decades.

Only a few of the first generation state that they are planning to return to Japan, and practically none of the second generation expressed such a desire.

TABLE 29

DISTRIBUTION OF JAPANESE POPULATION BY SEX AND AGE IN ORDER TO INDICATE PROBABLE NUMBER OF MALES IN GAINFUL OCCUPATIONS (I.E., TWENTY YEARS OF AGE AND OVER) IN 1910, 1920, AND 1930*

	Males		Females		
	Under Twenty Years	Twenty Years and Over	Under Twenty Years	Twenty Years and Over	Total
1910	3,295	31,821	1,965	4,275	41,356
1920	12,661	32,753	10,668	15,870	71,952
1930	23,607	32,833	22,174	18,842	97,456

* Based on United States Census.

Japanese high-school boys and, even more, college men feel handicapped in their occupational careers because of their race. Eight per cent of the former and 22 per cent of the latter feel it is a serious handicap, while 30 and 44 per cent, respectively, feel it is somewhat an obstacle to their plans. Their explanations as to why they were thus handicapped were for the most part vague. Evidently they have not given the matter much consideration, probably because they are not yet old enough to have actually encountered the effects.

INCOME, OWNERSHIP

Income reported by the few second generation now employed is slightly below that reported paid by a large public utility to whites of corresponding ages.

Eighteen per cent of the first generation interviewed in our survey reported that they own their homes, having a median value of $2,000. If ninety-one shacks owned by farmers are excluded from consideration, the median becomes $4,000. Of those engaged in business, 57 per cent reported that they are owners of their businesses, having a median value of $3,000. The average of $9,450 reflects the existence of eight large businesses between $60,000 and $500,000. Of those engaged in farming, about 11 per cent reported that they own their farms, having a median value of $8,500. All these values are as stated by the Japanese themselves.

The total value of the homes reported is $1,057,762; of the businesses, $6,912,230; and of the farms $949,082, totaling $8,919,074. It is rather surprising that the value of the farms is about one-seventh that of the businesses and slightly less than that of the homes. Undoubtedly not all the owners reported the fact of ownership of land, because of the anti-alien land laws. But unless the discrepancy is far larger than we suspect, the Japanese have more money invested in business than in farming. Yet we think of them as essentially farmers, and the occupational data support this view.

The totals above are based upon the returns from 2,087 men and 1,662 women. On the average, each of these has $282 invested in a home, $1,844 in a business, and $253 in a farm, a grand total of $2,379 per person, or $4,758 per married couple.

EDUCATIONAL AND OCCUPATIONAL PLANS

The school subjects that Japanese students like best and are planning to specialize in and the occupations they are planning to enter are given in detail in *Japanese in California*. When the various subjects are classified, the following order of preference for school subjects of Japanese high-school students results:

School Subject	Percentage	School Subject	Percentage
Mathematics	23.0	Physical sciences	7.8
Biological sciences	12.1	Agriculture	4.5
Shop work	11.7	History and philosophy	4.1
English, including literature	9.4	Art	4.1
Business of all kinds	8.4	Drawing	3.0
Foreign languages	7.9	Engineering	1.5

The remaining groups of school subjects are preferred by less than one per cent.

Among Japanese college students the subjects most liked are ranked as follows:

School Subject	Percentage	School Subject	Percentage
Business, including economics	37.5	Biological sciences	6.8
Medicine, including dentistry and pharmacy	13.6	Agriculture	4.5
Physical sciences	12.4	Mathematics	3.4
Engineering	10.1	History and philosophy	2.3
		Law and political science	2.2

Four additional subjects were preferred by one per cent each, namely, architecture, music, English, and education.

School subjects in which Japanese are planning to specialize.—The order of preference of Japanese high-school students is as follows:

School Subject	Percentage	School Subject	Percentage
Shop work	14.6	Agriculture	8.1
Business	12.9	Engineering	7.7
Mathematics	12.0	English and journalism	6.3
Biological sciences	11.0	Art	5.6
Physical sciences	8.1	Foreign languages	4.4

These ten groups of school subjects include the preferences of 91 per cent of the Japanese high-school boys.

The school subjects that Japanese college men are planning to specialize in are somewhat different; the order follows:

School Subject	Percentage	School Subject	Percentage
Business	31.2	Physical sciences	12.4
Medicine, including dentistry and pharmacy	18.8	Agriculture	6.3
Engineering	14.4	Law	5.2
		Biological sciences	4.1

No other group of school subjects is preferred by over one per cent.

When it is remembered that these Japanese come into more intimate contact with agricultural pursuits and with retailing than with any other vocational activity, it is surprising to find so little interest expressed here in these occupations. One explanation of this is, of course, that such occupations are hardly recognized in most school curricula and consequently, when choice of school subject is called for, are very unlikely to be mentioned. When we turn from "school subject most liked" to "subject to specialize in," it is apparent that business is a favorite subject but that only about 7 per cent plan to specialize in the study of agriculture.

Occupations which Japanese are planning to enter.—Agriculture is first choice of Japanese high-school boys (21.2 per cent prefer it). Business of all kinds is second choice (18.7 per cent). Then follow in order: skilled trades (16.2 per cent), engineering (11.9 per cent), medicine, including dentistry and pharmacy (11.4 per cent), aviation (6.7 per cent), architecture (2.9 per cent), and art work (2.7 per cent). These eight occupations account for 91.7 per cent of all the Japanese high-school boys. Except in the case of business, these occupations concern themselves with things, not people; they are based very largely on the applications of science.

In general, the occupational plans of the Japanese agree very closely with those of white high-school boys (correlation of over 0.80). But there are several differences between the two groups. First, the whites are more enthusiastic about aviation, engineering, and law than the Japanese, and less enthusiastic about skilled trades, all forms of medicine, and particularly agriculture (this last is seventh choice, not first). Second, whereas over 90 per cent of the Japanese choose one of the eight occupations listed above, only three-fourths of the whites choose them. This means that the whites are interested in a greater variety of occupational opportunities than the Japanese, such, for example, as law, chemistry, writing, and music. Third, although slightly more Japanese than whites are planning to enter business, proportionately more of the latter are selecting specific kinds of business (other than "business in general") and on the whole better-paid business activities, such as accounting, selling, banking, and brokerage.

Over 85 per cent of the Japanese college students are planning to enter one of five groups of occupations (see Table 30). Business is first choice (34.5 per cent prefer it); medicine, including dentistry and pharmacy, is second choice (21.5 per cent); engineering is third (14.7 per cent); agriculture is fourth (8.8 per cent); and the physical sciences of chemistry and geology are fifth (6.9 per cent). In addition, 2 per cent each are planning to enter law, teaching, the ministry, and skilled trades. These nine groups of occupations account for 94.4 per cent of the Japanese college men.

The occupational plans of Japanese and white college men agree very largely (correlation of over 0.65 between columns 1 and 2 of Table 30), but not so closely as do those of Japanese and white high-school boys. Fewer white college men are planning to enter business, medicine, and agriculture than Japanese college men, and more expect to enter engineering, chemistry, geology, law, teaching, writing, and biology. In other words, the Japanese are more concentrated in a few occupations than the whites and the concentration is decidedly in the direction of occupations dealing with things or with the application of the sciences. Practically none are interested in dealing with people except in a business connection. Half again as many Japanese expect to enter business as whites (34.5 and 23.3 per cent, respectively), but 22 per cent of the former have selected retailing and wholesaling in contrast to only 5 per cent of the latter. In other respects the plans of the two groups are about the same, with the exception that no Japanese is planning on banking, whereas 4.3 per cent of whites have selected it.

TABLE 30

OCCUPATIONAL PREFERENCES OF JAPANESE AND WHITE COLLEGE STUDENTS BORN IN THE UNITED STATES

Occupations	Japanese	Whites	Differences
Unskilled labor	1.0	0	1.0
Skilled trades	2.0	0.6	1.4
Agriculture	8.8	5.1	3.7
Mathematician	0	0.1	– 0.1
Chemist, geologist, etc.	6.9	10.6	– 3.7
Engineer	14.7	18.1	– 3.4
Architect	1.0	1.3	– 0.3
Artist	0	0.3	– 0.3
Actor	0	0.4	– 0.4
Musician	1.0	0.6	0.4
Aviation	0	0.8	– 0.8
Biologist	1.0	2.2	– 1.2
Physician	12.7	9.0	3.7
Dentist, pharmacist	8.8	0.7	8.1
Writer, publisher	1.0	4.6	– 3.6
Lawyer	2.0	12.0	–10.0
Politics, diplomatic service	1.0	0.7	0.3
Economist, historian	0	0.8	– 0.8
Accountant	2.0	1.4	0.6
Advertising	1.0	0.8	0.2
Wholesaler and retailer	21.6	4.8	16.8
Salesman	1.0	2.0	– 1.0
Business in general	5.9	8.0	– 2.1
Office work	2.0	0.8	1.2
Banker	0	4.3	– 4.3
Stock broker	1.0	0.8	0.2
Insurance	0	0.4	– 0.4
Teaching	2.0	7.5	– 5.5
Minister, priest	2.0	1.0	1.0
Physical director	0	0.7	– 0.7
Miscellaneous	0	0.3	– 0.3
All business occupations	34.5	23.3	11.2
Total in group	107	860	...
Did not reply	5	47	...
Total considered	102	813	...
Percentage who did not reply	5.0	5.5	...

College men are four years older than high-school boys; they are also a much more highly selected group. How, then, do these two groups differ regarding their occupational choices? The chief differences are given here in tabular form:

Occupational Choice	High School	College	Difference
Skilled trades	16.2	2.0	14.2
Agriculture	21.2	8.8	12.4
Aviation	6.7	0	6.7
Architecture	2.9	1.0	1.9
Engineering	11.9	14.7	− 2.8
Dentistry and pharmacy	5.1	8.8	− 3.7
Chemistry, geology, etc.	1.3	6.7	− 5.4
Medicine	6.3	12.7	− 6.4
Business	18.7	34.5	−15.8

The changes indicated are most natural. Skilled trades, agriculture, and office work are familiar to the high-school boy and are not so often entered by college men. It is most natural that the high-school boy should mention them more often than the college man. The reverse is the case with respect to architecture, engineering, dentistry, chemistry, geology, and medicine. All these are studied only in college and are hardly open at all to the high-school boy.

The belief that the Japanese are no longer planning to be farmers may well be based upon observation of Japanese college men. The college man has never entered agricultural work to any large degree, instanced here by only 8.8 per cent. However, 21.2 per cent of high-school boys say they are going to become farmers.

Relation between "Occupation Planning to Enter" and Vocational Interest Blank ratings.—It will be recalled (pp. 171–75) that all these students were scored on the Vocational Interest Blank.[8] At this point we may well ask the question, How do these ratings agree with the vocational programs of these young men? As the interest blanks have been scored for only nineteen occupational interests, comparisons are limited to these nineteen. As no students reported plans to become vacuum cleaner salesmen, one of the nineteen, this item has been omitted, leaving but eighteen possible comparisons. These are too few for a really satisfactory conclusion. But on this basis it appears that there is a rank order correlation coefficient of 0.81 between the test ratings (A and B+ combined) and the occupations Japanese eleventh-grade students are planning to enter. If all the Japanese high-school students are considered, the coefficient is 0.76; and if Japanese college students are considered, the correlation is 0.64. Corresponding figures for whites are 0.63, 0.63, and 0.49, respectively. Although singly these coeffi-

[8] See E. K. Strong, Jr., *Vocational Aptitudes of Second-Generation Japanese in the United States,* chapter v.

cients are not very reliable, nevertheless, because they all agree fairly well, they must be accepted as evidence of general agreement between Vocational Interest Blank ratings and occupational program.

Offhand one would expect the interest ratings to correlate more highly with present occupational plans among college students than among high-school boys, for the interests of the former are more nearly in agreement with those they will have as adults than is the case with the latter, who are four years younger. But the correlations quoted above are lower in the case of college men than in that of high-school boys. Personal contact with young men leads the writer to believe that many more college men than high-school boys are deliberately planning a career to make money and hence as a group are disregarding personal inclinations to a greater degree. Other things being equal they would prefer a certain career; but other things are seldom equal. With increasing age comes a realization of the conflict between inclination and remuneration. The high-school boy suffers less from this conflict of wishes, for he has had less opportunity to perceive the actual situation.

It would appear from the correlations given above that the Japanese student is at present planning to enter an occupation somewhat more in harmony with his Vocational Interest Blank ratings than is the white student (average correlation of 0.73 in the case of the former and of 0.58 in the case of the latter). This result agrees with the oft-expressed opinion that the second generation are following their inclinations and not seriously considering as yet the occupations open to them or the chances of success in different occupations.

The Japanese are less definite in their choices and less sure of those choices than the whites. In their day-dreaming of what they would like to do at age thirty-five they mention a life of luxury somewhat less than whites.

Recent college graduates.—Seventy-nine per cent of Japanese-American college graduates between 1920 and 1930 who replied to a questionnaire stated that they are now working at that for which they prepared in college. Included in this group are those who are pursuing graduate work as well as those actually practicing their professions. Two-thirds reported that they are entirely self-supporting; the remainder are largely still engaged in graduate work. The monthly incomes of those reporting range from $75 to $650, with an average of $209. As there is a tendency for the less well adjusted to fail to reply to questionnaires, the fair summary here is that at least half (51 per cent replied) of the second-generation college graduates are progressing satisfactorily.

RELIGIOUS AFFILIATION

The first generation prefer Buddhism to Christianity (77 per cent and 18 per cent, respectively). The reverse is the case with the United States–born, among whom 39 per cent prefer Buddhism, while 47 per cent of the males and 56 per cent of the females prefer Christianity. The Hawaii-born fall between the other two groups in this respect, the males having preferences rather similar to United States–born males and the females preferences quite similar to Japan-born females.

There is no evidence that the first generation tend to transfer their allegiance to Christianity as they continue to live in California. Their children clearly do so, as do the young Japan-born who are growing up in the state.

Preference for Christianity instead of Buddhism is associated with better education, better use of the English language, urban life, and greater ownership of farms but not of homes or businesses.[9]

---

[9] "When there is a Buddhist and a Christian element in a Japanese community, it usually appears that the Christian is more Americanized than the Buddhist element."—*Tentative Findings of the Survey of Race Relations* (1925), p. 22.

X. VOCATIONAL OPPORTUNITIES

The vocational adjustment of second-generation Japanese is affected considerably by where they live. If they scattered over the mainland, they would presumably encounter less prejudice and would have little or no competition among themselves. It is conceivable, for example, that hundreds of them might succeed under these conditions as dentists and physicians, whereas, if they concentrate in a few localities in California, this will be impossible.[1] On the other hand, such concentration makes possible a great many occupational openings in which they serve each other in one capacity or another, which is impossible if they are widely scattered.

EFFECT OF GEOGRAPHICAL DISTRIBUTION

In attempting to size up the vocational opportunities of the second generation, this matter of geographical distribution is therefore important. Are they likely to spread out over the country, i.e., go East, or will they leave this country and go to Japan, Brazil, or some other place? It is also important to determine whether or not the second generation in the Hawaiian Islands will come to the mainland in any considerable number.

The data presented in chapter iii make clear that the Japanese population has been steadily moving in the direction of Los Angeles, so that today 26 per cent of all in continental United States are in that county. So far they have shown no tendency to scatter over the country. The census figures make clear that they are not only moving toward Los Angeles but also moving away from rural communities toward the larger cities. We cannot be sure yet what will be the final outcome. During youth people move about only to settle down later on. There are still too few of the second generation old enough to leave home to have had any real influence upon the movements of the group.

Likelihood of going East.—In order to discover the attitude of the Japanese toward going East to live, all those over fourteen years of age who were interviewed in the survey were asked the question: "Would you go East, say, to Columbus, Ohio, if you were assured of $50 a month more income, in preference to staying here?" (In the tryout interviewing, each person was asked if he would go East if he could earn more money.

---

[1] There are a good many "ifs" involved here, such as, if they could secure patients, and so on.

Because nearly all said "No" and many raised the question of how much more money, it was decided to change the question and add the "$50 a month more income" phrase.) The question proved to be a very difficult one to handle. It was particularly difficult for the white interviewers to make the question clear; even the Japanese interviewers had difficulties in this respect. Many of those interviewed obviously had not grasped this speculative question even after the interviewer felt it had been understood. Because of this lack of comprehension, the answer to the question, in an unusually large number of cases, had to be reported as "Omitted."

Not all of the data were tallied, but three samples of about fifty each were taken from each interviewer. The data are segregated according to whether the persons lived in the three large cities, in the country, or at San Pedro and Monterey, engaged in fishing. They are further segregated according to whether the person belonged to the first or the second generation.[2]

Because of the wide differences reported by the eleven different interviewers the data for each are presented separately (see Table 31). It would appear probable that the white interviewers were misled in some cases and accepted the Japanese "Yes" to mean willingness to move when it meant no more than "I understand the question," which is a well-known usage of the term by Japanese. It would also appear probable that our Japanese interviewer No. 7 has reported fewer cases than another would find and that our Japanese interviewer No. 11 has reported more cases than another would discover. It is also possible that the data are correct as they stand and that there are peculiar conditions in the different districts which would account for these rather extreme variations. The figures in Table 31 must accordingly be accepted with some reservations.

We may conclude from the data in the table that from 10 to 15 per cent of the first generation would move East if they could materially improve their incomes and that from two to three times as many of the second generation would do likewise. The fact that they live in cities or country districts makes no difference respecting their readiness to move. There are, however, certain facts brought out in connection with the reasons advanced for going or not going East which throw additional light on the matter.

---

[2] The "young people" group was nearly all of the second generation but included a few born in Japan or Hawaii.

TABLE 31

PERCENTAGE OF JAPANESE WHO SAID "YES" TO THE QUESTION: "WOULD YOU GO EAST?" WITH DATA GROUPED ACCORDING TO RACE OF INTERVIEWER

Interviewer	Country Districts		City Districts		Fishing Districts	
	Young People	Older People	Young People	Older People	Young People	Older People
No. 1, white	44	22	..	..	..	..
No. 2, white	..	..	66	29	..	..
No. 3, white	..	..	45	24	..	..
No. 4, white (Japanese interpreter)	63	6	..	..	..	..
No. 5, white (Japanese interpreter)	34	9	35	12	..	..
No. 6, white (Japanese interpreter)	32	26	..	..	..	..
No. 7, Japanese	15	4	..	..	..	..
No. 8, Japanese	..	..	62	18	..	..
No. 9, Japanese	..	..	53	27	..	..
No. 10, Japanese	..	..	21	5	..	..
No. 11, Japanese	..	..	..	..	67	26
Average, white interviewers without interpreter	44	22	56	27	..	..
Average, white interviewers with interpreter	43	14	35	12	..	..
Average, Japanese interviewers	15	4	45	17	67	26
Average, all interviewers	42	14	40	16	67	26

Reasons against going East.—Of the 601 who gave a reason for not going East, 43 objected on the ground that their farm, business, or home was here or that they were well established and saw no advantage in making a change. Family reasons were advanced by 116, i.e., the family was settled here, it would cost too much to move under the circumstances, or there were advantages from being near one's family or relatives. The fact that one had no friends in the East was advanced by 40 more, some of whom urged, in addition, that there were few Japanese in the East with whom one could associate. "Too old to move" was advanced by 36, while 25 were planning to return to Japan and retire there.

The largest number (200 in all) were genuine boosters for California and voiced their objection in terms of its advantages. The climate was mentioned by 41 as superior to that in the East, 135 believed California was a better place in which to live, and 24 felt there were better opportunities to earn a living in California than in the East. Judging from the statements, several had had actual experience and others had heard reports of personal experiences upon which they based their opinions.

There were 96 who objected because of the unfamiliarity of the East, for example, "Don't like strange places"; "Don't know real conditions in the East"; "Too many chances in the East"; "No business to go to there"; "Used to it here"; "Familiar with farming here, wouldn't know how to farm there."

Reasons advanced for going East.—Of the 169 who gave reasons for going East, 53 expressed a real desire. Expressions such as these were recorded: "Sure"; "Anybody would"; "Certainly"; "Mean to go anyway"; "Prefer to live in the East"; "Have no friends in California"; "Don't want to live with Japanese"; "Don't want to stay here and it is better than Japan"; "Have heard favorable reports from aunt." Seven reported that they wanted to go but that their families were unwilling or very loath to have them leave. Five had in mind going to a particular place in the East.

There were others, 94 in all, who gave more definite reasons for making the change. Two-thirds of these considered the matter in terms of better opportunities. But many of them were far from sure that there were better opportunities awaiting them. In other words, they would go if there were, but that matter needed careful investigation. In a few cases this better opportunity was in terms of less race prejudice toward them. Eleven of this group emphasized the $50 aspect: "Would go anywhere for $50"; "Money the important thing"; "Would go for the money, but it's hotter there." Five thought $50 unimportant in their connection. They would go not for money but only if it were a better place in which to live, if they could be of greater social service to their race, or if they could get a professorship there.

The remaining 22 of the 169 were ready to go under the circumstances but were quite sure they would not stay. Remarks like the following were made: "Want to see new places"; "Want to see industrial conditions there"; "Would go temporarily"; "Go to Chicago a year to learn better methods in my trade [garage mechanic], and then return to California"; "Plan to go East to study; my uncle is there"; "Would go East for newspaper experience."

Conclusion.—There are two issues here: Would the Japanese go East if they could earn $50 more a month? and, second, Are the Japanese likely to go anyway; in other words, are they now planning to go?

The data in Table 31 indicate that from 10 to 15 per cent of the first generation and two to three times as many of the second generation would seriously consider going if they could earn $50 more a month. But judging from their expressed reasons this "if" is a very big one in their minds. They are far from sure that they can improve their lot by the change and they have many objections to leaving California.

As to the second issue, whether or not any number are really planning to go East, the evidence is overwhelming that few are considering the matter. Only 25 per cent (169 out of the 663 who said "Yes") had reasons favorable to going, in contrast to 37 per cent (601 out of the 1,630 who said "No") who had reasons against going even when $50 a month was included in the proposition. One would expect those planning to make a radical change to be well fortified with reasons for their action, but here it is the group who are unwilling to change who express themselves most freely. But more important still in support of the view that few are planning to go is the fact that among the 169 who gave reasons for going with a $50 bonus included, only 53 really expressed a genuine interest in going, and the remainder had serious questions about the advisability of the matter or were only going for a short time. Fifty-three from among 770 who gave reasons either for or against going seem to be all that are really likely to go under present conditions. They represent 7 per cent of the 770, or only 2.3 per cent of the 2,293 who were considered. It appears then that only a small proportion of the Japanese population in California is considering moving East as a way of improving their economic condition. Only if the Japanese discover that they can materially improve those conditions by going East will a considerable number do so, just as their parents immigrated from Japan to California. Even then, there are strong ties that hold them to California which must needs be broken before a change will be made.

Go to Japan.—Judging from the data in Table 32, only 3 per cent of United States-born Japanese high-school or college students prefer Japan as a place in which to live. About 10 per cent, in addition, indicate they have not decided whether to live in Japan or the United States. The great majority prefer to live where their home now is, but in each group there are some who prefer another locality.

Our interviewers were emphatic that the great majority of Japanese would stay here in preference to going to Japan. One summed it up in these words:

> The Japanese intend to stay here, as they feel they are better situated than in Japan and intend to stay here in spite of what America may do to discourage them and their culture, at the same time refusing to admit any superiority of American culture to theirs.

Another emphasized that the first generation came here to make money and then return to Japan. Many, of course, have returned, but most of those now here have settled down; some still dally with the thought of

TABLE 32

COUNTRY PREFERRED IN WHICH TO LIVE AND CARRY ON BUSINESS, IN PERCENTAGES

Country Preferred	Japanese High-School Students*			Japanese College Students		
	Born in Japan	Born in Hawaii	Born in United States	Born in Japan	Born in Hawaii†	Born in United States
Japan	11.8	0	2.4	49.6	2.8	3.7
Hawaii	0	6.7	0.2	5.0	68.2	0.9
United States	64.7	73.3	89.4	21.5	6.5	77.6
Other	5.9	0	0.9	0.8	3.7	0.9
Canada	0	0	0	1.7	0	0.9
Hawaii or United States	0	20.0	0.2	0	12.1	0
Japan or United States	17.6	0	5.5	19.8	5.6	14.0
Omitted	0	0	1.4	1.7	0.9	1.8
Numbered considered	34	15	634	110	107	107

* All living in California.

† Nearly all students at the University of Hawaii.

returning, but will stay on; others have definitely decided to remain with their children and their business. Still another of our interviewers wrote as follows:

> Most of the Japanese expressed the desire and intention to remain here rather than return to Japan. In giving reasons for this they compared their morale and well-being in the United States with that in Japan, pointing out their social and economic opportunities here, their educational opportunities, and the advantages of their children as citizens of the United States.
>
> In Japan it is difficult to move from one social stratification to another either by marriage or accumulation of money. Social customs are rigid. It is difficult both for social and economic considerations to engage in any industry other than that in which the individual's family has engaged. It is difficult for the bulk of the population to earn more than mere subsistence, much less accumulate capital to engage in agricultural expansion or in business.

Only one reference was made to immigration from the United States to any other foreign country aside from Japan; this was to Brazil.

Likelihood of Japanese emigrating from Hawaii to the mainland.—The evidence in chapter vi is that a relatively small number of the Japanese now in California have come by way of the Hawaiian Islands. During 1911–30, 1,582 went to the Islands from the mainland and 2,472 came to the mainland from the Islands. Travel both ways seems to be increasing slowly, particularly toward the mainland. During 1924–30 there was a net loss to the mainland of 205 first-generation and a net gain of 973 second-generation Japanese.

> The emigration of four or five thousand young men and women from Hawaii to the mainland would be for America a very minor matter in comparison with the numbers who come annually from Europe or from Canada and Mexico. But from the standpoint of the young people it is a serious matter. Family ties are strong in Hawaii. And then there is much real sentiment for Hawaii. Also there is fear of mainland race prejudice. Probably the great majority of the boys of Hawaii would prefer to remain in the Islands if they could secure economic opportunities somewhat superior to those of their parents. They have an exaggerated notion of the opportunity and status of the ordinary white man in America, but they would accept something inferior to this in order to remain with their parents in Hawaii.[3]

The writer found little or no indication in the Hawaiian Islands of any tendency for the Japanese to come to the mainland. They seemed to be unanimously of the opinion that they were better off there. They felt there was considerable prejudice against them in California on the part of both whites and Japanese, which appears to be the case. It is likely that some of the better educated will come this way in search of wider opportunities. But they will be too few to be noticed. It would appear there will be no great influx unless economic conditions in the Islands change for the worse.

Summary.—The second-generation problem will become more and more a California problem and particularly a Los Angeles problem. Furthermore, the problem will not be increased by any particular immigration of Japanese now in the Hawaiian Islands nor will it be decreased by any particular emigration of Japanese on the mainland to Eastern states or to Japan or to any other foreign country.

VOCATIONAL OPPORTUNITIES OF JAPANESE

What the second generation will do for a living is largely a speculative matter at the present time. There are too many conflicting factors to make it advisable for anyone to set himself up as a prophet in this

---

[3] Romanzo Adams and Dan Kane-Zo Kai, *The Education of the Boys of Hawaii and Their Economic Outlook* (University of Hawaii Research Publications, No. 4, January 1928), p. 24.

matter, and there are too few of the second generation of age to afford any real basis for judging what the remainder will do in terms of what these few are trying to do.

The matter can, however, be approached from several angles, and certain facts can be presented that will help to a better understanding of the whole subject.

Tendency to follow the way of first generation.—The data in chapter ix make clear that the first generation have followed very closely in the footsteps of their fathers in Japan, both before they left their native country and after their arrival here. The great majority have earned their living in agricultural pursuits and more recently in operating small retail establishments. Others have devoted themselves to fishing. It is true that they have worked at times in many different industries as common laborers, but essentially their work has been in the three fields named.

It is reasonable to suppose that many of their sons will continue in the same lines. Even though these sons profess indifference to agriculture, many will drift into the work they have learned under their parents' direction. Still others will try other activities and will discover by the process of elimination that agriculture is more interesting than they had supposed, or at least that a living can be obtained thereby more surely than in other ways.

It is not surprising that many sons of Japanese farmers wish to leave the farm. In most cases they do not own the land and must expect to move from time to time. There is little incentive to develop comfortable homes modern in style and with modern conveniences. The contrast between ranch homes and life in the city is great. The first generation lack also the knowledge, skill, and resources by which they can take full advantage of the situation; their income is largely a reflection of hard manual labor and not of good business management. The farmer's son thinks of agriculture as he knows it and not in terms of what he might make it if he were especially trained for it.

The typical Japanese farmer lives in what is pretty close to a mere hovel. He is clad in dirty overalls, for they are the most appropriate apparel for farming. He rises at about four-thirty or five in the morning and is out working in the fields before the clock strikes six. (He who takes his products to the market is up all night and sleeps uncomfortably during the day, when the flies buzz around so actively.) He takes about an hour for lunch, returns to the field, and labors until darkness prevents him from doing any more. Tired from the week's work, he usually rests on Saturday, the farmer's holiday, with apparently no interest in seeking recreation. On Sunday he goes back to the same routine. The farmer's son lives in this atmosphere year in and year out. He hears of pleasures elsewhere, and his youthful instinct of play boils over at his inability to engage in them. He knows that the profits of his father are small compared to the amount of time he spends at work. He continually hears of depressions, of bad years, of debts. Coupled with all this are the effects of the present business depression, which intensify the gloominess of the whole picture.

Nevertheless agriculture offers the greatest opportunity for employment, the establishment of homes, and the chance to prosper. Here the Japanese are wanted, for they are among the best workers and come into the least competition with the Occidental elements of the population. The second generation can lease and buy land and thus establish permanent homes and prosper according to their industry.

The recent agenda of a meeting of Japanese farmers and business men show they are interested in better procedures. Among other topics the following points were considered: better systems of management; formation of associations; better financing by Japanese themselves in order to obtain better control of marketing their products, now so extensively in the hands of commission merchants who extend credit; employment of experts; and better publicity in Japanese papers for agricultural news.

There is clear evidence that the trend on the part of the first generation toward ownership of retail establishments will be continued by their sons. These businesses have succeeded so far because they have catered to the needs of the first generation and to other racial groups in the neighborhood. The time is rapidly approaching when a readjustment must be made, for the second generation are trading elsewhere more and more. Can the Japanese stores overcome this tendency and succeed in competition with chain stores and all the other shopping facilities of the district? That their problem is appreciated is indicated by a clipping from a Japanese newspaper:

> Japanese owned and operated stores have not been able to compete with downtown stores owing to old methods and lack of specialization in their lines of business. Prices have been higher, stocks have not been complete or genuine, and most of all the appealing articles have been missing from the counters.
>
> The kind of service and sincere thoughtful attention which is necessary to maintain good-will and faith has been lacking. It is no wonder that most young people prefer to trade downtown. Any one of us would be glad to trade at Japanese stores if the prices were just as low and the quality uniform.

A decided change in this present defect of business policy is the aim of a group of young business men. They have organized to give to the young people the right quality of merchandise at the right price on the basis of comparison together with good service and sincere consideration. There is no reason why this cannot be accomplished with concentration along specialized lines, organized buying power, establishing of good-will and credit, and low overhead costs.[4]

Domestic service is another activity of the first generation which some second generation may follow, although it is without question the least appealing to them of all.

Out of all the trouble from the depression, we notice one thing and that is that more and more second generation members are entering domestic work for their living. In years gone by, the California raised girls have had the tendency of looking down upon domestic workers. They would have considered it an insult if anyone had offered them such employment. And this, despite the fact that their parents may be or may have been domestic workers. In other words, white collar job was their ideal.

Such an attitude was looked upon with misgivings. The first generation members were skeptical about the future of the growing generation and this was one of the reasons. We had assured them, however, that the young people would surprise them if an emergency should arise. And we feel that we were right.

When there is a scarcity of jobs, the young people are not afraid to earn their livings even through manual work. They are not living on empty prides. They can face reality when such an occasion should arise. By this, we do not mean that we desire to have the second generation remain as domestic workers. What we wish all to bear in mind is that any honest work is worth taking unless a better one is in store.

Domestic work may appear to have no future at first glance; but to the second generation members who are crying because of race prejudice and lack of opportunities, this type of work may be their very salvation. The employer may have a large business establishment and he may offer a position in his office once he learns of the education, qualification, and desire of the young man or lady serving in his home. We have heard of many instances of Japanese finding employment in their employer's business. So after all, even domestic works have possibilities. It helps to bring about contact with persons who are in a position to offer opportunities for better prospects.[5]

The Japanese have specialized in a particular phase of domestic service, that of house-cleaning, whereby usually a man comes for a half or a full day once a week and does such cleaning as is desired. This service meets a real economic need and quite likely will be continued by some of the second generation.

Occupations developing out of present first-generation activities.— Few men jump from one occupation to a radically different one; most

[4] Rio Kashiwagi, in the *Japanese-American Courier,* July 26, 1930.

[5] Editorial, *The Pacific Citizen,* March 1, 1932.

go gradually, step by step. Hence it is most plausible to expect that many of the second generation will start in where their fathers are now engaged and then slowly develop the various possibilities of that business until essentially they may achieve quite new undertakings.

The most successful occupation in which the Japanese are engaged is that of raising vegetables. Seemingly there are real opportunities of expanding this both horizontally and vertically, horizontally by increasing the production of vegetables, berries, and other agricultural products, and vertically by controlling the marketing of these products from producer to consumer locally and in the East. The Japanese have already established vegetable markets and grocery stores. Fish they should be able to add, as they catch so many. Similarly there should be more florist shops owned by them, as they raise flowers today most competently. Trucking of vegetables to market is another allied activity. There are many intimately related phases of wholesaling. Canneries might be opened for the stocks of fruit and vegetables. Here there is opportunity for those with a specialized knowledge of agricultural production, marketing, business practices, and efficient management.

Japanese excel in the gold-fish business. They are also excellent gardeners. Why should they not in time become nurserymen and enter landscaping? Their tea gardens are unique and should be popularized.

Until second-generation citizens enter fishing there is little likelihood of development there, for the first generation suffer from the fear that their livelihood may be taken from them by legislation.[6]

Interests and inclinations of the second generation.—Table 33 gives the percentage of Japanese and white high-school and college students (the two educational levels are averaged together) who received A and B+ ratings on the Vocational Interest Blank. Thus, 23.6 per cent of Japanese and 19.3 per cent of whites received such ratings for the interest of physicians. The second part of the table gives the percentage who expressed preference for the occupation. Thus 9.5 per cent of Japanese and 6.7 per cent of whites say they would like to be physicians. The differences between the two racial groups give some indication whether one or the other group is more likely to enter an occupation in large numbers, in so far as interest and preference are an indication of future action.

From this table it appears that proportionately a few more Japanese than whites will enter the occupations based on the biological sciences,

---

[6] See E. G. Mears, *Resident Orientals*, chapter x.

TABLE 33

VOCATIONAL INTEREST RATINGS AND OCCUPATIONAL PREFERENCES OF JAPANESE AND WHITES

Occupations	A and B+ Vocational Interest Ratings			Percentage Expressing Preference		
	Japanese*	Whites*	Difference	Japanese†	Whites†	Difference
Biological sciences and applications						
Physician	23.6	19.3	+ 4.3	9.5	6.7	+2.8
Dentist and pharmacist	...	...	...	7.0	2.2	+4.8
Farmer	35.1	26.5	+ 8.6	15.0	5.4	+9.6
Biologist	...	...	...	1.3	1.7	−0.4
Psychologist	1.6	2.9	− 1.3	...	...	...
Physical sciences and applications						
Chemist, geologist, etc.	21.0	15.6	+ 5.4	4.1	7.2	−3.1
Engineer	29.3	26.9	+ 2.4	13.3	16.1	−2.8
Architect	3.5	3.6	− 0.1	2.0	2.2	−0.2
Skilled trades	...	...	...	9.1	5.6	+3.5
Aviation	...	...	...	3.4	7.2	−3.8
Ministry, teaching, social service						
Teacher	17.4	8.5	+ 8.9	1.2	4.1	−2.9
Minister, priest	4.6	2.7	+ 1.9	1.2	0.6	+0.6
Y.M.C.A. secretary	9.1	4.0	+ 5.1	...	...	...
Physical director	...	...	...	0.2	1.3	−1.1
Art work	0	0.8	− 0.8	1.4	1.6	−0.2
Music	...	...	...	0.9	1.4	−0.5
Business, except advertising and selling						
Accountant	...	...	...	1.0	1.2	−0.2
Retailer and wholesaler	...	...	...	12.8	3.9	+8.9
Office worker	28.3	31.2	− 2.9	3.2	3.7	−0.5
Banker	...	...	...	0.2	2.9	−2.7
Broker	...	...	...	0.5	0.9	−0.4
Certified public accountant	1.2	1.1	+ 0.1	...	...	...
Personnel director	9.9	9.5	+ 0.4	...	...	...
Business man in general	...	...	...	7.0	4.7	+2.3
Advertising and selling						
Advertising man	0.5	3.2	− 2.7	0.5	0.5	0
Salesman	...	...	...	1.3	2.3	−1.0
Life insurance salesman	2.5	7.5	− 5.0	...	...	...
Real estate salesman	4.2	14.9	−10.7	...	...	...
Vacuum cleaner salesman	12.4	9.5	+ 2.9	...	...	...
Law, writing						
Writer, publisher	18.2	25.0	− 6.8	1.0	3.5	−2.5
Lawyer	8.4	19.4	−11.0	1.9	9.3	−7.4

* Some individuals are rated A or B+ in more than one occupation, hence these columns add up to 230.8 and 232.1, respectively.

† Percentages in these columns would add to 100 if miscellaneous occupations were included.

such as physician, dentist, pharmacist, farmer, and biologist. The interest-test results indicate that more Japanese than whites have the interests of men in these occupations. The Japanese population is too small and for the most part too scattered to support many medical men. Until it has been sufficiently demonstrated that such can secure patients from other racial groups, it would seem hazardous for too many to specialize here (over 20 per cent of Japanese college men are planning to become physicians, dentists, and pharmacists). It would seem that whites would patronize such Japanese specialists once their reputation was well established, but reputation is a plant of slow growth.

In the case of the occupations based on the physical sciences, as far as interests are concerned, there should be more chemists, geologists, and engineers among Japanese than among whites and an equal number of architects. But in terms of preference the Japanese are not planning to enter these activities to the extent that white youths are. When other aspects are taken into account one must question the advisability of many Japanese entering engineering and geology. These occupations necessitate the handling of white common and skilled laborers, who resent Japanese being placed over them. It is also problematic whether many Japanese students can acquire the intimate acquaintanceship with skilled activities open to many a white boy who works during vacation. It is in this respect that the nonexistence of Japanese skilled workmen on the mainland constitutes a serious obstacle to the plans of the second generation to become engineers. The same thing holds true of architecture. A Japanese might succeed as an office man but he would have difficulty in handling matters on the job. In Hawaii the presence of Japanese workmen, foremen, and even contractors eliminates this difficulty. The whole engineering field is today overcrowded, and there are too many experienced white men looking for work to warrant Japanese attempting to enter this field.

The interests of farmers (graduates of agricultural schools who earn their living as farmers) correlate 0.76 with the interests of engineers, 0.63 with chemists, 0.66 with dentists, and 0.41 with physicians. It is quite likely that some Japanese planning to enter these four professions really belong in farming. The writer has found this situation to be true among whites. They choose one of the four instead of farming because of encouragement to do so. It is natural also for those growing up on a farm to turn to engineering if they are interested in the machinery, trucks, radio, etc., on the farm. But such interests do not necessarily indicate engineering.

More Japanese than whites are interested in mathematics. Yet no one reports he intends to specialize in it. It would seem to the writer that really qualified Japanese would meet less prejudice in this field than in many others, for the work of actuary or statistician is an inside activity in which there is little need to contact the general public. Teaching college mathematics might be open, but the field is badly overcrowded today; there is always room here as elsewhere, however, for the outstanding man.

More Japanese than educated whites are planning to enter skilled trades, although the difference is not great. It is in this field that the Japanese population is most deficient. As indicated above, the lack of Japanese artisans interferes greatly with the chances for other Japanese to occupy more advanced positions. The evidence is clear that Japanese can do skilled work. But they must build from the bottom up in this regard. A few are entering the garage business. Possibly this is as good a place to begin as any, since they should be able to command considerable business from other Japanese in getting their start. Once efficiently run garages are established there would be opportunity for other Japanese to enter related skilled trades.

From certain tests, described in chapter vii, it appears Japanese are superior to whites in finger co-ordination and reaction time. It is hazardous to claim on this basis that Japanese are superior in work calling for fine finger co-ordinations, but the chances are favorable to this view. All this suggests the possibility of their becoming laboratory technicians for dentists and hospitals, since their interests run in that direction. Similarly one should expect to find Japanese becoming watch repairmen or engaging in other allied activities.

Japanese are fond of photography, and many produce most artistic results. The many ramifications of this industry should provide niches suitable for them.

Japanese have the interests of teachers, ministers, and social workers to a greater degree than whites, yet fewer of them are planning such careers. The chief difference, however, is in teaching, which is hardly open to the second generation in the public schools. It will be wiser for them to forego any possible opportunity in this field until the days of agitation have been practically forgotten. If the Japanese language could be introduced into the high schools as a substitute for French or German, this would provide an opening wedge into the teaching profession. A few Japanese are already so employed in colleges or universities. Until there is a demand for such instruction by the students, however, there will be few such opportunities.

Very few Japanese or whites have the interests of artists or musicians.[7] The prospects for a career in music, unless one is obviously gifted, are very slim, owing to the advent of the radio. The writer is convinced that there is an increasing emphasis upon beauty in every phase of life and that those qualified should consider carefully what part they may play here. The Japanese are generally thought of as an artistic nation. So far their representatives in this country have made little contribution to our art. Possibly those with artistic ability did not come here; possibly those here have had to work so hard for a living that they have had no excess energy or money to devote to artistic expression. The unique in landscaping, in interior decorating, and in merchandising is eagerly sought. Japanese art is so different from Occidental art that it seems certain that there is an opportunity for those who can properly introduce it into this country. Any contribution will meet with little or no resentment or competition.

The few data available suggest no particular difference between the two racial groups as to interest in business, omitting advertising and selling for the moment. More Japanese than whites say that they are going to enter business, but the difference is to be found among the larger number of the former going into retailing. The whites are evidently selecting a wider variety of business openings and on the average better-paid positions (see p. 220).

Japanese have much less the interests of advertising men and salesmen than whites. Very few are planning such careers, but then very few in school do make such plans. It is doubtful whether young Japanese would be successful in selling most commodities to whites; on the other hand, it would be quite appropriate for them to sell anything that is associated with them. A really good salesman would probably succeed in selling many other articles. Within their own group there are a considerable number of selling positions, particularly insurance of all kinds. There should be a need before long for several advertising men to direct the advertising of Japanese businesses and newspapers.

According to the interest test, Japanese have much less the interests of lawyers and writers than have whites. Although a few second-generation Japanese are practicing law and one at least has been admitted to practice before the United States Supreme Court, on the whole few have entered the profession or are now planning to do so. There seems to be a widespread feeling among the Japanese that white judges and

---

[7] See Table 33; also p. 171.

jurors are prejudiced against a Japanese lawyer and consequently they are better represented in court by white lawyers. This may be true, but there may well be a need for Japanese lawyers who would specialize in the problems most affecting members of their race and would at least handle such cases outside of court, if not in court.

There are a considerable number of Japanese newspapers on the Pacific Coast, some published in Japanese, some in English, and some in both languages. Offhand, it would appear that this field is well covered as far as number is concerned. The quality and quantity of material printed in English, however, can be greatly improved, for every issue furnishes good evidence that the English language has not yet been mastered by the Japanese.

Occupational openings due to Japanese ancestry.—It would seem that the second generation would have many advantages over whites in export and import business with Japan. But this presupposes mastery of the two languages, which we have seen is seldom the case for even one language. Those planning such a career should recognize that there is great competition for positions and should prepare themselves accordingly.

Retail outlets for Japanese goods and curios have not been developed to any great extent. Whether or not they can be advantageously increased is a question, considering the probable competition with all manner of existing stores.

The Chinese have given us novel eating-places in which chop suey and other dishes are served. These are not truly Chinese but are adaptations of Chinese foods to American taste. So far the Japanese have not succeeded in this sort of thing, although they operate many cheap restaurants. Can they not specialize in something novel and at the same time appetizing, served in a different setting from our other eating-places? This field again is comparatively small—only a few such restaurants in a city could be profitable.

The mere fact of being a Japanese is an asset in itself in certain situations, particularly if it is accompanied by a pleasing personality. Certain exclusive retail organizations employ Japanese to lend "atmosphere" to an establishment. Alert and pleasing proprietors of such undertakings as florist shops, stores for vending fancy fruits and vegetables, etc., have already gained an enviable popularity. Specialty shops of all sorts seem to hold similar promise for the striking personality further distinguished by Japanese attributes. Varieties of domestic service also seem feasible, though apparently less and less engaged in, in accordance with the reputed tendency away from "menial labor." There should similarly be a few such openings in the amusement industry.

Where Japanese are congregated in large numbers, a few openings will develop in large businesses for Japanese to serve their fellows. Thus one bank has a Japanese teller who specializes in Japanese accounts.

The Japanese are a clannish people. Though they resent the preference of whites for whites, they themselves prefer their own kind. Consequently, the second generation have the entrée to all the varied occupational activities which arise among the Japanese themselves. Many of these are already filled by the first generation, but their places will need to be taken over from time to time by the second generation. Unless these businesses expand in size (they now average one-half employee apiece), they will furnish future employment to only one son and his wife. Wages now paid to employees are extremely low and these openings are not attractive.

In our survey of 2,115 first-generation men, 296 were engaged in businesses rendering service and 267 in retail stores (see Table 27, pp. 209–11). Three-fourths of these men owned their business. Managing a restaurant or hotel was the most popular type of business; next come grocery stores, meat markets, and fruit and vegetable stands. Other fairly common types of such businesses are dry cleaning, barber shops, jewelry stores, and soft-drink establishments. Until the Japanese enter other types of business there is little prospect of their employing many of their own or of any other race.

Ownership.—Our findings in chapter ix make clear that the Japanese have a surprising tendency to achieve ownership. They own their own businesses and would like to own their farms, in decided preference to working for others. Many Japanese have confided to the writer that one of their greatest weaknesses is their inability to co-operate with one another—that their partnerships seldom endure. Seemingly, this must be peculiar to the Japanese who have come here or is a resultant of their experiences here, since their countrymen have demonstrated ability to build up large organizations in Japan. This view is supported by several of the second generation, who nevertheless intimate that when their generation comes along they will be able to co-operate as their fathers have not.

The only people the writer met in the Hawaiian Islands who were certain that the second generation having a high-school education could be induced to work on the sugar plantations were young second-generation leaders. They felt that the chief objection to such work was the impossibility of achieving promotion and, more important still, ownership. They felt that if the sugar planters really wanted this labor they could get it by appropriate changes from a highly paternalistic régime to one that fitted the new generation. This view is advanced here not in way of criticism of the sugar planters, for the writer does not know enough of the situation to hazard any view himself, but merely to emphasize the desire of the second generation for ownership.

To the extent that this is a dominant characteristic of the second generation it may be expected that the Japanese will seek occupations in which they can be their own bosses. The professions meet this requirement; also farming, retailing, even gardening and house-cleaning, as they carry it on, and in fact most of the activities in which they are now engaged. Even when working for others they tend to take the work on a share basis, as in farming. This tendency is a commendable one, but if it is too strong and too universal among them it will militate against the development of large undertakings. Whether the individual owner can succeed in the face of competition from large businesses is not yet settled, but it certainly is clear that he must be efficient to do so.

Lack of capital.—The Japanese came here without capital. They have acquired something, but after all not very much. It is true that a few have made fortunes and others will do likewise. Nevertheless, it is safe to say that for some time to come they will be greatly handicapped by lack of capital for the development of large business operations. However, as they gradually cease to send money back to relatives in Japan they will accumulate capital more rapidly. In the development of proper credit facilities there are opportunities for several competent and experienced business men.

Marriage for women.—There is such a strong emphasis upon marriage and family life among the Japanese that we may expect practically all the girls to marry. The first-generation women came to this country as wives or brides or with the expectation of marrying. This explains the exceptionally high percentage (98 per cent) who have been or are married. Our statistics indicate that the second-generation women are marrying to a greater extent and at an earlier age than white women.

Much has been made in certain circles of the fact that the oldest of the second-generation women are faced with a serious situation in that there are not eligible men for them to marry. Men of their own generation are of the same age or younger and have not established themselves to the point of supporting a wife. Men of the first generation are usually much older, have been brought up in Japan, and hold ideas as to the proper rôle of a wife entirely different from those held by second-generation women. Fortunately, the situation affects only comparatively few young women.

A much more serious condition results from the different points of view of the two generations regarding marriage. As one second-generation young woman puts it:

In our parents' days in Japan the young people were married without even seeing each other, the marriage being arranged between the two families by a go-between. Before consent was given by the parents of either party, the history of the other party's family was carefully examined in regard to social status, reputation, disease or other defects. The first generation now living in the United States have never experienced that romantic life that American boys and girls as well as our second generation Japanese have a tendency to enjoy. The first generation somewhat object to the American custom, and we think it perfectly natural. What the young people think good in a young man or young woman of their choice, the first generation consider unimportant and immediately begin investigating about the past record and family history in which the second generation have little thought. We like to, and have a tendency to live today, and look forward to building a future together, whereas the first generation considers the past more important.

Another girl, twenty-four years of age and a college graduate, reports she has already "stalled off" four proposals brought to her father by "friends" of comparatively unknown or personally repulsive men. Her father is fond of her and, unlike many first-generation fathers, has not forced her to marry against her wishes, but she says that if her father knew that she is holding off in the hope of arranging her own love marriage he would make her marry the next one that comes along. So saturated is she in the customs of obedience to her father that she seems to feel she would have to obey. The matter is made worse because of the girl's age, twenty-four, which is a terrible age for an unmarried Japanese daughter to be still on her father's hands—people are already beginning to ask what is the matter with her that she cannot secure a husband.

Still another girl, twenty years old, who went through high school in three years and was valedictorian of her class, has just been married by her parents to a young Japan-born and -raised farmer of thirty-eight, who has been to school but three months in his life.

This conflict in marriage customs only the Japanese can solve. They certainly would not appreciate any interference by whites in the matter.

As far as marriage is concerned it would seem that the Japanese women are better off than the whites, for many of the latter never have a real opportunity, whereas the former may not all have the romance they crave, nor be able to marry the right man, but evidently all will have proposals and can marry if they wish. There is still an excess of first-generation men as compared with women, but this does not hold for the second generation.

Possibly no group of women in this country have worked harder than the first-generation women, carrying on the functions of wife and mother and also of helper or partner in the field or shop. The indications are that the second-generation women have no intention of working outdoors on the farm. Our records show that some are planning a career independent of marriage.

NEED OF VOCATIONAL GUIDANCE

Occupations chosen by young people for their future work are restricted surprisingly to relatively few from all that are available. As previously pointed out, the range of choice of Japanese-Americans is somewhat less than that of whites but neither ever consider many occupations in which thousands are employed. In one rather extensive group of young second-generation Japanese none planned to become managers of barber shops, restaurants, confectionery stores, or bookstores in which some of their parents are engaged. Few considered any form of literary work, wholesaling, or teaching. A great variety of tasks are necessary in order that the work of the world may be performed. The attention of the young has, however, been directed to few of them.

It is obvious that all young people need vocational guidance. Too many believe that if they secure an education a good job will be supplied them. Many have only a hazy notion of what they want to do; evidently they have given little thought to the whole problem; many are not even interested in the subject.[8]

On the whole, the whites have more definite plans, are more sure they have selected wisely, have more second choices, show greater range or variety of choices, and have evidently thought more about the whole subject. The chief reason for this difference between whites and second-generation Japanese lies in the fact that the latter come in contact with fewer occupational activities. And for this very reason their parents and friends cannot help them so much. American schools supply some in-

[8] Twice the writer announced in Japanese newspapers that he would administer the Vocational Interest Blank free of charge to any Japanese who replied. Only one did so. A relatively poor return was received from Japanese college men when blanks were mailed them. See chapter vii.

formation, but they notoriously direct students away from the trades and agriculture into "white collar" jobs and they give pitifully little information about the economic life. It is unfortunate that what pertains to earning a living is viewed as vocational, not cultural, and that it is so often felt that only cultural subjects should have a place in high school or college. It is not surprising that there is a large minority graduating from college with no idea of what they are going to do to earn a living.

What shall be done?

Program of Akagi.—Akagi[9] urges that the Japanese organize vocational guidance bureaus in all the large Japanese centers, each of which is to be under the direction of a competent, technically trained, lofty visioned, and well-informed assistant director, with a director over all the bureaus. Each of these bureaus is to be correlated with an employment bureau. He very wisely advocates extensive research before launching the enterprise. "Before advising the choice of agriculture or engineering definitely, the director should be somehow certain of the future work, extent, and distribution in the respective field." Higher education and shorter technical training should be encouraged. To this end scholarships and loan funds should be established for needy students. "If we have no leaders today, why not start right now to educate and train them?"

Vocational-guidance problem.—Part of the vocational-guidance problem confronting the Japanese is identical with that confronting whites. Here is involved the analysis of the individual, on the one hand, and the analysis of all occupations, on the other hand, and, finally, the selection of the occupation for which the individual is best fitted. (This phase of the matter will be discussed a little later.) The part of the vocational problem which is peculiar to Japanese is the problem of what occupations not now open to them can be made available.

Japanese are living very largely within a Japanese community. The second generation naturally are finding their occupational careers within this circle and just without it in the outskirts of the white community. The complaint of many young Japanese is that they do not have free access to this white community. The complaint shows the naïve character of their thinking. No group gives away its privileges. If the young Japanese are to succeed in these new fields they must displace whites already entrenched. Some of the Japanese leaders perceive the true situation. One writes:

9 R. H. Akagi, *The Second Generation Problem* (Japanese Students' Christian Association in North America, 1926).

The continual pushing of the second generation may eventually make the barrier of race crumble away and they may be able to exercise their ability freely. The second generation is in the initial experimental stage and what it is able to accomplish will have consequences to bear on the third generation which will still be much of an experiment. My one hope is to see the second generation prepare themselves adequately in whatever line of activity the individual chooses and continue to exert themselves without ceasing. The success of the second generation lies in the drive they possess and in the perseverance they have in driving forward their powers and their abilities which are latent in them. Even if they are equal to the whites in ability, if they do not have the extra push, they are not going to get equal benefits. Dormant people do not get anything. It is live-wires who get what they want.

Knowing full well that this survey has done something to alleviate some of the difficulties to be encountered by the second generation, I am still a believer in the fact that only time will tell.

Two Japanese physicians who started in working at anything they could get expressed the same thought. One said: "The second generation needs to get out and do something for themselves." The other said: "The second generation must learn to dig for themselves, and seek to solve their own problems. At present they are not doing this; they are waiting for someone else to solve them for them." Another criticism of the same type is this:

Many of them [college graduates] have the idea that it is a disgrace to take positions their high school friends had occupied. Instead of accepting such offers, they idle their time until many years pass without their doing anything worthwhile. They remain as parasites to their parents or friends. The sooner one realizes the truth that large things have their foundation in small beginnings, the quicker will he be able to launch himself to his future career.[10]

Taking into account these criticisms and what we have learned of the ability and education and background of the second generation, what is the chance that they will break through the barriers that surround them? Without doubt, the chances are good. If there were no chance, vocational guidance would be a relatively simple matter, for it would involve merely the allocation of the second generation to the relatively few occupations in which Japanese are now to be found. Admitting the possibility that the second generation can break through the barriers that encircle them, the guidance problem becomes tremendously more complicated. Three more questions must be raised. If the second generation are going to extend their field, will they break all barriers or only some? And if only some, which ones? And, last of all, which second-generation individuals will break through?

---

[10] Editorial, *The Pacific Citizen,* March 1, 1932.

Suppose a Japanese physician should develop a particularly good treatment for tuberculosis. The writer feels certain that whites would seek his services, once his reputation were established. As a consequence, every other Japanese physician would find it easier to obtain patients outside his racial group. In other words, many Japanese may succeed or fail in medicine, depending upon whether or not a single Japanese achieves an outstanding success. The same situation holds more or less regarding each new occupation the second generation attempt to enter.

Under these circumstances it seems well-nigh impossible to advise the second generation. There is no way of determining what is the total number that can earn a living in a given pursuit, for there is no way of knowing beforehand whether or not this is to be one of the occupations in which the second generation will be outstanding successes.

When an infantry regiment is sent over the top the general knows full well that many will be killed and wounded, but he confidently expects some to reach the objective. Under a dictatorship the second generation could similarly be sent forth. The success of the few in the first wave would advance the cause, and future waves would find their going that much easier. Life is like this. From any group some succeed; once in a while, one makes a great success; most advance a little and then falter. It is seldom, however, that the really successful are spotted at the very beginning. Too many complicating factors enter in to make such prophecies of significance.

It seems, consequently, well-nigh impossible to give advice to the second generation as to whether or not they can succeed in an occupation now manned by whites. The chances are against them, yet success is possible. The writer remembers a man who was so blind he could only tell light from darkness and who stuttered terribly, yet he made a creditable living as a salesman to retail stores. He had developed a method of selling by displaying cards with pictures and reading-matter so unique that no one could fail to pay attention.

But what about the phases of vocational guidance which are common to Japanese and whites equally? Here we are concerned with four problems: (1) determination of each individual's abilities and interests; (2) analysis of occupations; (3) determination of which occupation, or occupations, each individual should plan to enter; and (4) placement of the individual in the occupation, or, if that is filled, in the next best one.

The fourth task is now being performed by various employment agencies with varying degrees of efficiency. There is nothing peculiarly difficult about the problem. Given a man wanting a certain kind of a job, it is possible to determine whether there is such an opening, and, if not, if there is an opening in an allied activity.

Some progress has been made toward solving the first problem relative to analysis of an individual's abilities and interests. We can tell certain individuals that they are so lacking in certain abilities that the chances are very greatly against success in such and such occupations. But we cannot prophesy that other individuals will be successful. They may have the general intelligence to acquire the necessary training, they may have certain qualities that are necessary, and they may have the required interests, and yet they may fail for other reasons. There is, for example, no way today of measuring the drive of the individual. Until we can foretell how hard he will struggle to achieve, we cannot prophesy with any accuracy what he will accomplish. Research is being carried on in many centers, and there is progress. But the problem is tremendous, and present research facilities are after all quite limited. Seemingly there is no other development of knowledge that will add so much to the welfare of society, making it possible for individuals to understand their capabilities and the rôle in which these can serve to best advantage.

The second problem, relative to analysis of occupations, is also a difficult one. The necessary methods exist, however, for such analysis and the data can be gathered as to how many men are available and how many are needed in each occupation. All that is lacking is money to do the job. But over and above the analysis of existing occupations is the greater problem as to which old occupations will disappear in the near future, which ones will radically change, and what new occupations will emerge. In other words, it is possible to determine supply and demand of human beings for the various occupations, and to make reasonably accurate estimates for the immediate future, on the basis of existing economic conditions. But in the realm of vocational guidance prophecies covering the period of a lifetime are essential. This no one would attempt today, for no one can foresee the inventions that will be made and their effects upon men's livelihoods. If we are to develop national planning of our economic life, as many now advocate, all this and more will be involved.[11]

The third problem of determining the occupation for which each

[11] The recent organization of the National Occupational Conference (1933) will result in a very distinct advance in our knowledge of occupations, particularly with reference to entry into them by young people. See *Occupations,* XII (February and June 1934 issues), 6 and 10.

individual is best fitted is dependent upon answering the first two problems. Consequently, it cannot be solved today with any real accuracy. The only proper procedure is for the so-called expert in this field to give the individual such available facts as bear on his case and then leave him to make his own decision. No man mindful of the woefully inadequate information available should dare to accept the responsibility of deciding another's career. But there should be concerted effort on the part of the state to place before each youth what is known so that he can make as good a guess as possible. And the state should undertake extensive research in order both to accumulate additional information and to determine the best manner of getting this information before young people.

Scientific versus practical approach.—The paragraphs above have been written from the point of view of the scientist who appreciates the very small chance of arriving at the "true" answer to a vocational-guidance problem. There is at the same time the practical aspect of the whole matter. Here we are confronted, for example, with a young man who cannot decide whether to go into engineering or into medicine, or with a second young man who thinks he wants to go into business, but isn't quite sure, and admits he doesn't know very much about business. What shall be done with these cases? Shall they be left to flounder alone, or shall society do the best it can with them? Just as there have always been medicine men and later on physicians to deal with sick people, even though the "true" cure was not known, so there should be established "guidance experts" who will have the best techniques available and will counsel with young people.

Such a guidance program involves, first, the analysis of the individual regarding his psychological characteristics, his physical condition (medical and psychiatric examination), and his industrial experiences. Second, the occupations for which he is seemingly best fitted should be called to his attention and information concerning them put at his disposal. When he has made his decision, a proper training program should be mapped out. If he is unwilling to undertake this, or cannot do so for financial or other reasons, then another occupation should be selected by him, as evidently the first is an incorrect choice. Finally, an employment bureau should be available to help him find a position.

As the state controls the education of youths, so it also should establish and maintain agencies whereby these youths may be guided into the type of education for which they are best fitted and should aid them in getting started in a beginning job. This is not all. Countless mistakes will be made today in such counseling and by the youths themselves. The agencies of the state should handle all ages of citizens, analyzing them again and again, prescribing new courses of training[12] and placing them in new positions, until the individual has found a place where he can earn a living. All this is actually much cheaper than the maintenance of our present relief agencies, including undoubtedly much of the cost of our criminal courts, reform schools, and penitentiaries.

VOCATIONAL GUIDANCE SPECIFICALLY FOR JAPANESE

The program outlined applies to second-generation citizens of Japanese ancestry, as well as to all other groups. All young people need such guidance and it should be supplied them.

But the Japanese group need special help regarding their own particular problem as to what new occupations they may enter and how that is to be accomplished. This problem is a phase of proper guidance and placement, but it will not be analyzed with any degree of merit by specialists who are handling whites primarily. Accordingly, it appears that the Japanese community must perform this function if it is to be well done. Some such organization as the Japanese-American Citizens' League should accept the responsibility.

The necessary program would require a full-time man who would study the occupational possibilities of the second generation and would travel about the state counseling the Japanese youths. Data should be kept up to date regarding the occupational plans of the second generation, also the occupations they are actually entering and their success. This would not be today a particularly onerous task, as there were only about 5,000 Japanese of age in 1932 and there will be only about 6,000 more coming of age during the next five years. A follow-up of these year by year would supply very valuable information as to what occupations are apt to be overcrowded and as to the occupations where successes and failures are most common.

There is an essential difference between this proposal and that of Akagi (p. 245). Akagi provides for a more or less complete system of guidance to care specifically for the second generation. Our program emphasizes the necessity of establishing proper guidance for all. But inasmuch as the Japanese-Americans have certain problems peculiar to themselves, we provide that one expert shall specialize in these problems and supply the necessary information not only to the Japanese directly

---

12 Emphasis is placed especially upon individual diagnoses and retraining in R. A. Stevenson, *The Minnesota Unemployment Project,* November (1931).

but also to all counselors in the school system, who in this way will be better prepared to handle the Japanese with whom they come in contact. It is fatal to the best interests of the second generation for the school authorities to believe that the Japanese guidance problem is so distinct that their own representatives must handle it.

One special warning needs to be sounded. It is quite possible that the first few of the second generation to seek jobs may have been quite successful merely because such jobs were more or less waiting for just such young people to come along. After these jobs have all been filled, it may be that the remainder of the second generation will have a harder time finding openings. The younger members of the second generation must investigate the possibilities ahead and not follow slavishly the educational and occupational programs of their older brothers.

XI. ECONOMIC OUTLOOK

How the second generation are going to earn a living and how they are going to get along with the whites are two questions so intimately related that they should be considered simultaneously. For the sake of convenience the two have been discussed separately, but what has already been presented on vocational opportunities in the preceding chapter must be kept in mind while the topics in this chapter are reviewed and the aspects of the subject discussed in this chapter must in turn be considered in relation to the statements that have previously been made.

JAPANESE-AMERICANS AND WHITES CONTRASTED

Mentally and morally the Japanese-Americans are similar to whites (chapter vii). The whites score slightly higher on tests of intelligence. This may be due to poorer acquaintanceship of Japanese-Americans with the English language in which the tests are given. It is also possible that the Japanese are actually less capable along linguistic lines. Morally the Japanese-Americans are possibly superior to the whites; at least their record in delinquency and crime is better (chapter vii). They are rated high for trustworthiness by housewives; the lower credit ratings assigned Japanese merchants are as likely to be a reflection of their inexperience in business as of their untrustworthiness in money matters.

Considering their opportunities, the second generation have so far made an excellent record. They are eager for education; and they obtain higher marks, at least in junior and senior high school, than the average pupil (chapter viii). Records based on half of those who have graduated from Stanford University and the University of California during 1920–30 indicate that they are progressing satisfactorily (see p. 223).

Physically there are differences between the two groups. The Japanese-American is shorter and scores lower in strength tests, but on the other hand his reactions are quicker. These differences are probably of little practical significance.

The only significant difference between the two groups is in physical appearance; the Japanese-Americans do not look like Americans. This was strikingly true in the case of the first generation, as it is true of most immigrant groups. The second-generation Japanese are not able to free themselves from the prejudice which is attached to their fathers, as do the second generation of Caucasian races, for they continue to look like their fathers and different from whites. There is no question but that this very greatly affects their problem.

The Japanese group has not striven to minimize this difference. Some second generation have been educated in Japan so that their Japanese mannerisms have been fostered, not eliminated. They have not mastered the English language, as do the second-generation Germans, Poles, or Armenians. Let us admit that the prejudice they have encountered has naturally kept them apart and has made them fearful to cut the bridge behind them and become entirely American. And all these factors have prevented genuine social intercourse whereby they would have had the opportunity to learn the language and customs of the country. Even when dress and mannerisms are acquired and mastery of the English language is attained, there will still remain the matter of physical size and appearance; here they are fundamentally different.

There is a greater unlikeness measured quantitatively between some blondes and brunettes of the same race than between short, dark-haired Americans and many Japanese. But the former difference is of little significance qualitatively, while the latter is intensified by the great variety of stereotyped reactions associated with the Japanese.

These stereotyped reactions have all been learned. It is entirely possible to replace them with new reactions of another sort. It is apparent that some change in this direction is taking place. The ugly things said about the Japanese, as quoted in chapter v, are less often encountered, particularly among the white children who are growing up in the public schools with Japanese-Americans. The latter are being reacted to much more distinctly as individuals than as mere members of a race.

CRUX OF THE JAPANESE-AMERICAN PROBLEM

The crux of the whole Japanese-American problem rests upon the answers to three questions: Will the whites radically change their conception of the Japanese as time goes on? If so, how rapidly will such a change take place? And, finally, how far will such a change go?

The answers to these three questions depend very largely upon how the second generation conduct themselves. They are unquestionably greatly handicapped, for their present economic and social position places them in an inferior status. In this regard they are no worse off than most immigrant groups; they are unquestionably better off than the Negro.[1] If they show the same adaptability and success in later life that

[1] A study of industrial conditions in Buffalo, for example, shows "the native white stock to be in control of the clerical, managerial, and supervisory positions;

they have already evidenced in school and in behaving themselves out of school, they will find the attitude toward them changing for the better. Every improvement in this attitude will mark a lessening in the handicap for all of them. Surely here is a great opportunity for 50,000 young people to co-operate and to see to it that each plays his proper rôle in ameliorating the unfavorable conditions affecting every one of them.

The answers to the three questions depend to some degree also upon how the Japanese in Japan conduct themselves. German-Americans suffered when their country went to war with Germany. The more Americans respect Japan as a nation, the better off the Japanese-Americans will be.

ASSIMILATION

Much of the argument against Japanese immigration of recent years has been in terms of whether or not they can be assimilated. Both sides to this controversy agree that the Japanese are capable of cultural assimilation, meaning, in the words of Jordan, "comprehension of political and social conditions," and in the words of Boddy, adoption of "the customs, practices, and mode of living prevalent in the country in which they reside" (see pp. 26 and 27).

But can they be assimilated in the sense of amalgamation into the larger group? It is this possibility which the advocates of exclusion deny, claiming that the Japanese tend to "develop foreign colonies which lead to friction and misunderstanding." Exclusionists hold that assimilation does not mean merely the living of two well-regulated groups in the same community but the fusing of the two into one. So far this has not been accomplished except through intermarriage. The sociologist, R. E. Park, is quoted in this connection, as follows:

> ". . . . Where racial differences are as marked, as they are in the case of the Japanese and the American, public sentiment opposes intermarriage. Where intermarriage does not take place assimilation is never complete and the difficulty of two races mentally accommodating themselves to one another, while maintaining each a separate racial existence, is bound to be very great. A racial group which is small in numbers, intimate, compact, and well organized, as is the case with the Jew and the Japanese, has, in the long run, great advantages in competition with

---

the immigrants and their sons and daughters to be concentrated in varying grades of manual labor; and the negroes to be confined almost exclusively to unskilled and general labor. There are overlappings between the several groups, but the main tendencies are quite clear."—N. Carpenter, *Nationality, Color, and Economic Opportunity in the City of Buffalo* (1927), p. 189.

a larger and less organized community. If there are already racial prejudices, this kind of competition intensifies them."[2]

There is at the present time little or no inclination on the part of either Japanese or whites to intermarry. This is particularly evident with respect to the former in the Hawaiian Islands, where intermarriage is possible (see p. 28). The attitude of the whites in continental United States is shown by the passage of legislation in nine states prohibiting such marriages.[3] The mere fact that this has been reduced to written law will make it that much harder to change the present custom upheld by both racial groups. On the other hand, history reveals that differences of race have never been a bar to marriage or to illegitimate relations. What will be the outcome: intermarriage and in time complete assimilation, or no intermarriage and great restriction of social contacts?

Berkson,[4] in discussing the possibility of a cultural group retaining its own national or racial characteristics while participating wholeheartedly in American life, asks two questions: "What place has the Jewish group in our democracy? May it retain its own identity or must it fuse with the total group? And, second, if it may retain its identity, under what limitations and through what agencies may it do so?" These questions make us recognize that in many respects the Jews and Japanese are in much the same position. The former can and the latter cannot intermarry with whites. But to a very large degree the former do not, so that practically neither group is amalgamating with the body of the citizenry.

This fact suggests another question. After all, is it desirable that amalgamation should be so complete that all units become approximately alike? A negative answer would be indicated by the following experience. A certain company made a careful study of their situation and decided that their executives needed a certain type of education. For many years they added to the organization only such men as fulfilled these requirements. Recently they woke up to the fact that there

---

[2] J. F. Steiner, "Some Factors Involved in Minimizing Race Friction on the Pacific Coast," *Annals, American Academy of Political and Social Science,* XCIII (January 1921), 117.

[3] Intermarriage between Orientals and whites is prohibited in Arizona, California, Mississippi, Missouri, Nebraska, Nevada, Oregon, South Dakota, and Wyoming (see C. G. Vernier, *American Family Laws* [1931], I, 204).

[4] Isaac Berkson, *Theories of Americanization* (Teachers College Contributions to Education, No. 109, 1920).

was no one available to succeed the president, who was ordered to retire by his physician. More careful analysis showed that no one was capable of handling the larger orders for their product, something the president had always done. They had standardized their executives so thoroughly in terms of their major requirements of production that there were none really fitted for sales, finance, or presidential functions. Too much today we are reducing a complex situation to some average and then assuming that that average represents, or should represent, each unit in the total. This particular business would be far better prepared to grapple with present-day problems if it were made up of capable men each of whom was as different as possible from all the others. From within the group then would spring a great variety of suggestions which, when worked over, would provide a far better basis for successful operation than could possibly originate from twenty men all making about the same proposals.

American culture is often stigmatized as "machine-made." There is standardization of the goods we buy, of the news we read, of the education we receive, to a large degree of the ideas we may and do express. The NRA is now strengthening our natural trend toward uniformity.

The elimination of differences is in harmony with the psychological principle that human beings dislike to change their ways of doing things. They object to differences, for differences necessitate readaptation. This is much truer of older men than of younger ones, for the habits of the former are more strongly established.[5] On the other hand, people crave some change, otherwise they suffer from boredom, ennui. These two strikingly opposite principles of psychology account for style. Each year's style is an outgrowth of some feature of last year's. In this way we change year by year our clothing, our autos, our belongings generally, but we never make a great change at one time. Such changes as take place represent a happy mean between uniformity and too great variety.

It is often desirable and pleasant to experience a more pronounced difference than that of this "happy mean." The value of travel lies largely in the fact that one is confronted with new experiences and is forced to adjust himself and his thinking to them. Certainly much of the value of an education is to be explained on this basis. Is there not then something to be gained in having within a nation various racial groups which maintain their customs and traditions? We enjoy the

---

[5] E. K. Strong, Jr., *Change of Interests with Age* (1931), p. 21.

deer in Kaibab Forest, the bears in Yellowstone, the Hopi Indians at Grand Canyon, and Chinatown in San Francisco. Why can't we enjoy the various nationalities as we meet them in everyday life just as we do when on a vacation to Honolulu or Quebec? We may well profit by being forced to adapt ourselves to new ways of living and new points of view.

The slow onward march toward political democracy has been marked by one struggle after another, because equality could not be recognized in the presence of some seemingly essential difference. Finally, it was realized that women could vote even though they were not men. Similarly, progress is being made toward industrial democracy. "But cultural and racial democracy we do not yet have in America, And until we do have it, our democracy is painfully and tragically incomplete."[6] Progress is slow because we all assume so absolutely that our own views are the only true ones; hence all differences are signs of inferiority. We must learn that practical equality can exist with essential differences and that differences do not imply inferiority.

Whether we like it or not the world is getting smaller every year; it has now been encircled in seven days. Nations should view each other as neighbors and must learn to live with one another. One way for the citizens of these countries to learn how to do this is to travel and meet other peoples. Another way is to know them as personal neighbors at home. Apparently the latter is harder and more disagreeable than the former. The point here is: Is there not genuine value in the learning? Is there not value in having different social cultures before one's eyes?

This point of view has been well expressed by one of our fiction writers.

> The future may bring a day when some enormously advanced civilization will welcome any alien race because a different race means a different culture and a different mode of looking at life. That is a precious thing—I should say the most precious thing, because when a man advances beyond a primitive concern about clothes for his back and food for his belly, the chief occupation and delight of man is the contemplation of life.[7]

There is another aspect of assimilation that cannot be ignored; that is, the numbers involved, or the velocity of changes, that are demanded. What is true of a few is not necessarily true of many; what is true

---

[6] Reginald Bell, *Public School Education of Second-Generation Japanese in California,* chapter ii.

[7] T. S. Stribling, *Clues of the Caribbees.*

of changes that may occur slowly is not necessarily true of similar changes that must occur very quickly. There should be no real objection to the presence of one hundred thousand Japanese, half of whom have been born here and are being educated in our schools. It is an entirely different matter to talk about assimilating large numbers coming yearly from Japan. It is not illogical to object to further immigration and at the same time to admit that the second generation are being assimilated to such a degree that they will be no menace to the rest of us. In other words, whether or not the fifty thousand second generation can be amalgamated into the total population is not essential: they can render a real service by remaining distinct provided they contribute something new and worth while to our civilization.

SIMILARITY OF PROBLEMS OF SECOND GENERATION AND OF WHITES

The great majority of problems confronting the second-generation Japanese are problems with which whites also must grapple. This is true because all human beings are far more alike than unlike. It is true because Japanese and whites are more similar in intellectual attainments than many other racial groups. And furthermore it is true because these two are living in the same environment and are being educated in the same school systems and practically to the same extent.

This point needs to be stressed because many who have written about the Japanese in America have unwittingly given the erroneous impression that the Japanese are faced with very peculiar conditions. These writers made few or no comparisons between the Japanese and other groups but merely listed the problems of the former. If they had similarly listed the problems of any other group, then the fact that most problems were common to both groups would have been apparent.

In studying the problems of the second-generation Japanese it is entirely feasible to compare them with the problems of all white young people; it is much fairer and more appropriate, however, to compare them with the problems of second-generation whites. The low economic and social status into which second-generation Japanese are born and their parents' relatively slight understanding of American civilization handicap them greatly. Both of these factors, plus that of their immigrant parents' inability to speak English, intensify the age-old conflict between parents and children, the young people early coming to believe they know more than their parents. It is unfortunate that the Japanese do not appreciate that other immigrant groups have had to contend with these problems, but attribute their troubles so largely to the fact that they are Japanese in origin. Thus one second-generation Japanese young woman writes:

> In regard to the young people's socials where dancing is involved our first generation usually disapprove by saying that it is not becoming for respectable young men and women to be seen in each others arms. Whereas the young people who do the dancing think not of the vulgar or indecent but of the rhythmic, graceful, gliding movements that are executed in response to music. Since our parents have never experienced dancing themselves, and have never seen it in Japan, when they are exposed to it here they think dancing indecent.
>
> Some of the first generation as they look upon our second generation boys and girls on the street, at church gatherings, at meetings, at socials, and on various other occasions, say that the young people think only of dressing and of looking up-to-date and think very little of economizing and saving. Especially of the way the girls dress now-a-days, some men say, "our wages can never support such young ladies and provide for a home too." So some of our first generation men prefer women of Japan who are reserved, conservative, say very, very little, and know how to cook and sew, because the women of Japan are brought up with that inferiority complex. The second generation women at least think they are equal and would like to have just as much to say about doing or acting as do the men. This the real Japanese men dislike.

There is nothing peculiar to the Japanese in this!

It is not surprising that many observers point out that the Japanese-American has an "inferiority complex," or in other words is "unusually sensitive" and prone to detect discriminations against his group which stimulate within him righteous resentment and audible demands for equity. The second-generation Citizens' League fosters these demands; in addition to encouraging its members to enter upon their civic duties, the latest conference of the League passed resolutions aiming at the rectification of certain matters that are felt to be discriminatory against Japanese as United States citizens and also against Japanese as nationals of Japan.

The "injured dignity" of the second generation is frequently accompanied by an extension of the individual's self-respect and personality to include marked solicitude for and pride in the Old Country. Thus, the second generation are not unaware of discrimination existing in relation to certain other sections of American society, but it is as if they feel that their Japanese ancestry should, if anything, exempt them from such unwelcome participation in this long-standing American difficulty. The argument of one young citizen begins in this manner: "A nation as much a world Power as Japan has become, should be on an equal immigration basis with the other Powers . . . ." In concluding, she feels that, though discrimination may abound even as between

Occidental citizens in political, economic, and social life in the United States, any such discrimination is of an entirely different "quality" from that of the discrimination—to which she is admittedly hypersensitive—involving Japanese.

Possibly the most serious handicap confronting the second generation is the chaotic state of mind that is induced by the welter of problems confronting them. Conflicting ideas, ideals, and aspirations result in the expenditure of much energy in one direction after another with little or no progress in any direction. Possibly in no age have all young people been more seriously handicapped by this condition. The solution is not, however, for the Japanese-Americans to attribute their troubles to the fact that they are Japanese in origin. To place all the blame for one's deficiencies upon an external fact over which one has no control rather than to a possible deficiency in one's own character is more gratifying to one's self-esteem, but it destroys the impetus to self-improvement which might mean future success.

It appears to the writer that the Japanese are particularly prone to blame the whites for all their troubles. For example, after discussion of their whole problem for an entire afternoon, in the early fall of 1933, a distinguished leader from Japan quoted the case of a young Japanese-American who had graduated four months earlier from an American university, having majored in chemistry. Because this young graduate had been unable to obtain a position immediately in his line, it was evident that Americans were very unfair to his countrymen. Previously this Japanese leader had recounted the difficulties confronting the Japanese nation because so many college graduates, out of jobs, were turning to socialism. He had also shown a surprisingly good grasp of the economic conditions in the United States and particularly their effect upon unemployment. But he apparently could make no application of this to a case involving a Japanese college graduate in this country. Such a college man, apparently, had a right to a first-class job, and when he did not get it within four months after graduation the wicked Americans were to blame! This same view seems to actuate the thinking of too many Japanese in this country, although fortunately this is not true of all.

In this connection one cannot but ask the Japanese what chance there would be of an American getting a job in a Japanese factory, or of a Japanese securing a position in England, France, or Italy. Tourists report that it is most difficult for an American even to visit these establishments abroad. Within the year the Japanese were greatly inflamed because two Americans took photographs of several public buildings in Japan to be used for advertising purposes in the United States!

Coupled with their proneness to blame Americans for their troubles, there is a surprising tendency to believe they themselves have a right to the "keys of the city." The writer only admires the Japanese the more for their insistence upon getting the best for themselves. But they should recognize that the whites also want the best and are out to get it. It is poor sportsmanship to blame their rivals every time a Japanese loses a trial heat.

Many college seniors, regardless of racial background, assume that the world owes them a first-class position upon graduation. Nearly all employers are agreed that the recent college graduate is a very difficult employee to handle. Possibly the view held by many young Japanese is no different from that of these white college men. If so, they will achieve a different point of view as time goes on. It is extremely important that they cease attributing all their troubles to race prejudice, that they size up their particular obstacles, and find ways to overcome them. At the same time they need to note their real deficiencies and to take steps to rectify them.

CAN RACE PREJUDICE BE OVERCOME?

Race prejudice is occasioned by concern, jealousy, and fear, arising from threatened or actual competition (see chapter iv). There results a magnification of the bad qualities and a minimization of the good characteristics of the out-group. All these defensive attitudes are associated with the physical differences between the in- and the out-group. Because of inability to distinguish between individuals of the out-group (they look so much alike), any unfortunate experience with one of them is unwittingly viewed as typical of the entire group and thus associated with the group's physical appearance.

Once race prejudice is established it is a question whether it can be overcome. Seemingly society is full of castes, cliques, fraternities, and the like whereby those within may look down upon those without. Unfortunately human beings would apparently rather hate than love; because of this it is far easier to establish prejudice than good-will. The latter does replace the former in individual cases; possibly such a change can occur within a whole group. Research is badly needed in this field.

Seemingly race prejudice should decline with decreasing competition. This has apparently occurred in California, following the exclusion of the Chinese and Japanese. It should decline also as the in-group come to know personally the members of the out-group. For when there is personal acquaintance there is less tendency to attribute to the entire out-group the characteristics of the individual who is known. And when the out-group has many fine qualities, as is the case with the Japanese, contact should further allay race prejudice toward them, if not eliminate it.

Our interviewers all noted the present lack of contact between whites and Japanese. They have emphasized that this situation is quite natural with respect to the first generation but that there is far less reason for such a condition existing as far as the second generation is concerned. Too much, they feel, the latter have accepted the view of their parents that only animosity is possible, and are unmindful of the change in attitude toward them since the exclusion act was passed. One of our Japanese interviewers reported:

> While educational progress must be made and high occupational hopes must be held, there is a need for the laying of the foundation for the future in amiable social ties which can only be accomplished if the Japanese wake up from the dreams of the past and benefit from the opportunities and privileges which are theirs today.

Lack of space prohibits our going into detail as to how contacts between whites and the second generation may be developed. Moreover, suggestions are not necessary, because articles and speeches by Japanese-Americans both in the Hawaiian Islands and in California testify to the fact that the young people are thoroughly able to solve this problem. When they come to appreciate how much they are handicapped by the present attitude toward them and at the same time how much they can do to change this attitude, the writer is convinced they will make genuine progress in this direction.[8]

ANSWER OF THE SECOND GENERATION TO ITS OWN PROBLEM

Despite all the handicaps that have been pointed out, the second-generation Japanese evidently believe they are better off where they are than anywhere else. All the Japanese in the Hawaiian Islands whom the writer met were unanimously of the opinion that the second genera-

---

[8] See, for example, Asayo Kuraya, "The Key to True American-Japanese Cordiality," *Nikkei Shimin,* June 1, 1930; and Dave Tstsuno, "What and How Can the Second Generation Contribute to the Life of America," *The Pacific Citizen,* June 1, 1931; also the oratorical contests sponsored by the Iolani Japanese Students' Association, Honolulu.

tion would not leave the Islands, even to go to California.[9] And the evidence, previously given, makes clear that those living in California will stay here. Clearly they believe there are greater opportunities for them in the United States than elsewhere. Comparable statistics are not necessary to prove that they can earn more here than in Japan, even if they could get jobs there.

The record of their educational achievement is sufficient to establish the fact that the second generation believe a good education is worth while.

The Japanese-American does not know, however, how he is to earn a living. But this is typical of young people everywhere. All the data that could be amassed on this point make clear that so far they have progressed satisfactorily.

THIS CHANGING WORLD

The Hawaiian Islands are isolated, two thousand miles from the mainland, and they are so small that it is humanly possible to take paper and pencil and calculate their economic situation in a way that is impossible for the United States as a whole. When this is done, it appears that 35 per cent of all workers are employed on the sugar plantations and 7 per cent more on the pineapple plantations, the two great industries of the Islands. Many more are employed in occupations which are more or less dependent upon these two. One can then learn from the Hawaiian Sugar Planters' Association that only 0.6 per cent employed (omitting managers from consideration) are college graduates, and 1.4 per cent are high-school graduates.[10] Now add to this picture the large number of children in the Islands who are attending high school and the considerable number who are going through college, and the question is forced home: What are these educated young people going to do for a living? The consensus is that if they go to high school they are lost to the plantations, except for a relatively few skilled positions. It seems perfectly clear that there are not and cannot be on the Islands sufficient positions to interest these young people.

Adams and Kai write in this connection:

> The number of boys is increasing so greatly that many of them will be unable to find employment in the secondary industries. But, by virtue of custom and

---

[9] For earlier discussion see p. 98.

[10] In these calculations the Filipinos are unclassified as to education, but few would fall in the college or high-school category. In terms of skill, there are 5.5 per cent skilled, 10.7 per cent semi-skilled, and 83.8 per cent unskilled.

education, and on account of general social influences, and especially because of the attitudes of their parents, all or nearly all of the boys are definitely aiming to improve their social and economic status through securing what is considered preferred employment. They expect to be skilled or semi-skilled laborers, independent farmers, clerks, bookkeepers, merchants, and professional men. For many, a pretty serious disillusionment lies ahead.

The problem relates to the future of the large numbers who will not be able to secure the expected opportunities in Hawaii. Will they change their attitude and accept work in the cane and the pineapple fields, or will they emigrate from the Territory—perhaps to the mainland of the United States? Will the owners and managers of plantations make agricultural work more attractive so as to keep Hawaii's native sons in Hawaii, or will they continue to depend almost exclusively upon foreign-born labor?[11]

Victor S. Kealoka, Hawaii's Delegate to Congress, was reported in the *Honolulu Advertiser* of June 6, 1931, in part as follows:

The school population of Hawaii is now approximately 80,000 and we have got to set some active plans in operation to take care of the yearly output of the schools. I am satisfied that serious thought is being given to this matter, and, meanwhile, the only thing to do is to develop the local labor supply for plantation work.

In commenting on Kealoka's remarks, a writer in the *Pacific Affairs* states:

"In this connection it is significant to note that the chairman of the newly created Territorial Board of Education, in his first public utterance, spoke of the primary importance of preparing the native youth of Hawaii to supplant alien imported labor on the plantations. Until the schools cease to prepare their students for non-existent or greatly restricted professional opportunities, and recognize that in order to create good *citizens* they must train good *workers,* Hawaii, essentially an agricultural community with a transient alien population tilling the soil, can advance no further, according to the board chairman's speech of June 15. 'Any program of instruction which does not, in the main, emphasize occupations in agriculture as the goal toward which the majority of our youth must travel, is a delusion and a snare, and only serves to build up hopes in the individual which are incapable of fulfillment in Hawaii,' he declared. Agitation in favor of vocational education and toward restricting the opportunities for higher education in the Territory has been mounting toward a climax of late months."[12]

Viewing this situation from two different angles, there result two very different proposals: First, educational opportunities should be re-

---

[11] Romanzo Adams and Dan Kane-Zo Kai, *The Education of the Boys of Hawaii and Their Economic Outlook* (University of Hawaii Research Publications, No. 4, January 1928), p. 8.

[12] Quoted from *The Pacific Citizen,* July 1, 1931.

stricted to the really superior and the remainder should be prepared for the only jobs that exist, mainly, plantation labor;[13] second, all children should be given every opportunity to obtain as good an education as possible and each should be treated as one's own child, namely, one who certainly is not going to earn his living at common labor if there is any way to avoid it. The stern actualities of life and the idealism of America cannot be reconciled today in these Islands. And yet they must be reconciled!

There has been no need in the United States to worry about harmonizing these two points of view, because since earliest days there has always been room beyond the frontier for anyone with enterprise. But conditions have changed. The frontier has disappeared. As production of economic goods now surpasses consumption, so the production of high-school and college graduates undoubtedly surpasses the number needed for the kinds of jobs such students have aspired to in the past.[14] The writer cannot help but believe that the condition existing on the mainland resembles that so easily seen in the Hawaiian Islands, though the factors are still so complex that the condition is not yet recognized.

Japan is faced with the same condition. Moulton points out:

The number of students enrolled in universities, colleges, higher schools and middle schools alike, has increased by leaps and bounds in the last twenty years, as is indicated by the following table:

Year	Middle Schools	Colleges and Higher Schools	Universities
1912	305,700	42,100	8,900
1916	375,500	50,400	9,700
1921	550,100	64,900	26,200
1925	829,800	87,600	46,700
1928	975,200	98,900	80,900

Although during this period the number of grammar school students increased by only 30 per cent, the number in the middle schools trebled, those in the colleges doubled, and those in the universities increased tenfold. In the year 1928 there were 21,400 university graduates.

Those who acquired superior training 30 or 40 years ago are still in the main in active service, and the new openings do not increase rapidly either in the higher or in the intermediate levels of opportunity. Thousands of young men are annually graduating from colleges into joblessness. An investigation recently conducted by the City of Tokyo shows that the number of college graduates who

[13] See *Report of Governor's Advisory Committee on Education* (1930).

[14] High-school enrollment has increased in the United States from half a million in 1900 to four million in 1930; college enrollment from two hundred thousand to a million in the same period of time.

procure positions is steadily decreasing. In 1923, as many as 97.8 per cent of college graduates obtained positions; in 1925 this percentage was reduced to 66.6; in 1927, to 64.7; and in 1929, to 50.2. Since the beginning of the depression in 1930, the condition is, of course, much worse. Moreover, the character of the jobs obtained has been growing steadily less satisfactory, increasing numbers of college graduates being forced to accept positions of the most menial character.[15]

In commenting on the large number of college and technical graduates unable to find work suitable to their education in Japan, Crocker paints even a gloomier picture:

> It appears that many of these will have to become clerks or even mechanics and manual laborers. That means an "intellectual proletariat." . . . . For an intellectual proletariat, armed with the weapons of socialist dialectic and socialist emotion, and living in the midst of large crowds of disappointed workless labourers, will be a bigger threat to social tranquillity than ever was the discontented aristocrat of the *ancien régime* who set out to engineer the passions of a hungry mob.[16]

What of the future? We need not discuss the effect of the industrial revolution, for its effect upon jobs has been largely within the range of common and skilled labor up to foremanship. The Japanese second generation within this range can earn a living, as have the first generation, in agricultural pursuits. They are too efficient to be displaced. It is the great majority of the second generation who are attending high school and college that concern us. How do the changing social conditions affect them? and also the whites of equivalent educational status?

The single word "overproduction" points to the answer. The frontier days which gave us freedom of opportunity, competition among employers for the workmen available, elimination of class distinctions, emphasis upon independence, resourcefulness, and, too often, brute force are gone. How far we can keep the best of these elements remains to be seen, now that the tables are turned and there are more men than jobs. The change from a seller's to a buyer's market has revolutionized industry and commerce. We have only recently become aware of the effect of this revolutionizing condition upon employment. Hence no one can see the end here. But certain results seem to be fairly clearly indicated.

---

[15] H. G. Moulton, *Japan, an Economic and Financial Appraisal* (1931), pp. 366–67, quoted by permission of the Brookings Institution, publishers.

[16] W. R. Crocker, *The Japanese Population Problem* (1931), p. 209; quoted by permission of the Macmillan Company, publishers.

First, freedom to move about from job to job will largely disappear. This was possible when there were more jobs than men but will become much more difficult in the future.

Second, jobs per se will become more valuable. They had little value when the worker could get one as good or possibly better elsewhere at any time. From now on a man will strive to secure the next job before quitting; he will desire some consideration before leaving from the man who is to succeed him.

Third, mere graduation from high school and college will become of less economic value because of the increasing supply of graduates. This will necessitate longer periods of preparation in order to secure an advantage through education over one's fellows.

Fourth, education will become more expensive, since it will necessitate a longer period of time and it will be harder for the average boy to obtain it, because odd jobs, by which he earns part of the expense, will become more and more the rightful property of another.

Fifth, educated men will be forced into less desirable positions. This may prove to be a great blessing to society, for many of these educated men will in time transform low-class jobs into real positions. Jobs are to a large degree neither good nor poor per se; the rank of a job is determined very largely by the caliber of the man holding it. Thus the common labor job of ditch-digging is rapidly becoming a machine-operator's position. In most cities men of a wide range of mental attainment enter the police force, but the better class quit before long, so that after five years there are left mainly men with intelligence-test scores much below the average.[17] If college men continued in the police force of a city, there would be an amazing change for the better in every police activity. The educated, professional type of man exhibits a pride in the quality aspects of his work that is largely unknown to the lower type of mentality.

Sixth, as we lose our zest for quantity, owing to overproduction, it will be natural for us to play up quality. Beauty is one most valuable phase of quality. Of late we have come to appreciate that the redwood groves, the Yosemite Valley, and many other places with natural scenery have economic value because people spend money to enjoy them. It would seem that we are on the eve of an era in which much attention will be devoted to beautifying our homes, our cities, our parks, and our

---

[17] L. L. Thurstone, "The Intelligence of Policemen," *Journal of Personnel Research* (June 1922), p. 64; Grace M. Fernald and Ellen B. Sullivan, "Psychology and Public Safety," *The California Monthly* (October 1924), p. 81.

highways. There should be many new openings here for men of artistic attainments, imagination, and resourcefulness.

Quantity production gives minimum employment per unit manufactured; whereas quality production necessitates the reverse, for the more distinctive each unit is the more individual is the attention its production demands. Possibly the solution of our unemployment problem will come about through an increasing demand by the public for the unique, the distinctive, and the beautiful.

Seventh, because no one can see far into the future, the best advice to the young is to prepare themselves as broadly as possible—this is not a time for extreme specialization. Then if a job, or a whole industry, disappears over night, they will be able to jump sideways into a related activity for which they have had some preparation. If their education, on the other hand, is all narrowly directed toward one thing and that proves to be valueless, they have no recourse but to start all over again.

Lastly, the second-generation group must recognize that their progress will come by climbing the ladder of success round by round.

> In this process of aspiring to better our social and economic standing, we have often been prone to set a goal, which from impartial eyes is too Utopian. From a generation of day laborers, some of the second generation seem to feel that they should take the place of Ford, of Rockefeller, or Edison and other captains of industry. In failing to attain this pedestal, too often we dodge the issue, and with sour taste say that it is all due to race prejudice. We think that we have not been given an equal chance when in reality we have been beaten by those who are superior to us. . . .
>
> Our task is infinitely harder than that faced by any European second generation; but in looking at the question from its broad aspects, there is a great similarity. If we are to use that analogy, we find that even in the vocational advance of European immigrants, there have been but few who have jumped from the lowest to the highest strata in one jump. There has been a Carnegie, a Schwab, a Bok, a Pupin, and a Riis, but as a whole the great mass of European immigrants are still of the middle class. Is it not true then, that we should not despair even if we fail to become the Captains of American industry, the judges of her benches, the doctors of her famous hospitals, and engineers in her gigantic constructions? Some of our number are going to make a rapid headway and through their ability, nothing will stop them, but as for the mass, we should not be too much disappointed if we do not vocationally reach the standard of our lofty dreams.[18]

Other second-generation immigrant groups have progressed beyond their parents. But for the most part they have not achieved the position

---

[18] Paul Aiso, "Vocational Opportunities of the Second Generation in America," *Nikkei Shimin,* May 15, 1930.

that their own children attained later on. The writer admires the ambition of many of the second-generation Japanese. He wishes them all success. But it is impossible to suppose that they will all be able to reach their goal. They will be a remarkable group indeed if many do not falter and some fall by the wayside. As a group, the second generation have no right to expect more than that a few will accomplish great things and the remainder will build upon the foundations established by their fathers. Their success will be measured by the distance they progress from where the first generation stop and by the variety of directions in which they advance.

XII. GENERAL STATISTICAL TABLES

Tables 34–43, which follow, comprise general population and immigration statistics for both continental United States and Hawaii, data on which much of the foregoing discussion has been based. For facility of reference these tables are here grouped in one section.

TABLE 34

JAPANESE POPULATION BY DIVISIONS AND STATES, 1900, 1910, 1920, AND 1930*

(United States Census, 1930)

Geographical Divisions	1900	1910	1920	1930
New England States				
Maine	4	13	7	3
New Hampshire	1	1	8	0
Vermont	0	3	4	1
Massachusetts	53	151	191	201
Connecticut	18	71	102	130
Rhode Island	13	33	35	17
Middle Atlantic States				
New York	354	1,247	2,686	2,930
Pennsylvania	40	190	255	293
New Jersey	52	206	325	439
South Atlantic States				
West Virginia	0	3	10	9
Maryland	9	24	29	38
Delaware	1	4	8	8
Virginia	10	14	56	43
North Carolina	0	2	24	17
South Carolina	0	8	15	15
Georgia	1	4	9	32
Florida	1	50	106	153

* Japanese population in continental United States for 1870 was 55; for 1880, 148; and for 1890, 2,039; in the Territory of Hawaii for 1890 it was 12,360.

Japanese population in Alaska for 1900 was 279; for 1910, it was 913; for 1920, it was 312; and for 1930, it was 278. These figures are not included in totals for continental United States.

Native-born Japanese in continental United States totaled 269 in 1900; 4,502 in 1910; 29,672 in 1920; and 68,357 in 1930. In the Territory of Hawaii they numbered 4,877 in 1900 ("foreign-born population born in Japan" subtracted from total, according to *United States Census of 1900,* I, 744); they were 19,889 in 1910; 48,586 in 1920; and 91,185 in 1930.

In continental United States there were 23,341 Japanese males and 985 Japanese females in 1900; 63,070 males and 9,087 females in 1910; 72,707 males and 38,303 females in 1920; and 81,771 males and 57,063 females in 1930. In Hawaii there were 10,219 Japanese males and 2,391 Japanese females in 1890; 47,508 males and 13,603 females in 1900; 54,784 males and 24,891 females in 1910; 62,644 males and 46,630 females in 1920; and 75,008 males and 64,623 females in 1930.

TABLE 34—*Continued*

Geographical Divisions	1900	1910	1920	1930
East North Central States				
Wisconsin	5	34	60	24
Michigan	9	49	184	176
Illinois	80	285	472	564
Indiana	5	38	81	71
Ohio	27	76	130	187
East South Central States				
Kentucky	0	12	9	9
Tennessee	4	8	8	11
Mississippi	0	2	0	1
Alabama	3	4	18	25
West North Central States				
North Dakota	148	59	72	91
Minnesota	51	67	85	69
South Dakota	1	42	38	19
Nebraska	3	590	804	674
Iowa	7	36	29	19
Kansas	4	107	52	37
Missouri	9	99	135	94
West South Central States				
Oklahoma	0	48	67	104
Arkansas	0	9	5	12
Texas	13	340	449	519
Louisiana	17	31	57	52
Mountain States				
Montana	2,441	1,585	1,074	753
Idaho	1,291	1,363	1,569	1,421
Wyoming	393	1,596	1,194	1,026
Nevada	228	864	754	608
Utah	417	2,110	2,936	3,269
Colorado	48	2,300	2,464	3,213
Arizona	281	371	550	879
New Mexico	8	258	251	249
Pacific States				
Washington	5,617	12,929	17,387	17,837
Oregon	2,501	3,418	4,151	4,958
California	10,151	41,356	71,952	97,456
District of Columbia	7	47	103	78
Total for mainland	24,326	72,157	111,010	138,834
Mainland outside California	14,175	30,801	38,058	41,378
Mainland outside three Pacific States	6,057	14,454	17,520	18,583
Territory of Hawaii	61,111	79,675	109,274	139,631

TABLE 35

JAPANESE POPULATION IN CALIFORNIA BY COUNTIES AND BY CITIES OF 25,000 OR MORE, 1900, 1910, 1920, AND 1930

(United States Census, 1930)*

Counties	1900	1910	1920	1930
Alameda	1,149	3,266	5,221	5,715
Alpine	0	1	0	0
Amador	0	2	17	2
Butte	365	295	423	307
Calaveras	4	3	0	0
Colusa	53	140	275	211
Contra Costa	276	1,009	846	796
Del Norte	0	0	0	0
Eldorado	30	31	47	9
Fresno	598	2,233	5,732	5,280
Glenn	14	33	122	9
Humboldt	0	6	0	0
Imperial	0	217	1,986	2,241
Inyo	0	41	82	20
Kern	48	273	338	712
Kings	156	293	594	746
Lake	3	3	0	0
Lassen	2	6	9	17
Los Angeles	204	8,461	19,911	35,390
Madera	19	32	136	208
Marin	52	199	140	158
Mariposa	0	3	0	0
Mendocino	23	77	56	82
Merced	43	98	420	768
Modoc	0	1	0	1
Mono	1	14	2	4
Monterey	710	1,121	1,614	2,271
Napa	6	103	79	68
Nevada	15	22	16	0
Orange	3	641	1,491	1,613
Placer	133	862	1,474	1,874
Plumas	0	20	22	10
Riverside	97	765	626	589
Sacramento	1,209	3,874	5,800	8,114
San Benito	15	286	427	559
San Bernardino	148	946	533	578
San Diego	25	520	1,431	1,722
San Francisco	1,781	4,518	5,358	6,250
San Joaquin	313	1,804	4,354	4,339
San Luis Obispo	16	434	501	868
San Mateo	46	368	663	1,169
Santa Barbara	114	863	930	1,889
Santa Clara	284	2,299	2,981	4,320

* The entire state population in 1900 was 1,485,053; it was 2,377,549 in 1910; it was 3,426,861 in 1920, and 5,677,251 in 1930.

TABLE 35—*Continued*

Counties	1900	1910	1920	1930
Santa Cruz	235	689	1,019	1,407
Shasta	20	42	3	0
Sierra	1	17	3	3
Siskiyou	8	24	14	10
Solano	870	894	1,017	1,350
Sonoma	148	554	506	716
Stanislaus	5	113	478	505
Sutter	155	134	373	399
Tehama	143	98	95	75
Trinity	1	0	0	0
Tulare	48	615	1,602	1,486
Tuolumne	2	6	3	2
Ventura	94	872	675	597
Yolo	410	789	1,152	1,423
Yuba	56	336	355	574
Total for state	10,151	41,356	71,952	97,456

Cities*	1900†	1910	1920	1930
Alameda	110	499	644	822
Alhambra	—	13	65	79
Bakersfield	—	160	153	239
Berkeley	17	710	911	1,320
Fresno	175	629	1,119	1,176
Glendale	—	36	177	408
Long Beach	—	127	375	596
Los Angeles	150	4,238	11,618	21,081
Oakland	194	1,520	2,709	2,137
Pasadena	17	253	383	842
Riverside	—	581	340	277
Sacramento	336	1,437	1,976	3,347
San Bernardino	—	94	110	124
San Diego	14	159	772	911
San Francisco	1,781	4,518	5,358	6,250
San Jose	44	345	321	463
Santa Ana	—	14	74	42
Santa Barbara	—	152	198	296
Santa Monica	—	66	80	432
Stockton	39	475	840	1,386
Total	—	16,026	28,223	42,228

* Over 25,000 population in 1930.
† Data for several cities not available.

TABLE 36

TOTAL POPULATION OF CALIFORNIA FOR THE YEARS 1850–1930 AND TOTAL JAPANESE AND CHINESE*

Year	Total Population		Japanese Population					Chinese Population				
	Number	Percentage of Increase	Males	Females	Total	Percentage of Increase	Percentage of Total Population	Males	Females	Total	Percentage of Increase	Percentage of Total Population
1850	92,597	...	....	....	....	....	....	.....	.....	.....	..	....
1860	379,994	310	....	....	....	....	....	33,149	1,784	34,933	..	9.19
1870	560,247	47	25	8	33	....	.006	45,404	3,873	49,277	41	8.79
1880	864,694	54	81	5	86	161	.01	71,244	3,888	75,132	52	8.68
1890	1,213,398	40	1,036	111	1,147	1,234	.09	69,382	3,090	72,472	–4	5.97
1900	1,485,053	22	9,598	553	10,151	785	.68	42,297	3,456	45,753	–37	3.08
1910	2,377,549	60	35,116	6,240	41,356	307	1.73	33,003	3,245	36,248	–21	1.52
1920	3,426,861	44	45,414	26,538	71,952	74	2.10	24,230	4,582	28,812	–21	0.84
1930	5,677,251	66	56,440	41,016	97,456	35	1.71	27,988	9,373	37,361	30	0.65

* Based on United States Census. Total Chinese population in continental United States was: 34,933 in 1860; 63,199 in 1870; 105,465 in 1880; 107,475 in 1890; 89,863 in 1900; 71,531 in 1910; 61,639 in 1920; and 74,954 in 1930.

TABLE 37

Immigration of Japanese to Continental United States during 1890–1900*

Date†	From Country of Japan	Of Japanese Race‡	Date†	From Country of Japan	Of Japanese Race‡
1890–91	1,136§	.....	1895–96	1,110	.....
1891–92	1,498§	.....	1896–97	1,526	.....
1892–93	1,380	.....	1897–98	2,230	.....
1893–94	1,931	.....	1898–99	2,844	3,395
1894–95	1,150	.....	1899–1900	12,635	12,628
Totals, 1890–1900				27,440	27,984

* Based on the *Annual Reports of the Commissioner-General of Immigration.*

† Fiscal year is from July 1 to June 30.

‡ Beginning with the 1898–99 *Report,* the race of the immigrant is given. Before this only the country from which the immigrant is coming was given. Thus, of the 3,395 Japanese reported in 1898–99, 2,737 came from Japan, 522 from British North America, 15 from the Hawaiian Islands, 42 from other Pacific Islands, and 79 from other countries. The totals of 27,440 and 27,984 probably include a few non-Japanese who entered from Japan and do not include some Japanese entering from ports other than those in Japan. Ichihashi reports that 32,528 Japanese were given passports to the country, according to statistics of the Japanese government (Y. Ichihashi, *Japanese in the United States* [1932], p. 55).

§ *Annual Report of the Superintendent of Immigration* (1891–92), p. 13, gives 2,634 for two years 1890–92; 1,136 is given for 1890–91 in the *Annual Report of the Commissioner-General of Immigration* (1925–26), p. 175. By subtraction, 1,498 is obtained for 1891–92.

TABLE 38

Immigration and Emigration of Japanese: Continental United States and Hawaii, 1900–1930*

Date	Immigrant Aliens Admitted	Non-Immigrant Aliens	Total Immigrant and Non-Immigrant	Emigrant Aliens Departed	Non-Emigrant Aliens	Total Emigrant and Non-Emigrant	Immigrant and Non-Immigrant Less Emigrant and Non-Emigrant
	(1)	(2)	(3)	(4)	(5)	(6)	(7)
1900–01..	5,249	.....	.....	.....	.....	.....	.....
1901–02..	14,455	.....	.....	.....	.....	.....	.....
1902–03..	20,041	.....	.....	.....	.....	.....	.....
1903–04..	14,382	.....	.....	.....	.....	.....	.....
1904–05..	11,021	.....	.....	.....	.....	.....	.....

* From the *Annual Reports of the Commissioner-General of Immigration* (fiscal year ends June 30). Reports refer to race or people, not country of last residence. Data in columns 1, 2, 4, and 5 supplied in tables; data in remaining columns based on these four.

TABLE 38—*Continued*

Date	Immigrant Aliens Admitted	Non-Immigrant Aliens	Total Immigrant and Non-Immigrant	Emigrant Aliens Departed	Non-Emigrant Aliens	Total Emigrant and Non-Emigrant	Immigrant and Non-Immigrant Less Emigrant and Non-Emigrant
	(1)	(2)	(3)	(4)	(5)	(6)	(7)
1905–06..	14,243	.....	.....	.....	.....	.....	.....
1906–07..	30,824	.....	.....	.....	.....	.....	.....
1907–08..	16,418	1,820†	18,238‡	5,323	3,865	9,188	9,050
1908–09..	3,275	1,168	4,443§	3,903	3,590	7,493§	−3,050
1909–10..	2,798	1,348	4,146‖	4,377	3,133	7,510¶	−3,364
1910–11..	4,575	1,915	6,490‖	3,351	4,982	8,333	−1,843
1911–12..	6,172	2,574	8,746‖	1,501	6,529	8,030	716
1912–13..	8,302	3,370	11,672	733	7,707	8,440	3,232
1913–14..	8,941	4,075	13,016	794	8,109	8,903	4,113
1914–15..	8,609	3,628	12,237	825	7,662	8,487	3,750
1915–16..	8,711	3,996	12,707	780	8,638	9,418	3,289
1916–17..	8,925	4,363	13,288	722	8,440	9,162	4,126
1917–18..	10,168	4,911	15,079	1,558	9,282	10,840	4,239
1918–19..	10,056	4,848	14,904	2,127	9,106	11,233	3,671
1919–20..	9,279	6,895	16,174	4,238	11,415	15,653	521
1920–21..	7,531	6,743	14,274	4,352	11,193	15,545	−1,271
1921–22..	6,361	6,476	12,837	4,353	10,925	15,278	−2,441
1922–23...	5,652	5,919	11,571	2,844	8,328	11,172	399
1923–24..	8,481	7,217	15,698	2,120	9,623	11,743	3,955
1924–25..	682	3,505	4,187	1,170	8,098	9,268	−5,081
1925–26..	598	5,180	5,778	1,201	9,190	10,391	−4,613
1926–27..	660	6,517	7,177	1,148	10,315	11,463	−4,286
1927–28..	522	7,190	7,712	1,055	9,614	10,669	−2,957
1928–29..	716	7,562	8,278	931	8,812	9,743	−1,465
1929–30..	796	7,423	8,219	1,004	9,331	10,335	−2,116
1907–10..	22,491	4,336	26,827	13,603	10,588	24,191	2,636
1910–20..	83,738	40,575	124,313	16,629	81,870	98,499	25,814
1920–30..	31,999	63,732	95,731	20,178	95,429	115,607	−19,876
1907–30..	138,228	108,643	246,871	50,410	187,887	238,297	8,574

† Not given in the *Annual Reports of the Commissioner-General of Immigration;* obtained by subtracting the figure in column 1 from that in column 3. (The figure 1,591 appears in table, "Country of Last Permanent Residence.")

‡ Given in the *Annual Report of the Commissioner-General of Immigration* (1907–8), Table A, p. 186.

§ Given in *ibid.* (1908–9), Table IV, p. 117. But the sum of the figures for 1908–9 in column 3 in Tables 39 and 40 gives 3,925, instead of 4,443; and the sum of the figures for the same year in column 6 in these two tables gives 7,382, not 7,493.

‖ The sum of the figures for 1909–10 in column 3 of Tables 39 and 40 gives 4,125, not 4,146; for 1910–11, 6,441, not 6,490; and for 1911–12, 8,589, not 8,746.

¶ The sum of the figures for 1909–10 in column 6 of Tables 39 and 40 gives 7,379, not 7,510.

TABLE 39

Immigration and Emigration of Japanese: Territory of Hawaii, 1900–1930*

Date	Immigrant Aliens Admitted—"Declared Destination Hawaii"	Non-Immigrant Aliens	Total Immigrant and Non-Immigrant—"Admitted to Hawaii"	Emigrant Aliens Departed—"Emigrated from Hawaii"	Non-Emigrant Aliens	Total Emigrant and Non-Emigrant—"Departures from Hawaii"	Immigrant and Non-Immigrant Less Emigrant and Non-Emigrant
	(1)	(2)	(3)	(4)	(5)	(6)	(7)
1900–01..	338	.....	.....	.....	.....	.....	.....
1901–02..	9,125	.....	.....	.....	.....	.....	.....
1902–03..	13,045	.....	.....	.....	.....	.....	.....
1903–04..	6,590	.....	.....	.....	.....	.....	.....
1904–05..	6,692	.....	.....	.....	.....	.....	.....
1905–06..	9,051	.....	.....	.....	.....	.....	.....
1906–07..	20,865	.....	.....	.....	.....	.....	.....
1907–08..	9,153†	?	8,694†	3,334	1,058	4,392	4,302
1908–09..	1,679†	?	1,493†	1,310	1,068	2,378	—885
1909–10..	1,239	288	1,527	1,632	723	2,355	—828
1910–11..	1,883	276	2,159	912	1,552	2,464	—305
1911–12..	2,816	415	3,231	517	2,076	2,593	638
1912–13..	4,062	839	4,901	216	2,577	2,793	2,108
1913–14..	3,817	737	4,554	215	2,388	2,603	1,951
1914–15..	2,625	583	3,208	100	2,420	2,520	688
1915–16..	2,797	810	3,607	58	2,438	2,496	1,111
1916–17..	3,178	951	4,129	84	2,497	2,581	1,548
1917–18..	2,856	1,080	3,936	249	2,900	3,149	787
1918–19..	2,384	1,116	3,500	174	2,731	2,905	595
1919–20..	2,138	1,168	3,306	229	3,762	3,991	—685
1920–21..	2,153	1,446	3,599	524	3,383	3,907	—308
1921–22..	2,212	1,644	3,856	730	3,375	4,105	—249
1922–23..	1,989	1,527	3,516	200	2,579	2,779	737
1923–24..	2,635	1,537	4,172	113	2,382	2,495	1,677
1924–25..	274	691	965	116	1,887	2,003	—1,038
1925–26..	61	1,065	1,126	56	2,584	2,640	—1,514
1926–27..	70	1,630	1,700	45	3,226	3,271	—1,571
1927–28..	25	1,752	1,777	23	2,630	2,653	—876

* From the *Annual Reports of the Commissioner-General of Immigration* (fiscal year ends June 30). Data in columns 1, 3, 4, and 6 given in the *Annual Reports.* Data in remaining columns based on these.

† Apparently an error here, as the figures in column 1 cannot exceed the figures in column 3. Consequently, totals cannot all be made to balance. These figures are from the *Annual Report of the Commissioner-General of Immigration* (1908–9), Table A, p. 196.

TABLE 39—*Continued*

Date	Immigrant Aliens Admitted—"Declared Destination Hawaii"	Non-Immigrant Aliens	Total Immigrant and Non-Immi-grant—"Admitted to Hawaii"	Emigrant Aliens Departed—"Emigrated from Hawaii"	Non-Emigrant Aliens	Total Emigrant and Non-Emi-grant—"Depar-tures from Hawaii"	Immigrant and Non-Immigrant Less Emigrant and Non-Emigrant
	(1)	(2)	(3)	(4)	(5)	(6)	(7)
1928–29..	58	1,927	1,985	21	2,441	2,462	—477
1929–30..	61	1,884	1,945	56	2,789	2,845	—900
1907–10..	12,071	288	11,714	6,276	2,849	9,125	2,589
1910–20..	28,556	7,875	36,531	2,754	25,341	28,095‡	8,436
1920–30..	9,538	15,103	24,641	1,884	27,276	29,160	—4,519
1907–30..	50,165	23,266	72,886	10,914	55,466	66,380	6,506

‡ In the *Annual Reports of the Governor of Hawaii* figures are given for Japanese immigration from and to the Orient. For 1910–20 the figures are 37,798 and 39,139, respectively; and for 1920–29 they are 27,025 and 39,660. The arrivals reported here exceed those in the table by 1,267 in 1910–20 and by 4,329 in 1920–29; the departures exceed those in the table by 11,044 in 1910–20 and by 13,345 in 1920–29. For 1900–1910, the Governor's *Reports* merely give all arrivals and departures presumably from and to both the Orient and the mainland. The arrivals are 77,421, which closely agrees with the total of 77,867 from the *Annual Reports of the Commissioner-General of Immigration* coming from Japan; the departures total 75,186. The *Reports of the Commissioner-General* give no corresponding information, except for the years 1907–10. During 1911–29, according to the Governor's *Reports,* the arrivals totaled 27,639 males, 28,467 females, and 6,469 children, and the departures 34,343 males, 18,923 females, and 22,042 children. Evidently 6,704 more males departed than arrived, whereas 9,544 more females and 15,573 more children arrived than departed.

TABLE 40

IMMIGRATION AND EMIGRATION OF JAPANESE: CONTINENTAL UNITED STATES, 1900–1930*

Date	Immigrant Aliens Admitted	Non-Immigrant Aliens	Total Immigrant and Non-Immigrant	Emigrant Aliens Departed	Non-Emigrant Aliens	Total Emigrant and Non-Emigrant	Immigrant and Non-Immigrant Less Emigrant and Non-Emigrant
	(1)	(2)	(3)	(4)	(5)	(6)	(7)
1900–01..	4,911	.....	.....	.....	.....	.....	.....
1901–02..	5,330	.....	.....	.....	.....	.....	.....
1902–03..	6,996	.....	.....	.....	.....	.....	.....

* From the *Annual Reports of the Commissioner-General of Immigration* (fiscal year ends June 30). Data in columns 3 and 6 supplied by the *Annual Reports.* The figures in column 1 are obtained by subtracting the figures in column 1 of Table 39 from the figures in column 1 of Table 38; the figures for column 4 are similarly obtained. The figures in columns 2 and 5 are based on the remaining columns.

TABLE 40—*Continued*

Date	Immigrant Aliens Admitted	Non-Immigrant Aliens	Total Immigrant and Non-Immigrant	Emigrant Aliens Departed	Non-Emigrant Aliens	Total Emigrant and Non-Emigrant	Immigrant and Non-Immigrant Less Emigrant and Non-Emigrant
	(1)	(2)	(3)	(4)	(5)	(6)	(7)
1903–04..	7,792	.....	.....	.....	.....	.....	.....
1904–05..	4,329	.....	.....	.....	.....	.....	.....
1905–06..	5,192	.....	.....	.....	.....	.....	.....
1906–07..	9,959	.....	.....	.....	.....	.....	.....
1907–08..	7,265	2,279	9,544	1,989	2,807	4,796	4,748
1908–09..	1,596	836	2,432	2,593	2,411	5,004	–2,572
1909–10..	1,559	1,039	2,598	2,745	2,279	5,024	–2,426
1910–11..	2,692	1,590	4,282	2,439	3,430	5,869	–1,587
1911–12..	3,356	2,002	5,358	984	4,453	5,437	–79
1912–13..	4,240	2,531	6,771	517	5,130	5,647	1,124
1913–14..	5,124	3,338	8,462	579	5,721	6,300	2,162
1914–15..	5,984	3,045	9,029	725	5,242	5,967	3,062
1915–16..	5,914	3,186	9,100	722	6,200	6,922	2,178
1916–17..	5,747	3,412	9,159	638	5,943	6,581	2,578
1917–18..	7,312	3,831	11,143	1,309	6,382	7,691	3,452
1918–19..	7,672	3,732	11,404	1,953	6,375	8,328	3,076
1919–20..	7,141	5,727	12,868	4,009	7,653	11,662	1,206
1920–21..	5,378	5,297	10,675	3,828	7,810	11,638	–963
1921–22..	4,149	4,832	8,981	3,623	7,550	11,173	–2,192
1922–23..	3,663	4,392	8,055	2,644	5,749	8,393	–338
1923–24..	5,846	5,680	11,526	2,007	7,241	9,248	2,278
1924–25..	408	2,814	3,222	1,054	6,211	7,265	–4,043
1925–26..	537	4,115	4,652	1,145	6,606	7,751	–3,099
1926–27..	590	4,887	5,477	1,103	7,089	8,192	–2,715
1927–28..	497	5,438	5,935	1,032	6,984	8,016	–2,081
1928–29..	658	5,635	6,293	910	6,371	7,281	–988
1929–30..	735†	5,539	6,274	948	6,542	7,490	–1,216
1907–10..	10,420	4,154	14,574	7,327	7,497	14,824	–250
1910–20..	55,182	32,394	87,576	13,875	56,529	70,404	17,172
1920–30..	22,461	48,629	71,090	18,294	68,153	86,447	–15,357
1907–30..	88,063	85,177	173,240	39,496	132,179	171,675	1,565

† In 1929–30, 8,219 Japanese were admitted. Of these, 3,108 were considered non-immigrants, as follows: 574 government officials and families, 854 temporary visitors for business and 681 for pleasure, 595 in continuous transit through the United States, and 404 to carry on trade under the existing treaty. The remainder, i.e., 5,111, were considered non-quota immigrants, as follows: 99 ministers and families, 13 college professors and families, 221 students, and 4,778 returning residents. Apparently the figure 735 is composed of those who were here to carry on trade (404), the ministers (99), the professors (13), and the students (221), which together made up 737.

TABLE 41

"JAPANESE ABROAD"*

Date	Territory of Hawaii	California†	Continental United States	Canada	Mexico	Total North America	Brazil	South America
1903......	68,740	23,246	38,908	.....	.....	.....	.....	.....
1911......	70,564	.....	?‡	*11,099*	.....	.....	1,426	.....
1913......	87,561	.....	*77,625*	12,252	2,737	*92,614*	7,367	.....
1916......	*96,749*	*71,651*	*100,955*	13,279	2,737	*116,971*	16,555	24,449
1918......	112,064	86,458	119,307	15,098	1,209	135,618	21,763	31,161
1920§.....	112,221	?	115,533	17,716	2,194	135,667	34,258	47,571
1925......	125,764	*95,004*	133,080	19,679	3,632	*156,391*‖	49,400	64,191
1928......	130,941	*106,951*	141,550	22,506	4,505	169,569	76 488	98,037
1932¶.....	146,764	.....	102,895	19,626	5,826	129,433	132,699	160,389

* Japanese Foreign Department figures, recorded in *Japan Year Books.* Figures in italics were obtained by adding subtotals. There are seemingly many errors in these *Japan Year Book* figures: e.g., for Portland, Oregon, in 1925 there were reported 1,502 males and 218 females, a total of 2,720; and for the whole of North America, 184,243 males and 110,399 females, a total of 295,641 (*Twenty-third Year Book,* p. 45).

† Data supplied by the Japanese consulates in Los Angeles and San Francisco, embracing the states of California, Nevada, Colorado, Utah, New Mexico, and Arizona, and Lower California in Mexico.

‡ The total of 23,729 was obtained by adding all the population figures given for the United States. It is obviously incorrect; apparently data from California were omitted.

§ McKenzie in Table B quotes figures from the Department of Foreign Affairs, Tokyo, giving 108,109 for Hawaii, 125,285 for continental United States, 17,688 for Canada, and 2,607 for Mexico. His figures agree with those above for 1913. (R. D. McKenzie, *Oriental Exclusion,* 1927.)

‖ The figure 295,641 occurs in the *Year Book.* It is obviously a total including the Hawaiian Islands, which are listed, however, under "Oceania." For 1924 the corresponding figure is 219,225, and for 1926, 158,412.

¶ *Annual Report of Department of Overseas Affairs* (Japan, 1933), pp. 609–10. Total abroad including Manchuria (135,507) and Kwantung (124,825) is 825,100.

TABLE 42

Arrivals in Honolulu of Japanese Steerage Passengers from the Mainland and Departures to the Mainland*

Date	Arrivals				Departures				Gain or Loss to the Islands
	Men	Women	Children	Total	Men	Women	Children	Total	
Jan. 1, 1902—Sept. 30, 1902	...	...	...	...	...	...	...	1,054	...
Oct. 1, 1902—Sept. 30, 1903	...	...	...	...	...	...	...	2,119	...
Oct. 1, 1903—June 30, 1904	...	...	...	...	...	...	...	3,665	...
July 1, 1904—Dec. 31, 1904	...	...	...	...	...	...	...	4,153	...
Jan. 1, 1905—Dec. 31, 1905	...	...	...	...	8,657	712	281	9,650	...
Jan. 1, 1906—Dec. 31, 1906	...	...	...	...	11,047	794	386	12,227	...
Jan. 1, 1907—Dec. 31, 1907	...	...	...	...	5,149	198	91	5,438	...
Jan. 1, 1908—Dec. 31, 1908	...	...	...	...	45	17	7	69	...
Jan. 1, 1909—Dec. 31, 1909	...	...	...	...	16	7	5	28	...
Jan. 1, 1910—June 30, 1910	...	...	...	...	21	6	2	29	...
July 1, 1910—June 30, 1911	3	0	0	3	23	7	5	35	—32
July 1, 1911—June 30, 1912	23	2	0	35	42	6	0	48	—13
July 1, 1912—June 30, 1913	25	1	1	27	37	3	2	42	—15
July 1, 1913—June 30, 1914	31	2	5	38	36	2	0	38	0
July 1, 1914—June 30, 1915	51	8	5	64	53	5	5	63	1
July 1, 1915—June 30, 1916	71	11	5	87	65	8	1	74	13
July 1, 1916—June 30, 1917	40	4	0	44	52	8	0	60	—16
July 1, 1917—June 30, 1918	47	3	6	56	58	5	1	64	—8
July 1, 1918—June 30, 1919	34	12	4	50	174	30	12	216	—166
July 1, 1919—June 30, 1920	57	9	5	71	299	67	24	390	—319
July 1, 1920—June 30, 1921	63	11	5	79	183	56	73	312	—233
July 1, 1921—June 30, 1922	44	8	3	55	28	9	2	39	16

* For 1902–11, based on *Reports of the Board of Immigration, Labor, and Statistics to the Governor of Hawaii*; for 1911–29, based on *Annual Reports of the Governor of Hawaii*. See also *Reports of the United States Commissioner of Labor on Hawaii* to Congress.

TABLE 42—*Continued*

Date	Arrivals				Departures				Gain or Loss to the Islands
	Men	Women	Children	Total	Men	Women	Children	Total	
July 1, 1922—June 30, 1923	50	11	7	68	104	9	4	117	—49
July 1, 1923—June 30, 1924	87	21	6	114	131	40	4	175	—61
July 1, 1924—June 30, 1925	45	6	8	59	97	10	5	112	—53
July 1, 1925—June 30, 1926	118	25	15	158	109	33	5	147	11
July 1, 1926—June 30, 1927	108	37	28	173	103	29	7	139	34
July 1, 1927—June 30, 1928	159	52	35	246	141	31	12	184	62
July 1, 1928—June 30, 1929	107	29	19	155	152	51	14	217	—62
Totals									
Jan., 1902—June, 1910	...	...	...	...	...	...	...	38,432†	...
Jan., 1905—June, 1910	...	...	...	...	24,935	1,734	772	27,441	...
July, 1910—June, 1920	392	52	31	475	839	141	50	1,030	—555
July, 1920—June, 1924	244	51	21	316	446	114	83	643	—327
July, 1924—June, 1929	537	149	105	791	602	154	43	799	—8
Jan., 1905—June, 1929	...	...	...	...	26,822	2,143	948	29,913	...
Jan., 1902—June, 1929	...	...	...	...	...	...	...	40,904	...

† Of this number, 375 were reported as Koreans and Chinese and 2,779 went to Canada, leaving 35,278 who went to the United States. There are probably a few other Koreans and Chinese included, and some others went to Canada or returned from there.

TABLE 43

ARRIVALS AT HONOLULU FROM THE MAINLAND AND DEPARTURES TO THE MAINLAND OF ALIEN JAPANESE AND CITIZENS OF JAPANESE ANCESTRY*

(After Romanzo Adams)

Date	Arrivals at Honolulu						Departures from Honolulu						Gain or Loss to the Islands					
	Aliens			Citizens			Aliens			Citizens			Aliens			Citizens		
	Male	Female	Total	Male	Female	Total	Male	Female	Total	Male	Female	Total	Male	Female	Total	Male	Female	Total
	(1)	(2)	(3)	(4)	(5)	(6)	(7)	(8)	(9)	(10)	(11)	(12)	(13)	(14)	(15)	(16)	(17)	(18)
1921–22	...	...	...	...	...	48	...	...	...	...	...	161	...	...	...	...	...	...
1922–23	...	...	...	...	...	34	...	...	...	...	...	128	...	...	...	...	...	...
1923–24	...	...	...	...	...	88	...	...	...	...	...	161	...	...	...	...	...	...
1924–25	99	37	136	48	35	83	82	17	99	108	32	140	17	20	37	− 60	3	− 57
1925–26	136	27	163	49	20	69	96	27	123	125	48	173	40	0	40	− 76	− 28	−104
1926–27	123	38	161	85	44	129	97	30	127	183	76	259	26	8	34	− 98	− 32	−130
1927–28	161	50	211	148	45	193	95	41	136	253	82	335	66	9	75	−105	− 37	−142
1928–29	163	62	225	167	64	231	161	63	224	345	117	462	2	−1	1	−178	− 53	−231
1929–30	132	49	181	203	68	271	122	41	163	421	159	580	10	8	18	−218	− 91	−309
Totals, 1924–30	814	263	1,077	700	276	976	653	219	872	1,435	514	1,949	161	44	205	−735	−238	−973

* Relatively few of the individuals covered are under sixteen years of age. Of those in this classification, the alien arrivals consist of 13 males and 18 females; the citizen arrivals, of 67 males and 78 females; the alien departures, of 11 males and 15 females; and the citizen departures, of 89 males and 88 females. There is a gain to the Islands of 5 aliens and a loss of 32 citizens.

The table includes both cabin and steerage passengers. Columns 6 and 12 are given in *Immigration Commission Report* for 1930, Table 111, p. 249.

INDEX